T0143346

Cloud Computing Technologies for Smart Agriculture and Healthcare

Chapman & Hall/CRC Cloud Computing for Society 5.0
Series Editors: ***Vishal Bhatnagar and Vikram Bali***

Digitalization of Higher Education Using Cloud Computing
Edited by: S.L. Gupta, Nawal Kishor, Niraj Mishra, Sonali Mathur, Utkarsh Gupta

Cloud Computing Technologies for Smart Agriculture and Healthcare
Edited by: Urmila Shrawankar, Latesh Malik, Sandhya Arora

For more information about this series please visit: https://www.routledge.com/Cloud-Computing-Technologies-for-Smart-Agriculture-and-Healthcare/Shrawankar-Malik-Arora/p/book/9781032068039

Cloud Computing Technologies for Smart Agriculture and Healthcare

Edited by
Dr. Urmila Shrawankar, Dr. Latesh Malik, and Dr. Sandhya Arora

CRC Press is an imprint of the
Taylor & Francis Group, an informa business
A CHAPMAN & HALL BOOK

First edition published [2022]
by CRC Press
6000 Broken Sound Parkway NW, Suite 300, Boca Raton, FL 33487-2742

and by CRC Press
4 Park Square, Milton Park, Abingdon, Oxon, OX14 4RN

CRC Press is an imprint of Taylor & Francis Group, LLC

Library of Congress Cataloging-in-Publication Data
Names: Shrawankar, Urmila, editor. | Malik, Latesh, editor. | Arora, Sandhya, editor.
Title: Cloud computing technologies for smart agriculture and healthcare / edited by Urmila Shrawankar, Latesh Malik, Sandhya Arora.
Description: First edition. | Boca Raton : Chapman & Hall/CRC Press, 2022. | Series: Chapman & Hall CRC cloud computing for society 5.0 | Includes bibliographical references and index. | Summary: "Cloud Computing Technologies for Smart Agriculture and Healthcare aims to cover the cloud management and framework. It discusses how cloud computing framework can be integrated with fog computing, edge computing, deep learning and IOT. This book will be divided in two application parts: Agriculture and Healthcare. Discusses fundamentals theories to practical and sophisticated applications of Cloud Technology for Agriculture and Healthcare Includes case studies Concepts are illustrated well with appropriate figures, tables and simple language This book is primarily aimed at graduates and researchers to understand the echo system of cloud technology for agriculture and healthcare"-- Provided by publisher.
Identifiers: LCCN 2021032157 (print) | LCCN 2021032158 (ebook) | ISBN 9781032068039 (hardback) | ISBN 9781032156071 (paperback) | ISBN 9781003203926 (ebook)
Subjects: LCSH: Agriculture--Data processing--Case studies. | Medicine--Data processing--Case studies. | Cloud computing--Case studies.
Classification: LCC S494.5.D3 C56 2022 (print) | LCC S494.5.D3 (ebook) |
DDC 338.10285--dc23/eng/20211007
LC record available at https://lccn.loc.gov/2021032157
LC ebook record available at https://lccn.loc.gov/2021032158

ISBN: 978-1-032-06803-9 (hbk)
ISBN: 978-1-032-15607-1 (pbk)
ISBN: 978-1-003-20392-6 (ebk)

DOI: 10.1201/9781003203926

Typeset in Palatino
by MPS Limited, Dehradun

Contents

Section III Cloud for Healthcare

Preface

The Cloud computing technology is now the essential part of our life. Cloud computing offers numerous benefits, because many applications have migrated to the cloud.

As it provides cost-effective service-oriented architecture, many society-based applications receive benefits, especially agriculture and healthcare applications.

This book covers details about Cloud-based applications related to the agriculture and healthcare domain.

This book is divided into three sections: 1. Cloud Management, 2. Cloud for Agriculture, and 3. Cloud for Healthcare; this book includes 19 chapters.

Chapter 1: This chapter provides a detailed overview of Cloud computing along with virtualization technology. It also explains the role of virtualization technology in Cloud resource management and its associated components. Further, this chapter discusses the various characteristics and components of Cloud computing, which plays a key role in multiple areas, like healthcare, agriculture, etc.

Chapter 2: This chapter gives a solution to the interoperability problem which would in turn be a helping hand for customers as well as resource providers. The aim is to provide an interoperable Cloud environment that will allow customers to compare and choose among resource availability when they switch between Cloud providers as and when needed so that their data and applications are not compromised.

Chapter 3: This chapter presents details about elasticity, which is one of the important features that allows resources to be scaled dynamically based on resource demand. It has to be efficiently implemented in order to meet Service Level Agreement (SLA) requirements as well as keeping the costs low. Automatic provisioning of resources a few minutes prior to actual demand helps maintain quality of service at the provider end. VM bootup time needs to be considered in auto scaling techniques.

Chapter 4: This chapter introduces the community Cloud service model for the hearing and speech impaired. These people with special needs can use Cloud-based services for education, healthcare in any disastrous condition and in daily workouts. This helps them to overcome the hesitation to communicate with others. Use of the community Cloud model separates this group of people and offers special services as per their needs. Use of Cloud services makes them more independent. It also helps them to obtain education more effectively, use telemedicine services for healthcare, and improves the engagement and collaboration with the outside world.

Chapter 5: This chapter features the capabilities of smart agriculture using IoT and wireless sensors. The primitive farm practices are changing by integrating and implementing sensor applications. Major agriculture applications are using wireless sensors, information communication technologies, and IoT are analyzed in detail. The sensors are used in various agriculture operations like irrigation, land preparation, land protection, weed management, nutrition management, planting, harvesting, etc. Also, the advancements in farm management, with the help of unmanned aerial vehicles and remote sensing, determine the area under cultivation to determine the relative health of agriculture fields, to estimate agriculture yield, and to strategize plantation and irrigation design and watershed management are discussed in detail.

Chapter 6: This chapter gives a quick survey of current SAR agricultural remote sensing techniques and their applications. The study includes techniques to retrieve biophysical parameters from SAR data and then to utilize these parameters for precision farming applications. The study reveals the benefits and limitations of available methods for precision agriculture. From the literature survey done in this study, it is identified that the generalized model needed for smart agriculture.

Chapter 7: In the current Cloud computing environment, technology and software tools are very useful in order to centralize the database of all farming crops (associated to soils, weather conditions, research, crops, farmers, agricultural promotion, composts, and knowledge on pesticides) in Cloud computing. This chapter discusses the computer model, qualities, execution prototype, Cloud facility prototype, Cloud benefits, and challenges of Cloud computing in farming fields.

Chapter 8: This chapter explains the IoTs Cloud-MANETS framework of a clever device collected to IoT's Cloud computing and MANETS. The creator fundamentally directs the reasons for difficulties and challenges identified with security, dependability, protection, and accessibility of administrations from the Cloud perspective. The significant commitment relates another approach to guarantee secure correspondence with the 5G organization of savvy gadgets utilizing the web. The methodology utilizes ideal reports and exact and successful re-enactments and can be provided to the IoT framework. Cloud computing is an application based on infrastructure that stores data on remote servers that access data through Internet. An effective implementation of the Cloud is encouraging in the agricultural sector.

Chapter 9: This chapter discusses "The Hybrid IDS Method for agricultural activities over Cloud Computing" and is implemented on the Weka tool. The proposed method is used to decrease the false alarm rate, toward refining a recognition rate. The presented method has several applications, such as the Cloud can store zone-specific weather, the weather forecast for a specific time, emerging agricultural security threads, as well as effective information sharing for agricultural activities.

Chapter 10: This chapter presents cluster-based real-time scheduling framework for healthcare applications on the Cloud computing environment. The different industrial case studies used for the Cloud environment are for real-time healthcare services, as presented in this chapter.

Chapter 11: This chapter describes the main objective to prepare a smart healthcare system so as to help separate the sleep disorder subjects and normal subjects and the alcoholic subjects and normal subjects based on fractal dimension calculations with minimum complexity and less time. The real-time EEG data can be uploaded on the hospital's Cloud. The Cloud-based healthcare system is trained with the algorithms for finding various features that are given to the classifier automatically to detect whether the person is suffering from a sleep disorder, alcoholic disorder, or is absolutely normal.

Chapter 12: This chapter defines Cloud computing and Internet integration of medical monitoring and management platform to provide new opportunities for the hospital, even in social fields. In the last few years, Cloud computing technology has been used in the healthcare industry. The Cloud is helpful in collecting more patient information than ever before. The healthcare industry and savvy entrepreneurs must learn how to secure data. Collaboration of different technology insights contain many challenges and opportunities. It is also evolving needs, business models, technology, and emerging evidence in healthcare efficacy.

Chapter 13: This chapter proposes various methodologies for the design and development of remote healthcare systems. These methodologies are based on data science and artificial intelligence (AI), and Cloud technologies also suggest leveraging the IoT-enabled medical data capturing through sensors, in addition to the location tracking and Cloud-based secured data storage mechanism.

Chapter 14: This chapter analyzes natural neighbor to identify the density of a data object, RNN-DBSCAN method, DPC-KNN method, A-DPC method, and LP-SNG algorithm. In the RNN-DBSCAN method, the performance depends upon the value of k. This paper proposes a method efficient in accessibility in Cloud databases of health networks with a natural neighbor approach for RNN-DBSCAN using the concept of natural neighbor.

Chapter 15: This chapter discusses a Cloud-based storage that assists doctors in analyzing the health of patients. As doctors and healthcare workers are naïve technology users, the system has a cross-platform interface.

Privacy of the patients' data is also an essential aspect of the system. It should be accessible to authorized healthcare workers.

Chapter 16: This chapter describes Parkinson disease (PD) as one of the most serious diseases. Hence, diagnosing it at an early stage lessens the effects. To predict the early stage, it's been discovered that the machine learning classification algorithm is one of the pleasant methods. In this work, we illustrate how Amazon SageMaker's algorithm-solving applications require machine learning models for prediction.

Chapter 17: This chapter discusses that in order to locate the area where the tumor is present, an average of codes is considered after every result to form the end MRI. This approach brings the model to the sensitive data owners and requires only the model updates to be sent to the central server, thereby preventing leakage of data and preserving privacy. While doing so, faulty updates from malicious clients can be discarded, thereby preventing them from hindering the central model. The challenges and considerations that need to be addressed while dealing with healthcare data for brain tumor segmentation are also highlighted in this chapter.

Chapter 18: This chapter describes the development, work, and efficiency of a smart system that will inform users about the guidelines issued by the government, enable him to determine his COVID-19 susceptibility via an SpO2 test, risk exposure status taking into account various factors and symptoms observed, and mask detection and maintaining social distancing to verify user compliance against these precautions, all using a smartphone which is owned by 99% of the population. The said system, after successfully running on numerous test cases, is found to be 97% accurate in calculating the SpO2 measure, risk status, and detecting masks and keeping record of the crowd exposure. Cloud computing is the on-demand availability of computer system resources, especially data storage and computing power, without direct active management by the user. The benefit of Cloud-based services to individual organizations is that they allow fast implementation and upscaling across a range of settings, as they do not need the organization to purchase additional hardware and they can be implemented remotely.

Chapter 19: This chapter discusses the attributes of policy data drawing from three measurements: social data, textual data, and contextual data. Effective attributes, like the theme distribution and hot data significance, are recognized by verifiable analysis. The effective attributes are input to the forecast and modeled to foresee the trending data related to COVID-19. The precise forecast outcomes could profit policy producers, permitting them to settle on better choices and understand and control people's judgments. To achieve such functionally, a powerful model, the "Rapid-Miner" simulator, is used and the proposed model is known as "Framework for Trending Data Prediction." This method provides great efficiency, performance, accuracy, and this model requires less execution time to predict the data over social media networks related to COVID-19.

Editors

Dr. Urmila Shrawankar received a PhD degree in computer science and engineering from SGB Amravati University and an M.Tech. degree in computer science and engineering from RTM Nagpur university. Her areas of interest include high-performance computing, advanced operating systems, distributed and parallel computing, Cloud computing, real-time computing, algorithms, assistive technology, etc. She is the author of two books, three books as an editor, nine book chapters, and around 200 research papers in international journals and conferences of high repute. She has published 16 patents. Her biography was selected and published in the Marquis *Who's Who in the World.* She received an international travel grant award from DST, Govt. of India, awarded a UGC Minor Project Grant, and RGSTC: Rajiv Gandhi Science and Technology Commission, Government of Maharashtra, India, Science and Technology Research Grant Scheme for two projects. She is serving on many journals as an editorial board member and as member of an international advisory board. Moreover, she is serving as a reviewer for many refereed journals and reputed conferences. She participated in many international conferences worldwide as a core organizing committee member, technical program committee member, special session chair, and session chair. She has delivered 50+ expert lectures on various topics for different universities. Dr Urmila is member of IEEE, ACM, CSI, ISTE, IE, IAENG, etc. Under her guidance, 15 industry-based projects, 51 UG (BE) Project Groups, 72 (PG) MTech Project Scholars, and one ME by Research Scholar completed their projects and 03 PhD Research Scholars are working. At present, Dr. Urmila is a professor in the Department of Computer Science and Engineering, G H Raisoni College of Engineering, affiliated to RTM Nagpur University Nagpur (MS), India.

Dr. Latesh Malik is working as an associate professor and head in the Department of Computer Science and Engineering, Government College of Engineering, Nagpur. She completed a Ph.D. (Computer Science and Engineering) from Visvesyaraya National Institute of Technology in 2010, an M.Tech. (Computer Science and Engineering) from Banasthali Vidyapith, Rajasthan, India, and a B.E. (Computer Engineering) from the University of Rajasthan, India. She is a gold medalist in B.E. and M.Tech. She has been teaching for 20+ years. She is life member of ISTE, CSI, ACM, and has more than 160 papers published in international journals and conferences. She is a recipient of 2 RPS and 1 MODROBs by AICTE. She guided 30+ PG projects and 8 students completed their Ph.D under her. She is an author of three books, *Practical Guide to Distributed Systems in MPI* and *Python for Data Analysis* on Amazon Kindle Direct Publishing and *R Programming for Beginners* by University Press India.

Dr. Sandhya Arora is a professor in the Department of Computer Enginering, MKSSS's Cummins College of Engineering for Women, Pune. She completed a Ph.D. (Computer Science and Engineering) from Jadavpur University, Kolkata in 2012, an M.Tech. (Computer Science and Engineering) from Banasthali Vidyapith, Rajasthan, India, and a B.E. (Computer Engineering) from the University of Rajasthan, India. She has extensive teaching experience of more than 22 years. She is a life member of ISTE, CSI, ACM, and has published papers in thoroughly acclaimed international journals and conferences. She is guiding PG and Ph.D. students. She has received prestigious awards in the field of computer science. She authored two books *Practical Guide to Distributed Systems in MPI* and *Python for Data Analysis* on Amazon Kindle Direct Publishing.

Contributors

Manasi Agrawal
MIT College of Engineering
Pune, India

G. Aishwarya
Department of Information Science and Engineering
Jyothy Institute of Technology
Bengaluru, Karnataka, India

Sandhya Arora
Cummins College of Engineering for Women
Pune, India

Shweta M. Barhate
Dept. of Electronics & Computer Science
Rashtrasant Tukadoji Maharaj Nagpur University
Nagpur, India

Siddhi Belgamwar
Department of Computer Science & Engineering
Shri Ramdeobaba College of Engineering and Management
Nagpur, India

Vaishali G. Bhujade
VJTI
Mumbai, India

Sumedha Borde
Marathwada Institute of Technology
Aurangabad, India

Rakshanda K. Borikar
Sant Gadge Baba Amravati University
Amravati, India

Advait Brahme
MIT College of Engineering
Pune, India

Bhargavi S. Chinchmalatpure
Bharatiya Mahavidyalaya
Amravati, India

Shaunak Choudhary
MIT College of Engineering
Pune, India

Priya Deokar
SKN College of Engineering
Pune, India

Mahendra P. Dhore
SSESA's Science College
Rashtrasant Tukadoji Maharaj Nagpur University
Nagpur, India

Chetan Dhule
Department of Computer Science and Engineering
G H Raisoni College of Engineering
Nagpur, India

Bharati Dixit
MIT World Peace University
Pune, India

Poonam A. Gaikwad
Sant Gadge Baba Amravati University
Amravati, India

Deep Gandhi
J. Sanghvi College of Engineering
Mumbai, India

Arvind S. Kapse
Department of ISE
New Horizon College of Engineering
Bengaluru, India

Avinash S. Kapse
Anuradha Engineering College
Chikhli, India

Atharva Kukade
Student, MIT College of Engineering
Pune, India

Pranay Kuthe
Student, Government College of Engineering
Nagpur, India

Jyoti Lagad
Smt Kashibai Navale College of Engineering
Pune, India

Latesh Malik
Government College of Engineering
Nagpur, India

Ramchandra Mangrulkar
J. Sanghvi College of Engineering
Mumbai, India

Jash Mehta
J. Sanghvi College of Engineering
Mumbai, India

Prachi Patil
Student, Government College of Engineering
Nagpur, India

Preeti V. Patil
Department of Information Science and Engineering
Jyothy Institute of Technology
Bengaluru, Karnataka, India

Shreya Rathi
Department of Computer Science & Engineering
Shri Ramdeobaba College of Engineering and Management
Nagpur, India

Sohan Rathod
Student, Government College of Engineering
Nagpur, India

Varsha Ratnaparkhe
Government College of Engineering
Aurangabad, India

Mohit Sawal
Department of Computer Science and Engineering
Shri Ramdeobaba College of Engineering and Management
Nagpur, India

Nemil Shah
J. Sanghvi College of Engineering
Mumbai, India

Ameya Shahu
Student, Government College of Engineering
Nagpur, India

Swati S. Sherekar
Sant Gadge Baba Amravati University
Amravati, India

Shrijeet Shivdekar
Department of Computer Science & Engineering
Shri Ramdeobaba College of Engineering and Management
Nagpur, India

Urmila Shrawankar
Department of Computer Science and Engineering
G H Raisoni College of Engineering
Rashtrasant Tukadoji Maharaj Nagpur University
Nagpur, India

Shiji K. Shridhar
Department of Information Science and Engineering
Jyothy Institute of Technology
Bengaluru, Karnataka, India

K. R. Sinchana
Department of Information Science and Engineering
Jyothy Institute of Technology, Bengaluru
Karnataka, India

Girish Talmale
Department of Computer Science and Engineering
G H Raisoni College of Engineering
Nagpur, India

Vilas M. Thakare
Department of CSE
Sant Gadge Baba Amravati University
Amravati, India

Harshvardhan Tiwari
Centre for Incubation, Innovation Research and Consultancy
Jyothy Institute of Technology
Bengaluru, Karnataka, India

Shubham N. Ugale
Sant Gadge Baba Amravati University
Amravati, India

Manjiri Vairagade
Department of Computer Science and Engineering
Shri Ramdeobaba College of Engineering and Management
Nagpur, India

Rupali J. Wadnare
Research Scholar
Sant Gadge Baba Amravati University
Amravati, India

Sampada Wazalwar
Department of Computer Science and Engineering
G H Raisoni College of Engineering
Nagpur, India

Rashmi Welekar
Department of Computer Science and Engineering
Shri Ramdeobaba College of Engineering and Management
Nagpur, India

Section I

Cloud Management

1

Virtualization Technology for Cloud-Based Services

Urmila Shrawankar and Chetan Dhule
Department of Computer Science and Engineering,
G H Raisoni College of Engineering, Nagpur, India

CONTENTS

1.1 Cloud Computing Overview

Cloud is the most advanced and fastest-growing technology in the world of computers. Cloud computing delivers unique IT proficiencies as services. Cloud-based services offer more system independence, demand, reusability, and reliability than traditional data centers. Cloud computing is the most recent evolution of computing for organizing and delivering services throughout the web. Utility computing, parallel computing, virtualization and service-oriented architecture are the key characteristics of cloud computing. The word "Cloud" jointly refers to the whisk of networks, interfaces, storage and hardware to deliver good assistance.

DOI: 10.1201/9781003203926-1

Cloud computing isn't a brand new notion. After August 2006, Amazon established a subsidiary, Amazon Internet Services, and launched its Elastic Compute Cloud (EC2) (Emeras et al., 2019) accompanied with the launch of the beta version of Google application Engine from Google in April 2008 (Prodan et al., 2012). At this time, lots of Information Technology (IT) organizations such as Amazon, Yahoo, Google, etc., were supplying cloud services to their customers.

Cloud provides distinct IT advancements and applications over the web through third parties. Computational resources, such as storage space and CPU power etc., are provided as basic utilities rented out to and released by the end consumer over the web as a pay-as-you-go and per order basis. It is very economical for business people who have just floated their startup company to service their small and growing need for resources, especially when there is demand in the market, using cloud services. Thus, cloud computing plays a key role in multiple areas like healthcare, agriculture, etc.

1.1.1 Features of Cloud Computing

The characteristics of cloud computing are:

i. On-demand Self Services:
The Cloud computing services do not require any individual administrators, because the consumers themselves can supply, monitor and manage computing resources, as need.

ii. Uniform Access to Broad Network:
The Computing solutions are usually provided over conventional networks and heterogeneous devices.

iii. Quick Elasticity:
The Computing services must have IT resources which can scale out very fast and align with needs. Thus, whenever the farmers need services, they scale up with services supplied; and when the requirement is over, they scale down with services stopped.

iv. Resource pooling:
The IT sources (e.g., storage, networks, servers, software and services) are pooled as if one resource bank available for servicing multiple programs and many tenants in an uncommitted manner. Numerous clients are supplied services from the identical physical source.

v. Measured support:
The resource utilization is kept track of for every program and tenant, and both the consumer and the resource provider are updated with an account of what's being utilized and how much. This can be done for a variety of reasons like monitoring, billing and efficient utilization of resources.

1.1.2 Impact of Cloud Computing on Business and Its Ecosystems

High-Performance Computing (HPC) is characterized by a cluster of systems functioning together smoothly as a single unit to attain performance goals impossible with disparate or monolithic systems. Consequently, organizations are eager to embrace HPC to keep ahead of their opponents because HPC enables ideas of brand new products, markets, and opportunities to open up if businesses possess the resources to analyze data that were not previously available. HPC is currently useful for solving a broad range of issues, and across industries, because of its capacity to fix large scale computational problems within acceptable time and cost parameters. Increasing computational power or high efficiency of HPC powered systems permits organizations to compute problems faster and efficiently.

HPC can be carried out on premise, in the cloud, or in a hybrid model which has features of both. Within an on premise HPC setup, a company or research institution assembles an HPC cluster filled with servers, storage solutions, and other infrastructure that they handle and update over time. In a cloud HPC set up, a cloud service provider oversees the infrastructure, and organizations only use it in a pay-as-you-go mode. Some organizations utilize hybrid deployments, particularly where they are already in an on-premise infrastructure but need to benefit also from the flexibility, time and cost efficiency of the cloud. For example, the organization may use the cloud to conduct a few HPC workloads on a continuous basis, and whenever queue time becomes a problem on premise, the tasks become cloud services on an ad hoc basis.

Organizations with on premise HPC surroundings gain end to end control over their operations, however, they need to contend with several challenges (Elnawawy, 2020; Mauch et al., 2013), such as:

- Investing substantial funds for computing equipment, which has to be constantly updated.
- Paying for real time ongoing management and different operational costs.
- Agreeing to time delay, or queue, from a couple of days to months before consumers can conduct their HPC workload, particularly when demand increases.
- Postponing upgrades to more effective and powerful computing components because of lengthy purchasing cycles, which slows down the speed of research and business.

Due to other challenges such as overall cost and energy consumption incorporated in on premise environments, cloud based high performance computing is found to be more reliable.

Acting as the main driving forces behind adoption of cloud computing by most of businesses, the following facilities are provided to businesses by cloud computing and it leads to the phenomenal growth of cloud.

i. **Business Agility**
Cloud computing has provided a great deal of flexibility to both the companies and their employees. While today, the employees can work from where they need, while for businesses it has become easier to obtain the resources they want. It has also helped in providing jobs quicker and reducing the time to advertise. These concerns offer a competitive advantage to grow and to thrive in business.

ii. **Less Operational Issues**
Cloud enables easy communication and cooperation between employees. This implies multiple people in different locations may work on a single project in real-time, supply their opinions, and make sure end choice is ideal.

iii. **Accessible 24×7**
Cloud Computing 24×7 availability is far simpler for employees. They could access data, apps, or anything saved in the Cloud from anywhere. All they require is a device and an active online connection.

iv. **Best Use of Tools**
In the traditional approach, software licensing and yearly renewals are riddled with complications. Additionally, monitoring the progress of workers and making certain they're contributing to our success is tough. But with the assistance of cloud computing, we could keep tabs on exactly what workers are up to and guarantee they're completing their jobs in time. This enhances business productivity.

v. **Less Capital Expenditure**
Cloud computing is useful in that it eliminates costly hourly rates you have to cover hiring expensive IT professionals, installing costly applications and asking for a consultation. With cloud computing, there's not any need to fret about upfront consulting charges, neither any need to sign costly maintenance and support contracts. Again, traditional IT requires keeping up with the newest technology and infrastructure to outdo competition and provide best service to clients. Cloud computing takes care of IT needs of the company and let's them devote time to core business. Alternatively, businesses may register for ready-to-use IT cloud solutions which need little if any entry cost. This finally contributes to less capital expenditure.

vi. **Managing Physical Servers**
With the everyday busy life, to carry each important data through physical storage devices is tedious; and also the hardware setup is not portable which makes every task very slow and processes difficult to maintain and keep organized. On the other hand, in cloud computing, the personal data or the important service in the form of a software is already installed and configured on to the cloud, and anyone with his needs to access created for him and with proper authentication can access this service from anywhere in the world with just a fast internet connection.

1.1.3 Deployment Models for Cloud Based Agriculture Services

Following are the cloud deployment models.

i. **Public Cloud**
The public cloud allows systems and services to be easily accessible to the general public. Public cloud may be less secure because of its openness.

ii. **Private Cloud**
The private cloud allows systems and services to be accessible within an organization. It is more secured because of its private nature.

iii. **Community Cloud**
The community cloud allows systems and services to be accessible by a group of organizations.

iv. **Hybrid Cloud**
The hybrid cloud is a mixture of public and private cloud, in which the critical activities are performed using private cloud while the non-critical activities are performed using public cloud.

1.2 Virtualization Technology

Virtualization creates virtual instances of a machine's resource on physical infrastructure. It can create a single virtual instance of a machine resource or combine multiple machine resource options like OS, Network, computing and storage devices, etc into one machine instance. Hypervisor working as a link or mediator between physical hardware and the virtual environment which facilitates access to the physical and virtual machines and plays a key role in distribution of multiple physical resources like memory, storage and CPU between multiple virtual machines.

Virtualization is conceptually defined as a unit acting like a physical component i.e., it'll be "behaving" and "working" like a separate hardware unit. Thus, with the absence of actual hardware, still, it will function as if it were currently present there (Spruijt, 2013).

Virtualization technique allows the company to use a single existing hardware system to run more than one Operating System at a time which greatly reduces the operating cost of individual hardware systems without affecting the overall efficiency of the current system. Thus, it is known for boosting the concept of cloud computing by emulating hardware like functionalities.

Virtualization plays a very crucial role in defining cloud computing, given cloud users share and store their data on the cloud like they are using a separate physical storage hardware when actually with virtualization many customers securely share the common Infrastructure located at a distinct place anywhere in the world.

Virtualization helps to create customer's resources such as data and storage, but it's only later with the help of cloud computing that it will be delivered to the end user on-demand (Khajehei, 2014).

Virtualization technology is mainly used for supplying the application in its original version to the cloud consumers. For example, if the latest version of a particular application is made available in the market, then the cloud service provider has to upgrade the old one and deliver the latest one to the cloud consumers, when practically it were more expensive given buying that many licenses as number of consumers would have made cost prohibitive.

To solve this issue, the cloud service providers take the benefit of virtualization and deploy the latest version of all applications, where virtualization creates instances of the updated software and lets consumers use the updated software. Clients using cloud-based services need not worry about updating software to latest version every time when a new version of the software is released.

1.2.1 Advantages of Virtualization

Virtualization provides the following advantages to cloud based businesses:

i. The number of servers gets reduced as instances of a server are getting created and not the physical server.
ii. The capabilities of the technology gets improved.
iii. The business continuity also gets raised due to the use of virtualization.
iv. A mixed virtual environment is created.
v. The development and test environment efficiency is improved.
vi. The Total Cost of Ownership (TCO) falls.

1.2.2 Benefits of Virtualization

Virtualization offers following benefits to companies:

i. Removal of special hardware and utility requirements.
ii. Effective management of resources.
iii. Increased employee productivity as a result of better accessibility.
iv. Reduced risk of data loss, as data is backed up across multiple storage locations.

Virtualization offers following benefits to data centers.

i. Maximization of server capabilities, thereby reducing maintenance and operation costs.
ii. Smaller footprint as a result of lower hardware, energy and manpower requirements.

1.2.3 Components Associated for Implementation of Virtualization

Following components are associated with the implementation of Virtualization as depicted in Figure 1.1:

a. *Host Machine*
A Host Machine is said to be any physical medium or hardware on which the virtualization is taking place. Host Machine allows the Hypervisor to set up and manage different virtual machines on it. Different physical components of the physical machine such as processor, memory and storage individually meet different needs of each virtual machine running on it. Typically, all of these actual physical resources are masked from Guest Machines. Hypervisor thus plays a leading role in creating this simulation effect. The end motive of the physical machine is to just provide all the raw resources such as the CPU power, Storage Space and Network Connection Requirements.

b. *Virtual Machine (Guest Machine)*
A Virtual Machine or the Guest Machine is a type of Operating System Software designed to run in a virtual environment on the physical Host Machine. Using single physical host, one can run more than one virtual machines at a same time. Various types of Storage Mediums, Database and Other computational resources can also be virtualized over a single physical system.

With the invent of Cloud and Virtualization Technology, it is now possible to simulate a single piece of hardware to deploy different types of environments such as Desktop or Server as per the wish. After all, behind all of this, from setting up the virtual environment to the actual request sent to the real hardware, everything is managed by the "Hypervisor". Whatever the hardware plans to do is requested via feedback using hypervisor and is applied on to the Virtual Environment.

Although all the virtual machines are running separately on their personal virtual space still each virtual machine believes that it is operating on it's separate Hardware System.

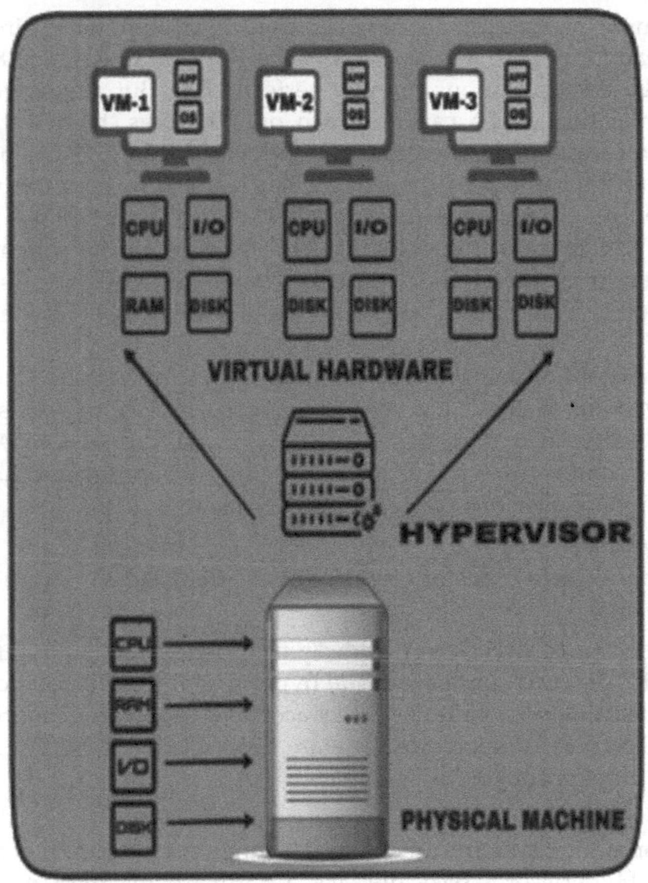

FIGURE 1.1
Components Associated with Implementation of Virtualization.

It is also possible to simulate another Hardware system apart from the existing one. For example, one of the virtual machines is using a storage array of 20 simultaneous storage locations emulating on standard physical server. In this scenario too, the storage array will act like the virtual machine is using 20 distinct Storage Hard Drives physically wired to the Network Interface. The end motive of the Guest Virtual Machine is just to run different Software and User Environments for individual virtual machines.

c. *Hypervisor*
A Hypervisor is not necessarily a software. It can be a firmware or hardware which binds to create and manage different virtual machines at the same time, along with resource allocation between them, as needed. Here the computational resources required for running the VMs are thus completely taken from the Host Machine. The Hypervisor is also known as VM Monitor because its task is to monitor the requirements of different VMs, according to which the resources of the physical hardware are divided as many times as needed.

For example, if you are using a Computer System with Linux Operating System already installed, and the system has the overall RAM of 8 GB, you will find Linux-based applications running perfectly fine. But, if you want to run any specific application which can only run on Windows, then it's here that hypervisor comes into play. It creates a Windows Virtual System on the existing computer and then allocates the current hardware resources to the new VM as per the application-specific requirements.

A major advantage of hypervisor is that it keeps all the concurrent running VMs isolated from each other because though all VMs are using the same hardware for resources, but still, they should ideally be separated from one another.

Another benefit of using hypervisor, along side of Virtual Machine, is from the security point of view. VM security protocol allows hypervisor to create a separate security layer in between actual OS and Virtual OS. Any malicious content downloaded from web is limited to the VM running and has not a single percent of impact over Primary Computer System.

d. *Types of Hypervisor*

There are mainly two types of Hypervisors as depicted in Figure 1.2:

i. *Type-1 Hypervisor*

Hypervisor runs directly on underlying host system. It is also known as "Native Hypervisor" or "Bare metal hypervisor". It does not require any base server operating system. It has direct access to hardware resources. Examples of Type 1 hypervisors include VMware ESXi, Citrix XenServer and Microsoft Hyper-V hypervisor (Figure 1.3).

ii. *Type-2 Hypervisor*

A Host operating system runs on underlying host system. It is also known as "Hosted Hypervisor". Basically, it's a software installed on an operating system. The hypervisor asks the operating system to make hardware calls. An example of Type 2 hypervisor includes VMware Player or Parallels Desktop. Hosted hypervisor is depicted in Figure 1.4.

1.2.4 Benefits of Virtualization to Cloud Data Centers

Virtualization offers following benefits to cloud data centers:

i. Prevention from System Failure

Just as virtualization creates a separate layer of security in between the primary system and the virtual system for preventing harmful content affecting core functionality, the same benefit is also seen for system failures. Any unlikely event of virtual system corruption will not risk data corruption on the primary system. Thus, it is very convenient to test or debug any new type software on the virtual environment without worries of risk to the underlying physical hardware, like virus, malware or system crash of the main system.

ii. Easy Transfer of Data or System

Hardware Maintenance is a tedious process, if it has to be carried out regularly. With the intent of data transfer or complete system migration from one place to

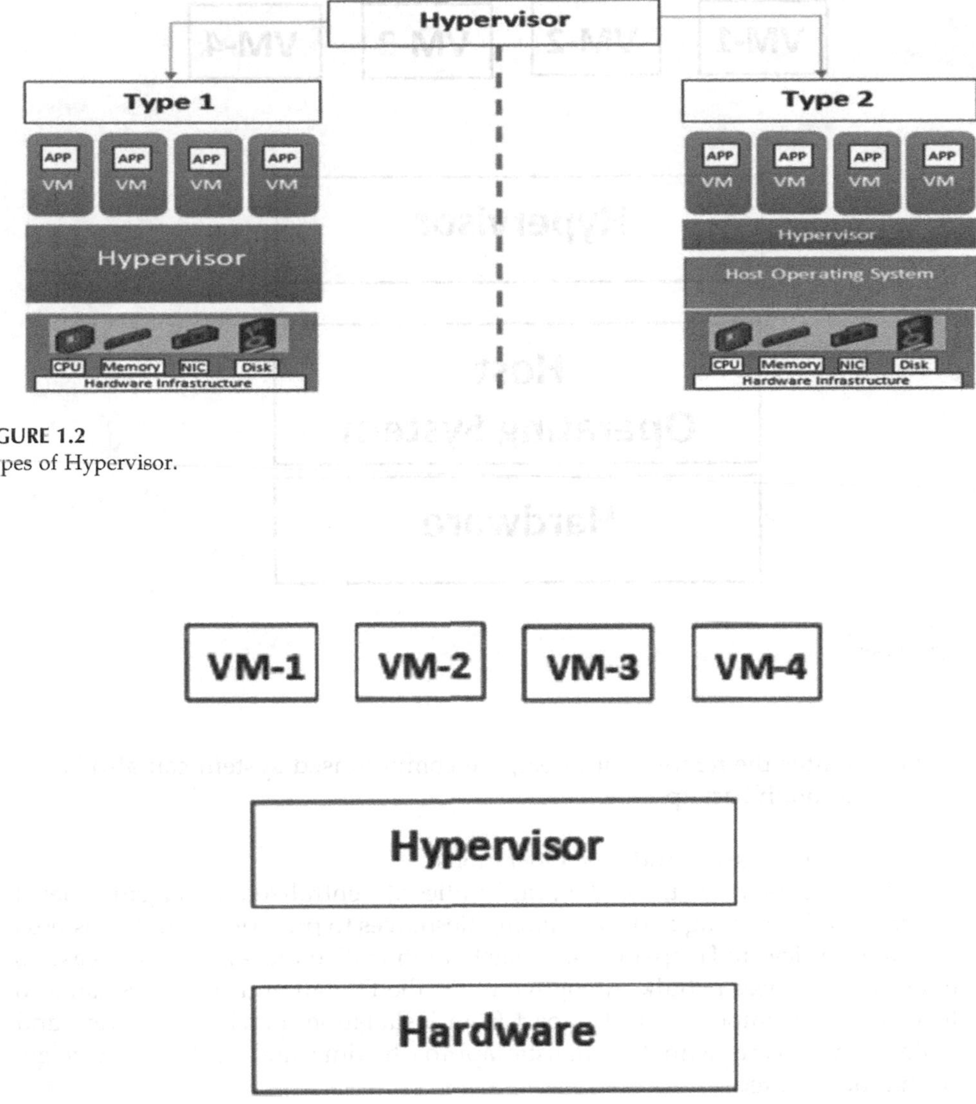

FIGURE 1.2
Types of Hypervisor.

FIGURE 1.3
Type-1 Hypervisor.

another, virtual system transfer takes everything to another physical infrastructure as per requirement without just moving any of the infrastructure from its place.

iii. Advanced Security Measures
Apart from additional security barrier between guest and Host Machine, the cloud along with virtualization also provides various core security protocols to prevent system from being exposed to external threats. It is totally impossible to hijack the complete infrastructure from a single loophole in any one of the virtualized systems because one compromised part cannot infect other secured

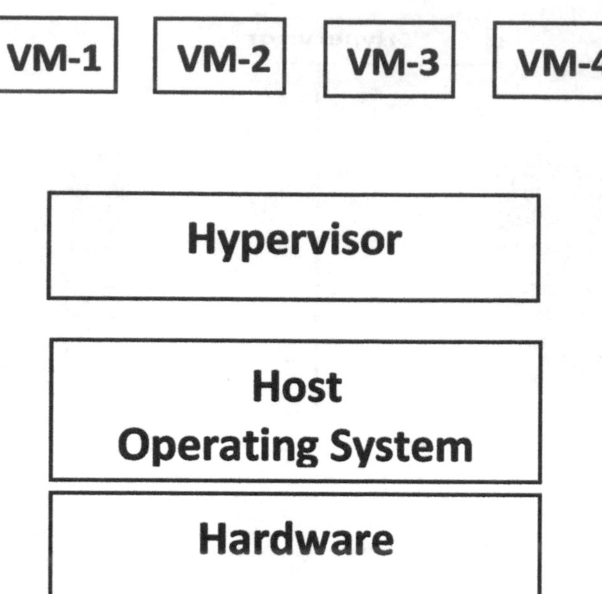

FIGURE 1.4
Type-2 Hypervisor.

portions. After the removal of threat, the compromised system can also be recovered through backup data.

iv. Centralized Processing and Fast Operations
Cloud Providers utilize the system capabilities at Centralized Management level which includes Pooling and Virtualizing Resources to provide accurate business oriented services to IT operators. At such a rationalized level, it is very easy to manage all devices in bulk. Along with this, the IT staff and resources can also focus on other important tasks apart from installation, patching software and maintenance. Thus with this holistic approach, time and cost efficiency get continuously lifted.

v. Low Operating Cost
Cloud Computing offers a hassle-free set up without being worried about physical platforms. With virtualization, it becomes very convenient to handle virtual environments or storage needs with less or no physical infrastructure. This eliminates hidden charges in terms of rental fees and power supply.

1.2.5 Role of Virtualization in Cloud Resource Management

By allowing response isolation, specific customization, enhanced security and ease of management, virtualization allows the cloud to deliver the services on demand. Its role is crucial for performing computing virtually. Cloud data centers mostly adopt hardware and programming language virtualization. Virtual hardware is considered as IaaS and virtual programming is PaaS.

Thus, both of these offer highly customized and virtual environments to businesses without the need of maintaining in-house infrastructure.

The highest degree of resource isolation offered by virtualization allows service providers to use the same set of resources for multiple services without any interference.

This plays a crucial role in reducing all underutilized hosts by migrating all Virtual Machines (VMs) on such underutilized hosts to some other moderately utilized hosts. This terminology is called server consolidation. The process of moving the virtual machines is called virtual machine migration. The migration can be done by temporarily stopping the VMs or by migrating live VMs.

The live migration-based server consolidation helps to achieve the maximum resource utilization and reduce the resource wastage.

1.3 Virtual Machine Migration

The process in which the complete virtual machine is going to be moved from one physical system to another for load balancing without interrupting the ongoing cloud services is known as Virtual Machine Migration. After migration, all the preliminary components like storage and network connectivity are transferred to the Destination Guest Machine.

1.3.1 Types of VM Migration

There are two types of VM Migration:

a. Cold/Regular Migration
   In this process, the virtual machine is completely turned off from the current Source Host Machine and then transferred to the new Destination Host Machine. After the completion of transfer process, the old Guest Machine from Source Host is deleted completely and the new Guest Machine on Destination Host is powered on for further service. Here, since after migration, there is no connection between Guest Machine and Old Source Host Machine, all the associated data need not be on shared storage.
b. Hot/Live Migration
   In this process, the Virtual Machine is continuously powered on during migration from Source Host Machine to Destination Host Machine. During migration to destination host, the Guest Machine at Source Host is halted for a very limited time until all the content from the RAM of Guest Virtual Machine along with some of the working CPU registers gets copied to the Destination Host Machine. This is a very fast process in which active cloud users cannot even distinguish between the interruption of availability and return to it. After copying all the live working content, within a few seconds, the actual virtual machine gets transferred to the destination address. One of the main reasons for live migration is to allow Administrators to carry out VM Maintenance or Upgradation without allowing for system downtime.
   Thus, proactive maintenance gets convenient with the intent of Live/Hot Migration. Live Migration can also be implemented for balancing overall load on

Source Host Machine in which, most of the time, the live working content is only transferred to the destination host and remaining resources get shared between the two host machines. This will greatly optimize CPU Resource Utilization due to a shared environment.

1.3.2 Cost of VM Live Migration

Before Live Migration, it is necessary to understand the overheads from data transfer during migration so that the customer should not face any downtime during normal operations. It is very important to consider some of factors in Host Machine such as CPU States, Storage Contents and Memory Contents.

i. **CPU State**
CPU State represent minimal information and is the lower bound of service downtime. The CPU State associated with Virtual Machine must be context switched between source and destination host. It has very low impact on migration downtime.

ii. **Storage Content**
It is an optional part of migration. It is not necessary to transfer storage contents to the Destination Host because LAN connections like CDC and Cluster utilizes Network Attached Storage type (NAS). If it is difficult to transfer all the storage contents due to large volume, then the cloud provider has to create a secondary Virtual storage medium on the Destination Host Machine and then needs to synchronize it with original source content. Due to high storage volume, storage contents need a considerable amount of time for transfer. One solution for overcoming this situation is to filter out unnecessary contents with the help of Hypervisor and then transfer only the important contents to destination Virtual Disk.

1.3.3 Applications of VM Live Migration

i. **Hassle Free Hardware Maintenance**
Cloud Services are provided around the globe and lots of customers are using it simultaneously which sometimes leads to sudden failure of systems and several times. Thus, to prevent these unknown system halts, VM Migration is performed in which complete overloaded system is temporarily transferred to the new Host Machine and, after completion of source hardware upgrade, the system is as is moved back to its original physical location (Cisco Systems, Inc., 2021).

ii. **Load Management**
Physical Hardware on which different VM's are simultaneously running needs to be completely load free because overloaded physical machines reduce overall server lifespan and also diminish Quality of Service (QoS) (Hu et al., 2010). On the other hand, unoccupied server spaces result in wastage of energy. Thus, main outcome of migration should focus on maintaining overall Quality of Service. One of the ways of load balancing is to evenly distribute content among different geo-located data centers during VM Migration.

iii. **Server Consolidation**
As per the needs and requirements, VMs are constantly created and destroyed within a particular data center. Whenever there is need for creating Virtual Machine, a new Virtual Setup is assigned by Hypervisor and after the completion of task, Hypervisor itself is instructed to permanently free up all associated hardware resources. In some cases, VMs are created and kept in idle or suspended state. It is very important to properly consolidate servers; else, VMs will leave a complete disarray. The two main purposes of server consolidation are to accomplish VM Migration for load balancing and for communication scenarios to reduce network traffic (Hu et al., 2015).

iv. **Prescient Fault Tolerance**
System failure is a recurrent issue during managing multiple VMs at the same time in data centers. These systems faults should be presciently addressed to reduce failure impact caused to system and application execution. To tackle all of these, various Fault Tolerance techniques are implemented (Bala and Chana, 2012).

v. **Energy Efficiency**
As discussed before, the server may be in Busy (Overloaded) State, Free (Idle) State or Off (Sleep) mode. As per requirement, if server is overloaded, then VM Migration helps to reduce this stress; else, if the server is in idle state, then switching it off so that it enters in sleeping mode will save more than 70% of energy. Thus, VM Live Migration is the most energy-efficient technique in Cloud Computing (Dhule and Shrawankar, 2017, 2019, 2020; Fan et al., 2007; Ge et al., 2014).

vi. **Resource Distribution**
Various performance issues arise with limited supply of computational resources like CPU Cycles, Memory Space and Cache. This problem of resource insufficiency can be solved by VM reallocation from overcrowded server to uncrowded server. Also resource sharing reduces overall cost due to switching off unused servers (Ghutke and Shrawankar, 2014), (Talmale and Shrawankar, 2017), (Dong et al., 2013), (Zanjal and Girish, 2016).

1.4 Applications of Cloud-Based Services in Agriculture Sector

Cloud computing is very helpful in agriculture by providing real-time information across multiple locations. Following are a few of these specific areas where clouds are useful.

i. **Crop-related information**
The cloud can provide historical information related to crops; this information can be used by farmers to take accurate decision about which crop to cultivate.

ii. **Weather information**
The forecast of weather in a specific region can help farmers to make crop-related decisions accordingly.

iii. **Soil Information**
The cloud-based information about the soil profile combined with the information about past prediction of future trends can be very helpful to farmers.

iv. **Monitoring Growth**
Cloud combined with IoT can monitor the growth of crops. This will help farmers to plan the activities accordingly.

v. **Farmers' Data**
Policymakers can use the region-wise cloud-based data of farmers while framing agricultural strategies.

vi. **Expert Consultation**
Cloud can provide real-time expert consultation facility for local farmers.

vii. **E-commerce**
The cloud can help farmers from rural areas who are unable to sell their own produce directly to the market without the intervention of middlemen to sell online. Cloud based e-commerce system for agricultural products can allow the farmers to sell their products directly to the end users/retailers.

1.5 Conclusion

Cloud computing offers services in the most flexible and scalable way. Thus, it provides industries more and more control over their data and allows businesses to pay only for services they use, which reduces overall operating costs, and also runs infrastructure more efficiently by providing a scalable set of resources as businesses must change to adapt to changing business environment. This leads to a big shift from the traditional computing paradigms to cloud-based services. This chapter provided a detailed introduction to cloud computing. Further, this chapter provided the details of cloud infrastructure and components associated. It also provided an overview of Virtualization Technology which makes easy the organizations' significant shift from traditional computing paradigms to cloud-based services. It also explained the role of Virtualization Technology in cloud resource management and its implementation-associated components. Further, this chapter discussed the various characteristics and components of cloud computing which plays a key role in multiple areas like healthcare, agriculture, etc.

References

Bala, Anju and Inderveer Chana. "Fault Tolerance-Challenges, Techniques and Implementation in Cloud Computing." *International Journal of Computer Science Issues (IJCSI)* 9, no. 1 (2012): 288.

Cisco Systems, Inc. "Virtual Machine Mobility with Vmware Vmotion and Cisco Data Center Interconnect Technologies." VMware 2009. Accessed Feb 21, 2021.

Dhule, Chetan and Urmila Shrawankar. "Performance Analysis for Pareto-Optimal Green Consolidation Based on Virtual Machines Live Migration." *International Journal of Grid and High-Performance Computing (IJGHPC)* 9, no. 4 (2017): 36–56.

Dhule, Chetan and Urmila Shrawankar. "Energy Efficient Green Consolidator for Cloud Data Centers." In *2019 6th International Conference on Computing for Sustainable Global Development (INDIACom)*, IEEE (2019): 405–409.

Dhule, Chetan and Urmila Shrawankar. "POF-SVLM: Pareto Optimized Framework for Seamless VM Live Migration." *Computing*102 (2020): 2159–2183.

Dong, Jiankang, Xing Jin, Hongbo Wang, Yangyang Li, Peng Zhang and Shiduan Cheng. "Energy-Saving Virtual Machine Placement in Cloud Data Centers." In *2013 13th IEEE/,ACM International Symposium on Cluster, Cloud, and Grid Computing*, IEEE (2013): 618–624.

Elnawawy, Hussein. "Analyzing and Mitigating the Cost of Persistence in High-Performance Computing Systems." (2020).

Emeras, Joseph, Sébastien Varrette, Valentin Plugaru and Pascal Bouvry. "Amazon Elastic Compute Cloud (EC2) Versus In-House HPC Platform: A Cost Analysis." *IEEE Transactions on Cloud Computing* 7 (2019): 456–468.

Fan, Xiaobo, Wolf-Dietrich Weber and Luiz Andre Barroso. "Power Provisioning for a Warehouse-Sized Computer." *ACM SIGARCH Computer Architecture News* 35, no. 2 (2007): 13–23.

Ge, Chang, Zhili Sun, Ning Wang, Ke Xu and Jinsong Wu. "Energy Management in Cross-Domain Content Delivery Networks: A Theoretical Perspective." *IEEE Transactions on Network and Service Management* 11, no. 3 (2014): 264–277.

Ghutke, Bhushan and Urmila Shrawankar. "Pros and Cons of Load Balancing Algorithms for Cloud Computing." In *2014 International Conference on Information Systems and Computer Networks (ISCON)*, IEEE (2014): 123–127.

Hu, Jinhua, Jianhu Gu, Guofei Sun and Tianhai Zhao. "A Scheduling Strategy on Load Balancing of Virtual Machine Resources in Cloud Computing Environment." In *2010 3rd International Symposium on Parallel Architectures, Algorithms and Programming*, IEEE (2010): 89–96.

Hu, Rongdong, Guangming Liu, Jingfei Jiang and Lixin Wang. "A New Resources Provisioning Method Based on QoS Differentiation and VM Resizing in IaaS." *Mathematical Problems in Engineering* 2015 (2015): 1–9.

Khajehei, Kamyab. "Role of Virtualization in Cloud Computing." *International Journal of Advance Research in Computer Science and Management Studies*2, no. 4 (2014): 15–23.

Mauch, Viktor Marcel Kunze and Marius Hillenbrand. "High Performance Cloud Computing." *Future Generation Computer Systems* 29, no. 6 (2013): 1408–1416.

Prodan, Radu, Michael Sperk and Simon Ostermann. "Evaluating High-Performance Computing on Google App Engine." *IEEE Software* 29 (2012): 52–58.

Spruijt, Ruben.*"Application Virtualization Smackdown."* Solutions Overview and Feature Comparison Matrix Whitepaper, PQR Corporation (December 2013): 1–53.

Talmale, Girish and Urmila Shrawankar. "Dynamic Clustered Hierarchical Real Time Task Assignment & Resource Management for IoT Based Smart Human Organ Transplantation System." In *2017 Conference on Emerging Devices and Smart Systems (ICEDSS)*, IEEE (2017): 103–109.

Zanjal, Samir V. and R. Girish Talmale. "Medicine Reminder and Monitoring System for Secure Health Using IOT." *Procedia Computer Science* 78 (2016): 471–476.

2

Hybrid Cloud Architecture for Better Cloud Interoperability

Shweta M. Barhate[1] and Mahendra P. Dhore[2]
[1]*Dept. of Electronics & Computer Science RTM Nagpur University, Nagpur, India*
[2]*Shri Shivaji Science College, Affiliated with RTM Nagpur University, Nagpur, India*

CONTENTS

2.1 Introduction

Clouds are basically known for their service delivery over the internet along with the infrastructure. These services are provided by its hardware and systems software in data centres. This facilitates clouds with ubiquitous and wireless networking, less storage costs, and progressive improvements in internet computing software. The clients will be able to get value added services ubiquitously at reduced costs, optimised resource utilization, etc. The current technical governing of cloud computing infrastructures and services is done by virtualization.

DOI: 10.1201/9781003203926-2

The clients can avail cloud services like Infrastructure-as-a-service (IAAS), Platform-as-a-service (PAAS), or Software-as-a-service (SAAS) where they pay on the basis of use. The customer requests for Cloud services and are allocated to them dynamically. The workloads in the clouds are varying in nature, due to it the clouds should be able to manage with easy management of these workloads. The cloud infrastructure is designed to be flexible in getting tuned with loose tied CPU clusters.

Cloud technology is like an umbrella which provides the customer with the numerous resources with the power of virtualization technology. Cloud consists of physical machines under which several virtual machines are created which provides users with umpteen numbers of resources. But when such a large environment is being implementing naturally the cloud platform setting gets very costly. Hence it is very necessary that there is efficient reuse of the cloud resources so as to make it more cost efficient. This reuse is possible when there is interoperability among heterogeneous cloud environment. But interoperability is the most overlooked branch of cloud computing. Thus, there was an immense need of interoperability study so that customers get the advantage of full resource provisioning in a very cost efficient way.

Here we provide needed solution to the interoperability problem which would in turn be a helping hand for customers as well as resource providers. The aim is to provide an interoperable Cloud environment which will make customers able to compare and choose among resource availability when they switch between Cloud providers as and when needed so that their data and application are not compromised (Barhate et al. 2018).

2.2 Super Five Technologies of Cloud

2.2.1 Standardization Technology

There can be an efficient share and use of data which can be transferred from one cloud to another. This forms the basis of Interoperability. Data management interface in clouds is supported by standardization. Many cloud storage providers support data and storage management interfaces which makes use of Simple Object Access Protocol (SOAP) and Representational State Transfer (REST). Cloud Standardization can be thought of as an suitable solution to issues such as data migration and interoperability. Standards in cloud consist of OVF (open virtualization format) that provisions universal language to describe metadata and relevant virtual machines configuration parameters thereby facilitating networking. This VM networking helps to function the virtual machines in a smooth way. Standardization focuses on enabling resource exchange and information between multiple clouds. This ultimately provides the way for the clouds to observe mutual consent for the data and resource share.

2.2.2 Virtualization Technology

Virtualization is the base technology of cloud computing. It is the most efficient technology for IAAS deployment. It provides plentiful benefits to cloud architecture through its abstraction technique. The virtualization divides the architecture in physical and logical view. A cloud works as an umbrella where under a physical machine various dissimilar virtual machines work parallel. Virtualization reduces number of physical components thereby less number of components to manage and maintain. This technology works under the idea that the operating system is isolated from underlying hardware resources and functionalities. Multiple logical computers take birth virtually from one physical computing unit through this powerful technology where each logical unit uses its guest software. The technology at server level can be implemented by introducing thin layer of hypervisor layer called **virtual machine monitor**. The hypervisor multiplexes the access to resources so that the multiple logical resources can be shared effectively. It can be implemented in various ways and depending on the ways there is no need that the guest operating system and host operating system should be same.

2.2.3 Intercloud Technology

Cloud computing can be visualized as a collection of umpteen number of resources situated at different data centres residing in different regions. These resources are shared among different users as per need. But as there are large numbers of resources, subsequently there are number of users also. In cloud computing concept of graceful degradation also in non-tolerable as this generally introduces customer dissatisfaction because of imprecise waiting time and also degraded seek time. Thus an idea of powerful combination of multiple clouds floated and which was ultimately termed as intercloud technology. The intercloud architecture works on the logic that clouds are reciprocally compliant for resource sharing amongst them which means that they are prudent in using a gateway via standardized interface.

The super powerful Intercloud technology took a birth due to the fact that one cloud is not capable of providing adequate physical resources and thereby not adhering to ubiquity which is the biggest power of cloud. The important trait of cloud is that it supplies the clients with customer desirable computational and storage resources via infrastructure ubiquitously. Ultimately cloud makes available the users services in the like platform, software, and infrastructure. The Intercloud technology offers the clients the independence to switch between host cloud or the federated other clouds as the need be. The federated technology provides an architecture parallel to internet wherein a service provider would provide services to the user independent of the geographical location of the users using Internet routing protocols with other service providers as they have established relation to share resources mutually.

2.2.4 Fault Tolerance

Fault tolerance in cloud computing relates to keep the working in cloud on even if there is failure in some part of cloud. We can relate fault tolerance technique to graceful degradation of the system working in cloud (Zeeshan Amin April 2015). Following are some of the important parameters considered while conducting the research which are tabularized as follows (Table 2.1):

2.2.5 Energy Efficiency

The international use of cloud computing is predicted to convey with it few disadvantages like high energy consumption which ultimately adds to global warming due to the emission of harmful and undesirable gases which creates an intolerable problem to the users. Hence the need of the hour is at least an optimal energy efficient architecture. Thus the first successful move towards efficient energy consumption came to be provisioning of the virtual machines dynamically and then implementing optimal energy consumption techniques.

TABLE 2.1
Fault Tolerance Metrics

Fault Tolerance Metrics	Approach of Metric Towards Fault Tolerance
Performance	Has to be improved at Reasonable Cost
Response Time	Parameter should be minimized
Scalability	This Metric Should be Improved
Throughput	It should be high to improve the performance of the system
Reliability	Correct Result should be given in less time.
Availability	As reliability Increases Availability also increases
Cost Effectiveness	Should be an optimized monitory cost

There are two types of techniques to optimize energy efficiency in cloud computing as follows:

- **Software Based Energy Reduction Techniques**: Techniques here implement a range of algorithms in software to reduce energy consumption.
- **Hardware Based Energy Reduction Techniques**: Popularly used techniques for energy efficiency are as follows:
  - Data Distribution
  - Server Consolidation

Data distribution and server consolidation work on the logic that "The more the resource utilization more would be the Energy consumption". Then the next approach was to think of the way the above to techniques would go hand in hand which was really challenging. After lots of exploration it was a conclusion drawn regarding above two golden techniques that the data is so optimally distributed that there is no over utilization or underutilized of the data centres. The underlying logic was to switch the data from the underutilized data centres to the other data centres and close the ones which are less used. **Server Consolidation technique is the one which** works by reducing energy consumption by agglomerating the Virtual Machines in such a way that the ones who have no requests are combined to work together such that all work optimally.

2.3 Architecture of Interoperable Clouds

Interoperability, decoupling and just in time integration are the key services of cloud computing. Cloud to cloud interface provides communication with other clouds and services by interoperability. Thereby interoperability remains a big challenge for cloud computing. The use cases which emerged as big issues in cloud computing are user authentication, data migration, workload management and load balancing. Then emerged a way that interoperability can be managed by solving these four use cases. User authentication with respect to interoperability deals with security in cloud with respect to interoperability. Managing the above four issues along with fulfilling the QOS requirements is the focus of this research work (Buyya et al. 2009). The present work focuses on problems such as vendor lock-in, high cost due to inability to reuse the code or resources etc. After deep exploration of issue the solutions towards interoperability emerge out as follows:

1. Standardization
2. Hybrid Cloud

Previous studies suggest standardization aspects with respect to interoperability. Some studies suggest a middleware layer in the architecture for ease of interoperability. Here the focus is done on interoperability with respect to the use cases of interoperability along with the standardization initiatives. The cloud configuration is such that provisioning of the data centres is implicit and the user request is answered quickly. Hypervisor is used as a middleware by the data centres based on virtualization for resource delivery. So, implicit cloud provider for resource provisioning was implemented. With umpteen number of high speed, powerful, costly resources, resource reuse came up as one the feasible solutions. The resource reuse here can also be called as interoperability (Parmeswaran and Chaddha 2009) (Srinivasana et al. 2015). While implementing interoperability in cloud environment security emerged out as a big challenge in public clouds. In private clouds the issue of high security but restriction to access the resources and high waiting time due to limited number of resources continues to challenge the interoperability solution. So to overcome the problem of limited resource access in powerful private clouds and security problems in public clouds standardization rose up as an ideal solution to various such important issues including ease of access, ease of mobility, resource utilisation, throughput, and cost and most important is time (Ghanam, Ferreira, and Maurer 2012) (Kostoska, Gusev, and Ristov 2013) (Lee, Park, and Yang 2015).

This research working focusing upon interoperability as a need of the hour in cloud environment came up with a feasible solution that Hybrid Cloud which is a potent combination of large and resourceful public clouds and fast and secured private clouds. Hybrid cloud can be thought that it will be able to prevail over all the major issues discussed earlier along with the wrapped up advantages of both the clouds (Srinivasana et al. 2015).

Real world implementation or testing of cloud is not feasible due to the huge cost incurred in resource usage and so the interoperability or hybrid cloud architecture is studied using cloud simulators like Cloudsim, (Calheiros et al. 2010) (Sheshasaayee and Swetha 2015) Cloud Analyst (Singh, Sharma, and Kumar 2016), Cloud Reports.

2.4 Hybrid Cloud Interoperability Methodology

Interoperability architecture for hybrid cloud was designed spotlighting on the following parameters (Buyya, Ranjan, and Calheros 2010):

1. Throughput (Low response time w.r.t. more work done)
2. Execution Time (Data centre processing time)
3. Cost Efficiency (Grand total cost for cloud modelling)
4. Efficient Resource Utilization

5. Energy Efficiency
6. Heterogeneity of Hybrid clouds
7. Security.

2.5 Modelling of Hybrid Interoperability Cloud Methodology

Interoperability focused Hybrid cloud methodology involves following steps:

1. Hybrid cloud modelling by appropriate grouping of private and public cloud data centres.
2. Central idea is based on the logic that hybrid cloud is made up of small sized private clouds, with limited resource access and advanced configuration and big sized public clouds with mediocre configuration.
3. While modelling public cloud or private cloud for simulation the virtual machines would be the deciding factor for big sized clouds and the number of hosts would be deciding factor for modelling configuration in small but higher end clouds.
4. So according to logic decided above private cloud will be modelled with more number of hosts and public cloud would be modelled having less number of hosts.
5. Accessibility of private cloud would be only for users of that specific region and accessibility of public cloud would be for the users of any region.
6. By default request sent by the user is forwarded to the private cloud and as the threshold is reached then the request is dynamically sent to public cloud if the need be.
7. Interoperability hybrid cloud framework engages first 1 private cloud with more number of hosts and less number of virtual machine and adding 2 public clouds with vice a versa combination of virtual machines and hosts per region.
8. Service broker policy which is the key role player provisioning interoperability.
9. At the last the VM load balancing algorithm is considered which advances selecting the ideal virtual machine for job allocation as per the need of the user.
10. The framework is finally modelled region wise that is across the world with varying region wise time slot.

2.6 Tools Used to Design Hybrid Interoperability Methodology

The real world modelling and design of hybrid cloud is very difficult as there are various restrictions in real world cloud implementation. So this work proposes use of cloud simulators for design and development of hybrid cloud methodology.

Hence the work proceeds considering CloudSim as the main simulator for modelling and implementation of hybrid cloud. For analysing the performance of any architecture, modelling and simulation technologies are very useful. So, there was a need of appropriate software system techniques and tools to test and analyze cloud performance. CloudSim simulator has a complete package of powerful toolkits and classes built on the cloud platform for resource utilization and parallelization.

This simulator provides near to real world implementation and working of clouds. CloudSim consists of User Interface Structure, Virtual Machine Interface, cloud Services such as VM Provisioning, CPU allocation, Memory Allocation, Storage Allocation, Bandwidth Allocation etc, Cloud Resources like hosts, data centre, etc (Barhate and Dhore 2018).

The proposed hybrid cloud interoperability framework was designed with the help of Cloud Analyst Tool which is an extended toolkit and a GUI of CloudSim. The reason behind using Cloud Analyst was that it provides an easy, transparent cloud modelling and experimentation. The main advantage is that simulations can be easily repeated as many number of times as needed even with slight change in parameters (Mahajan and Dahiya 2014).

Netbeans environment is used to model GUI of CloudSim 3.0.3 with Jdk 1.7.0 in windows 7 (64 bit) environment. The research work realises that CloudSim a very helpful simulator for modelling real cloud infrastructure with flexible scalability and repeatable testing model facility. GUI of CloudSim 3.0.3 i.e. Cloud Analyst Toolkit is used NetBeans (Wickremasinghe, Calheiros and Buyya 2010).

2.7 Proposed Framework for Hybrid Cloud Interoperability

As pointed out above cloud analyst is used to model the proposed hybrid cloud interoperability framework. As discussed in methodology modelling was done as a package of one private and two public clouds which goes on scaling the public and private data centres region wise. We lock the logic as private clouds will be considered as small and higher configured ones and public clouds to be large and lower configured. Then the framework moves ahead considering the appropriate service broker policy which has key role cloud environment and especially hybrid clouds. The work advents with independent modelling of public and private clouds and then contrasting the hybrid cloud performance (Figure 2.1).

2.8 Working Philosophy of Hybrid Cloud Framework

Interoperability is the key focused in the framework and all the modelling of data centres, working of virtual machines and moving across the data centres redirected by service broker policy and appropriate load balancing algorithm work accordingly. Framework underlines the ideology that hybrid cloud modelling with fully work with respect to interoperability issues. It also forms as a basic logic that data would first move to private cloud which is dominant cloud and as the need be users implicitly are routed to large public clouds which are of lower configuration.

The work analyzes the supportiveness of hybrid cloud towards interoperability. Brokers stand up as the most important part as interoperability enabler. A request is first processed by appropriate service broker policy implemented by data centre brokers and accordingly redirecting the resource request to available and appropriate data centre. A

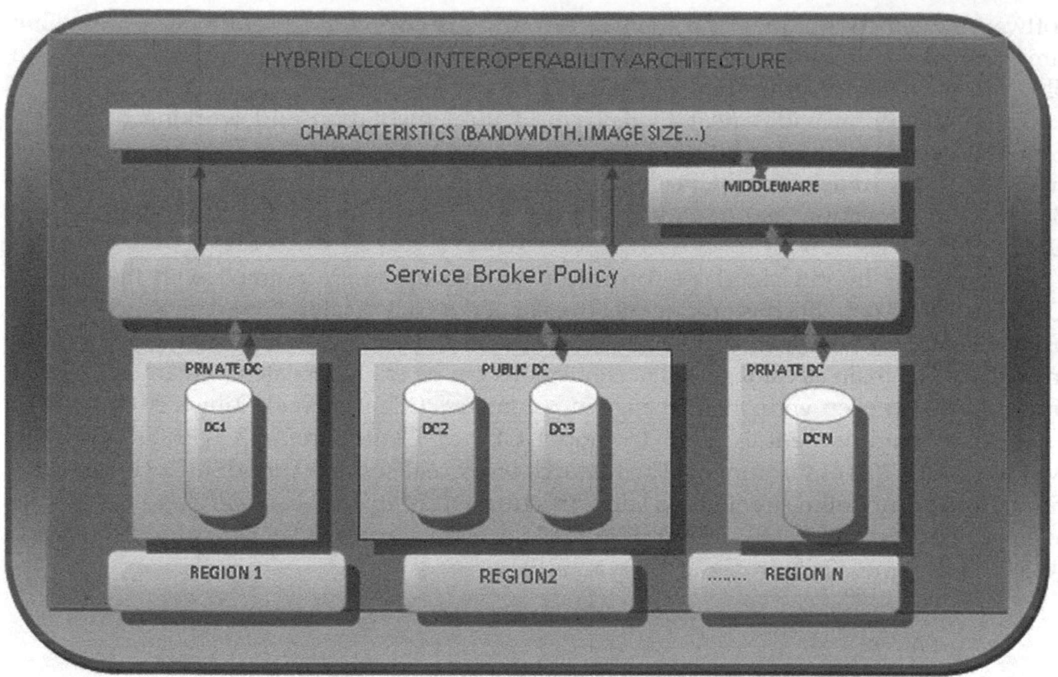

FIGURE 2.1
Hybrid Cloud Interoperability Methodology.

data centre has a combination of hosts and virtual machines. These virtual machines accepts and takes care of the user request. The implementation of hybrid cloud is then analyzed considering different interoperability issues like data migration, work load management and load balancing.

The parameters affected while moving around in hybrid cloud:

1. Resource Utilization
2. Power Consumption
3. Throughput (Response time is less in ideal condition)
4. Data centre Processing Time
5. Grand Total Cost (GTC)

2.9 Simulation of Hybrid Cloud in Cloudsim

Cloud computing while moving ahead confronts with many issues which needs to be addressed by the user efficiently. Interoperability is one of the most important challenges in them.

The work now keeps the focus on interoperability use cases and makes a detailed analysis of the performance of proposed hybrid cloud for enhanced interoperability.

Of the above discussed affecting parameters list this work considers following parameters for analysis:

1. Average Response Time (ART)
2. Average Data Centre Processing Time (ADCPT)
3. Grand Total Cost (GTC)

A relative study of all these considered parameters in hybrid clouds is done (Barhate and Dhore 2018).

The work chooses Cloud Analyst Toolkit for simulation (Mishra and Bhukya 2014) (Mahajan and Dahiya 2014) (Wickremasinghe, Calheiros and Buyya 2010).

Private Cloud: Private cloud is modelled with only one data centre in a user base region so that the data centre of that region can be viewed private for user bases in that region.

Public Cloud: Public clouds modelling has larger sized data centres. To contrast with private clouds, public clouds are bigger and have more number of virtual machines.

Hybrid Cloud: Hybrid cloud is a pack of 1 private and 2 public clouds respectively.

Region Wise Distribution of Data Centres (Tables 2.2–2.5, Figures 2.2–2.5):

It is evident from the above graph that in hybrid cloud the average response time gives optimised values. Private cloud gives 77.13 ms as the cloud is small, where in case of public cloud has 81.63 ms as clouds are larger. The hybrid cloud gives 78.99 ms which is very much optimised value even when using secured private and resource packed public clouds. Hybrid cloud gives Average Response Time (ART) value as optimised which is the first achievement

TABLE 2.2

Region Wise Distribution of Data Centres (Wickremasinghe, Calheiros and Buyya 2010)

Regions	Location
R0	United States of America
R1	North American Countries
R2	European Union
R3	India, China
R4	Africa
R5	Australia

TABLE 2.3

Hybrid Cloud Configuration

Main Configuration | Data Center Configuration | Advanced

Data Centers:

Name	Region	Arch	OS	VMM	Cost per VM $/Hr	Memory Cost $/s	Storage Cost $/s	Data Transfer Cost $/Gb	Physical HW Units
DC1	0	x86	Linux	Xen	0.1	0.05	0.1	0.1	3
DC2	1	x86	Linux	Xen	0.1	0.05	0.1	0.1	1
DC3	1	x86	Linux	Xen	0.1	0.05	0.1	0.1	1
DC4	2	x86	Linux	Xen	0.1	0.05	0.1	0.1	3
DC5	3	x86	Linux	Xen	0.1	0.05	0.1	0.1	1

Add New

Remove

TABLE 2.4
ORT of Hybrid Cloud

Service Broker Policy: Optimise Response Time

Data Center	# VMs	Image Size	Memory	BW
DC1	100	10000	512	1000
DC2	175	10000	512	1000
DC3	200	10000	512	1000
DC4	100	10000	512	1000
DC5	400	10000	512	1000

TABLE 2.5
Parameters Affected for Public, Private and Hybrid Cloud

Parameters	Private	Public	Hybrid
Average Response Time (ART) in ms	77.13	81.63	78.99
Average Data Centre Processing Time in ms (ADCPT)	0.66	4.99	2.34
Grand Total Cost (GTC) in $	95.71	248.21	123.21

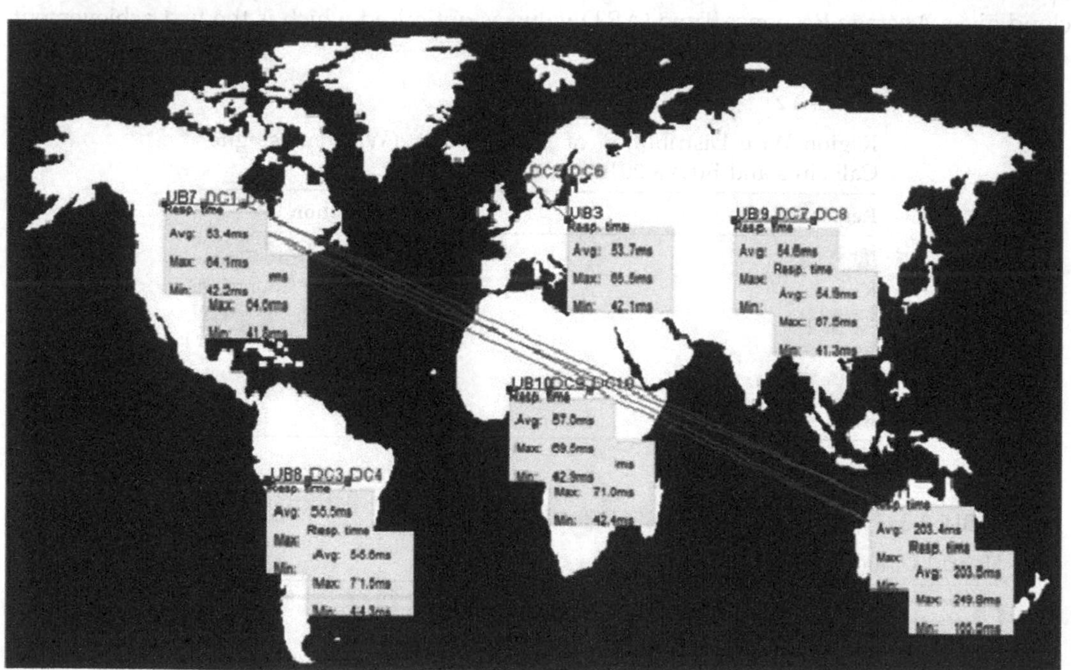

FIGURE 2.2
Cloud Analyst Snapshot for Public Cloud Modelling.

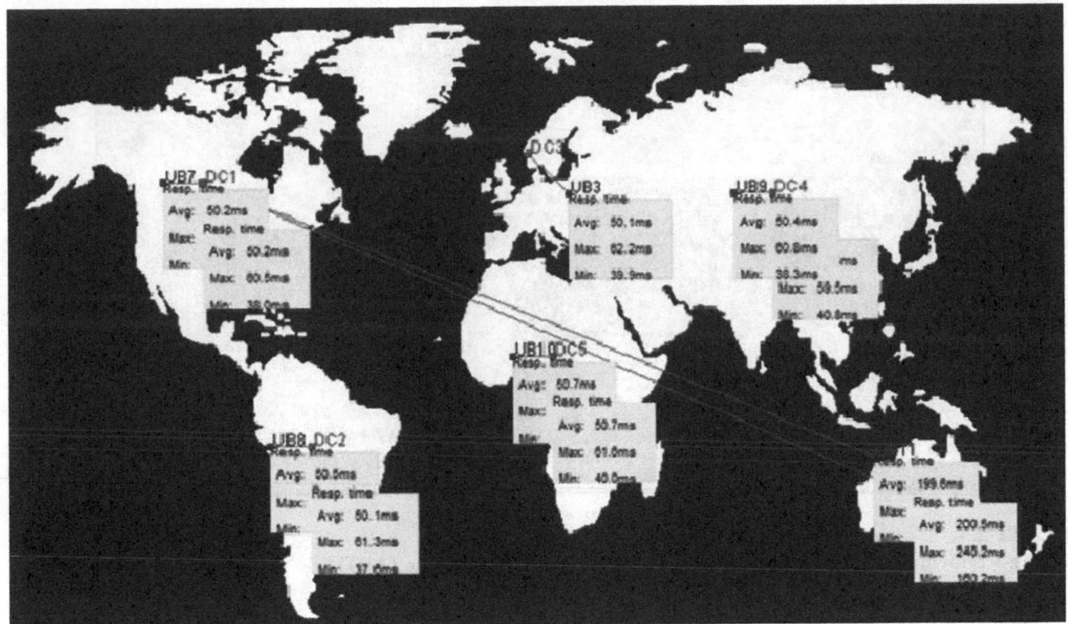

FIGURE 2.3
Cloud Analyst Snapshot for Private Cloud Modelling.

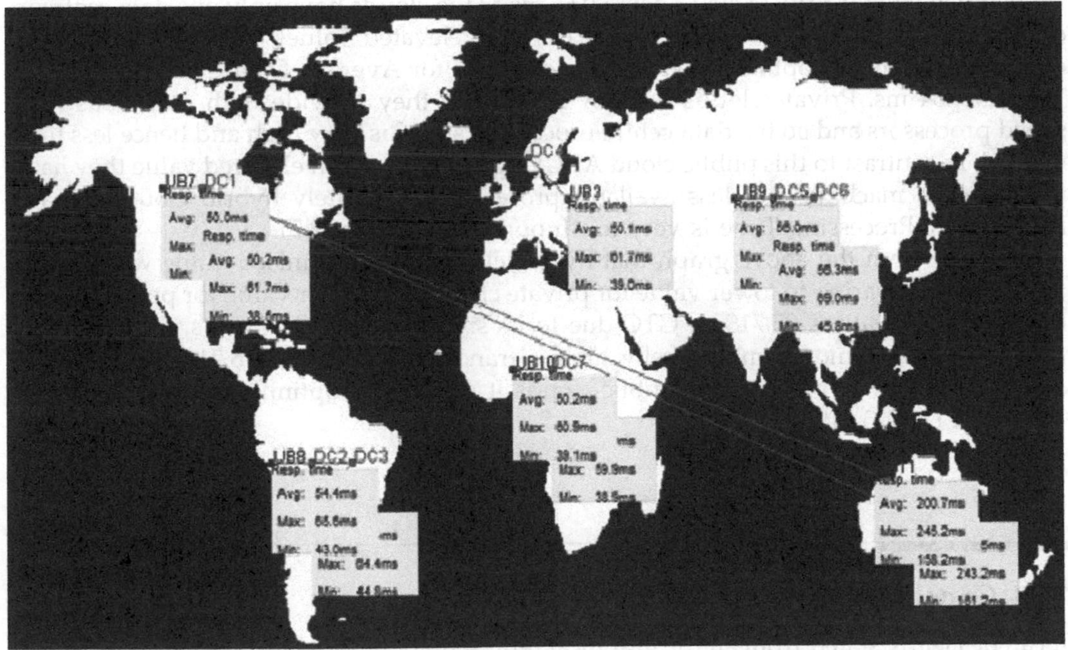

FIGURE 2.4
Cloud Analyst Snapshot for Hybrid Cloud Modelling.

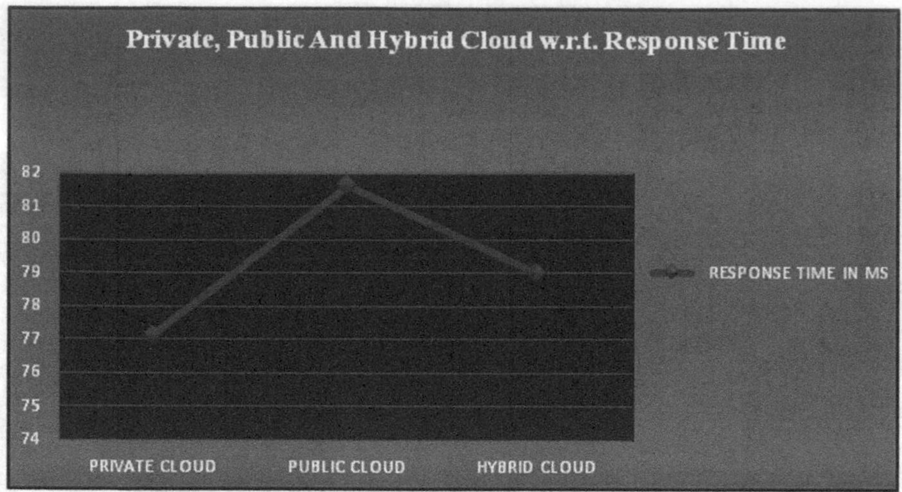

FIGURE 2.5
Graph 1 Showing Effect of Hybrid Cloud on Average Response Time (ART).

in terms of time for Hybrid Cloud interoperability. Hybrid cloud ART indicates that hybrid cloud is capable even after combining private cloud and big public clouds (Figure 2.6).

From the above graph it can be clearly stated that Average Data Centre Processing Time is too much low for private cloud being 0.66 ms as the clouds have only one data centre in one region. In case of public cloud ADCPT gives elevated values 4.99 ms. Where as in case of hybrid cloud optimised values are obtained for Average Data Centre Processing Time is 2.34 ms. Private clouds has low ADCPT as they provide with numerous high speed processors and so the data centre processing speed is very high and hence less time needed. In contrast to this public cloud ADCPT gives very much elevated value they have more virtual machines but less available processors. Ultimately hybrid cloud Average Data Centre Processing Time is very much optimised (Figure 2.7).

It is clear from the above graph that hybrid cloud gives optimised value w.r.t. grand total cost. Comparing to lower value for private cloud and higher value for public clouds. Private cloud realises 95.71$ as GTC due to its small size and less vm's. Contrastingly public cloud has more vm's thereby higher grand total cost i.e. 248.21$. Since hybrid clouds has pack of private and public clouds it gives very optimised value for Grand Total cost i.e. 123.21$.

2.10 Conclusions

It can be clearly stated from all the graphical representation for ART, GTC, & ADCPT that hybrid cloud proves to be an ideal solution as far as the interoperability issue is concerned. It gives optimised results for all the three parameters under consideration. So hybrid cloud can be considered to be implemented in the real world also as time and cost are the two most important metrics to be considered for any computing architecture to be

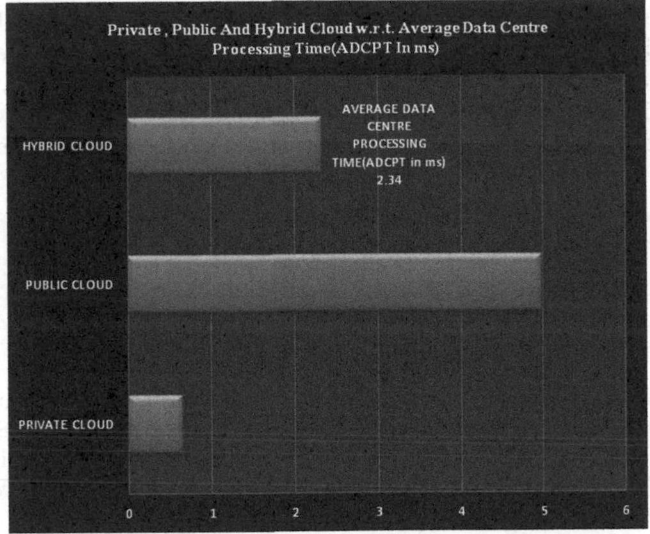

FIGURE 2.6
Graph 2 Showing Hybrid Cloud Average Data Centre Processing Time (ADCPT).

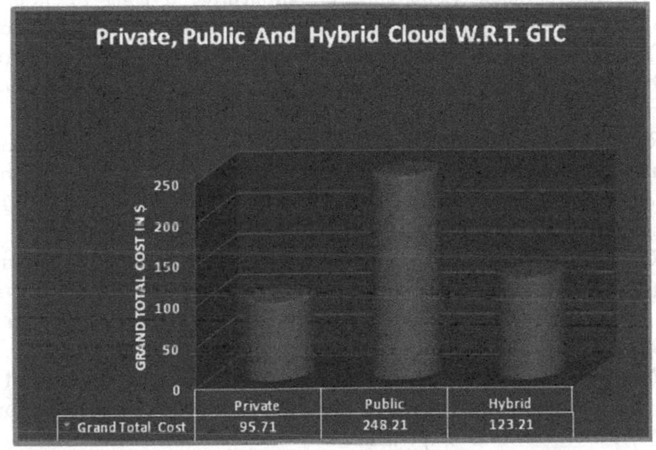

FIGURE 2.7
Graph 3 Showing Hybrid Cloud Grand Total Cost (Barhate and Dhore 2020).

successful. Since Hybrid Cloud gives wonderful results on the considered metrics thereby provisioning efficient interoperability.

To conclude it can be stated that simulation results show that hybrid cloud framework successfully addresses interoperability issue in cloud environment. The proposed Hybrid cloud architecture has been realised to be a good and efficient solution towards interoperability. Hybrid cloud architecture facilitates in achieving better interoperability being a combination of large public and dominant private clouds which also can be have better and fast access to resource with the important facility of security of private clouds.

Relative study of private, public and hybrid cloud signifies that all the three parameters under consideration show very low values in Private Cloud. Whereas public clouds shows high end values for all the parameters in consideration. Finally hybrid cloud gives all the values optimised. Hence the research work concludes that hybrid cloud can be a very efficient and ideal cloud with respect to time and cost considerations in cloud interoperability.

References

Amin, Zeeshan, Nisha Singh and Harpreet Singh. "Review on Falut Tolerance Techniques in Cloud Computing." *International Journal of Computer Applications* 116, no.18 (2015): 11–17.

Barhate, S.M. and M.P. Dhore. "Intercloud Architecture for Interoperability: A Review." *International Journal of Advanced Computational Engineering and Networking* 3, no. 12 (2015): 78–82.

Barhate, S.M. and M.P. Dhore. "Hybrid Cloud: A Solution To Cloud Interoperability." *Second International Conference on Inventive Communication and Computational Technologies*, doi: 10.1109/ICICCT.2018.8473006. IEEE Xplore (2018).

Barhate, S.M. and M. P. Dhore. "Hybrid Cloud: A Cost Optimised Solution To Cloud Interoperability." *International Conference on Innovative Trends in Information Technology (ICITIIT)*. Kottayam (2020): pp. 1–5: doi: 10.1109/ICITIIT49094.2020.9071563.

Barhate, S. M., P. Yende and M.P. Dhore. "Review of Workload Management Issue for Better Interoperability in Cloud Environment." *Global Journal of Engineering Science and Researches* 5 (2018): 65–70.

Buyya, Rajkumar, Rajiv Ranjan and Rodrigo N. Calheiros. "Modelling and Simulation of Scalable Cloud Computing Environments and the CloudSim Toolkit: Challenges and Opportunities." *International Conference on High Performance Computing & Simulation* (2009): 1–11, doi: 10.1109/HPCSIM.2009.5192685.

Buyya, Rajkumar, Rajiv Ranjan and Rodrigo Calheros. "InterCloud: Utility-Oriented Federation of Cloud Computing Environments for Scaling of Application Services." *International Conference On Algorithms and Architecture For Parallel Processing, ICA3PP 2010, Lecture Notes In computer Science* Vol. 6081 (2010): 13–31.

Calheiros, Rodrigo N., Rajiv Ranjan and Anton Beloglazov. "Cloudsim A Toolkit for Modeling and Simulation of Cloud Computing Environments and Evaluation of Resource Provisioning Algorithms." *Software-Practice & Experience* 41 (2010): 23–50.

Ghanam, Yaser, Jennifer Ferreira and Frank Maurer. "Emerging Issues & Challenges in Cloud Computing—A Hybrid Approach." *Journal of Software Engineering and Applications* 5 (2012): 923–937.

Kostoska, Magdalena, Marjan Gusev and Sasko Ristov. "A New Cloud Services Portability Platform." *24th DAAAM International Symposium on Intelligent Manufacturing and Automation* (2013).

Lee, Kangchan, Chulwoo Park and Hee-Dong Yang. "Development of a Cloud Computing Interoperability-Based Service Certification." *International Journal of Security and Its Applications* 9, no. 12 (2015): 11–20.

Mahajan, K. and D. Dahiya. "A Cloud Based Deployment Framework for Load Balancing Policies." *2014 Seventh International Conference on Contemporary Computing (IC3)* (2014): 565–570.

Mishra, Rakesh Kumar and Sreenu Naik Bhukya. "Service Broker Algorithm For Cloud Analyst." *International Journal of Computer Science and Information Technologies (IJCSIT)* 5, no. 3 (2014): 3957–3962.

Parmeswaran, A.V. and Asheesh Chaddha. "Cloud Interoperability and Standardization." *SET Lab Briefings* 7, no.7 (2009).

Sheshasaayee, Ananthi and Margaret T.A. Swetha. "Cloudsim: A Software Framework for Modelling Cloud Computing Environment." *International Journal of Advance Research In Science And Engineering(IJARSE)* 4, no. 01 (2015): 1369–1375.

Singh, Simar, Anju Sharma and Rajesh Kumar. "Analysis of Load Balancing Algorithms using Cloud Analyst." *International Journal of Grid and Distributed Computing* 9, no. 9 (2016): 11–24.

Srinivasana, Aishwarya, Abdul Quadir Mdb and V.C. Vijayakuma. "Era of Cloud Computing: A New Insight to Hybrid Cloud." *2nd International Symposium on Big Data and Cloud Computing (ISBCC'15)* (2015): 40–51.

Wickremasinghe, B., R. Calheiros and R. Buyya. "CloudAnalyst: A CloudSim-Based Visual Modeller for Analysing Cloud Computing Environments and Applications." *24th IEEE International Conference on Advanced Information Networking and Applications* (2010).

3

Autoscaling Techniques for Web Applications in the Cloud

Priya Deokar[1,2] and Sandhya Arora[2]
[1]*SKN College of Engineering, Pune, India*
[2]*Cummins College of Engineering for Women, Pune, India*

CONTENTS

DOI: 10.1201/9781003203926-3

3.1 Introduction

Cloud computing has emerged as a boon to business owners because it allows them to rent and utilize services and resources on a need basis in a pay-as-you-use manner. It also allows optimal use of resources and infrastructure. Virtualization technology along with ubiquitous network connectivity has made cloud computing possible. Cloud computing has various merits over the conventional data center such as the illusion of infinite computing resources on demand, pay-as-you-use and elasticity (Menascé, 2003).

Elasticity is one of the important features that allow resources to be scaled dynamically based on resource demand. This is particularly important because both over-provisioning and under-provisioning hamper the utility of the cloud. Overprovisioning leads to wastage of resources and additional costs to users. Under provisioning causes SLA (Service Level Agreement) violation and also leads to performance degradation. Automatic provisioning of resources a few minutes prior to actual demand helps maintain Quality of Service at the provider end. For the cloud administrator, VM bootup time needs to be considered in auto scaling techniques. The time required for VM to become operative, which includes bootup time, spans between 5 and 10 minutes. During this time, as the system does not have enough resources, some of the requests cannot be served resulting in penalty to the cloud providers. Prediction techniques allow to proactively boot up the VM and make resources available before they are actually required.

Achieving elasticity for web applications deployed in cloud is a challenging task. Various techniques are available in the literature to address this problem. We will discuss available techniques and related terms in this article.

3.1.1 Service Models

Cloud providers offer various services but IaaS, PaaS, SaaS are few important ones.

3.1.1.1 IaaS

With this service, infrastructure is provided to the consumers. Infrastructure includes resources such as servers, storage, networks and other fundamental computing resources (Chadwick et al., 2011). Consumers have complete control over the operating system and softwares installed on that infrastructure and can run and deploy any arbitrary software on it. Consumers, however, do not have any control over the underlying cloud infrastructure.

3.1.1.2 PaaS

With this service, various development platforms are provided to the consumers. These platforms provide support for programming languages, libraries and services (Islam et al., 2012). Consumers can create their own applications using platforms provided by cloud service providers.

Consumers need not manage all the infrastructure resources such as network, servers, operating system or storage. Consumers still have control over the configuration settings and of the deployed applications. PaaS provides consumers with limited freedom than IaaS but it provides much more ease to the consumers without theirs worrying about managing the platform including web servers/application servers and other services.

3.1.1.3 SaaS

With this service, on-demand software is provided to end users to access. Consumers have to pay only for utilizing the software and not for its development (Chadwick et al., 2011). Consumers need not install the software and these softwares are usually in the form of services. Google Doc is the best example of SaaS where users can edit documents online which is similar to Microsoft Word. Google Doc is a powerful web service with a lot of features provided free of cost by Google but more advanced features are available in the paid version. SaaS applications are accessible through the web browser and consumers need not be aware of the operating system, platform or where these applications are hosted. SaaS removes the burden on consumers to download and install the software and can seamlessly access it through a web browser. All the hardware and software resources required for hosting this service are managed by cloud service providers.

3.2 Deployment Models

When organizations decide to move their applications to the cloud, they must take the critical decision, one of many, as to which deployment model to choose.

Major deployment models are Public, Private and Hybrid Cloud. Organizations need to carefully select the deployment model considering the security, available resources, infrastructure, sensitivity of data and applications, volume of data etc.

3.2.1 Public Cloud

Service provider provides the cloud infrastructure for any of the services discussed earlier to anybody who wants to opt for it. These services are offered either free of cost or pay-by-use by the cloud service provider. As these services are available to the public, anybody who opts for it has to share the infrastructure resources with other participants. Public clouds are hosted by third parties and often hosted at a location away from the customer premises. These clouds are believed to be less secure compared to other deployment models because customers have to share infrastructure resources with other participants.

3.2.2 Private Cloud

Private clouds are hosted for the exclusive use of an organization. The applications and the data deployed on this cloud are completely under the control of the owner. These clouds provide utmost security, reliability and flexibility in management of resources.

There are two categories of private cloud: Externally Hosted Private Clouds and On-Premise Private Cloud. Externally hosted private clouds are used solely by the organization but are hosted and managed by third parties. On-Premise private clouds are used, hosted and maintained by the organization.

Private clouds are costlier than public clouds.

3.2.3 Hybrid Cloud

This model is a combination of Private and Public Cloud. It has advantages of both the Public Cloud and Private Cloud. Sensitive applications and data could be stored securely in the private cloud and everything else can be deployed on the public cloud. Private clouds are costlier than public clouds, so, storing everything on the private cloud is not an economical option. Hybrid cloud is a better option in such scenarios.

3.2.4 Community Cloud

Community cloud is a cloud shared by multiple enterprises with identical regulatory requirements, restrictions or compliance. Apart from participating enterprises, nobody else can avail resources of this cloud. It is a kind of non-shared public cloud where consumers are relieved from security and reliability issues of the public cloud. This provides great benefits to individual organizations as well as the groups.

3.3 Pricing Models

There are different types of pricing models as described below.

3.3.1 On-Demand Instances

Customers have to pay for the instances they have used as per the specified hourly rate (Menascé, 2003). Customers do not need to make any long-term commitments in this case. Customers can also opt for an auto scaling feature which allows them to adjust resources as per requirement.

3.3.2 Reserved Instances

Customers have to pay for the resource for a longer duration usually for a year or three (Menascé, 2003). With the requirement to make one-time upfront payment for these resources, the instance is reserved for the specified duration and ensures availability of the resource during that period. They are usually cheaper than other models.

3.3.3 Spot Instances

Customers specify the maximum rate per hour that they are willing to pay (Menascé, 2003). Without any requirement to make any upfront commitment, these are usually cheaper than on-demand rates. Their prices fluctuate depending upon demand and supply.

3.4 Scaling in the Cloud

Web applications might work well with regular traffic but when there is a sudden spike in the incoming traffic, these applications can give degraded performance or might just stop responding (Gandhi et al., 2012). Provisioning additional resources to the application as per requirements can serve the purpose. Resources could be provisioned in two ways: vertical scaling and horizontal scaling.

3.4.1 Vertical Scaling

As shown in Figure 3.1, in vertical scaling or scaling up, more resources which include CPU, memory, I/O, and network are added to your existing machine. Vertical scaling has its limitations because of which it is not considered suitable for highly scalable applications. Maximum capacity of a physical machine is the limit for vertical scaling. Vertical scaling may involve some downtime while adding new resources.

3.4.2 Horizontal Scaling

In Horizontal scaling or scaling out, more machines are added into your system, thereby distributing the workload across all the resources (Gandhi et al., 2012). When web applications are deployed with horizontal scaling, load balancing is employed to redirect the traffic to newly added resources. Horizontal scaling is particularly useful for highly scalable applications and does not involve any downtime while adding new resources.

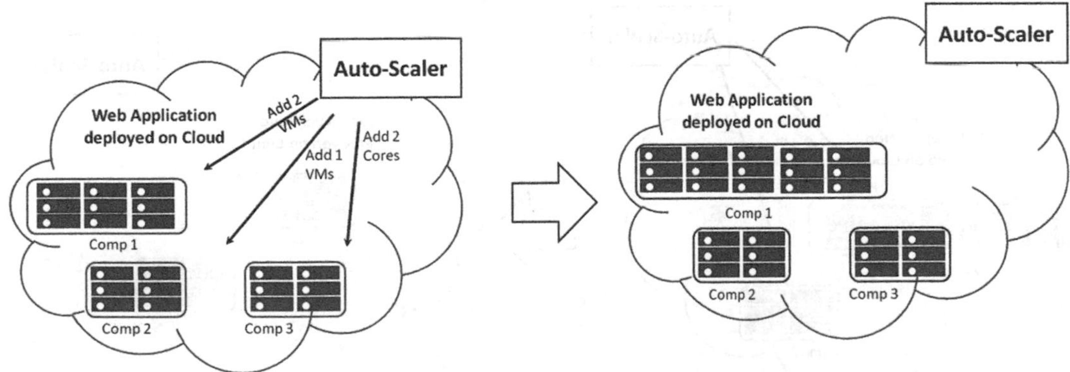

FIGURE 3.1
Scaling Up.

4.5 Auto Scaling Techniques

Scaling the application at the right time decides the efficiency of the auto scaling technique, and estimating the resource requirement precisely is the key for appropriate resource provisioning (Dutreilh et al., 2010). Lots of research is being done in this area. Auto scaling techniques can be broadly categorized into reactive resource provisioning when need arises, and proactive resource provisioning considering the future resource requirement. Lots of these techniques use metrics such as CPU utilization, memory, network consumption, memory swap and cache miss rate. Along with these, other parameters such as average response time, throughput, request rate, session creation rate and service time are also important in resource estimation.

Figure 3.2 shows scaling down when resource requirement is less.

4.5.1 Reactive Approach: Threshold-based

It is the simplest form of auto scaling technique. Many cloud service providers such as Amazon make use of these techniques.

Rules based on threshold values specified against metrics such as CPU utilization, memory, network consumption, memory swap and cache miss rate are used for scaling the application (Menascé, 2003). Two threshold values could be set for the metric with upper and lower bounds which is used for scaling out or scaling in respectively. For example, If CPU utilization is above 80% add more instances to the application infrastructure or if CPU Utilization goes below 40% remove instances from the application infrastructure. Many cloud service providers provide step scaling along with threshold values. In step scaling resources are added stepwise. After adding resources at every step, performance is monitored and, if required, the next step of resources are added.

3.5.2 Proactive Approach

Resource estimation is the key towards success of auto scaling techniques. When there is a sudden spike in the incoming traffic for the web application, it is necessary to provision

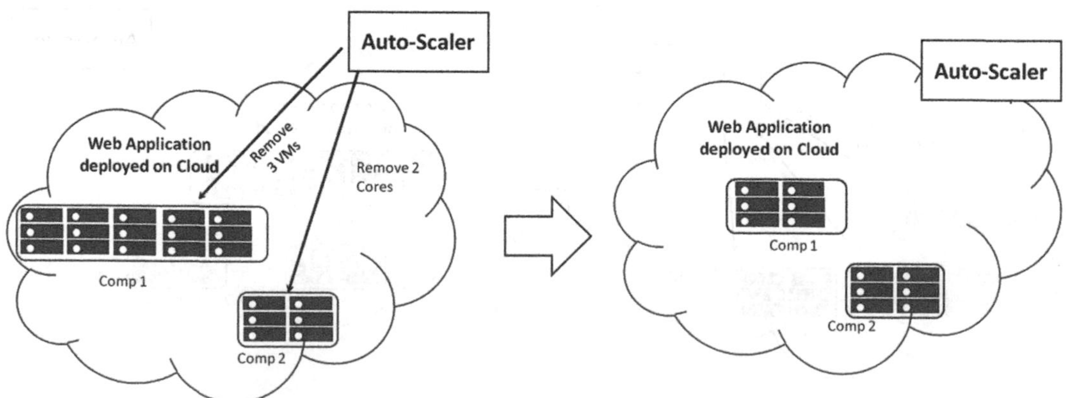

FIGURE 3.2
Scaling Down.

the resources immediately. When new resources are to be provisioned, it is necessary to consider time required to acquire VM, boot up and configure. Prediction is useful in resource estimation.

3.5.3 Time Series Analysis

Time Series constitute a continuous sequence of observations at regular time intervals. With time series, analysis patterns could be detected and future values could be predicted on data point sequences. This property of time series is used for finding out resource utilization patterns in the cloud and to predict future resource requirements.

Time Series Analysis algorithms for the prediction task use following approaches:

3.5.3.1 Linear Regression, Neural Network, SVM

Islam et al. (2012) developed prediction based resource measurement and provisioning strategies using a combination of neural networks and linear regression to satisfy future resource demands, while our work considers only the time series prediction models. Machine learning techniques such as Neural Network, Linear Regression and SVM are used for prediction. Ajila and Akindele (2013) compared performance of these techniques for prediction and concluded that SVM outperformed the other two.

3.5.3.2 Autoregressive Models (ARs)

These schemes make use of ARIMA along with Kalman filters for prediction. Fetzer and Yazdanov (2012) used an AR method to predict short-term CPU usage.

3.5.3.3 Signal Prediction

This scheme converts each time interval into a wavelet-based signal thereby applying signal prediction techniques on it. Nguyen et al. (2013) proposed this method which uses signal prediction along with time series analysis.

3.5.4 Control Theory

Control theory creates an application's model. The aim of these schemes is to define a controller which makes use of the model to adjust the resources based on application demands. The efficiency of such schemes depends on both the controller and the application model. Many researchers believe it to be a promising approach when combined with prediction of resources (Dutreilh et al., 2010).

3.5.5 Reinforcement Learning

RL automates scaling by learning without using prior models or knowledge of the application. For each particular state, it learns with a trial-and-error approach. As it doesn't consider any a priori knowledge and processes each state independently, it usually takes longer time for learning which makes it infeasible in practice (Dutreilh et al., 2011).

3.5.6 Queuing Theory

Queuing theory finds the relationship between the arriving jobs and leaving jobs. It has been largely applied to computing systems. In this simple approach, a queue is created for requests from each VM which helps to estimate various performance metrics (Salah et al., 2016; Gandhi et al., 2012). The main drawback of this approach is that they are not dynamic enough to accommodate changes in the workload and re-computation is required when workload changes.

3.6 Proactive Auto Scaling Technique Using SVM: A Case Study

This case study is done for prediction of resources for TPCW web application which emulates online book shopping and which is deployed on Amazon Cloud instances with the database on another instance of Amazon. Traffic to this application can be generated using Remote Browser Emulator which is part of the TPCW application. Resource usage from cloud instances is collected using Amazon CloudWatch APIs. This data is used to train Support Vector Regression (SVR) model. It is then used for prediction of future resource requirements.

3.6.1 Solving Approach

Traffic to web applications is not always uniform. It can be either steady or busty. Based on the data of the previous 10 h, a pattern of traffic is found out and that is done using Support Vector Machine technique. SVM model is trained using this behavioral pattern.

3.6.2 Experimental Setup

Amazon micro instances are used to setup TPCW web application. One instance is used for application server setup based on Ubuntu Linux platform. Another instance is used for MySQL database server.

Client component is installed on the local machine. Also the auto scaling tool which contains data collection, training, testing and auto scaling components are installed on local machine.

3.6.3 Client Infrastructure

TPC-W RBE is deployed on local machine.

- TPC-W web application has a tool called remote browser emulator which can emulate multiple clients in a single node (Islam et al., 2012).
- By adjusting the number of emulated clients, changing workload can be created.

3.6.4 Architecture

Figure 3.3 shows an Architecture Diagram Using TPC-W Web Application.

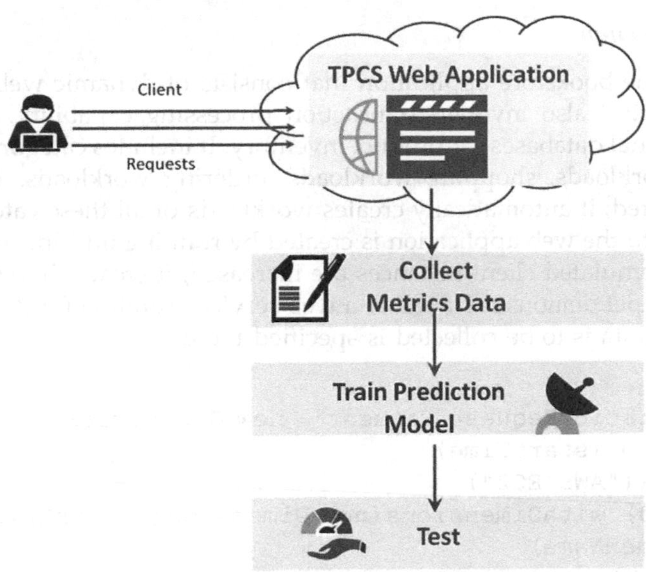

FIGURE 3.3
Architecture for Training and Testing Using TPC-W Web Application.

3.6.4 Algorithm

1. Start.
2. Collect data using the TPC-W benchmark.
3. Pre-process data files to scale input features to values between 0 and 1.
4. Split processed data files into two datasets 60:40%.
5. Train SVM model using 60% dataset.
6. Test trained SVM model using the remaining 40% of the dataset.
7. If desired accuracy is reached, then use the model for prediction.
   There can be two conditions: either resource requirement is less or more than current resources.
   a. If less requirement then
      Scale-down resources
   b. Else if more requirement
      Scale-up resources
   c. Else go to step 5.
8. At every scheduled time go to step 2.
9. SUCCESS.

3.6.6 Implementation

Following are the implementation details at every step:

3.6.6.1 Data Collection

TPC-W is an online bookstore application that consists of dynamic web pages complex application logic and also involves transaction processing capability, as well as connectivity to relational databases for product inventory. It includes categories of workloads viz. browsing workloads, shopping workloads, ordering workloads. When the client emulator is executed, it automatically creates workloads of all these categories.

Random traffic to the web application is created by running multiple emulated clients. If the number of emulated client instances are increased, it creates bursty traffic.

Below code snippet demonstrates call to a web service, duration for data collection and metric for which data is to be collected is specified there.

```
GetMetricStatisticsRequest request = new GetMetricStatisticsRequest
().withStartTime(startTime)
.withNamespace("AWS/EC2")
.withPeriod(60).withDimensions(new Dimension().withName
(Constants.dimenName)
.withValue(Constants.dimenValue))
.withMetricName("CPUUtilization")
.withStatistics("Average")
.withEndTime(endTime);
GetMetricStatisticsResult result = awc.getMetricStatistics
(request);
```

3.6.6.2 Data Preprocessing

All the data values collected are scaled to values between -1 and 1. This normalizing step has an advantage of avoiding higher numerical range values dominating lower numerical range values.

3.6.6.3 SVM Training

SVM model is trained with preprocessed data. Radial Basis Function (RBF) is most promising among four kernels of SVM and that's the reason we used RBF kernel for training.

3.6.6.4 Process for Scaling

1. Call the CreateLaunchConfiguration action by specifying the following parameters:
   I. Launch configuration name: my-test-lc
   II. Instance type: m1.small
   III. Image ID: ami-0078da69
2. Call the CreateAutoScalingGroup action by specifying the following parameters:
   I. Auto Scaling group name: my-test-asg
   II. Launch configuration name: my-test-lc

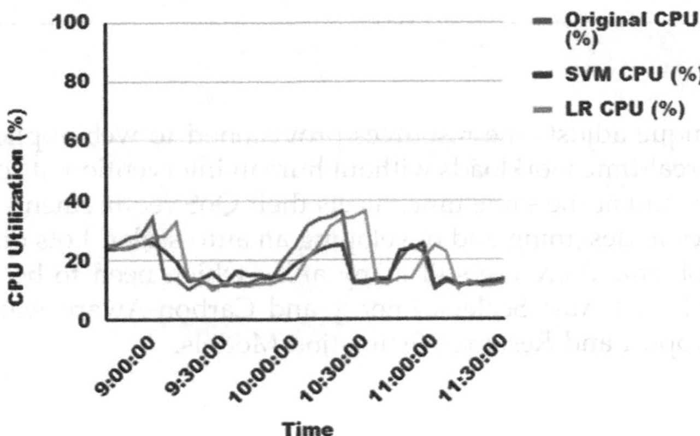

FIGURE 3.4
Testing Results with LR and SVM.

Model	MAPE	RMSE
SVM	21.06	10.43
LR	34.91	18.67

FIGURE 3.5
SVM and LR Comparison.

III. Availability Zone: us-east-1a
IV. Minimum size: 1
V. Maximum size: 10

3. Call SetDesiredCapacity to set the capacity to the desired number of instances based on prediction results of the application.

3.6.6.5 Results

Prediction model is trained using a normalized sampled dataset. SVM prediction results are compared with prediction results using Linear Regression. MAPE (Mean Absolute Percentage Error) and RMSE (Root Mean Square Error) are the performance metrics used to measure the performance accuracy.

Data is collected from Amazon instances running TPCW application for the past 24 h. Varied workload is created by running multiple instances of client emulator and generating mixed traffic. 60% of data from this is used for training and 40% is used for testing purposes. Figure 3.4 shows the results.

Figure 3.5 indicates that the values of MAPE and RMSE of SVM are lower than those of LR. Higher accuracy is indicated by lower values in both of these metrics.

Thus experimental results show that SVM outperformed the Linear Regression technique.

3.7 Discussion

Auto-scaling technique adjusts the resources provisioned to web applications deployed on cloud based on real-time workloads without human intervention. It costs cloud users a minimum resource, and at the same time, meets their QoS requirements. However, there are many challenges in designing and developing an auto-scaler. Lots of research is done to address this problem. There are still many areas which need to be explored further such as Container-Based Auto-Scalers, Energy and Carbon-Aware Auto-Scaling, Better Vertical Scaling Support and Resource Estimation Models.

References

Ajila, Samuel A. and A. Akindele. "Bankole: Cloud Client Prediction Models Using Machine Learning Techniques." In *Proceedings IEEE 37th Annual Computer Software and Applications Conference* (2013).

AWS Auto Scaling From http://aws.amazon.com/autoscaling/

Chadwick, David W., Stijin F. Lievens, Jerry I. den Hartog, Andreas Pashalidis and Joseph Alhadeff. "My Private Cloud Overview: A Trust, Privacy and Security Infrastructure for the Cloud." In *Proceedings of2011 IEEE 4th International Conference on Cloud Computing*, Washington, DC (2011): 752–753, doi: 10.1109/CLOUD.2011.113.

Dutreilh, Xavier, Aurélien Moreau, Jacques Malenfant, Nicolas Rivierre and Truck Isis. "From Data Center Resource Allocation to Control Theory and Back." In *Proceedings of 2010 IEEE 3rd International Conference on Cloud Computing* (2010): 410–417.

Dutreilh, Xavier, S. Kirgizov, Olga Melekhova, Jacques Malenfant, Nicolas Rivierre and Isis Truck. "Using Reinforcement Learning for Autonomic Resource Allocation in Clouds: Towards a Fully Automated Workflow." In *Proceedings of 2011 International Conference on Autonomic and Autonomous Systems* (2011): 67–74.

Fetzer, Christof and Lenar Yazdanov. "Vertical Scaling for Prioritized VMs Provisioning." In *2012 Second International Conference on Cloud and Green Computing*, Xiangtan (2012): 118–125.

Gambi, Alessio, Giovanni Toffetti, Cesare Pautasso and M. Pezzé. "Kriging Controllers for Cloud Applications." *IEEE Internet Computing* 17, no. 4 (2013): 40–47. 10.1109/MIC.2012.142.

Gandhi, Anshul, Yuan Chen, Daniel Gmach, Martin Arlitt and Manish Marwah. "Hybrid Resource Provisioning for Minimizing Data Center SLA Violations and Power Consumption." *Sustainable Computing: Informatics and Systems*2 (2012): 91–104. https://doi.org/10.1016/j.suscom.2012.01.005.

Google App Engine from https://cloud.google.com/appengine/.

Islam, Sadeka, Jacky Keung, Kevin Lee and Anna Liu. "Empirical Prediction Models for Adaptive Resource Provisioning in the Cloud." *Future Generation Computer Systems* 28 (2012): 155–162.

Menascé, Daniel A. "TPC-W Benchmark, Transaction Processing Performance Council (TPC)." *IEEE Internet Computing* 6, no. 3(May 2003): 83–87. https://doi.org/10.1109/MIC.2002.1003136.

Nguyen, Hiep, Zhiming Shen, Xiaohui Gu, Sethuraman Subbiah and John Wilkes. "Agile: Elastic Distributed Resource Scaling for Infrastructure-as-a-Service." In *Proceedings of the USENIX International Conference on Automated Computing (ICAC'13)* (2013).

Salah, Khaled, Khalid Elbadawi and Raouf Boutaba. "An Analytical Model for Estimating Cloud Resources of Elastic Services." *Journal of Network and Systems Management* 24 (2016): 285–308.

4

Community Cloud Service Model for People with Special Needs

Sampada Wazalwar and Urmila Shrawankar

Department of Computer Science and Engineering, G H Raisoni College of Engineering Nagpur India

CONTENTS

4.1 Introduction

Cloud computing is gaining more and more importance as it helps more and more to offer on demand services anywhere-everywhere to a person. There are many cloud services available which are cost-effective. Cloud services offered are database, storage, processing and networking applications. With the availability of computers and internet, people are now becoming technocrats and prefer to use technology for many types of work instead of following the conventional path. People, nowadays, prefer e-commerce for marketing, e-payments, use various online healthcare services, prefer to go for online/distance learning and, even, prefer to work online. In a pandemic situation like COVID-19, we were all eye witnesses to the hike in use of all such services and, now, it seems, people will continue to use this for convenience.

DOI: 10.1201/9781003203926-4

Society has both people who are physically able and people with special needs. The latter are the disabled. We are specially focusing on the people with speech and hearing impaired. The physically able can make use all types of available services and have no difficulty communicating using their chosen language. But, the speech and hearing impaired hesitate to go out to the outside world as their ways of communication, the sign language, is not understood by all. This restricts them from utilization of many services. However, cloud services help them to overcome their hesitation and work effectively using online platform through single login.

4.2 Deployment Models of Cloud

Different types of cloud deployment models are shown in Figure 4.1. There are mainly two types of clouds: private and public. Cloud Service Providers also offer nowadays hybrid cloud which combines the properties of both private and public clouds. In this set of cloud types, the community cloud is the latest variant of hybrid cloud which is used to serve the need of a group of people.

Private Cloud: The cloud which is meant for a single business company is a private cloud. It includes and offers the applications which are private to that company only. The disadvantage of the private cloud is that all developmental changes have to be done by the company and is expensive.

Public Cloud: Where an individual company uses the infrastructure provided by the cloud service provider as well as shares the services with other companies is a public cloud. These are very cost effective but requires high security to be imposed to be beneficial to the organizations that use its services.

Hybrid Cloud: If a company deploys the cloud in two types of provisions i.e. private and public, then it is called a hybrid cloud. The important and sensitive information is kept within the private cloud, and the rest is kept within the public cloud. The hybrid cloud helps the company to implement diverse application in public cloud while keeping data in private cloud as secure.

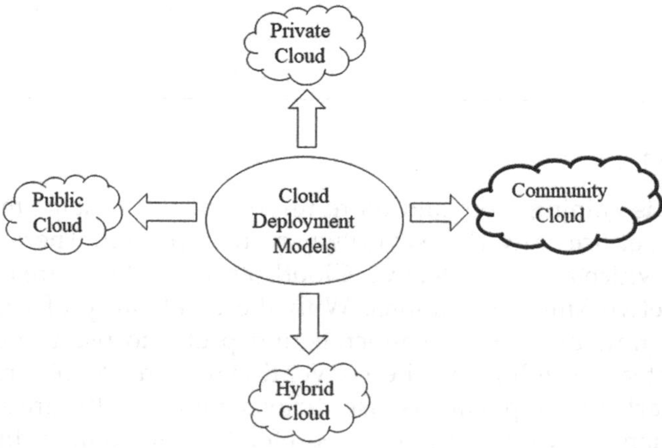

FIGURE 4.1
Cloud Deployment Models.

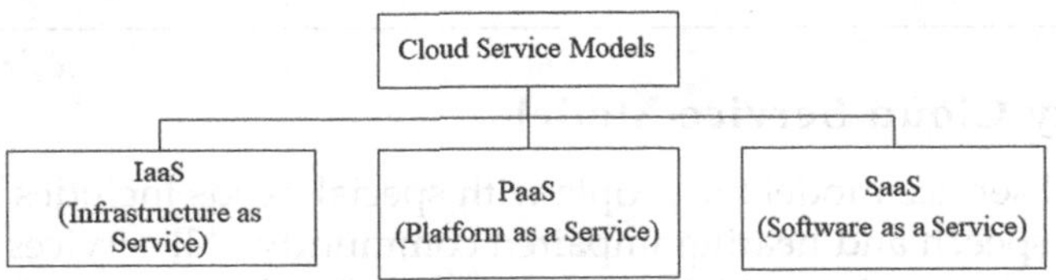

FIGURE 4.2
Cloud Service Models.

Community Cloud: Used by a community, this cloud offers the infrastructure including software and developmental tools required by the particular community. This specially includes the services required by a group of people.

With cloud deployment models, cloud computing also has a service model which is again divided into three types i.e. IAAS, PAAS & SAAS as shown in Figure 4.2.

In this chapter, we introduce the community cloud for people with special needs. This community cloud will offer all the required services for the hearing and speech impaired group of people.

4.3 Main Objectives to Develop Community Service Model

People with special needs encompass all who are disabled with the type of disability restricting a person from various activities which are done by the able very efficiently. This results in a person with special need to hesitate from doing his/her activity freely. We are introducing a community cloud for the speech and hearing impaired. They cannot communicate with ease in their language and, hence, use the sign language for communication. The sign language is mimetic and so the people with speech and hearing impaired cannot communicate effectively with the vocal people and vice versa. It results in a communication gap which adversely affects the spontaneous growth of the speech and hearing impaired in many areas like education, healthcare and, even, in employment. These people, though, they cannot communicate effectively in the vocal way can, still, use computing technologies very efficiently. Thus, there is a need of community cloud service model for people with special needs due to following reasons:

1. To communicate effectively with the outside world.
2. Gain the access to online telemedicine/healthcare services.
3. To take advantage of online education.
4. Gain the services from a single login anywhere-everywhere.
5. Convenient employability.
6. Continue services during pandemic or any adverse condition.
7. Gain the access to assistive technologies.
8. Overall empowerment.

4.4 Community Cloud Service Model

Community cloud service model for people with special needs includes many services to the person under speech and hearing impaired community. All services can be benefited through a single login. Services which are included under this community cloud are listed below:

1. Sign language dictionary.
2. Sign language learning applications.
3. Tools for translation of sign language into spoken language, and vice versa.
4. Distance learning education system for the disabled.
5. Telemedicine and healthcare service for the deaf and mute.
6. Employment opportunities for the disabled.

The community cloud model is shown in Figure 4.3.

Every service in the model is explained in detail below.

4.4.1 Sign Language Dictionary

Every language has its own standard dictionary. Sign language is used by the hearing and speech impaired for communication. The standard sign language dictionary keeps on updating day by day by the ISLRTC (http://pib.nic.in/newsite/PrintRelease.aspx?relid=177900). The speech and hearing impaired are not aware of all these updations from time to time. To make these people aware about available standard signs for a given word, the sign language

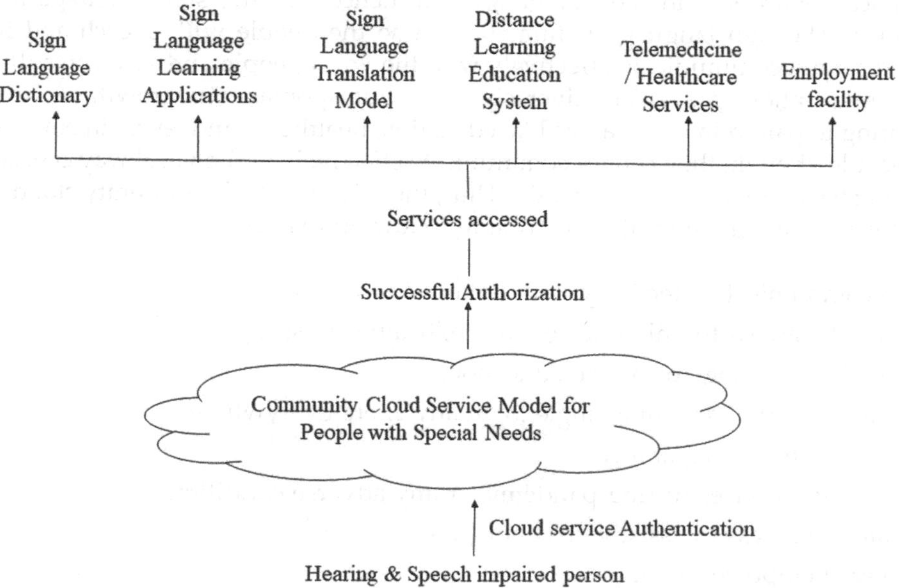

FIGURE 4.3
Community Cloud Service Model.

dictionary can be made available in their own login. Many other sign language dictionary links can also be provided in the login for reference (https://indiansignlanguage.org/). So if someone wants to search a standard sign, he/she can search it in dictionary.

4.4.2 Sign Language Learning Applications

The hearing and speech impaired people can use many other modes of communication like leap reading, finger spelling, air writing, etc. (Wazalwar and Shrawankar, 2019). So for the person of any age, whenever he/she wants to learn the sign language, he/she can learn it easily from various sign language learning applications. There are many sign language learning applications available and some are listed below:

- Sign Language for Beginners.
- Sign School.
- Indian Sign Language.
- Lingvano: Learn Sign Language.
- Person can access above and additional applications through the cloud for learning sign language.

4.4.3 Tools for Translation of Sign Language into Spoken Language and Vice Versa

Communication between a speech and hearing impaired and a vocal person requires the language translator which will convert sign language into spoken language, and vice versa. Many researchers are working on the development of a fully functional sign language translation system (Cheok et al., 2017; Qiao et al., 2015; Wazalwar and Shrawankar, 2017; Sobhan et al., 2019). Some of the applications are already there which can be linked into the services provided by cloud. It helps to improve the communication between the speech and hearing impaired and the vocal person effectively. Some of the available applications for translation are listed below:

4.4.3.1 Distance Learning Education System

- Hand Talk Translator.
- MotionSavvy's.
- Signall.
- Mimix Sign Language Translator.

The pandemic situations like COVID-19 has now turned the world towards equipping the online education as an essential part of education from almost February 2019 till today. This has raised many challenges in the education field because it requires hardware, software resources along with technical educators as well (Shrawankar and Shireen, 2020; Abdallah and Fayyoumi, 2016; Wazalwar and Shrawankar, 2021). Still while the able has managed to adjust to this change in such an anomalous situation, the disabled face the gap in education with difficulty because of system requirements to overcome their disability. In such a situation or in any adverse situation when the people cannot adjust to a

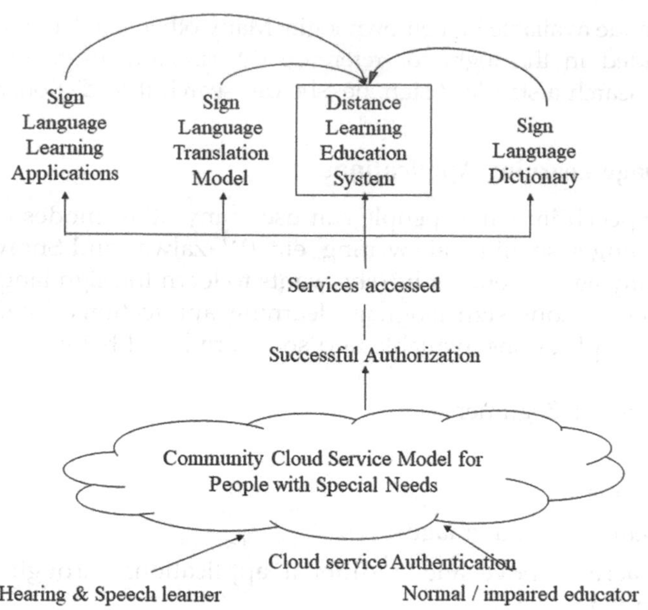

FIGURE 4.4
Community Cloud Model for Distance Learning.

difficult situation, the website: https://www.smartdatacollectiveeet, for classroom teaching cloud service, as shown in Figure 4.4, can be used, where the educator and the students, both, can login in to the same platform and utilize the tools to get in gear for online education.

4.4.4 Telemedicine and Healthcare Service for the Deaf and Mute

Like todays pandemic condition of COVID-19, we all experience shortage of healthcare services, unavailability of physicians as they are engaged in other work and patients who cannot visit hospitals to avoid the spread of the corona virus. In such conditions, telemedicine or online healthcare services are like a blessing in disguise (Wazalwar and Shrawankar, 2020). The physically able take the benefit of telemedicine system as they can interact with physician online over the system. On the other hand, the hearing and speech impaired need a telemedicine system to work with the sign language to allow free communication amongst patient and the physician. In this context, the sign language dictionary for medical terms is also important as many a times doctors may not be knowing a sign for a term, so, help of a dictionary can be indispensable to tide over the situation. The model for telemedicine service is shown in Figure 4.5:

Some of the popular telemedicine apps are listed below:

- MDLIVE
- LiveHealth
- Doctor on Demand
- Teladoc

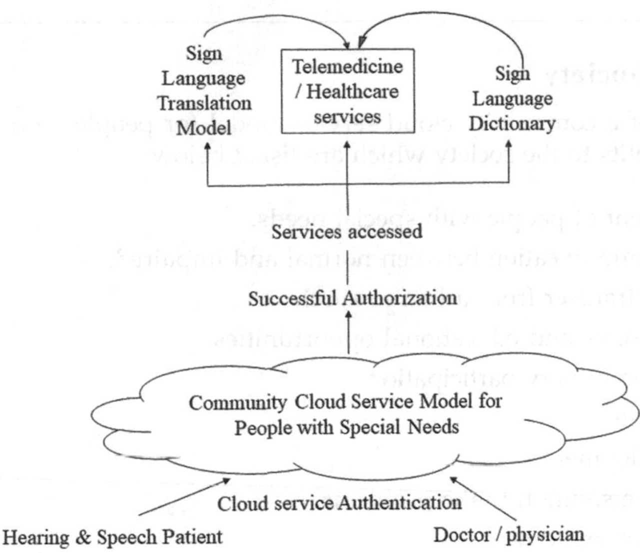

FIGURE 4.5
Community Cloud Model for Healthcare.

- DocsApp

4.4.5 Employment Opportunities for Disabled

Technology has improved the quality of life to a certain extent from home services to finding the workplace. But in this goal, people with special needs generally struggle to find a job. This struggle is not because of their disability but because very few jobs can accommodate their impairment. So a platform is really needed for providing employment to these people with special needs on the basis of their technicality. The National Institute on Disability & Rehabilitation Research (NIDRR) is working on many cloud services for the disabled. These cloud services are work from home service for the disabled so that people with mobility problem can empower themselves. Even people who hesitate to communicate effectively with others, he/she can also overcome the employment problem by opting to work from home. Few cloud based services are listed below (https://www.smartdatacollective.com/how-cloud-creating-employment-blind-and-disabled/).

- Microsoft's roaming profile.
- TCN's 3 VocalVision.

These are all different services which are offered in a community cloud service model for people with special needs.

4.5 Benefit to Society

Implementation of a community cloud service model for people with special needs includes many benefits to the society which are listed below:

1. Empowerment of people with special needs.
2. Effective communication between normal and impaired.
3. Technology transfer from urban to rural.
4. Online economic and educational opportunities.
5. Increased community participation.
6. Quality of life.
7. Online Employment.
8. Cost effective solution to the problems.
9. Overall nation building.

4.6 Conclusion and Future Scope

Cloud computing has a distributed architecture which can be used to provide the services to people with special needs under single login anywhere-everywhere. All the services which are explained in Section III proved to be helpful to the disabled to empower them. The biggest advantage of using this community cloud service model is its cost effectiveness. The user can take the benefit of all services from anywhere on any device which makes it platform agnostic which is a huge benefit for the mobile. This facility helps the community to grow and overcome their handicap with respect to the physically able. Though we are concentrating on the hearing and speech impaired, however, such community cloud services can be developed for other types of physically challenged people.

The future scope of this work includes the addition of more services under this community cloud service model. Services like online voting (NIDRR is working on this), agriculture related services and information, e-commerce services can also be explored. The updations to policies of the government for people with different types of disability can also be included for the knowledge of the person. Cloud services can do miracles if used properly and made available to the society at low cost.

References

Abdallah, Emad and Ebba Fayyoumi. "Assistive Technology for Deaf People Based on Android Platform." *Procedia Computer Science*94 (2016): 295–301. 10.1016/j.procs.2016.08.044.

Cheok, Ming Jin, Zaid Omar and Mohamed Hisham Jaward. "A Review of Hand Gesture and Sign

Language Recognition Techniques." *Springer International Journal of Machine Learning and Cybernetics*10 (2017): 131–157. 10.1007/s13042-017-0705-5.

https://indiansignlanguage.org/

http://pib.nic.in/newsite/PrintRelease.aspx?relid=177900

https://www.smartdatacollective.com/how-cloud-creating-employment-blind-and-disabled/

Qiao, M., W. Bian, R. Y. D. Xu and D. Tao. "Diversified Hidden Markov Models for Sequential Labeling." *2016 IEEE 32nd International Conference on Data Engineering (ICDE)* (2016): 1512–1513, doi: 10.1109/ICDE.2016.7498400.

Shrawankar, Urmila and Azra Shireen. "Suggesting Teaching Methods by Analysing the Behaviour of Children with Special Needs." *Bio-Algorithms and Med-Systems* 16, no. 1 (2020): 1–20, 20190038, ISSN (Online) 1895-9091 / 1896-530X, 10.1515/bams-2019-0038, Publisher © 2020.

Sobhan, Masrur, Mehrab Zaman Chowdhury, et al. "A Communication Aid System for Deaf and Mute using Vibrotactile and Visual Feedback." *International Seminar on Application for Technology of Information and Communication (iSemantic)* (2019): 184–190, 10.1109/ISEMANTIC.2019.8884323.

Wazalwar, Sampada S. and Urmila Shrawankar. "Interpretation of Sign Language Into English Using NLP Techniques." *Journal of Information and Optimization Sciences* 38, no. 6 (2017): 895–910, 10.1080/02522667.2017.1372136.

Wazalwar, Sampada and Urmila Shrawankar. "Multimodal Interface for Deaf & Dumb Communication." *6th International Conference on Computing for Sustainable Global Development (INDIACom)*, 978-93-80544-34-2$31.00_c 2019. IEEE (2019).

Wazalwar, Sampada and Urmila Shrawankar. "Online Healthcare Consultation System for Deaf & Dumb During Pandemic Situation." *Bioscience Biotechnology Research Communications* 13, no. 14 (2020): 213–216, 10.21786/bbrc/13.14/50.

Wazalwar, Sampad S. and Urmila Shrawankar. "Distributed Education System for Deaf and Dumb Children and Educator: A Today's Need." In: Singh Mer K.K., Semwal V.B., Bijalwan V., Crespo R.G. (eds) *Proceedings of Integrated Intelligence Enable Networks and Computing. Algorithms for Intelligent Systems*. Springer, Singapore (2021). 10.1007/978-981-33-6307-6_35.

Section II

Cloud for Agriculture

5

Sensor Applications in Agriculture – A Review

Jyoti Lagad[1] and Sandhya Arora[2]
[1]Smt Kashibai Navale College of Engineering, Pune, India
[2]Cummins College of Engineering, Pune, India

CONTENTS

5.1 Introduction

India is considered to be a developing country where the majority of the population, more than 60%, is still employed in agriculture. Though the contribution of the agriculture sector in GDP is less as compared to other sectors, it still gives employment to many small marginal and landless families. Indian agriculture is characterized by fragmented land holding, climatic variation, high dependency on monsoon, unavailability of irrigation resources, and poor adaptation of technology which are inhibiting growth to less than flourishing in the farming sector. If the farming community and the government promote the adoption of new technologies, then the farming business will become more and more profitable. Effectively, it will contribute heavily to the GDP and the progress of

DOI: 10.1201/9781003203926-5

the country. Advanced emerging technologies such as machine learning (ML), spectral data analysis (SDA), application of sensor, Deep Learning, Support Vector Machine, Multiclass Support Vector Machine (MCSVM) are applicable to every citizen in the world. Internet of things (IoT), with its influence over the traditional system of cropping, irrigation, etc., has vast applications in the agriculture and farming sector and reduces the manpower and complex work into simple one (Zeyada et al., 2017). Supplying water by artificial means to the crops is known as irrigation and, provided we have skilled labor and basic knowledge of irrigation, IoT application to improve the various techniques of irrigation such as deep irrigation, sprinkler irrigation, furrow irrigation, surface flooding, etc becomes a reality worth considering. With more time being consumed to understand the technique, it's IoT that has promising solutions related to various tasks of irrigation such as field preparation, seed preparation, handling, ploughing the crop, applying various compost to nurturing of the crop, harvesting, etc. Global Positioning System (GPS) which is the wireless base technique mounted in the tractor is more beneficial to prepare the land (Kayad et al., 2019). The agriculture industry having implemented various sensor technologies will bring benefits for E- farming as farmers begin to sell the crop product all over India.

Technology plays an important part in the advancement of plants and farm practices for it has the ability to be the primary factor to uphold and maintain agricultural systems. Nowadays, updated and modified sensors with advanced features are available with a wide scope to improve data and information by its implementing and integrating into the production system. This is the need of the hour even as future trends look towards promoting smart farming and precision agriculture using digital transformation. The application of sensors had a remarkable impact on agricultural practices. To name a few, soil moisture sensors used for irrigation practices support farmers to make informed decisions about optimum and accurate irrigation to plants (Torabian et al., 2019). The remote sensing technology with its advanced satellites and applications are being used to map an area under crop cultivation, yield prediction, crop health, and crop stages. Since ICT and the sensor revolution have a decisive impact on the way crop is produced, we are witness to how they have impacted the whole farming system. Digital technology is helping farmers to take more accurate decisions based on real-time and accurate information about weather, crop condition, soil condition, etc. Section II illustrates the basic key role of the Internet of Things (IOT) in the modern era of agriculture. Section III gives insights into key application of IoT in the agriculture sector and advanced technology, and its application and utilization in the field of agriculture. Section IV elucidates IoT with a case study and enumerates forthcoming developments in farm management. Section V concludes the work.

5.2 IOT in Agriculture

The conventional farming strategies can be changed at a very basic level by implementing advanced IoT technologies in farming practices. The leveraging of IoT and integration of wireless sensors in E-Farming can lift agribusiness to incredible heights. For example, smart agriculture technology like the internet of things (IoT) will improve upon the various traditional issues related to farming such as drought problems, optimization of crop yield, fertility of the land, methods of irrigation, and crop diseases by bringing in foresight from

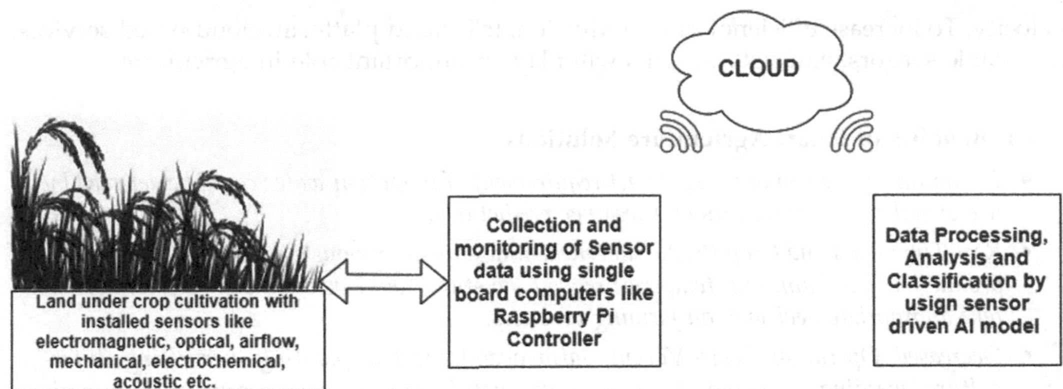

FIGURE 5.1
IoT and E-Farming.

managed cultivation practices that take feedback from data and plan before carrying out cultivation. As an agricultural equipment being implemented independently wherever essential, wireless sensors play a crucial role in collecting data related to the crop condition such as permanent wilting of the crop, rotten fruits, etc. Further, it is an urgent need to overcome the traditional heavy machinery and use new cutting-edge agricultural tools for further improvement of the agriculture sector. With a full-fledged range of better and more powerful IoT solutions in this area, fog computing and cloud computing can be built into Wireless Connections (Peteinatos et al., 2014). The Sensor Network has proved to be an economically feasible option for rural activities with features including detector combination, digital delivery, low power usage, interoperability, and protection in applications like irrigation, field surveillance, regulation of pesticide use, environmental agreements, monitoring of intruders, monitoring of environmental quality, etc. (Reiser et al., 2019). Figure 5.1 shows application of IoT and E-Farming.

Sensors play an important role in obtaining information on numerous variables, such as land, water, atmosphere, etc., for agricultural development. With the aid of data gathered from various sensors, the IoT stakeholders can help farmers understand the current state of their agricultural production and how to improve their crop yield. To date, a variety of analysis techniques have been established to assist producers in decision-making on agricultural production in order to increase their profits. It has been shown that there is a significant role for sensors in measuring nature. These sensors contribute to the smart farming system, particularly in the management of suitable irrigation systems to support farmers.

5.3 Major Applications in Agriculture

There are numerous motivations and benefits to implementing modern agricultural solutions into profitable and local farming. The crop yield and efficient use of water can be improved by monitoring and processing data for the intensity of sunlight, atmospheric temperature moisture present in the soil, humidity, rainfall, sunshine hours, and wind velocity. To increase efficiency and production, IoT based platform, cloud-based services, affordable sensors, and data insights will play an important role in agriculture.

5.3.1 Benefits of Smart Agriculture Solutions

- *Optimum utilization of water–Exact requirement of irrigation water could be detected by use of soil moisture sensors and weather predictions.*
- *Real-Time Data and Crop Production–Real-time data on various aspects which affect crop production like humidity, temperature, soil moisture, wind velocity etc. help farmers to take appropriate decisions on farming practices.*
- *Decreased Operation Costs–Various farm operations like planting, harvesting, interculture, weeding, spraying etc., can be automated reducing source consumption, accidental error, and total cost.*
- *Increased Quality of Production–Timely and accurate management of irrigation, nutrition, protection, fruit care, and harvesting with the help of various technological appliances will certainly improve the quality of product.*
- *Prevent Environmental Loss–Judicious utilization of resources for crop production will eventually reduce the loss to environment.*
- *Remote Monitoring–A farmer, vigilant, at one place can monitor various factors affecting the crop production for multiple farms at various locations on real time basis and can take appropriate decisions on irrigation, nutrition, protection, harvest or any other farm operation.*
- *Equipment Monitoring–One can monitor the performance, efficiency, and effectiveness of various equipment and machineries used for various farm operations.*

These are some of the key areas in which integration and implementation of sensors act as primary factor to support farmers in agriculture practices; and are depicted in Figure 5.2 Smart Farming Applications. Some important applications are discussed in a further section.

5.3.2 Soil Moisture Sensing

An accurate soil moisture assessment is essential in flood and drought prediction, meteorological forecast, agriculture, and water budgeting. Conventional techniques normally give point-like estimations; however, the ill effects of soil textures often leads to the critical error of the soil moisture estimation. Recently, cosmic ray neutron sensing (CRNS) has proven to be the finest methodologies to detect soil moisture (Stevanato et al., 2019). Physical properties of the soil and surrounding environment are important factors that impact soil moisture level, where soil moisture levels are one of the crucial factors for crop growing conditions. To determine the soil moisture content, numerous techniques were developed amongst which the CRNS based sensors were proposed in cultivation to monitor wide areas. Another type of sensor like capacitance sensors are affordable and could provide real-time soil moisture level giving, whenever required, an accurate calibration. The paper by Stevanato et al. (2019) presents an innovation in the development of an instrument that permits soil moisture assessment from environmental epithermal neutron counts. A subsequent article was authored by Nagahage et al. (2019), in which the capacitive soil moisture sensor model: SKU: SEN0193, DFRobot was calibrated under lab conditions. The sensor is integrated with a data acquisition system for analysis and

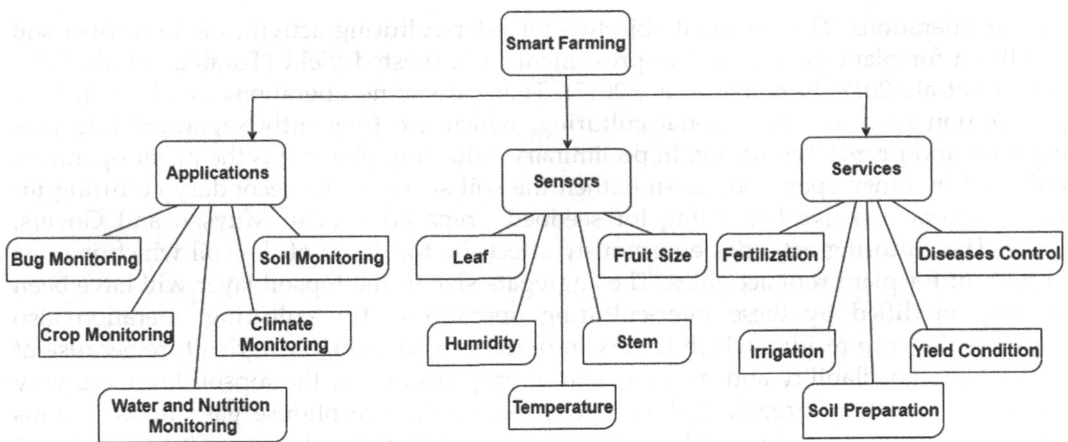

FIGURE 5.2
Smart Farming Applications.

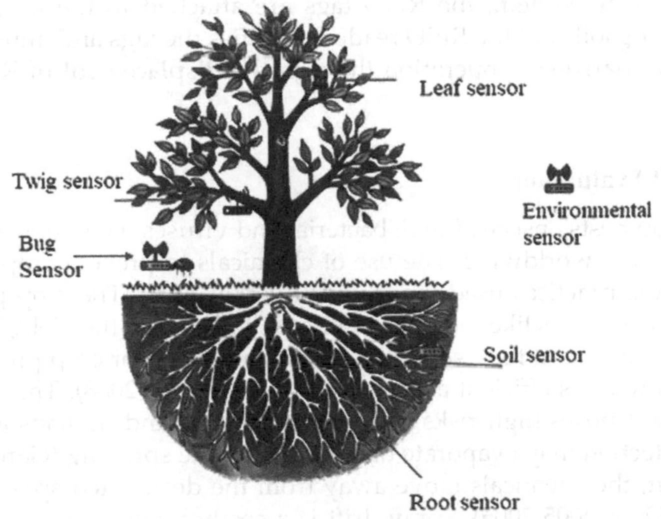

FIGURE 5.3
Sensors Used in Crop Production.

studied under lab conditions. The conventional gravimetric technique and other calibrated sensor model: SM-200 were used to compare sensor data. The results elaborate that the SKU: SEN0193 sensor can assist in nourishing the readily-available moisture present in the soil. In indoor systems, it limits the hazard of both excess water application and soil moisture strain. Figure 5.3 shows use of sensors in crop production.

5.3.3 Land/Seedbed Preparation

Land preparation to make changes to soil properties and crop properties is one of the major activities in crop production which involves plowing, tilling/culturing, and other similar operations. The principal objective for inter-culturing activities is to recover soil condition for plant growth and improvement in harvested yield (Torabian et al., 2019; Zeyada et al., 2017; Pezzuolo et al., 2017). There are some operations involved in land preparation such as conventional culturing, which are frequently separated into preliminary and primary culturing. In preliminary culturing, plowing is the major operation followed by other operations to smoothen the soil surface. The secondary culturing involves operations like harrowing for seedbed preparation (Van Muysen and Govers, 2002). The culturing activities enormously affect the top layer of the soil which is most important for plant root activities. The aggregate size in the topsoil layer will have been suitably modified by these inter-culturing operations. The culturing operation also manages the crop residue which is very important for sustainable agriculture because of the fact that availability and management of crop residue in the topsoil layer are very important to ensure organic carbon levels, reduce the greenhouse gas effects, humus contents in the soil, reduce soil erosion, and maintain the soil texture (Cherubini and Ulgiati, 2010; Cillis et al., 2018). The soil attributes, the amount of crop residue in the topsoil, the depth and speed of inter-culturing operation are some of the factors which affect how effective was the inter culturing operations. An article by Kayad et al. (2019) suggested using RFID systems to assess the topsoil movement after the rotary harrowing operation. In the RFID system, the RFID tags are attached to the targeted object and distributed in the topsoil, and the RFID reader identifies the tags and, thus, the movement in the topsoil after harrowing operation through the displacement of RFID tags can be measured.

5.3.4 Spray Drift Evaluation

The attacks by crop pests, insects, fungi, bacteria, and viruses have reduced crop yield by as much as up to 40% worldwide. The use of chemicals to prevent crop loss from these attacks is one of the practices used worldwide (Oerke, 2006). The crop protection using chemicals has some benefits like reduced labor cost, increase in the yield, improvement in the quality of the crops, and food security. To use chemicals for crop protection in fields, the method of spraying is efficient and low cost (Giles et al., 2008). Though it is efficient and low cost, still it poses high risks to the environment and humans as the chemicals used for crop protection may evaporate or drift during the spraying (Garcerá et al., 2017). During spray drift, the chemicals move away from the designated spraying area due to air current (ISO 22866:2005 2005). Spray drift is a costly affair as it increases the cost of plant protection drastically, and also impacts the result-producing effects of spraying, and, consequently, yield and quality production. During spray drift, the chemicals could be deposited in off-target areas like other crops, soils, surface water bodies, animals, humans, and thus could bring in serious consequences like air pollution, water pollution, direct or indirect effect on domestic animals, and other crops (Nuyttens et al., 2007). The factors which add to spray drift are interrelated, and some can be controlled and some cannot be controlled.

These factors can be classified as (Balsari et al., 2019):

- *Equipment and application strategies.*
- *Climate conditions during application.*
- *Spray attributes.*

- *Operator's expertise.*
- *Crop canopy* (Balsari et al., 2019).

Advanced equipment such as electromagnetic sprayers could be used to improve spray efficiency. Also, the use of sensors for monitoring and predicting of weather conditions like temperature, humidity, and wind speed could help farmers in deciding on spraying slots with optimum weather conditions. This will also reduce the spray drift due to environmental conditions (Bourodimos et al., 2019).

5.3.5 Weeding Robot

Weeds are the undesirable plant growth that competes with the main crop for sunlight, water, and nutrition, thus, causing reduced yields anywhere on earth. For better crop production and higher yields, one has to eradicate the weeds during the crop cycle for as many times as necessary. Weeding is either done by employing human labor or with mechanical implements or by the use of chemicals. The weeding operations using human labor, though effective, is a costly affair and highly dependent on the availability of labor. The unavailability of labor, in time, for weeding operations will result in reduced crop yield (Peteinatos et al., 2014; Andújar et al., 2016). The weeding operation using farm implements and types of machinery, though cost-effective, is not a very efficient method given the implements and machinery used may affect the main crop. Also, there is a requirement of human labor while using the implements and machinery. Many farmers, these days, choose the third method to eradicate weeds from the fields, that is, the use of herbicides. Though herbicides are economical and efficient, they can cause disastrous effects on the activities of microorganisms in the soil. This results in soils becoming, day by day, more and more unproductive. Also, some of the chemicals used as herbicides are cancer-causing chemicals.

Thus, the use of weeding robots that will identify the weeds and remove them mechanically is the most effective and economical method for the eradication of weeds. These mechanical weeding robots could be used any time at the farmer's ease with less resource and less energy (Balsari et al., 2019). The manuscript by Reiser et al. (2019) reports the use of an electric tiller weeder for automatic inter-row weeding in vineyards. According to the report, the robot consists of a rotary weeder with an electric tiller head and a 2D laser scanner to follow the rows, and the crops or trees were detected and evaluated by feeler and sonar.

5.4 Cloud Based Air Quality Monitoring: Case Study

Air contamination can prompt exceptionally destructive conditions that ominously affect living things. Air contamination is a universal issue with the concerned including the mass media, international organizations, and governments. The use of somewhat natural resources at an advanced rate than nature's capacity to restore can accomplish contamination of water, air, and plants. Next to human-made exercises, a cataclysmic event like volcanic emission could bring about the pollution of air. Rapid industrialization, urbanization, global warming, deforestation, agricultural activities, and burning of fossil fuels are the important reasons for the contamination of air (Dhingra et al., 2019):

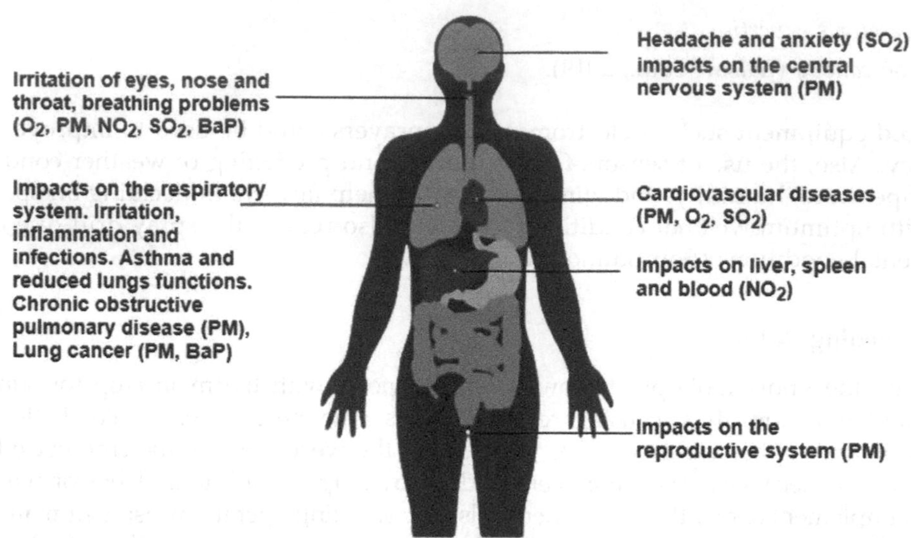

FIGURE 5.4
Consequences of Air Pollution on Human Health.

- *Carbon Monoxide: Carbon monoxide is generated by the devouring of petroleum derivatives, for the most part in cars, autos. Carbon monoxide has a great affinity towards the hemoglobins and forms carboxyhemoglobin which has no use in the respiration system and starts blood clotting. Due to more concentration of carbon monoxide, heart attack may occur. The human being may suffer from cerebral pains.*
- *Toxic air toxins: Due to the burning of fossil fuel, emission of various gaseous matters from the chemical factories such as Hydrogen Sulphide (H2S), carbon dioxide (CO2), nitrous oxide (N2O), and ammonia (NH3), the air is getting contaminated. These poisonous gaseous matters are responsible for cancer and causing birth defects.*
- *Nitrogen Dioxide (NO2): Produced from the ignition of fuel, for example, automobile fuel, electric utilities, coal burnings, and mechanical boilers, the quality and quantity of NO2 produced is the main source of lung-related illnesses.*
- *Sulphur Dioxide (SO2): It is produced from the burning of sulfur fuel, open burning of domestic waste, and natural disasters such as volcanoes.*

Figure 5.4 shows consequences of air pollution on human health.

5.4.1 Role of IoT

In every walk of human life, life is full of innovations and advancements. To fulfill individual and industrial interest and to meet their needs, it is advisable that all respective activities are done by upgrading existing systems and by using novel innovations. In the last decade, IOT has been one of the most important developments in communication which enables the interfacing of numerous low powered, smart embedded devices to one another and to the Internet. Several wireless techniques such as Radio Frequency Identification labels, actuators, sensors, and smart phones establish the IoT concept. The main purpose is to transmit and receive data autonomously, therefore opening new

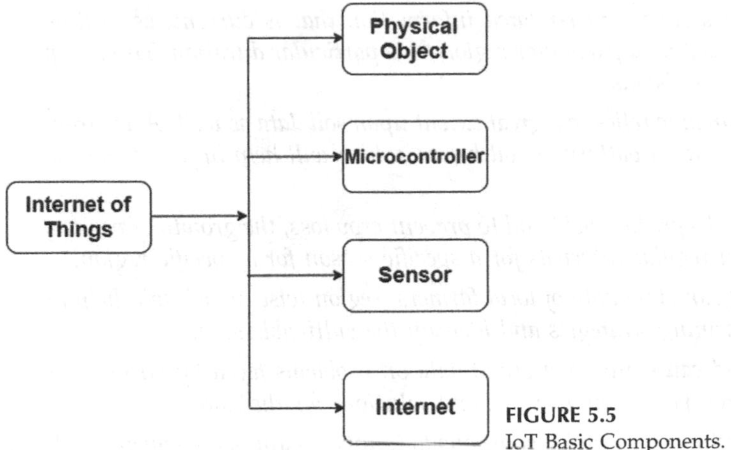

FIGURE 5.5
IoT Basic Components.

horizons for household, health, and industrial applications. Internet of things will associate things or devices with one another via the internet, that means everything will have the ability for communication.

The basic IoT model has four layers as follows:

- *Application layer: Contains numerous services and applications that the IoT provides.*
- *Perception Layer: Includes different types of sensors such as gas sensor, temperature sensors, and vibration sensors, to name some.*
- *Network Layer: It is composed of physical components and the network communications software.*
- *Physical Layer: It includes the hardware components like smart appliances or power supplies.*

Figure 5.5 shows basic components of IoT.

5.4.2 Role of Cloud Computing

Cloud computing is an IT paradigm that allows users to access shared pools of configurable system resources and services over the internet. Sharing of resources is rational and scalable with next to no administrative exertion. The user can likewise decide on choices: Software as a service (SaaS), Platform as a service (PaaS), or Infrastructure as a service (IaaS). Cloud computing facilitates users with real-time processing, storage, and data access without knowing the actual physical location and the configuration of the system or resource that provides different services.

5.4.3 Applications of Cloud Computing in Agriculture

- *Analysis of Previous and existing cropping patterns: Cloud computing helps store and analyze cropping data over a period of time which will help farmers to take appropriate decisions on which crop in which season to be cultivated will give incomes on a sustainable basis.*

- *Weather Data: Cloud can store weather-related information that is current, as well as past, and also weather forecast for a particular region for a particular duration. These help the farmers in crop-related decisions.*
- *Soil Data: Yield-related dynamic relies to a great extent upon soil data as well. Aside from soil profile, it can likewise give a pattern of soil before, which will help in foreseeing the pattern in the future.*
- *Crop Growth Monitoring: To predict yield and to prevent crop loss, the growth of various crops can be monitored on regular intervals for a specific season for a specific region.*
- *Farmers' Data: The cloud can store data of local farmers, region wise, which will help in making decisions about farming strategies and identify the cultivable area.*
- *Expert's Advisories: Cloud can store a variety of data on problems faced by farmers for nutrition management, crop pest, crop diseases, and solutions for the same.*
- *E-commerce: Cloud computing can provide solutions for supply chain management, real-time demand assessment, and traceability.*
- *R & D Data Hub: Research fellows can share their innovations, recommendations, conclusions, and experiences on the research studies on various aspects of farming such as irrigation management, nutrition management, protection management, canopy management, fruit care, etc.*

5.4.4 Overview of Air Quality Monitoring System

IoT devices are formed by using devices which has ability to connect to the internet and has integrated sensors, network connection support, on and off switches, software, and actuators. Devices such as this include laptops, cell phones, smart watches, smart gadgets, home appliances, lights, almost everything. Internet of Things (IoT) involves all the web-empowered gadgets that send and receive data they get from their enveloping environmental factors using sensors, processors, and hardware equipment. These devices, at times, can communicate with different devices and process the data transmitted by other devices (Dhingra et al. 2019).

The new IoT advances ensure fine-grained information, better precision, and flexibility in the gadgets. Effective determining requires detailed knowledge and adaptability in range, instrument type, organization, and course of action. This ensures early acknowledgment, discovery, and early responses to forestall death toll and property loss.

Three fundamental phases were involved in the design are:

Phase I. Application of sensors to detect the concentration of air contaminations in a particular area.

Phase II. Easy and simple interface – User friendly Android application to recognize the contamination level in a specific region.

Phase III. Application of the analytical model to predict the air quality.

The executed details can be proposed in Figure 5.6.

The air pollution detection system is implemented as follows (Stankovic, 2014; Uckelmann et al., 2011):

Gas detecting sensors are connected to the Arduino board. Data is generated by these gas sensors (like Carbon dioxide (CO2), Carbon monoxide (CO), Methane (CH4)) that declaim the gas concentration around there. In first step this data is collected and

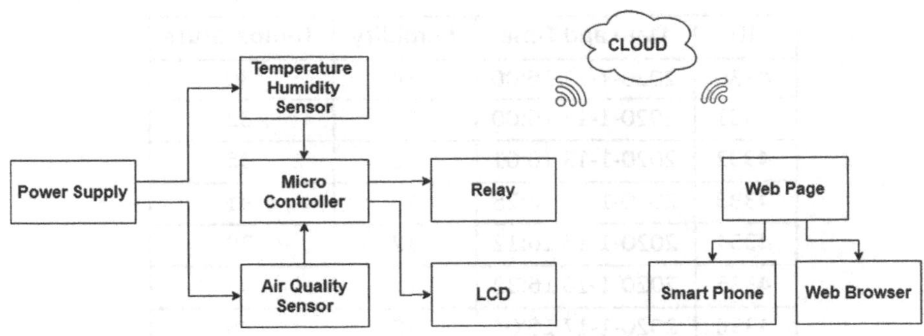

FIGURE 5.6
Architecture of Air Quality Monitoring System.

processed and stored in cloud platform. Subsequently, the Android platform is used to access this information. IoT Kit is developed in such a way that the data produced by sensors is directed to the cloud, then it is processed and made available to the user in the suitable form.

Vast and versatile data is generated by the sensor system. Thus, it is important to have high information loading and data processing capacity. Right now, different cloud systems are accessible which can be utilized to handle sensor information. To make this data available on the internet it requires a dwelling to access and store data, and communication way with it. Normally, these comprise the web server and an application programming interface (API) (method of conveying). Web server applications, which run locally on personal computers up till now are located on the web (e.g. Google Maps, Yahoo Mail). An Application Programming Interface, in this framework, stipulates the rules and explains how data is exchanged or transferred with the web based application. The architecture of Air Quality Monitoring System is given in following Figure 5.6

The system uses the ESP32 Development Board as the microcontroller for the system which carries out all the automation and data collecting work of the system, MQT135 Air Quality Sensor detects the smoke, H2, CH4, Alcohol, and propane available in the atmosphere, the DHT-11 is a Temperature and Humidity sensor, the MQ-09 sensor is used for the detection of the Carbon Monoxide and LPG, the system consists of an LCD 1602 I2C for the displaying the current condition live and the HLK-5M05 5V/5W is used for the AC to DC conversion(Dhingra et al., 2019).

The Real-Time Dataset

The information utilized in this work is gathered from the DHT11 sensor for producing humidity and temperature dynamically. A dataset is prepared by the data generated from sensors. Figure 5.7 delineates the data set generated by the system.

Data is stored to the cloud when the accurate sensor values are retrieved. This is done by creating an Arduino HTTP client which in turn calls a JSON service. The application is configured using a web interface after creating the Arduino HTTP user to send data along with a verification code. Web interface stores data collected from sensors in different variables. Data can be sent to the cloud after the configuration of variables and stored with ID. The data like longitude, latitude, and concentration of various gases are stored for every location which has a unique ID with the installed sensors. In view of the gas

ID	Date and Time	humidity	Temperature
4330	2020-1-11 16:06	14	30
4331	2020-1-12 16:00	14	32
4332	2020-1-13 16:01	16	35
4333	2020-1-14 16:25	13	31
4334	2020-1-15 16:12	12	28
4335	2020-1-16 16:32	15	34
4336	2020-1-17 16:04	15	36

FIGURE 5.7
DHT11 and MQ135 Sensor Dataset.

concentration, the AQI is determined. The air quality basically depends upon the various parameters present in the air such as suspended particular matters (SPM) having a diameter of fine impurities in the range of <10–<2.5 µm, nitrogen dioxide (NO2), carbon monoxide (CO), Ozone (O3). These parameters are very important because on the basis of these ingredients purity of air is measured. Determination of air quality is generally known as Air Quality Index (AQI). From the cloud technology, the concentration of mentioned pollutants was determined and is retrieved. If the pollution level is increased above the standard norms given by the central pollution control board (CPCB). The Indian government gives warnings messages to alert the public and to minimize pollution (Dhingra et al., 2019). Figure 5.8 shows the AQI color codes and health effects.

5.5 Future Advancements in Farm Management

For agriculture, need to use a fleet of drones and sensors to calculate the total area under cultivation, to determine the relative health of agriculture fields, to estimate agriculture yield, and strategize irrigation design & watershed management. Current methods rely on conventional tools, human deployment to plan the agriculture yields. Limitation of human accessibility and lower resolution & obsolete data leads to inefficient decision making. The use of drone-based data and high-resolution satellite image data helps to have an up-to-date and high-resolution land record that can be used as the base imagery to overlay other information such as land ownership, crop type, crop growth stages, and canal network. This will help in quick decisions on analyzing & predicting yields and effect on the performance of agricultural fields like, calculating the total area under cultivation, determining the relative health of agriculture fields, estimating agriculture yield, and strategizing plantation and irrigation design & watershed management.

Existing methods involve deploying manpower on the ground to check for cropping identification and crop cutting experiment. With no high-resolution visual data, it becomes difficult for decision-makers to completely comprehend the ground reality leading to decisions with limited data. With drone data, it becomes possible to access precise

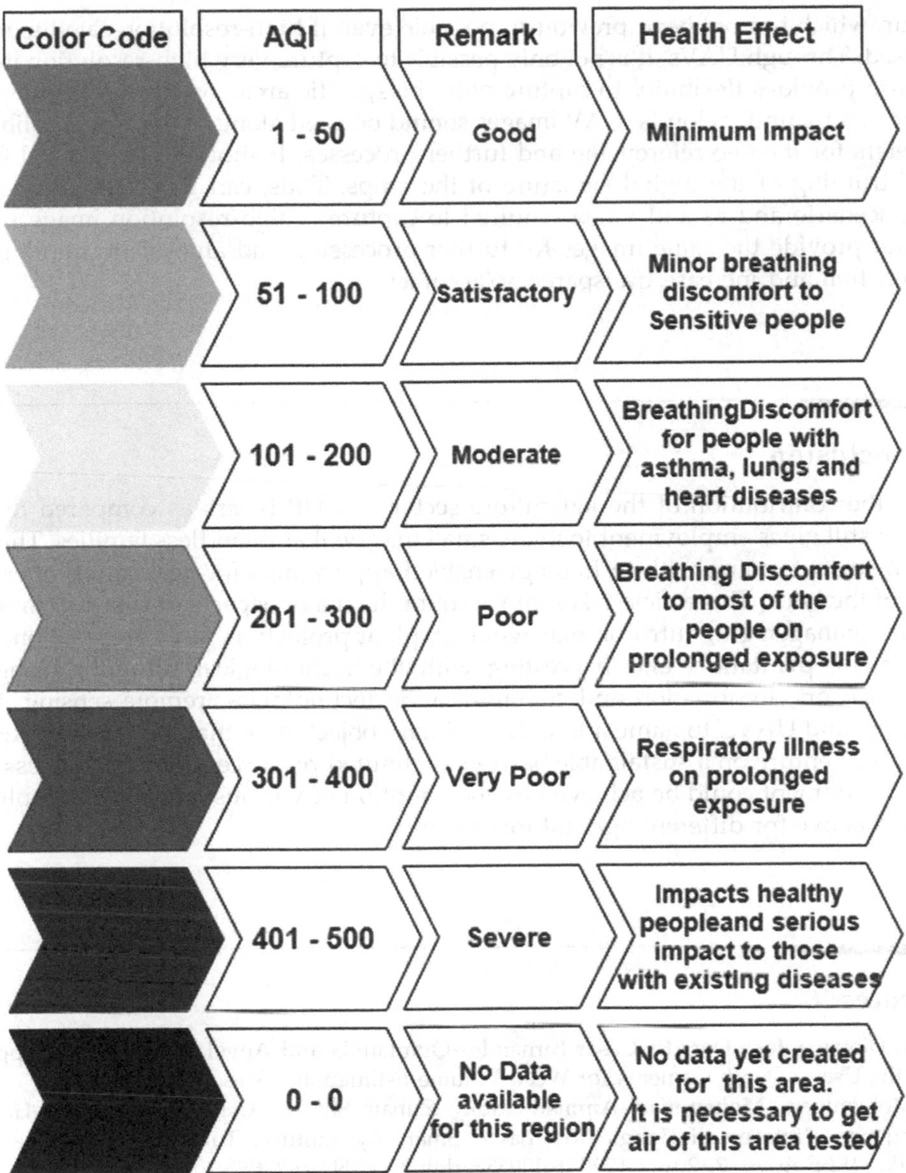

Color Code
AQI
Remark
Health Effect
1 - 50
Good
Minimum Impact
51 - 100
Satisfactory
Minor breathing discomfort to Sensitive people
101 - 200
Moderate
BreathingDiscomfort for people with asthma, lungs and heart diseases
201 - 300
Poor
Breathing Discomfort to most of the people on prolonged exposure
301 - 400
Very Poor
Respiratory illness on prolonged exposure
401 - 500
Severe
Impacts healthy peopleand serious impact to those with existing diseases
0 - 0
No Data available for this region
No data yet created for this area. It is necessary to get air of this area tested

FIGURE 5.8
AQI Color Codes.

on-ground information without having to travel to the agriculture fields and thus allows for taking quick & better decisions.

Unmanned Aerial Vehicles (UAVs) provide flexibility to capture a high-resolution image of a particular area of interest under the cloud and during a disaster like a landslide, hailstorm, flood, etc. The exclusive and enormous use of Unmanned Aerial Vehicle could be used for crop damage or loss assessment. Within the defined boundaries and in order to cover the maximum area in the shortest period of time with maximum transparency, the practice of UAV is essential. Crop monitoring at the farm level is the need of the hour, which has not been previously possible even if high-resolution satellite images were used. Through UAVs, it is not only possible to capture very high-resolution images, but it also provides flexibility to capture only the specific areas where we are interested and also can fly under clouds. UAV images should be used along with camera calibration parameters for the geo-referencing and further processes. It should also be used for the ground-truthing of the digital signature of the crops. Thus, can use UAV during such type of scenario and as and when required to capture a high-resolution image in such cases and provide the same images for further processing and analysis to minimize the time of action and increase transparency/accuracy.

5.6 Conclusion

Though the contribution of the agriculture sector in GDP is less as compared to other sectors, it still gives employment to many small marginal and landless families. Thus, the focus on smart farming with technology-enabled applications for agriculture operations is need of the hour. This article takes into account the major aspects of smart farming like irrigation management, nutrition management, plant protection, land preparation, weed management, plantation, and harvesting with the technological solutions using IoT, wireless sensors, information and communication technologies, remote sensing, image processing, and UAVs, to name a few. The primary objective of making farming business a profitable venture on a sustainable basis using limited resources and causing less harm to the environment could be achieved by the adoption of various technological solutions discussed above for different agriculture operations.

References

Andújar, Dionisio, Jose Dorado, Cesar Fernández-Quintanilla and Angela Ribeiro. "An Approach to the Use of Depth Cameras for Weed Volume Estimation." *Sensors* 16 (2016): 972.

Ayaz, Mohammad, Mohammad Ammad-Uddin, Zubair Sharif, A. Mansour and El-Hadi M. Aggoune. "Internet-of-Things (IoT)-Based Smart Agriculture: Toward Making the Fields Talk." *IEEE Access* 7 (2019): 129551–129583, doi: 10.1109/ACCESS.2019.2932609.

Balsari, Paolo, Marco Grella, Paolo Marucco, Fabio Matta and A. Miranda-Fuentes. "Assessing the Influence of Air Speed And liquid Flow Rate on the Droplet Size and Homogeneity in Pneumatic Spraying." *Pest Management Science* 219, no. 75 (2019): 366–379.

Bourodimos, Georgios, Michael Koutsiaras, Vasilios Psiroukis, Athanasios Balafoutis and S. Fountas. "Development and Field Evaluationof a Spray Drift Risk Assessment Tool for Vineyard Spraying application." *Agriculture* 9 (2019): 181.

Cherubini, Francesco and Sergio Ulgiati. "Crop Residues as Raw Materials for Biorefinery Systems—A LCA case study." *Applied Energy* 87 (2010): 47–57.

Cillis, Donato, Maestrini Maestrini, Andrea Pezzuolo, Francesco Marinello and Luigi Sartori. "Modeling Soil Organic Carbon and Carbon Dioxide Emissions in Different Tillage Systems Supported By Precision Agriculture Technologies Under Current Climatic Conditions." *Soil Tillage Res.* 183 (2018): 51–59.

Dhingra, Swati, Rajasekhara Babu Madda, Amir H. Gandomi, Rizwan Patan and Daneshmand Mahmoud. "Internet of Things Mobile–Air Pollution Monitoring System (IoT-Mobair)." *IEEE Internet of Things Journal* 6, no. 3 (June 2019): 5577–5584, doi: 10.1109/JIOT.2019.2903821.

Garcerá, Cruz, Carla Román, Enrique Moltó, Raquel Abad, Jose Antonio Insa, Xavier Torrent, Santiago Planas and Patricia Chueca. "Comparison between standard and drift reducing nozzles for pesticide application in citrus: Part II." *Effects on Canopy Spray Distribution, Control Efficacy of Aonidiella Aurantii (Maskell), Beneficial Parasitoids and Pesticide Residues on Fruit, Crop Protection* 94 (2017): 83–96, ISSN 0261-2194, 10.1016/j.cropro.2016.12.016.

Giles, D., N. Akesson and W. Yates. "Pesticide Application Technology: Research and Development and the Growth of the Industry." *Trans. ASABE* 51 (2008): 397–403.

ISO 22866:2005. Equipment for Crop Protection-Methods for Field Measurement of Spray Drift International Bureau of India Standards, New Delhi (2005): 1–17.

Kayad, Ahamed, Riccardo Rainato, Lorenzo Picco, Luigi Sartori and Francesco Marinello. "Assessing Topsoil Movement in Rotary Harrowing Process by RFID (Radio-Frequency Identification) Technique." *Agriculture* 9 (2019): 184.

Nagahage, Ekanayaka Achchillage Ayesha Dilrukshi, Nagahage, Isura Sumeda Priyadarshana and Takeshi Fujino. "Calibration and Validation of a Low-cost Capacitive Moisturesensor to Integrate the Automated Soil Moisture Monitoring System." *Agriculture* 9 (2019): 141.

Nuyttens, David De, Mieke De Schampheleire, Katrijn Baetens and Bart Sonck. "The Influence of Operator- Controlled Variables on Spray Drift from Field Crop Sprayers." *Trans. ASABE* 50 (2007): 1129–1140.

Oerke, E. "Crop Losses to Pests." *The Journal of Agricultural Science* 144, no.1 (2006): 31–43. doi:10.1017/S0021859605005708

Peteinatos, Gerassimos G., Martin Weis, Dionisio Andújar, Victor Rueda Ayala and Roland Gerhards. "Potential Use of Ground-Based Sensortechnologies for Weed Detection." *Pest Manag. Sci.* 70 (2014): 190–199.

Pezzuolo, Andrea, Benjamin Dumont, Luigi Sartori, Francesco Marinello, Massimiliano De Antoni de Antoni Migliorati and Bruno Basso. "Evaluating the Impact of Soil Conservation Measures on Soil Organic Carbon at the Farm Scale." *Computers and Electronics in Agriculture* 135 (2017): 175–182.

Reiser, David, EI Sayed Sehsah, Oliver Bumann, Jorg Morhard Morhard and Hans W. Griepentrog. "Development of an Autonomous Electricrobot Implement for Intra-row Weeding in Vineyards." *Agriculture* 9 (2019): 18.

Stankovic, John A. "Research Directions for the Internet of Things." *IEEE Internet Things J.* 1, no. 1 (2014): 3–9.

Stevanato, Luca, Gabriele Baroni, Y. Cohen, Francesco Cristiano Lino, S. Gatto, Marcello Lunardon, Francesco Marinello, Sandra Moretto and Luca Morselli. "A Novel Cosmic-Ray Neutron Sensor for Soil Moisture Estimation over Large Areas." *Agriculture* 9 (2019): 202.

Torabian, S., S. Farhangi-Abriz and M.D. Denton. "Do Tillage Systems Influence Nitrogen Fixation in Legumes? A Review". *Soil Tillage Res.* 185 (2019): 113–121.

Uckelmann, Dieter, Mark Harrison and Florian Michahelles. "An Architectural Approach Towards the Future Internet of Things." *Architecting the Internet of Things*, Springer, 2011, pp. 1–24.

Van Muysen, W. and G. Govers. "Soil Displacement and Tillage Erosion During Secondary Tillage Operations: The Case of Rotary Harrow and Seeding Equipment." *Soil Tillage Res.* 65 (2002): 185–191.

Zeyada, Ahmed M., Khalid Ali Al-Gaadi, E. Tola, Rangaswamy Madugundu and Ahmed G. Kayad. "Impact of Soil Firmness and Tillage Depth on Irrigated Maize Silage Performance." *Appl. Eng. Agric.* 33 (2017): 491–498.

6

Crop Biophysical Parameters Estimation Using SAR Imagery for Precision Agriculture Applications

Vaishali G. Bhujade
Computer Engineering, Veermata Jijabai Technological Institute, Mumbai, India

CONTENTS

6.1 Introduction

Precision farming is the approach of gaining as much information from the crop as possible and used this information effectively to build a strategic decision support system for the management of crops and resources. Precision farming is done by observing the plants on time with different methods and then extract essential information from observations. The ultimate aim of precision agriculture is to automate the farming activities and to accelerate the productivity with minimum utilization of input resources. In this, the farmers are in charge of making strategic decisions based on environmental care and

DOI: 10.1201/9781003203926-6

production needs. Nowadays, several methods are available to access the status of the crops and to retrieve growth parameters using their biophysical parameters, namely, plant area index (PAI), wet biomass (WB), leaf area index (LAI), canopy height, canopy volume, and so on.

Remote sensing is a method of gaining statistics about a feature or an entity without actually get in touch with the element or object. Remote sensing is used to develop information about objects, classes, and topographies on the exterior of the ground, atmosphere, and oceans from the acquired geospatial data. This data collected by several sensors can be of any form and investigated to get statistics about the entities beneath attention. The method by which we gather land observations from quantities of electromagnetic radiation (EMR) from the soil's exterior is known as remote sensing. This EMR can either be radiated or redirected from the Earth's surface. Remote sensing can be defined in another way as it is the process of sensing and determining electromagnetic power imitated or radiated from detached entities prepared by various constituents for classifying these entities by their nature or class, material, and spatial distributions. There are two types of remote-sensing systems as follows:

1. Active Remote Sensing: This sensing technique has a power source. Therefore, active sensors emit their energy to scan areas and objects. Then the target emits or reflects the radiations, which are captured by the sensor to analyze them. Example: LiDAR and RADAR.
2. Passive Remote Sensing: This technique does not have its energy source; therefore, it depends upon the sun for energy.

Examples: Film photography, radiometer, infrared, and charge-coupled devices.

Figure 6.1 represents components of remote sensing systems as follows:

1. Energy Source: The sun act as an energy source in the remote sensing system. It emits electromagnetic radiations on the Earth's surface comprising targets.

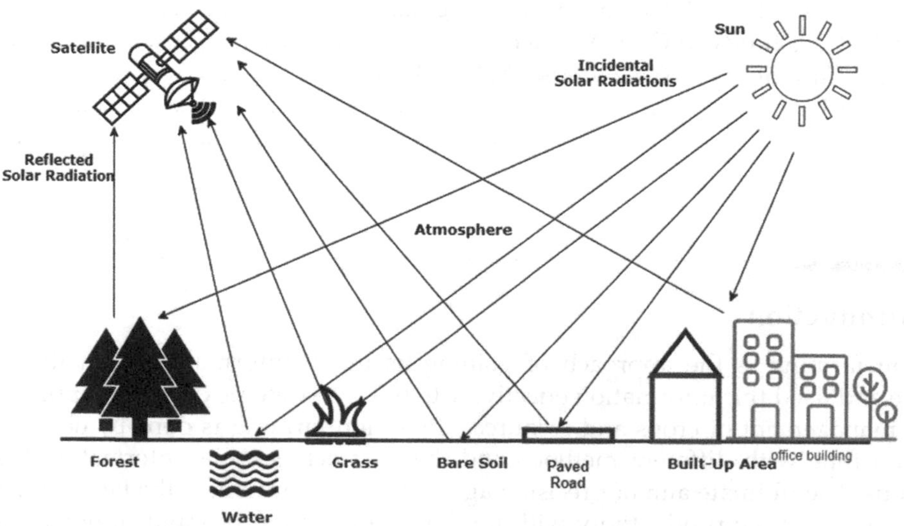

FIGURE 6.1
Remote-Sensing Process.

2. Atmosphere: It is used to transmit and energy from the source to the corresponding target.
3. Interaction of EMR with the target: The emitted energy is passing through the atmosphere and interacts with the object on the surface.
4. Transmission of Energy: As a result of interaction in the previous step, some amount of energy is absorbed by the object, and the rest will be transmitted toward the sensors located on satellite.
5. Recording by Sensors: The energy coming towards sensors is recorded by the sensors, and passed it to the ground stations.
6. Data Processing: Ground stations are responsible for processing the information coming from sensors.
7. Data Analysis: After processing, the information is analyzed to use with specific applications.

Nowadays the world's population is growing so fast, but the agricultural land and resources are limited. To fulfill the need of a growing community, we need efficient techniques for crop management. With this goal, it is common to use UAVs, satellites, and drones to capture crop images and gather insights about it, which help farmers to use the right quantity of fertilizers, water, and pesticides to the crop to increase productivity.

There are two well-known methods to access vegetation development information, i.e., biophysical parameters and NDVI. The NDVI is used to calculate and provide an overview of the plant development status quickly. Biophysical parameter estimation is a more advanced method of obtaining vegetation development information. As it is advanced, it needs more efficient algorithms for processing. Table 6.1 provides the list of biophysical parameters with corresponding meaning.

For retrieving vegetation development information from observations captured by SAR satellites, the method first understands the backscatter intensities of crop canopy. Figure 6.2 represents the SAR scattering mechanism and the classical polarimetric SAR scattering types. This method is then reversed to retrieve characteristics of the canopy (Prevot et al., 1993). A

TABLE 6.1
Biophysical Parameters and Their Meaning

Sr. No.	Name of Parameters	Meaning
1	LAI (Leaf Area Index)	Number of meters of leaves in one square meter of ground
2	WB (Wet Biomass)	Represents water content of canopy and carbon accumulation
3	fCover (fractional cover of green vegetation)	% of the surface of the ground occupied by the plant
4	GLAI (Green Leaf Area Index)	Represents green leaf area per unit ground from one side of leaf
5	FAPAR (Fraction of Absorbed Photo Synthetically Active Radiation)	% of sunlight absorbed by the plant in the domain of photosynthesis.
6	Chlorophyll Content	Content of Chlorophyll A and B per unit of leaves.
7	PAI (Plant Area Index)	Represent average active radiation of photosynthesis at various height inside the canopy.
8	fNPV (fractional cover of non-photosynthetic-brown-vegetation)	% of the surface of the ground occupied by brown leaves, seen from above

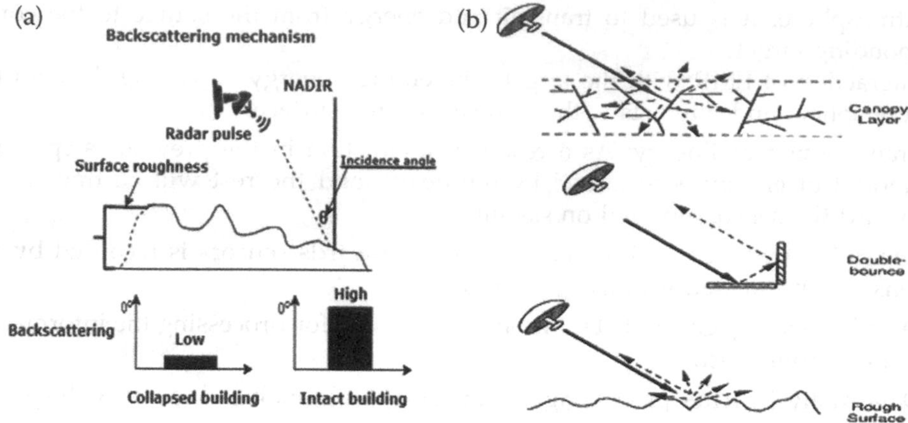

FIGURE 6.2
The SAR Polarimetric Scattering Mechanism: (a) The Backscattering Mechanism; (b) The Scattering Types of Polarimetric SAR.

model proposed by Attema and Ulaby (Attema et al., 1978), i.e., the backscattering coefficients are determined by a semi-empirical water-cloud model (WCM).

- **Specular reflection-** This type of scattering occurs when the radar signal encounters a very smooth surface, like pavements or water. The smooth surface reflects the radar signal like a mirror, sending most of it away from the SAR sensor. This type of reflection results in a low backscatter and creates dark areas in the SAR scene.
- **Volume/diffuse scattering-** This type of scattering occurs when the radar signal encounters a rough surface, like vegetation canopy or dirt. The rough surface scatters the radar signal in many different directions, and a small portion of it is returned to the SAR sensor. This type of reflection results in moderate levels of backscatter, and appear as medium gray areas in considered SAR scenes. In the case of volume scattering in a forest, leaves reflect radar signals onto other leaves and branches, resulted in multiple scattering.
- **Double bounce scattering** - It occurs in areas like cities where a large number of human-made features exist. In urban areas, the radar signal is first reflected in a specular way as it encounters roads and sidewalks. The specularly reflected signal then bounces off the sides of buildings and is returned to the SAR sensor. Double bounce reflection causes most of the radar signal to return to the sensor, resulting in high backscatter and bright areas in the considered SAR scene.

   a. **Backscattering Mechanism:** The method in which the backscatter is formed when the radar frequency hits the target. The notation sigma is used to measure the reflective strength of a radar target. This mechanism depends on the roughness of the surface and dielectric properties of the medium. All the factors of backscattering depend on the incidence angle, frequency, and polarization of the radar.
   b. **Scattering Types:** There are three different types of scattering described as follows:

Precision agriculture applications are categorized as follows:

1. **Plant/Fruit Detection:** It is the process of detecting an accurate position of the object of interest from the considered scenario. It is necessary for some automated farming activities such as seeding, harvesting, and pruning. To achieve these activities, several features such as temperature, shape, and color are needed.
2. **Structural Characterization:** It is the process of extracting structural parameters such as leaf area index, plant area index, canopy volume, canopy height biomass, etc. which are useful for making strategic decisions to enhance the agricultural process.
3. **Pesticides and Fertilizer Management:** The process of supplying minimal input parameters such as pesticides and fertilizer to the crop according to their need is known as pesticides and fertilizer management. It is used to decrease the harmful impact on the environment.
4. **Crop Growth Monitoring:** It the process of monitoring the overall growth of crops. It is used to access the global status of plants, such as the proper use of water, pesticides, fungicides, and disease detection, etc.
5. **Pruning Directives:** Pruning is the process of removing unwanted parts of a plant such as a particular bud, branch, etc.
6. **Breeding:** The process of creating new plant varieties from the old one is known as breeding. These new varieties are more resistant to pests, diseases, and environmental changes.

This study elaborates several sensing methods to capture the information about crops needed for precision farming. Following is the list of various sensors.

6.1.1 Morphological Characterization Sensors

Several sensors retrieve the information needed for crop characterization. Here we have a list of sensors that are used for the above precision agricultural applications.

1. **Time-of-Flight Sensors:** It is used to measure intensity and distance by using a source of light and an array of detectors. These are compact, very much accurate, and have a high frame rate.
2. **Ultrasound Sensors:** These sensors emit the high-frequency pulses, which are of short duration on the target and receives echoes generated by the target. These are of low cost and are robust to dust and fog.
3. **LiDAR:** It is a light detection and ranging sensor. These are also used to measure distances. These are widely used for farming activities to estimate several structural parameters such as PAI, biomass, etc.
4. **Color Cameras:** These are used in farming applications for characterization and detection. We can retrieve additional parameters from color information as shape and texture.
5. **Structured Light Cameras:** These types of sensors provides accurate distances. They project an IR pattern over the target and measure the distortion coming from the target. These are effective in indoor environments.

6.1.2 Physiological Assessment Sensors for Vegetation

1. **Hyperspectral and Multi-Spectral Cameras:** This categorization depends on the number of bands, resolution of bands, and span of the electromagnetic spectrum. Multi-spectral cameras have few bands, and they are not necessarily contiguous; whereas hyperspectral has more bands, and they all are contiguous.
2. **Thermal Cameras:** These are used to measure the temperature of the considered target. Nowadays, heat acts as a critical parameter for farming activities such as disease diagnosis and stress identification. The temperature of the plant is a useful indicator of water quantity, which is used for irrigation system development. These are used to identify water stress by examining the temperature of leaves. It is also used for detecting fruits from other parts of the plant as fruit irradiate and absorb the radiation in a different way compared with other components.

6.2 Motivation

To build a nation's economy, agriculture plays a vital role. Agriculture is dreadfully crucial as it gives food, clothes, and shelter to human lives, and it is also a key element for social stability and economic development of the nation. To fulfill the needs of the growing population, agricultural production must be double by the year 2050. Therefore, it is essential to timely access and monitor crop growth and forecast the crop yield.

Timely and accurate techniques are the demand of the current era for crop growth monitoring, crop disease detection and recognition, stress identification, and yield production. Remote sensing is a promising way to fulfill these needs, but it suffers from a few limitations as it is weather and sunlight dependent. Therefore, the most promising method for agriculture is synthetic aperture radar (SAR).

SAR data has several potentials in the field of agricultural remote sensing. Remote sensors, spaceborne radar observations, and observation of the Earth from space provide vital information about vegetation or precision agriculture. Hence, the extraction of this crucial information from SAR data could lead to an improvement in crop management, yield production, and ultimately reduction in economic losses of the country. Therefore, every research in agriculture requires extract and estimate biophysical parameters to generate timely and accurate results. Thus, the study focuses on biophysical parameters estimation techniques.

6.3 Literature Survey

This chapter reviews the result and existing theory of the earlier studies according to the need of the research area. The extraction of biophysical parameters from crop images, crop disease identification and prediction, crop classification, and crop growth predictions are introduced to give background knowledge about the research topic. According to the available results, precision agriculture research problems are carried out using the image processing approach, remote-sensing approach, and radar imagery approach. This chapter highlights the gaps between the state-of-the-art material.

Yushan Zhao et al. proposed a model for automatically recognizing crop diseases by the multi-context fusion network method deployed in the agricultural Internet of Things in 2020. The model considers 50,000 images from in-field observations and extracts visual features using the standard CNN model. The contextual features are extracted from image acquisition sensors. For recognizing crop diseases, the proposed model combines the extracted contextual and visual elements. Experiments consider 19 different crops of three different categories with 77 common crop diseases. Results showed that MCFN achieves 97.5% of recognition accuracy using a deep fusion model (Yushan Zhao et al., 2020).

An efficient model for classifying and estimating the severity of leaf biotic stress for the coffee plant using deep learning techniques was proposed by Jose G.M. Esgario et al. in 2020. The proposed model consists of CNN architecture with multi-task capabilities for classifying the stress and estimating the severity of it. The standard and mixed type of data augmentation methods are incorporated into the model to improve the model's accuracy and efficiency. The authors collected their data set with different smartphones, which categorized as image data set (372 images), and symptom data set (2722 copies). The model focuses on four various biotic stresses as rust, leaf miner, Cercospora leaf spot, and brown leaf spot. Five different CNN architectures (AlexNet, GoogleNet, VGG16, MobileNetV2, and ResNet50) have experimented, and results showed that ResNet50 outperforms over others with a classification accuracy of 95.24%, and severity estimation accuracy of 86.51% (Esgario et al., 2020).

An ensemble-based technique for detecting the maize leaves diseases using two pre-trained CNNs was developed by Darwish et al. in 2020. The technique was using pre-trained VGG16 and VGG19 architecture. CNN is sensitive to a variety of hyperparameters; therefore, to select optimal values of hyperparameters, an orthogonal learning particle swarm optimization(OLPSO) method was used. To prevent the CNN model from falling into the local minimum, an exponentially decaying learning rate was used. To avoid the drawback of imbalanced data set random majority under-sampling, and random minority oversampling methods were used. The model experimented on a public data set with 12,332 maize leaf images with four disease categories as common rust, gray leaf spot, healthy, and northern leaf blight. The results were compared against two pre-trained CNN models, namely InceptionV3 and Xception. The proposed model outperforms with an accuracy = 98.2%, recall = 0.97, F1-score = 0.97, and precision = 0.98 (Darwish et al., 2020).

Yanfen Li et al. in 2020 proposed a convolutional neural network-based model for crop paste recognition. The proposed CNN-based model can recognize ten different pests on crops. The model was experimented on the manually collected data set by authors by capturing the images by smartphone and downloading the pictures from search engines, which consists of 5,629 images representing ten crop pest species. A GoogLeNet model uses Watershed, and the GrabCut algorithm to remove complicated background from collected images. The proposed model achieves improvement in accuracy by 6.22% as compared to the ResNet101 (previous) model. For performance improvement, the data augmentation method was implemented by performing rotation, translation, flipping, mirroring, noise addition, and zooming operations. After data augmentation, the size of the data set was changed from 5,629 to 14,475. The training and testing were applied with a 9:1 ratio. The computational complexity of five models, namely ResNet50, ResNet152,

VGG16, VGG19, and GoogLeNet, were tested. The model gives an average accuracy of 98.91% (Yanfen Li et al., 2020).

Kim et al. proposed an automatic model for detecting downy mildew of onion plants using a machine-vision technique. The model periodically captures the images of the onion field using a PTZ camera, located in the area of the "National Institute of Crop Sciences, Muan, South Jeolla Province." The technique trained the deep neural network model by providing collected images as input, and the performance of the model was evaluated using the mAP metric. The proposed model focused on the six disease classes and consists of components such as tilt, pan, PTZ camera, and motor system. The model has three main functionalities as identified by an infected portion of plant image, infected phenotype area, and yield loss due to infection caused by disease. The data set contains 584 images of size 4,000 $*$ 3,000 pixels. The performance of the developed disease detection system is in between 74.1 to 87.2 (Kim et al., 2020).

Maimaitijianga et al. have used the model for yield prediction of soybean crops using a deep learning approach from UAV by combining the data from several sensors. The method combined all four types of features: canopy structure information (canopy height, vegetation fraction), canopy spectral information (VIs, raw band data), canopy thermal information (temperature), and canopy texture information for predicting yield. The method is evaluated for numerous deep learning models such as input-level feature fusion-based DNN (DNN-F1), Support Vector Regressor (SVR), Partial Least Square Regression (PLSR), Random Forest Regressor (RFR), and intermediate-level feature fusion-based DNN (DNN-F2) and three soybean genotypes. The results have shown that the DNN-based model outperforms over other models in terms of RMSE and coefficients of determination (R2) (Maimaitijianga et al., 2020).

The technique for estimating nationwide yield using carbon accumulation and meteorological stress indices was developed by Chen et al. in 2020. The proposed semi-empirical model (crop-SI) comprises the multiple linear regression (MLR) algorithm and support vector regression (SVR) to estimate the yield of numerous crops such as barley, wheat, and canola using remotely sensed data. The Crop-SI combined crop-specific meteorological stress indices (temperature, cold stress, and precipitation, etc.) and carbon fixation during the dangerous crop-growth stage. Experiments have shown that the model reduces relative error for every considered crop (Chen et al., 2020).

Tong et al. developed a technique for classifying the Sahel region into the fallow and cropped field using Sentinel-2 data in 2020. The proposed method used the Random Forest algorithm and Google Earth Engine (GEE) to process the images taken from Sentinel-2 imagery. The techniques effectively classify the fallow fields and determine the extent of how many fallow fields are present within the cropland. The reference data needed for classification was created from seasonal metrics obtained from MODIS NDVI data, which indicates the maximum spectral difference between fallow and cropped fields. Due to the integration of Landsat and Sentinel-2 data, the proposed technique is highly accurate and can be applied to map fallow fields for multiple years of data. It also efficiently understands the dynamics of fallow-crop rotation cycles in a similar region like the Sahel (Tong et al., 2020).

The model for jointly estimating the wet biomass and Plant Area Index (PAI) from the SAR polarimetric data of C-band for soybean and wheat crop was proposed by Dipankar et al. in 2019. The technique used the Multi-Target Random Forest Regression (MTRFR) method to determine both critical parameters required to estimate the growth of the crop. The model considered data from the RADARSAT-2 satellite for analysis and validation captured during the SMAPVEX16 campaign. The system has presented a novel joint approach for biophysical parameter retrieval, which determines low estimation errors and a high correlation for three combined polarizations (HV+VV+HH). The proposed technique gives the correlation coefficient as 0.6 to 0.8 (Dipankar Mandal et al., 2019).

Dipankar Mandal et al., in 2019, developed a technique for estimating a critical biophysical parameter leaf area index from corn plants using SAR data of the C-band. This key parameter can effectively be used for the classification of several crops, determining productivity, and for monitoring crop stress. For validation and performance evaluation, the data is collected from two different satellites, namely Sentinel-1 and RADARSAT-2. The techniques evaluate several algorithms such as Look-up Table (LUT), Iterative Optimization (IO), Random Forest Regression (RFR), and Support Vector Regression (SVR). As a result of the performance evaluation, this technique gives the best method, i.e., Support Vector Regression to retrieve LAI form corn plants with the root mean square error 0.677 m2 m−2 and correlation coefficient of 0.92 (Mandal et al., 2019).

Bruno et al. developed a deep learning–based technique for counting corn plants using Unmanned Aerial Vehicle (UAV) images in 2019. Plant density is the crucial element for estimating the yield of the crop. The proposed method captures the UAV images of large fields, followed by image labeling. In the segmentation process, the corn plant images are differentiated from ground images using a U-net deep learning algorithm. Different colors are used to represent corn plants and ground. A blob detector algorithm is used to detect and count the plants from ground images. The authors have evaluated the performance of the model for three different approaches of plant densities and growth stages. As a result, it is shown that the best results are achieved for the early growth stage (V4, i.e. four leaves), plant density 70,000 plants/hectare, and 20-meter flight height (Kitano et al., 2019).

Roberto et al. gave an automatic technique for estimating crop yield and mapping crops using Landsat data. The proposed method effectively monitors and classifies the available crops based on phenological data extracted from Landsat imagery collectively with agroecological zoning (AEZ) and crop calendar. The model retrieved the phenological stages of cultivation and used it as input to the classification algorithm. The Multivariate Decision Tree (MDT) classification algorithm uses prior knowledge about the crop calendar for the classification process. The model was evaluated on maize and wheat crops. The proposed technique gives a high classification accuracy of 91.35% as it follows a combined approach using AEZs and phenological data (Luciani et al., 2019).

Yonghao Xu et al. participated in the data fusion contest organized by IEEE GRSS. They developed a novel algorithm Fusion-FCN (Fully Convolutional Network) for land cover and land use classification. The authors are provided with three data sets, namely hyperspectral imagery, multispectral LiDAR imagery, and VHR color imagery. The model used computer vision and machine learning algorithms to classify the extracted objects into 20 individual classes. The model improves the classification results using post-classification processing, which determines the relationship between different objects and categorizes the objects. The proposed method outperforms for almost all classes with OA for LiDAR-FCN-post = 81.07%, Kappa coefficient for LiDAR-FCN-post, and Fusion-FCN-post = 0.80 (Yonghao Xu et al., 2019).

An automated method for identifying and classifying paddy crop stresses as biotic and abiotic was developed by Anami et al. in 2019 using computer vision algorithms. The method focuses on five varieties of rice crops comprising nine abiotic and two biotic stresses. The field images are captured for identifying crop stress during the booting growth stage. The color descriptors are used to analyze responses of stress in terms of color variations. This method is evaluated on three classifiers, namely SVM, Back

Propagation Neural Network (BPNN), and K-Nearest Neighbor (KNN). To improve the overall classification accuracy, the Sequential Forward Floating Selection method is used in the feature selection phase. The BPNN algorithm outperforms SVM and KNN with a classification accuracy of 89.12% (Anami et al., 2019).

A system for classification of multiple plant diseases using convolutional neural networks was developed by Artzai Picon et al. in 2019. The data set was created by acquiring images from the real field using a smartphone camera, consisting of 121,955 images representing five different crops (corn, rape-seed, barley, rice, and wheat) comprised of 17 diseases. The model possesses two different approaches two solve the classification problem. The first approach is to use a separate model for every single crop and achieve a balanced accuracy of 0.92. The second approach is to classify diseases by considering a single model for multiple crops and achieve a balanced accuracy of 0.93. By incorporating the visual features for the classification, balanced accuracy can be increased up to 0.98 and improves the misclassification rate by removing 71% classification errors as compared to the previous model. The proposed model not only considers leaves but also consider stem and pinnacle for disease classification. The model used 8:1:1 criterion for training, testing, and validation resp. (Artzai Picon et al., 2019).

Peng Jiang et al. in 2019, implemented a real-time apple disease detection technique. The authors combined two deep neural network frameworks, InceptionV3 and VGG-16, with a developed proposed model called VGG-INCEP. The model was experimented on the manually collected data set, i.e., ALDD (Apple Leaf Disease Dataset) by authors by capturing the images from real-field, and laboratory by smartphone, which consists of 2,029 images representing five different diseases of apple plants. For performance improvement, the data set was annotated by experts, and augmented by operations such as rotation, vertical and horizontal flips, and disturbing intensity of the original image. After data augmentation, the size of the data set was 26,377 images. The proposed model was trained with two approaches: before data augmentation and after data augmentation. The model possesses the accuracy of 71.89% mAP and 78.80% mAP before and after data augmentation resp. The model can identify several diseases from a single image and is also able to detect a separate illness with different shapes and sizes. The model was evaluated against eight different DCNN frameworks, and the results showed that the performance of the developed disease detection system is 78.80% mAP and has a very high detection speed of 23.13FPS, which is much better than state-of-the-art models (Peng Jiang et al., 2019).

A hyperspectral imaging-based approach for identifying plants affected by cold damage using the convolutional neural model was developed by Wei Yang et al. in 2019. Due to severe injury, plants stop growing, and it resulted in yield loss. Therefore, the proposed model captures ten hyperspectral images of corn using a camera and extracts spectral features (abstract and invariant features) for identifying cold damage. The model focuses on five different varieties of corn. The preprocessing of images was done by the Savitzky-Golay smoothing method and Gaussian low-pass filter. For every type of corn, samples of 3,600 pixels were considered as regions of interest. For performance evaluation of the model, a CNN model with 10 layers was used. The model has identified the level of cold damage for each variety as B73:25.6%, W22: 41.8%, PH207: 20%, BxM: 35%, and Mo17: 14%. The experimental results were compared against chemical method results. The correlation coefficient between the chemical method and the CNN model was 0.8219 (Yang et al., 2019).

A novel method for selecting the features subset based on phenology information was proposed by Siddarth et al. in 2018. The estimated features were used for classifying several crops. As the phenological stage of crop changes, there is a change in the scattering behavior. The proposed technique incorporates this knowledge. The Random Forest algorithm is used to select a set of features from five different crops. Multitemporal data of the L-band was collected by the E-SAR satellite from the AgriSAR-2006 Campaign for experimentation and validation. The partial probability plot was used to determine the consequence of SAR polarimetric parameters on the considered crop. This consequence helps to decide parameters with a unique range for a specific date and individual plant. The proposed technique has better classification accuracy, i.e., 99.12% over traditional approaches (Hariharan et al., 2018).

Murugan et al. gave a combined approach using satellite and drone data for monitoring agricultural activities with adaptive thresholding in 2017. The technique monitors and classifies fields into a sparse and dense category. The ultimate aim of the proposed method is to reduce the repetitive use of drones for data acquisition without disturbing the accuracy of the method. The data obtained by Landsat-8 and drones are segmented, and cloud-affected data is corrected using masking. Drones collect the ground truths for model evaluation, and numerous bands required for classification are selected. To avoid repetitive use of drones to collect ground truths, adaptive thresholding is used. The model is evaluated by providing an image with different acquisition dates and locations to the model (Deepak et al., 2017).

Susan et al. presented a review of numerous techniques for precision agriculture using radar remote sensing in 2017. The purpose of this survey is to understand available techniques for precision agriculture and to successfully identify challenges and opportunities in the area of radar remote sensing. The study reveals the understanding of backscattering concerning agriculture and developments in PA applications. The considered methods focus on spaceborne SAR for data acquisition because of its more excellent spatial resolution and independency on cloud and weather. The study adequately describes the ways of data acquisition, such as airborne radar instruments and ground-based scatterometer, with their pros and cons. It also reveals the understanding of data collected in experimental campaigns such as Soil Moisture Active Passive Experiments (SMAP), which are needed for model training and evaluation. The review presents the most common ways of retrieving backscatter parameters from vegetation canopies (Steele-Dunne et al., 2017).

Mustafa et al. (2020) presented the method for the identification of plant diseases using an image processing technique in a support vector machine, naive Bayes. The plant disease detection is very critical in the agriculture. The outputs are interpreted in a number of ways that is difficult to analyze and requires lots of data for developing the system (Mustafa et al., 2020).

Nuttakarn and Masahiro developed drone and IoT-based architecture for detecting rice diseases in its early development stage and positioning the location of the diseased plant in the real field using GPS. The system acquires real-time information from data acquisition and analysis for the detection and classification process. The system captured the rice plant images using a drone and camera and extracted color and shape features, and then the ground control station transfer captured images to a server for disease analysis. Lastly, disease detection is followed by disease mapping in the real field by locating the diseased plant using GPS sensors. The server has a Support Vector Machine algorithm and the Gray-Level Co-occurrence Matrix (GLCM) for classification and detection. The model was evaluated on only four diseases of rice as sheath blight, leaf blast, bacterial blight, and brown spot from the IRRI database (Kitpo and Inoue, 2018).

Singh et al. gave the method for predicting late blight disease of potatoes using weather parameters such as maximum and minimum temperature, humidity, and rainfall. The proposed method used an extreme learning machine classifier for prediction and evaluated on AICRP data set, comprising five attributes. The technique identifies the occurrence and severity of the disease. The method experimented over several activation functions, and results showed that the random basis function gives high performance in terms of accuracy (Singh and Singh, 2018).

Thomas et al. (2018) have utilized hyperspectral sensors. The hyperspectral sensors are valuable tools for the plant disease detection, identification, quantification, on different scales from the tissue to the canopy level. The basic principle of the hyperspectral measurements and the different types of the available hyperspectral. The merits of the method are the entire spectrum is acquired at each point that the operator needs no prior knowledge of the samples and the post-processing allows all available information from the data set is to be mined and the demerits are low throughput and the small number of wavelengths considered (Thomas et al. 2018).

Federico Martinelli et al. gave a review of smartphone-based sensors used for agricultural applications. The authors also described several sensor-based tools or methods as BaiKhao, PocketLAI, Magri's, VillageTree, mKRISHI, SOCiT, etc. This also explains the use of sensors in farming applications like water and soil study, and crop water needs estimation, fertilizer calculator, disease diagnosis and detection, and so on. It also surveyed information systems and farm management applications. The study also identified challenges and research opportunities in the same area (Martinelli et al., 2015).

From the literature survey done above, the following are the general observations:

1. **Traditional methods are too specific:** It is identified that most of the available techniques required for precision agriculture are crop-specific, i.e., they have considered only either one or two crops. If the technique is for disease identification, then they have considered only one or two crop types with limited varieties. And if the technique is for crop mapping or classification, then it has a maximum of ten crops. Therefore, the generalized model is the need for the current scenario.
2. **Traditional data set collection methods are too restricted:** Most of the data sets are collected in a specific environment such as particular lighting conditions, angle, etc. Again, most of the data sets are created under a controlled environment. Therefore, we need to generalize a data set that should consider a variety of crops and diseases and create an outdoor environment.
3. **Most of the techniques are using image processing** to identify and classify diseases. Therefore, we can consider other data acquisition techniques, such as thermal imaging or SAR data.
4. **Earlier methods are either classifying the crops or recognizing the disease:** We can implement a general model for both tasks.
5. **Model Training:** In some systems, the model is trained using samples from specific sites, so the model should be trained using an equal proportion of samples from every considered site.
6. **Severity Estimation:** The disease detection techniques can be extended to determine the severity of the disease in a particular scale so that farmers should get insights about giving priority to treat that disease (Figure 6.3).

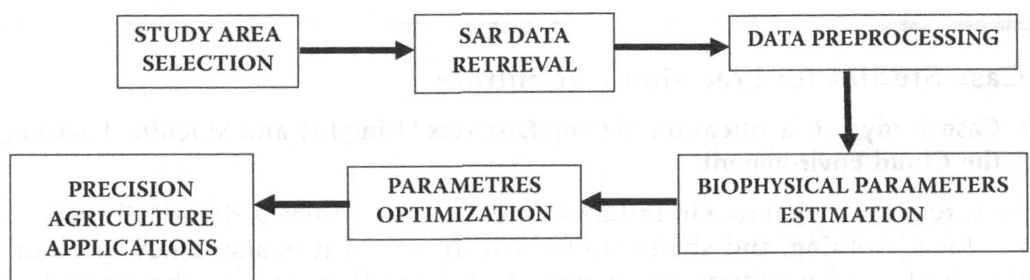

FIGURE 6.3
Proposed Architecture.

6.4 Proposed Systems

The proposed model consists of the following phases:

4.1. **Study Area Selection:** In this, we have to select the location of the study area, i.e., latitude and longitude of real-field. These latitudes and longitudes are used to collect data from satellites. We need a study area for data set collection and ground truths required for model validation.

4.2. **SAR Data Retrieval:** SAR is a technique for capturing extremely high-resolution radar images, typically of Earth's surface from a satellite, airplane, or using UAV. The radar beam is focused on a single patch of the Earth in spotlight mode, as the satellite moves from one point to another. The returned signals are captured using a backscattering mechanism to create a high-resolution image. Various satellites are available to capture the SAR images such as TerraSAR-X, Envisat, JERS-1, Radarsat-1, Radarsat-2, Sentinel-1, Sentinel-2, RISAT, TanDEM-X, ALOS, etc.

4.3. **Data Preprocessing:** The collected SAR images need some enhancement to remove errors or distortions generated during data acquisition. Preprocessing removes these distortions, noise, corrects phase errors, etc.

4.4. **Biophysical Parameters Estimation:** The interaction of solar radiation with vegetation or crops are represented by canopy properties or surface biophysical elements called biophysical parameters. These are the key input parameters for understanding crop dynamics. Therefore, surface parameter retrieval from SAR data is a crucial task to obtain vegetation properties. Several techniques are available in the literature to extract these parameters.

4.5. **Parameters Optimization:** After retrieval of several parameters, we have to select only optimal parameters to reduce the complexity of the proposed model. We have several optimization techniques, such as iterative optimization (IO).

4.6. **Precision Agriculture Applications:** Precision agriculture has a variety of applications. They are crop monitoring, crop classification, disease prediction, soil monitoring, yield prediction, fertilizer monitoring, etc. After parameter estimation, we can develop any application using extracted parameters such as data mining, deep learning, and machine learning techniques.

6.5 Case Studies for Precision Agriculture

6.5.1 Case Study 1: Classification of Crop Diseases Using IoT and Machine Learning in the Cloud Environment

Agriculture plays a vital role in India's economy. Agriculture is dreadfully crucial as it gives food, clothing, and shelter to human lives, and it is also a key element for social stability and economic development of the nation. Due to the limited agricultural land, adverse environmental factors, crop diseases, and lack of technological resources, the production of agricultural products are decreasing day by day. To fulfill the needs of the growing population, agricultural production must be double by the year 2050. Therefore, it is essential to timely access and monitor crop growth and forecast the crop yield. To overcome this situation, the Internet of Things along with machine learning and Cloud computing play essential role. In these kinds of systems, the sensor networks are created on agricultural sites using the Raspberry Pi model. The images of the crop site are taken from SAR, thermal cameras, or digital cameras and will be sent to the Cloud server. On the server side, the machine learning or deep learning techniques are used for disease identification and classification.

The Internet of Things is the collection of various sensors and electronics devices, used to detect and sense internal and external environmental parameters such as temperature, pH value, humidity, etc. They are also communicating with the Cloud environment and connected devices. The considered system is the real-time IoT-based application for crop disease classification using machine learning in the Cloud computing environment. The diagram below shows the system architecture (Figure 6.4).

The system collects the data from agricultural land using IoT sensors. The Raspberry Pi model is installed in the farm. These data are converted into a data set. After conversion, the data set is sent to the Cloud server using th Raspberry Pi model. The Raspberry Pi model is consists of the Raspbian operating system with Noobs. On the server side, the K-means machine learning algorithm is applied on the available data set. Cloud uses the Tomcat Apache WAMP for storing live data coming in the form of data set and images coming from agricultural land. Using machine learning techniques, the crop diseases are identified and classified. The system follows image processing approach for identification and classification with steps: image acquisition, image processing, image segmentation, feature extraction, and lastly classification of diseases.

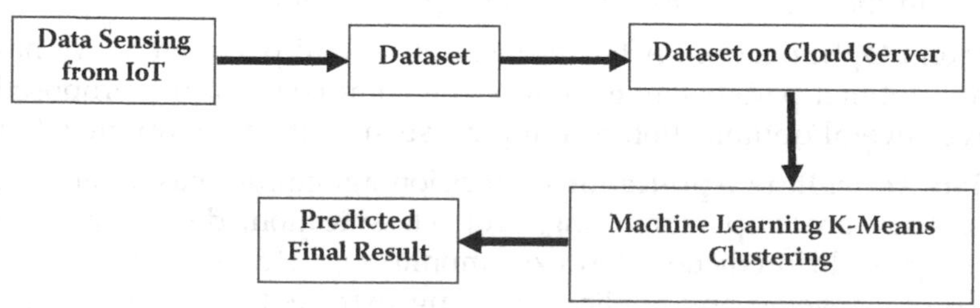

FIGURE 6.4
System Architecture for Case Study 1.

6.5.2 Case Study 2: IoT-Based Smart System to Support Agricultural Parameters

Nowadays, agricultural activities are facing water shortages due to climate change and population growth. Therefore, water retention is important. The IoT-based smart agriculture system is designed for proper allocation of water for farming activities in all conditions. The environmental parameters such as pH, temperature, turbidity, and soil moisture are collected by several IoT devices and sensors equipped in the agriculture. The system collects the data and is sent over the Cloud platform using ThingSpeak and a wireless system. The Cuckoo Search Algorithm on the server side uses data collected by ThingSpeak from sensor devices, allowing the selection of appropriate crops for particular soil. The system uses hardware sensors like soil moisture sensors and temperature sensors to capture the data. These values are converted into a data set. The sensed data sent over the Arduino goes to the Cloud. Then the generated data set is used for prediction. The figure below shows the block diagram of the system (Figure 6.5).

6.5.3 Case Study 3: Climate Monitoring

In these systems the sensors are located across the agricultural land. These sensors are responsible for collecting various parameters as temperature, humidity etc. from the environment and send these values to the Cloud server. The data understood by the server maps to several climate conditions, and proper decisions are made by various algorithms. These decisions improve the productivity in all aspects. (i.e., precision farming). Following are a few examples of such smart agriculture IoT devices: **allMETEO** (https://allmeteo.com/), **Pycno** (https://pycno.co/), and **Smart Elements** (https://incyt.io/).

6.5.4 Case Study 4: Crop Management

The most common case of precision agriculture is crop management. Similar to climate monitoring the sensors are planted in the crop land at several locations to capture environmental parameters. It collects the data related to crops such as precipitation to leaf water potential, temperature, and to identify overall crop growth and health. By monitoring the crop growth parameters system, we are able to identify anomalies for efficiently preventing diseases at an early stage that could harm the yield.

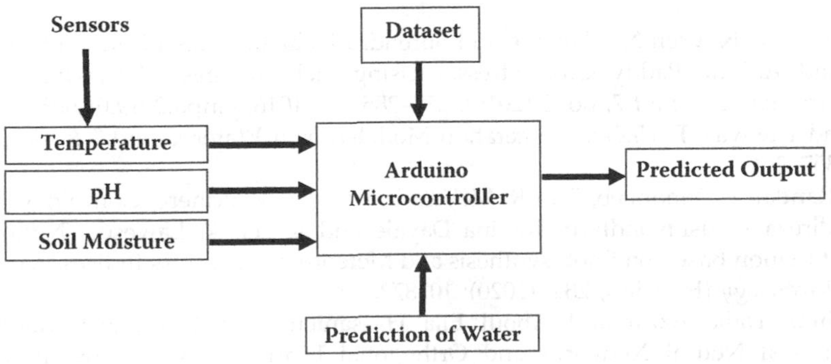

FIGURE 6.5
System Architecture for Case Study 2.

6.5.5 Case Study 5: Greenhouse Automation

Traditional systems used a manual method to control the greenhouse environment. But nowadays IoT sensors enable farmers to get accurate and timely information about greenhouse parameters such as temperature, soil condition, lighting, pH value, and humidity. Also, the located sensor devices are able to automatically adjust these parameters according to the requirements of crops. **Growlink** (https://growlink.com/) and **Farmapp** (https://farmappweb.com/) are IoT-based products available for smart agriculture. **GreenIQ** (https://easternpeak.com/works/iot/(GreenIQ)) is a smart irrigation system used to control the farm, lawn lighting, and irrigation remotely. It can save 50% of water required for actual irrigation.

6.6 Conclusion

This study efficiently understands remote sensing, SAR data, precision agriculture applications, and biophysical parameters. The report reveals a survey of sensing systems needed for accomplishing several tasks in precision agriculture. The techniques like image processing, machine learning, and deep learning are used in precision agriculture applications. Some techniques have used passive sensors, whereas others used active sensors for data acquisition. The report also presented different sensors and satellites for data collection. Retrieving biophysical parameters using the radar backscattering mechanism is a crucial element for modern precision agricultural practices. This paper presented the survey of numerous ways for BP estimation and identified how these parameters are used in PA applications. The study identified some gaps between the state-of-the-art methods. According to the literature survey done in Chapter 2, we can conclude that we need to generalize a data set and model, which should be applicable for most of the precision agriculture applications. The study also presented a few case studies of Cloud computing technologies for smart agriculture.

References

Anami, Basavaraj S., Naveen N. Malvade and Surendra Palaiah. "Classification of Yield Affecting Biotic and Abiotic Paddy Crop Stresses Using Field Images." *Information Processing in Agriculture, Science Direct* 7, no. 2 (2019): 272–285 , 10.1016/j.inpa.2019.08.005.

Attema, E. and Fawwaz T. Ulaby. "Vegetation Modeled as a Water Cloud." *Radio Science* 13 (2) (1978): 357–364.

Chen, Yang, Randall J. Donohueb, Tim R. McVicarb, François Waldnerc, Gonzalo Matad, Noboru Otad, Alireza Houshmandfard, Kavina Dayale and Roger A. Lawesd. "Nationwide Crop Yield Estimation Based on Photosynthesis and Meteorological Stress Indices." *Agricultural and Forest Meteorology* (Elsevier), 284, (2020): 107872.

Darwish, Ashraf, Dalia Ezzat and Aboul Ella Hassanien. "An Optimized Model Based on Convolutional Neural Networks and Orthogonal Learning Particle Swarm Optimization Algorithm for Plant Diseases Diagnosis." *Swarm and Evolutionary Computation* 52 (Elsevier 2020): 100616.

Esgario, Jose G. M., Renato A. Krohling and Jose A. Ventura. "Deep Learning for Classification and Severity Estimation of Coffee Leaf Biotic Stress." *Computers and Electronics in Agriculture* 169 (Elsevier January 2020): 105162.

Hariharan, Siddharth, Dipankar Mandal, Siddhesh Tirodkar, Vineet Kumar, Avik Bhattacharya and Juan Manuel Lopez-Sanchez. "A Novel Phenology Based Feature Subset Selection Technique Using Random Forest for Multitemporal PolSAR Crop Classification." *IEEE Journal of Selected Topics in Applied Earth Observations and Remote Sensing* 11, no. 11 (2018). doi: 10.1109/JSTARS.2018.2866407

https://allmeteo.com/

https://incyt.io/

https://pycno.co/

https://growlink.com/

https://farmappweb.com/

https:/./easternpeak.com/works/iot/(GreenIQ)

Jiang, Peng, Yuehan Chen, Bin Liu, Dongjian He and Chunquan Liang. "Real-Time Detection of Apple Leaf Diseases Using Deep Learning Approach Based on Improved Convolutional Neural Networks." *IEEE Access, Special Section on Advanced Optical Imaging for Extreme Environments* (May 6, 2019): 59069–59080. DOI: 10.1109/ACCESS.2019.2914929.

Kim, Wan-Soo, Dae-Hyun Lee and Yong-Joo Kim. "Machine Vision-based Automatic Disease Symptoms Detection on Onion Downy Mildew." *Computer and Electronics in Agriculture* 168 (Elsevier 2020): 105099.

Kitano, Bruno T., Caio C. T. Mendes, André R. Geus, Henrique C. Oliveira and Jefferson R. Souza. "Corn Plant Counting Using Deep Learning and UAV Images." *IEEE Geoscience and Remote Sensing Letters, Digital Object Identifier*, IEEE (2019):1–5 10.1109/LGRS.2019.2930549.

Kitpo, Nuttakarn and Masahiro Inoue. "Early Rice Disease Detection and Position Mapping System using Drone and IoT Architecture." *2018 12th South East Asian Technical University Consortium (SEATUC)*, 12–13 March 2018, Yogyakarta, Indonesia, IEEE 2018.

Li, Yanfen, Hanxiang Wang, L. Minh Dang, Abolghasem Sadeghi-Niaraki and Hyeonjoon Moon. "Crop Paste Recognition in Natural Scenes Using Convolution Neural Networks." *Computer and Electronics in Agriculture* 169 (Elsevier January 2020): 105174.

Luciani, Roberto, Giovanni Laneve and Munzer JahJah. "Agricultural Monitoring, an Automatic Procedure for Crop Mapping and Yield Estimation: The Great Rift Valley of Kenya Case." *IEEE Journal of Selected Topics in Applied Earth Observations and Remote Sensing* 12, no 7 (July 2019): 2196–2208. DOI: 2196 - 2208, DOI: 10.1109/JSTARS.2019.2921437

Maimaitijianga, Maitiniyazi, Vasit Sagana, Paheding Sidikea, Sean Hartlinga, Flavio Espositoc and Felix B. Fritschi. "Soybean Yield Prediction from UAV Using Multimodal Data Fusion and Deep Learning." *Remote Sensing of Environment*, 237-111599-2020.

Mandal, Dipankar, Vineet Kumar, Heather McNairn, Avik Bhattacharya and Y.S. Rao. "Joint Estimation of Plant Area Index (PAI) and Wet Biomass in Wheat and Soybean from C-band Polarimetric SAR data." *Int J Appl Earth Obs Geoinformation* 79 (2019): 24–34.

Martinelli, Federico, Riccardo Scalenghe, Salvatore Davino, Stefano Panno, Giuseppe Scuderi, Paolo Ruisi, Paolo Villa, Daniela Stroppiana, Mirco Boschetti, Luiz R. Goulart, et al. "Advanced Methods for Plant Disease Detection. A Review." *Agronomy for Sustaunable Development, Springer Verlag /EDP Sciences/INRA* 35(1) (2015): 1–25.

Murugan, Deepak, Akanksha Garg and Dharmendra Singh. "Development of an Adaptive Approach for Precision Agriculture Monitoring with Drone and Satellite Data." *IEEE Journal of Selected Topics in Applied Earth Observations and Remote Sensing* (2017): 1–7. 10.1109/JSTARS.2017.2746185.

Mustafa, M. S., Z. Husin, W. K. Tan, M. F. Mavi, R. S. M. Farookand Stefan Thomas, Matheus Thomas Kuska, David Bohnenkamp, Anna Brugger, Elias Alisaac, Mirwaes Wahabzada, Jan Behmann and Anne-Katrin Mahlein. "Development of Automated Hybrid Intelligent System for Herbs Plant Classification and Early Herbs Plant Disease Detection." *Neural Computing and Applications* 32.15 (2020): 11419–11441.

Picon, Artzai, Maximiliam Seitz, Aitor Alvarez-Gila, Patrick Mohnke, Amaia Ortiz-Barredo and Jone Echazarra. "Crop Conditional Convolutional Neural Networks for Massive Multi-crop Plant Disease Classification Over Cell Phone Acquired Images Taken on Real Field Conditions." *Computers and Electronics in Agriculture* 167 (2019): 105093.

Prevot, L., I. Champion and G. Guyot. "Estimating Surface Soil Moisture and Leaf Area Index of a Wheat Canopy Using a Dual-frequency (c and x Bands) Scatterometer." *Remote Sensing of Environment* 46, no. 3 (1993): 331–339.

Singh, B. K. and R. P. Singh. "Tejasvee Bisen, Shweta Kharayat, "Disease Manifestation Prediction from Weather Data Using Extreme Learning Machine." IEEE 2018.

Steele-Dunne, Susan C., Heather McNairn, Alejandro Monsivais-Huertero, Jasmeet Judge, Pang-Wei Liu, and Kostas Papathanassiou. "Radar Remote Sensing of Agricultural Canopies: A Review." *IEEE Journal of Selected Topics in Applied Earth Observations and Remote Sensing* 10 (2017): 2249–2273.

Thomas, Stefan, et al. "Benefits of Hyperspectral Imaging for Plant Disease Detection and Plant Protection: A Technical Perspective." *Journal of Plant Diseases and Protection* 125.1 (2018): 5–20.

Tong, Xiaoye, Martin Brandt, Pierre Hiernaux, Stefanie Herrmann, Laura Vang Rasmussen, Kjeld Rasmussen, Feng Tian, Torbern Tagesson, Wenmin Zhang and Rasmus Fensholt. "The Forgotten Land Use Class: Mapping of Fallow Fields Across the Sahel Using Sentinel-2." *Remote Sensing of Environment* 239 (2020): 111598.

Xu, Yonghao, Bo Du, Liangpei Zhang, Daniele Cerra, Miguel Pato, Emiliano Carmona, Saurabh Prasad, Naoto Yokoya, Ronny Hänsch, and Bertrand Le Saux. "Advanced Multi-Sensor Optical Remote Sensing for Urban Land Use and Land Cover Classification: Outcome of the 2018 IEEE GRSS Data Fusion Contest." *IEEE Journal of Selected Topics in Applied Earth Observations and Remote Sensing* 12, no. 6 (2019).

Yang, Wei, Ce Yang, Ziyuan Hao, Chuanqi Xie and Minzan Li. "Diagnosis of Plant Cold Damage Based on Hyperspectral Imaging and Convolutional Neural Network." *IEEE Access* 7 (2019), 10.1109/ACCESS.2019.2936892.

Zhao, Yushan, Chengjun Xie Liu, Wang Rujing, Wang Fangyuan, Bu Yingqiao and Zhang Shunxiang. "An Effective Automatic System Deployed in Agricultural Internet of Things Using Multi-Context Fusion Network Towards Crop Disease Recognition in the Wild." *Applied Soft Computing Journal* 89 (2020): 106128, 10.1016/j.asoc.2020.106128.

7

Importance of Cloud Computing Technique in Agriculture Field Using Different Methodologies

Arvind S. Kapse[1], Avinash S. Kapse[2], and Vilas M. Thakare[3]
[1]*Department of ISE, New Horizon College of Engineering, Bengaluru, India*
[2]*Anuradha Engineering College Chikhli, Maharashtra, India*
[3]*Department of CSE, Sant Gadge Baba Amravati University, Amravati, Maharashtra, India*

CONTENTS

7.1 Introduction

Cloud computing is the facility of having a computer system, complete with everything that one could want, like storage, networking, software and utilities, as a service through internet. Thus, the vision of distributed computing where the user is at his office with a computer and the data center with computing resources, like software, applications, and

DOI: 10.1201/9781003203926-7

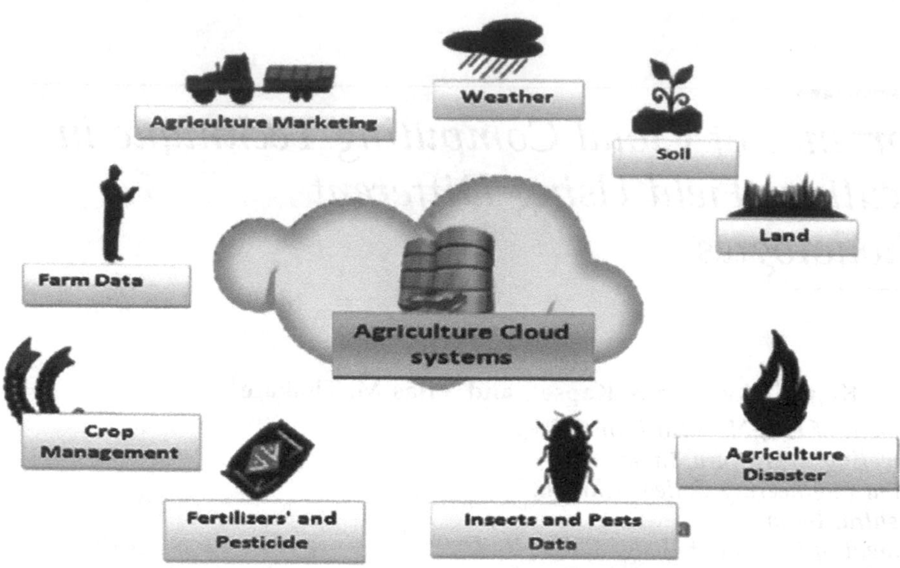

FIGURE 7.1
Agriculture Cloud System.

networking are located somewhere in the cloud available through the internet becomes a possibility. In the context of agriculture, cloud computing becomes a necessary technology to have because even though India is one of the biggest producers of foodgrains and related other products, still the activities of farming and its production methods are lacking in modern methods of cultivation with outdated and below-par equipment, dependence on rainfall for irrigation, and tied to manual labor to carry out its agricultural tasks.

The aim of cloud computing technology in agriculture is to close the gap between demand and supply chains for farming products. Thus, if the demand chain looked at analyzing the extant and potential customer requirements to meet his expectations, then supply chain looked at aligning the product to this demand. The widening gap between these two had an undesirable effect on the financial situation of the farmers as well as on the nationalized revenue of the nation.

This gap can be removed by implementing Cloud Computing technology in agriculture. A central location will collect data. Data can contain multiple independent records or files in the databases. Land, climate, soil, crop management, fertilisers and pesticides, insects and pests data, agriculture disaster and contingency planning, and farmer data can be kept in one place and can be made available for use of anyone with access rights. Any user, like agriculturalists, specialists, advisers, scholars, scientists, etc. can easily access this data anytime and from anywhere via a device connected to the cloud. Figure 7.1 shows the process of Agriculture Cloud Computing System.

7.2 Methods and Values of Agriculture Entry to the Field of Cloud Computing

7.2.1 Agriculture and Cloud Computing

So far, the adoption of IT in agriculture has become the exception rather than the norm where farmers were more or less forced to take it up to conform to government regulations and the allocation sector. For example, for filing tax returns and maintaining tracking registers. It cannot be said with certainty that IT was beneficial in creating opportunities for real farming invention. By concentrating on the succeeding two opinions, we examined the computer systems that should be advantageous for creation of farming invention (Hori et al., 2010).

- Improved productivity of farming by means of an attitude for manufacturing
- Agronomic skill succession

Consequent to research associated towards tackling this problem on the farm site, we foremost proved the requirement by providing an example where the agricultural working method themselves were changed. Through the adoption of a manufacturing process, the example showed how the improvement plan-do-check-act (PDCA) cycle was implemented as well as how it contributed to increased knowledge distribution and transmission.

- Better PDCA sequence (interpretation of workflows for example delivering guidelines and recording)

We have the information that the planning, structuring and execution of farm tasks are memorized rather than recorded as tangible data by farmers who inherit the knowledge base and awareness of their forefathers contributing to a huge pool of non-collated and non-organized knowledge accumulated, assimilated and distributed by word of mouth and field demonstration over the years. Such knowledge accrues through the method of guidelines. For example "If A happens, do B." It's a mixture of experience direction that has fought aimed at durations among invention development and IT in the subordinate industry, where sufficient effort is deemed beneficial and effectiveness is being developed. In terms of knowledge management, since it is ideal to turn implicit experience into explicit experience, there is a trend to focus on how to produce tastier vegetables. However, though such type of farming skill is obviously essential, it has proved extremely hard to apply computers towards such intuitive guidelines. So we started by focusing on themes that are seriously related to operations and supervision, and points associated to how data will be kept and used.

- Improve transmission and information spreading (during enterprise discussions, etc.)

We have presented this with the help of projector to demonstrate content on a laptop or computer system. It is possible to provide usual work reports and distribute data among skilled and unskilled agricultural employees, with detailed information on farmers, pests or emerging circumstances, and pass on professional advice.

7.2.2 Cloud Computing Mechanisms to Support Agricultural Operations

On the basis of results of fieldwork found after undergoing real agricultural work in the fields for additional one month in the total work (Figure 7.2), we argue that agricultural work can be supported by software around the flow structure illustrated in Figure 7.3 (input →data storage → visualization → instruction → analysis).

We used a web application and a smartphone application to prototype the four operations planned below, and we conducted a authentication experiment with a co-operative agricultural company in two places in Japan (an outside vegetable farm in Miyazaki Prefecture, and rice fields/dryland farms in Shiga Prefecture) to verify their technical and commercial effectiveness.

1. **Selling/planting (manufacture) preparation**
   Selling to clients and planning for planting (manufacture) agricultural soil can be done together.
2. **Working preparation/outcomes management**
   Management of growth and functions inspections will be carried out based on pre-arranged work on site and usual collection of outcomes.
3. **Patrol assistance**
   Descriptions and commands will be issued simply and consistently by distributing photos and comments on the site among all administrators and employees.

FIGURE 7.2
Farmer's Working Experience.

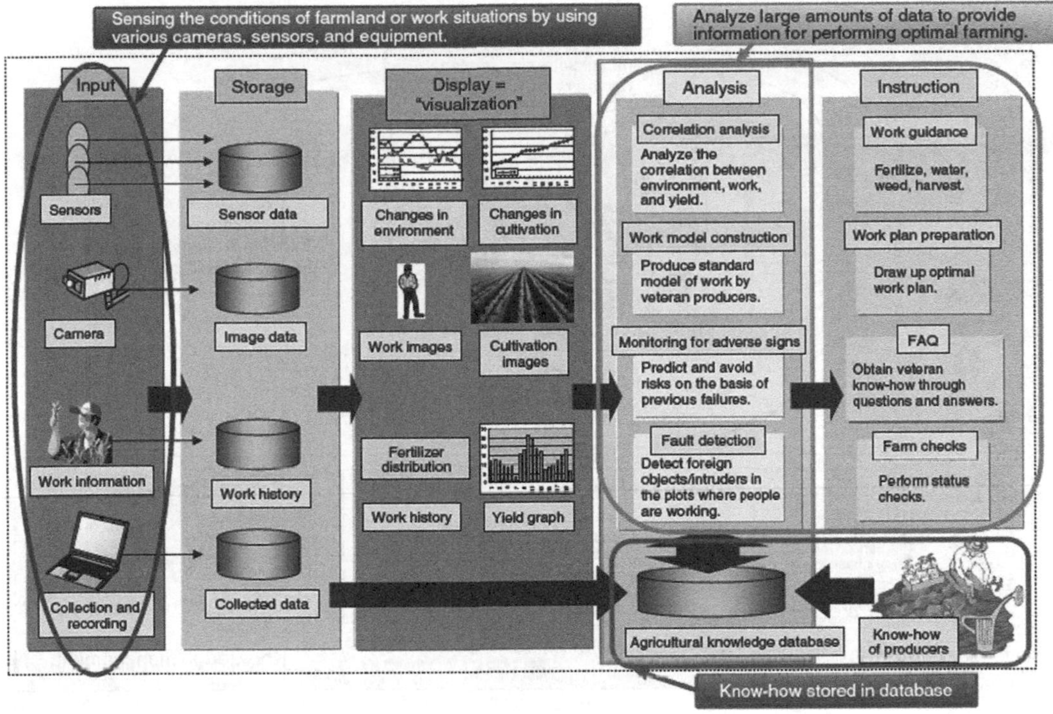

FIGURE 7.3
Cloud Computing Mechanisms to Support Agricultural Operations.

4. **Management of sophisticated land property data**
   Administration of entire types of related information on sophisticated land property, involving place of the land, land property privileges, region, land features and possible land property incorporated.

The above four functionalities are favored through two database management systems, and they rely on tools such as sensor devices (weather, earth, global positioning system [(GPS)], network [wireless local network, third generation (3G)] and management knowledge.

7.3 Farmer's Attraction with the Cloud Computing Technology

Prior to the investigation process for the application of cloud computing to the agricultural field, we created five common values for the cloud computing technology as follows:

- Reduction of original expenses.
- Infinite distribution of the resources on request.

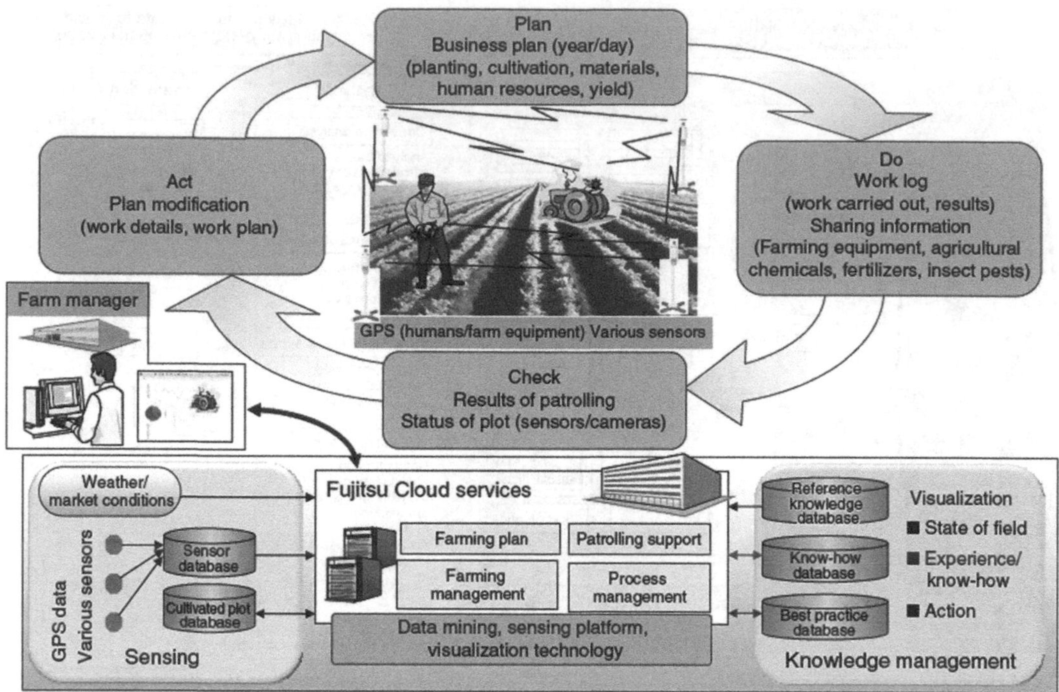

FIGURE 7.4
PDCA Cycle is Applied to Agricultural Work.

- Maintenance and updates are carried out in the backend.
- Fast and easy improvement, comprising association with other systems of the cloud computing.
- Greater chances for worldwide service expansion.

For example, for a special service oriented on such values, we have estimated the methodology displayed in Figure 7.4, where the PDCA cycle is useful on the farming field, which then plans to carry it out and get feedback from the following actions:

- **Plan:** draw up a production and operational plan.
- **What to Do:** Gather the results of the work (it includes executing the real effort on place, even if IT service cannot be offered for this).
- **Control:** Carry out improvement supervision and keeping a watch on agricultural land.
- **Take Action:** Make the necessary changes to your strategies.

As per such working style, basic knowledge detection and supervision methodologies will most likely be pivotal which are useful as cloud services.

7.4 Proposed Cloud Computing Platform for the Farmers

We were also instrumental in creating proposals for the Fujitsu cloud computing platform. Even when assuming single farming service software, the mandatory operations contain fundamental authentication and billing operations which can be used in conjunction with various domains such as GPS data handling and mapping techniques (Yamashita, 2020).

Figure 7.5 shows the proposed layer structure of cloud computing platform. Further operations that have to be shared with other arenas are many to indicate but contain image/sound processing and data mining. These operations can be useful not only in the farming field but also in other activities where on-site work is required, e.g. medical/nursing and maintenance work.

Currently, in our verification tests, we are applying a technique with a vertically integrated structure, but from the very commencement of our model improvement we have concentrated on the fact that it is achievable to progress parallel within the platform as-a-service level (PaaS) and below.

In the upcoming discussion, together with having a special discussion about building the optimal platform internally, we similarly propose to certify better exposure of Fujitsu's basic technologies that remain hidden today.

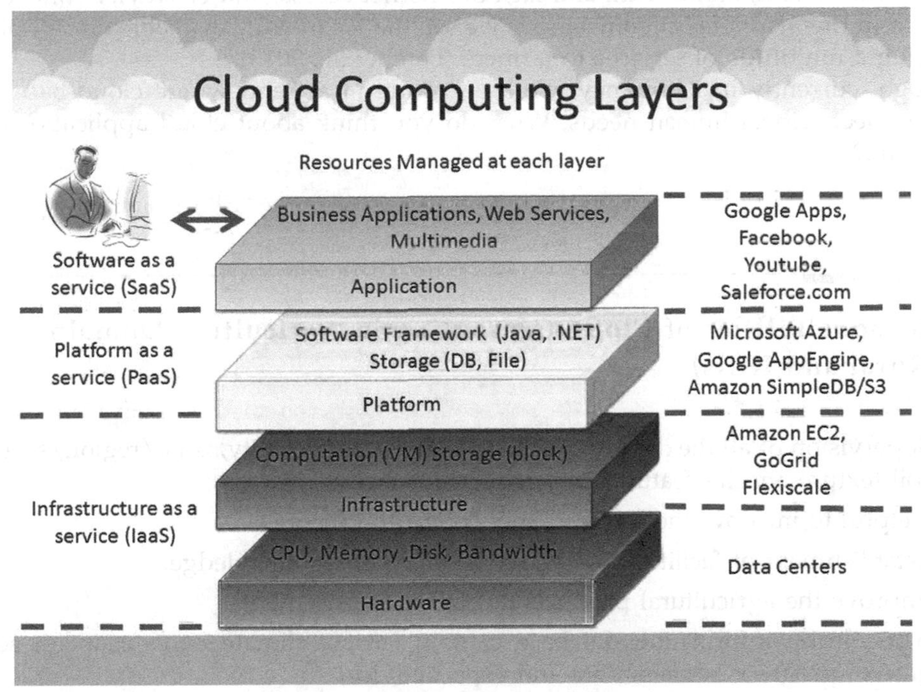

FIGURE 7.5
Proposed Layer Structure of Cloud Computing Platform.

7.5 Cloud Computing is Helping the Agricultural Sector to Grow

We are witnessing a continuing trend of loss of cropland and biodiversity around the world. If we consider that there are real-time usages with the help of cloud computing technology to produce entire ecosystems, then using respective sensors and supervising software to gather information from the field as photos of farmer's terrains and annotations of human actors in the field feed data repositories with their GPS coordinates with precision. For example, sensors can now detect the location of hay bales in the field, as well as the amount of moisture they contain.

Farmers can be made capable to apply cloud computing technique to access the data from prognostic analytics institutions, which allows them to get accurate predictions of products demanded by various markets and modify production accordingly (Kamath et al., 2011).

Farmers are also encouraged to use a knowledge-based repository that contains a wealth of information on agricultural practices, crop inputs, agricultural novelties, insecticides, seeds, composts, nutrition and weed resistance, and tools. All of this is accompanied by expert advice from various sources, for example on agriculture and agricultural product processing.

Although these facilities can be used in advanced nations with ubiquitous internet browsing, this is not easily achieved in developing countries where there are problems with internet access, bandwidth, and lack of internet access, and electricity connections. But even in these adverse circumstances, we see the technology available on cell phones providing a multitude of services to farmers (Patel et al., 2013).

Though, currently in its infancy, we are looking at a trend where cloud-based ecosystems meet critical human needs. What do you think about cloud applications with agriculture?

7.6 Responsibilities of Cloud Computing in Agriculture Domain (Rural and Hills)

- Supervision of all the data related to property land, locality, zone/region/sector, soil texture and it's features through a centralized software.
- Helpful to improve the farmers' knowledge and incomes.
- Establishment of facilities and agricultural expertise knowledge.
- Improve the agricultural products through advertisement.
- Agricultural information database contain (crops, climate circumstances, soil, growth progress, farmers data and expert advice).
- Resourceful usage of agricultural assets.
- Keep all the farming related knowledge in a centralized place called cloud computing, where it will be very useful to extract the data by the farmers or users from anywhere, anytime.

7.7 Advantages of Cloud Computing Technology in Agriculture

- Guarantee in the food quality.
- Inspiration to agriculturalists and scholars.
- Reduction of technical issue.
- Rural-Urban movement.
- Obtainability of data at any time and at any location at very fast rate.
- Develop a market price of food, seeds, other product.
- Related data can be accessible by the farmers or users at any time, any location.
- To improve worldwide communication.
- Increase financial situation of the country.
- Helpful to enhance the GDP of the country.

7.8 Challenges of Cloud Computing Technology in Agriculture

- Farmers need to learn about cloud computing methodology.
- A smaller amount of actual control.
- Training in such technology is required for the farmers.
- Not useful in less than adequate speedy internet.
- Management and supervision of this cloud computing is done by some third party agent, so, there is no guarantee that our data is safe and secure.
- Internet connection is mandatory.
- Needs a stable Internet connectivity.

7.9 Applications of Cloud Computing Technology in the Field of Agriculture

In a simple word, cloud computing is useful in actual computing, data retrieving and storing the farmer's data at remote location also.

Some of its specific uses are as follows:

- **Crop-related information**
  It can capture information about all crops grown in the past and, thus, can help farmers create choices about what to plant next. Climate news: the cloud is capable of storing the region-wise climate news as well as weather forecasts for an exact length of time.

- **Land and mud related Information**
  Plant-related decision-making also relies heavily on land- and mud-related knowledge. Besides, the land and mud texture, it also gives insight into past soil quality trends, which will help predict future trends. As an example, a query may be formulated as: has the land mud become acidic/alkaline, or what composition and variations in land mud texture will be detected?
- **Monitor development of the plants**
  The development of the plants will be observed in various areas; and periodically. It will be very easy to compare the past and current development of the plants.
- **Farmer data**
  Zone-wise farmer's data can be collected, tracked and analyzed with contribution of native farmers. It will be helpful to detect basic agricultural zones, to take decisions for developing their strategy.
- **Expert consultation**
  Here, we are going to provide the keys for general problems that farmers regularly face. This apart, the experts also provide solutions for a specific problem, in a very short time span.
- **E-commerce**
  Farmers in the rural area cannot directly sell their products to the market. Many agents emerge between the retailers and the production; the agents cause loss for farmers because they devour the margins that could have accrued to farmers from selling products at market price. Thanks to cloud computing technology, farmers can now sell their products directly to end retailers/ users.
- **Sharing practical information**
  Agriculture scientists or agriculture experts can share their own views and share the advice related to current planting methods, fertilizer use in the cloud, among other information.

7.10 Conclusion

Farms are conventionally supported by people and societies where the transmission and distribution of knowledge is considered as very essential. Collecting and distributing the awareness takes improved competency and inclusive throughput. In the agriculture field, the awareness of cloud computing technology is very thin. If the influence from the outcomes of cloud computing can be expanded, we should be able to produce additional hike in agriculture output. So, cloud computing technology can assist such types of developments in agriculture. Cloud computing is useful in actual computing, data retrieving and storing the farmer's data from remote location also.

References

Hori, Mitsuyoshi, Eiji Kawashima and Tomihiro Yamazaki. "Application of Cloud Computing to Agriculture and Prospects in Other Fields." *Fujitsu Science and Technology Journal* 46, no. 4 (October 2010): 446–454.

Kamath, S. and A. A. Chetan. "Affordable, Interactive Crowd Sourcing Platform for Sustainable Agriculture: Enabling Public Private Partnerships." *Cloud Computing Journal* 9, no. 2 (2011): 46–54.

Patel, Rakesh and Mili Patel. "Application of Cloud Computing in Agricultural Development of Rural India." *International Journal of Computer Science and Information Technologies* 4, no. 6 (2013): 922–926.

Yamashita, K. *The Pitfalls of Agricultural Cooperatives*, First edition, Takarajimasha, Japan (2020): 23–29.

8

Optimal Clustering Scheme for Cloud Operations Management Over Mobile Ad Hoc Network of Crop Systems

Poonam A. Gaikwad, Swati S. Sherekar, and Vilas M. Thakare
Sant Gadge Baba Amravati University,
Amravati, India

CONTENTS

8.1 Introduction

In the gadget-to-gadget communications in Cloud, a MANETs framework of the IoTs is a new method to discover and connect smart gadgets without centralized infrastructures (Abu-Sharkh, 2017). In this investigation, the projected explore exertion is the improvement and execution of flow versatile impotent organization correspondence utilizing the Cloud inside the web of things climate (Airehrour and Gutierrez, 2015). These gadgets will converse with each other (Allam, 2018a, b). A truth of articles that are associated is that they can convey between the gadget to the gadget (Allam, 2018a, b). Such a development would not depend on the number of inhabitants of mankind, or on the way that we routinely utilize brilliant gadgets (Allam, 2019).

In this Cloud computing based environment, the focus is on sharing computation Cloud computing network access to the pool of configurable, server storage, applications. Cloud computing is the network-based environment over the Internet that meets the elastic demand of the customer with minimum efforts or interaction with the service

DOI: 10.1201/9781003203926-8

provider. This examination gives a methodology that can build up another system for the safe correspondence of brilliant gadgets on the web. This exploration was utilized and is an effective reproduction of the focus to investigate and can be applied inside the IoT system. The present remote organization is made out of cells in a particular region inside its reach. Each cell incorporates a base location, which can be connected via cable or remote organizations. These days, brilliant gadgets give valuable, direct Wi-Fi usefulness (Allam, 2020). The First is an SaaS platform, as help is proposed basically for customers who utilize the product as a component of their regular day-to-day existence. Furthermore, platform as an assistance (PaaS) is fundamentally proposed for programming designers who need advancements to build up their product just as in execution. The chief point of IaaS (Infrastructures as a -Service) is to arrange engineers who need framework usefulness (Allam, 2017). To perceive the actual article, houses, individuals' pictures, area, and so on, the structure utilizes picture acknowledgment strategies. The web of things is currently moving from data innovation to operational innovation, for example IPV4 (man-to-machine) - IPV6 (machines-to-machine) (Allam, 2019).

This methodology of Cloud-based administrations in the ad-hoc models to the gadget-to-gadget correspondence can be an exceptionally helpful way to deal with upgrading the capacities of keen gadgets in the web of things climate. MANET is associated with the 5G heterogeneous organization and gadgets are likewise ready to utilize Cloud administration to find neighborhood gadgets and trade data. The Propos Approach incorporates MANETs and distributed computing on the web of shrewd gadgets that is valuable.

8.2 Background

At the point when at least two savvy gadgets wish to impart in the Cloud-MANETs models in the web good holdings, then correspondence protection is the primary test.

All through the Cloud: MANETs models the brilliant gadgets that are powerfully joined and made organizational alone. Additionally, they can get to the Cloud administration. In any case, there are so many difficulties for protection, correspondence is a self-made organization that entrance Cloud administrations. Clouds: MANETs is a sort of remote organization that is self-organizing and auto associated in a de-centralized framework also. Every gadget in MANETs can be moved uninhibitedly, starting with one area then onto the next in any direction inside the scope of Wi-Fi. A few MANET associate with similar Clouds and they can be utilizing Cloud administrations. MANETs models of keen gadgets in neighborhood correspondence can function admirably; utilizing the Cloud it can bomb associates in exist-organizations. Each brilliant gadget necessities look for neighborhood gadgets. A most significant inquiry emerges. Correspondence secured in the public: Clouds and MANETs? The appropriate response is indeed it's conceivable via the Cloud ad-hoc model and is executed and coordinated through portable applications.

Cloud: Ad-hoc portability scheme is a coordinated system of Cloud figuring and ad-hoc organizations.

Area I Introduction. Segment II talks about the Background. Area III examines past work. Segment IV talks about existing procedures. Segment V talks about and examinations the ascribes and boundaries of the strategy and how these are influenced. Segment VI gives the proposed strategy, Section VII is the results and discussion section and conclusion of the survey paper. At last, Section X gives future scope.

8.3 Previous Work Done

The savvy gadgets that partake a MANETS organization can be very unique in relation to each other. The network can be installed with sensors, portable applications, home apparatuses, or different kinds of gadgets, and should cooperate to increment and improve consumer loyalty. A portion of these apparatuses may have restricted assets to run, at times even non-existent asset requirements, they should attempt to enhance network traffic. The writers were zeroing in consideration on unconstrained organizations in this article. They were proposed a safe specially appointed unconstrained organization, in light of direct distributed communication in the IoTs. An obtained and confirmed unknown information accessed on Cloud: MANET network is introduced in the article. In an article, the zones-based MANET Routing Protocol with a calculation is introduced.

Airehrour and Gutierrez (2015) created different secured directing conventions for MANET that be utilized to set up secure steering conventions for the IoTs so the investigation of these safe MANET directing conventions is to give a guide to the turn of events and execution of safety in the IoTs and Cloud computing. On paper, the creators additionally give secure steering conventions in MANET while offering protected directing highlights IoT's directing to guarantee classification and honesty. They additionally talked about researched patterns and future headings in the area of IoT network security (Airehrour and Gutierrez, 2015).

The (IoTs) innovation across ship ad-hoc, networks (MANET) as a sea information securing and map-making framework the ships were prescribed to convey across VHF that is now accessible on maximum ship and are built with various sensors, for example, ocean level, heat, wind rapidity, and heading, etc. A 5G base station hub coastal worker sinks for the information gathered and are built with total information and preparing capacities for mobile edge environment. At last, the tactile information is amassed on the web in a focal archive to produce state-of-the-art advanced map making arrangements.

Tanweer Alam et al. (2017) have distributed literature where they presented a system that they can get to, convey Cloud administrations to the MANETS clients via their shrewd gadgets in the IoT. Likewise, the anticipated structure was completed wherever all calculations, information, and assets were given to the executives. MANETs can associate with the Clouds and can utilize Cloud administrations. The fundamental commitment in this examination interfaces another philosophy for giving secure correspondence on the web of brilliant gadgets utilizing MANET. In this exploration, the technique utilizes the right and proficient reproduction of the ideal examination and can be executed in a structure of the Internet of Things later on.

8.4 Existing Methodologies

Finding the brilliant gadgets in MANETs in the covered-up models is used in two dimensions. The structure is associated space, savvy gadgets can interchange intimate space and find another savvy gadget. The change grid is shaped in the space of MANETs, for finding every one of the brilliant gadgets. A few boundaries are utilized for finding savvy gadgets as follows.

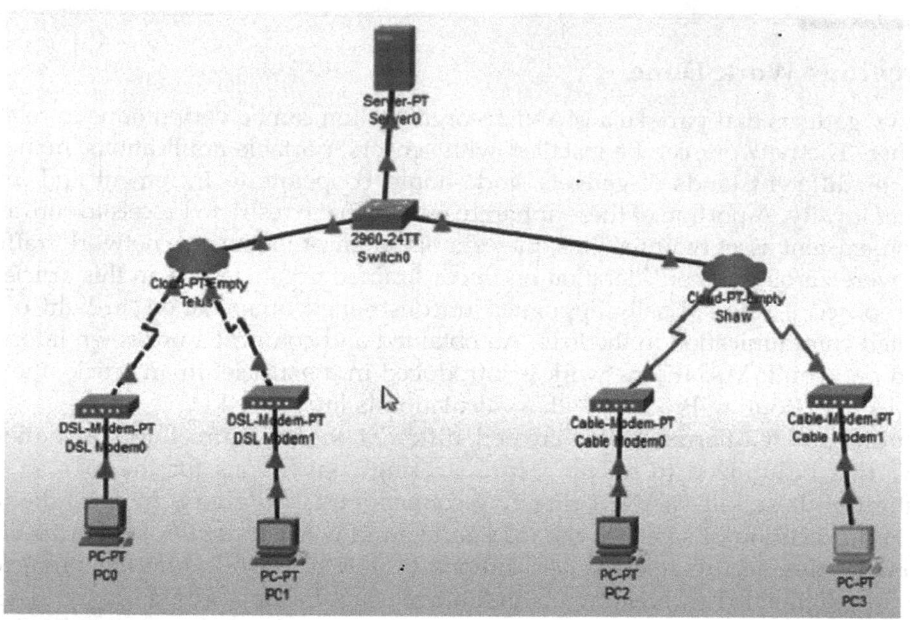

FIGURE 8.1
Packet Transfer with the Help of the Cloud.

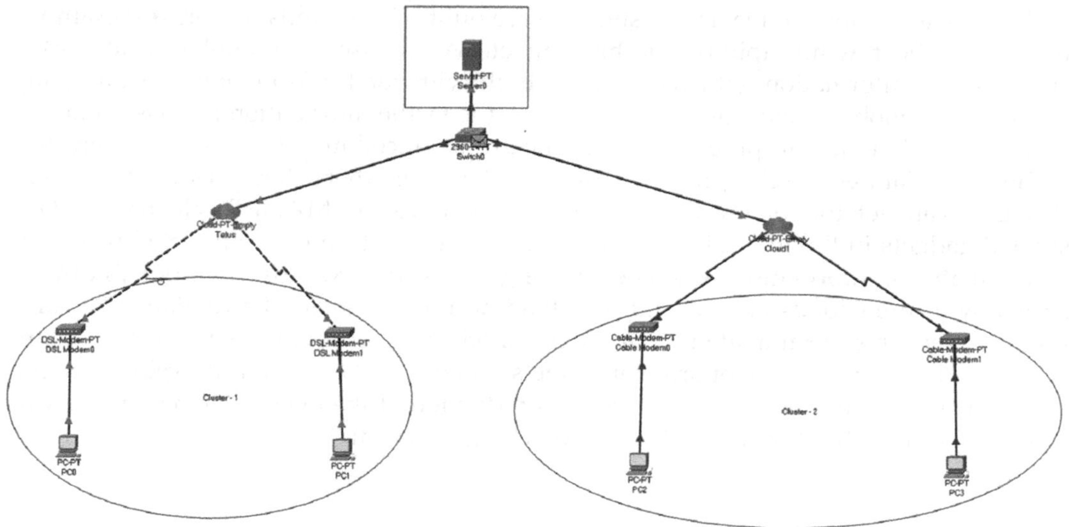

FIGURE 8.2
Design of the Proposed Cloud Framework.

Assume, S = S1:S2: _ _ SN. Where, S is the stage; S1
is The _rst stage; S2 is the subsequent stage; and So forth individually Cell
relies upon 1state, in S.
Progress network likelihood p = pij (one <= I <= n)

PDU List Window

Fire	Last Status	Source	Destination	Type	Color	Time(sec)	Periodic	Num	Edit	Delete
	Successful	Server0	PC1	ICMP		0.000	N	0	(edit)	(delete)
	Successful	Server0	10.10.10.4	ICMP		12.000	N	1	(edit)	(delete)
	Successful	PC2	Server0	ICMP		8.406	N	2	(edit)	(delete)
	Successful	Server0	PC2	ICMP		20.399	N	3	(edit)	(delete)
	Successful	Server0	PC1	ICMP		22.399	N	4	(edit)	(delete)
	Successful	PC3	PC1	ICMP		23.103	N	5	(edit)	(delete)

Time: 00:30:53.941 PLAY CONTROLS

FIGURE 8.3
Simulation Result.

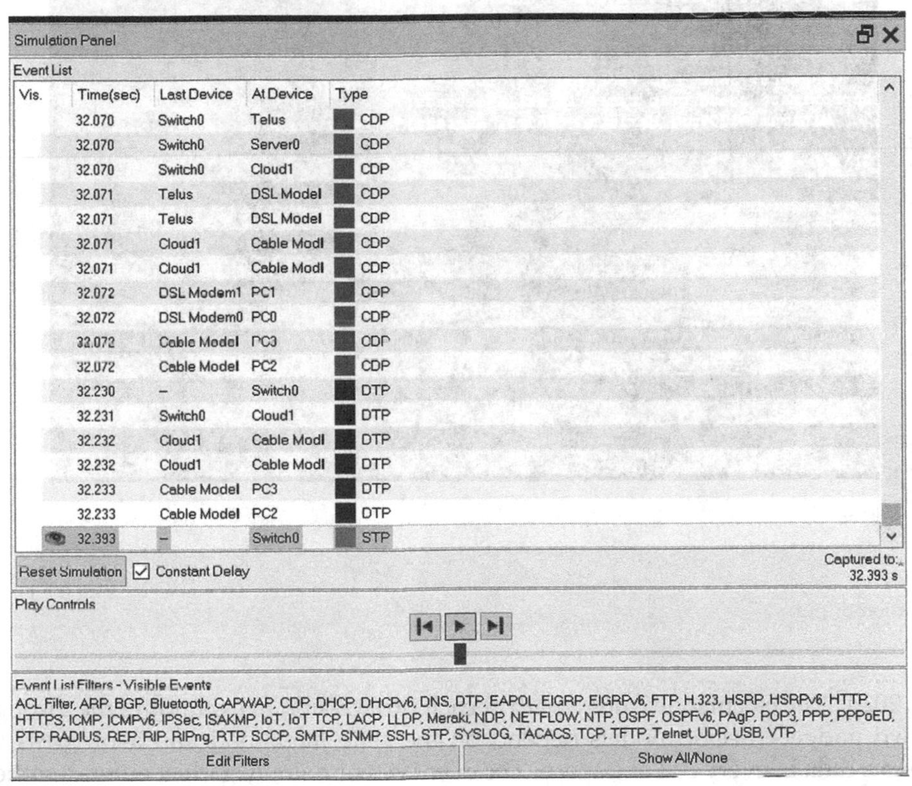

FIGURE 8.4
Simulation panel using the Cloud model.

where pij described to moved probability from si - sj

The likelihood Pij is simply significant is Si; Sj is the neighborhood state in the 2D plane. The state works to climb, down left and right in the 2D Level (14). The left part inside the structure is each of 0-s at first. The secret model is addressed in the accompanying progress grid.

The keen gadget in every cell is addressed by_ _ = _i(one<= i<= n).

Keen gadgets in MANETs: Can be utilized to find the signal utilizing the viterbi calculation in the 2D plane. Assume O1; O2;:::;On are The perception finding the gadgets in the 2-D Plane. Each shrewd gadget sends a reports of perceptions during a time frame

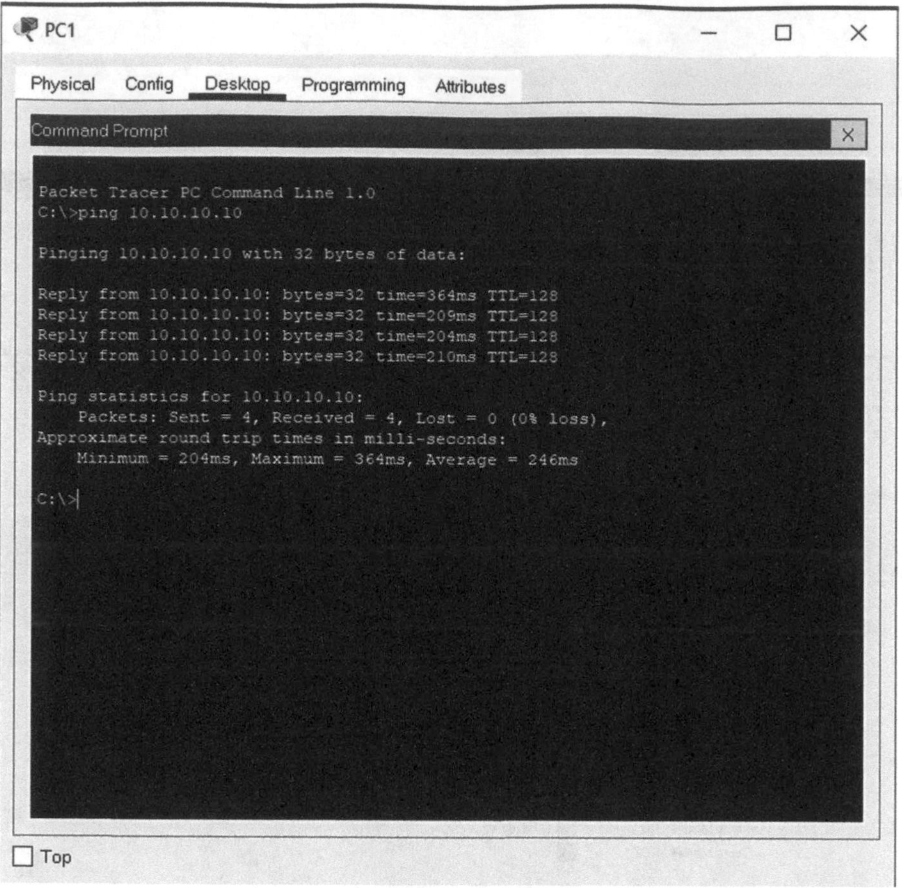

FIGURE 8.5
Configuration of pc1.

(Allam, 2020). The calculation finds a path at each progression in expanding the throughput of shrewd gadgets. Secret models depend on the state likelihood and a progress lattice addresses a data in every cell of a space. The event is that a savvy gadget enters another cell nd then it eliminates past information and updates the data. Finding the keen gadgets, the slope model works gadgets and divide the data between the brilliant gadgets. In the end, when a keen gadget perceives another brilliant gadget, the angle worth will set to one and additionally find another brilliant gadget in the space where MANETs are framed. An application in the actual laws and the distance between the two shrewd gadgets is corresponding to one upon the distance of the occasion. Gadget (distances/one/event-dista).

8.5 Proposed Methodology

In the up-and-coming age of processing, mobile specially pointed organization (MANET) will assume in the Internet of Things (IoT). The MANET is a sort of remote organization

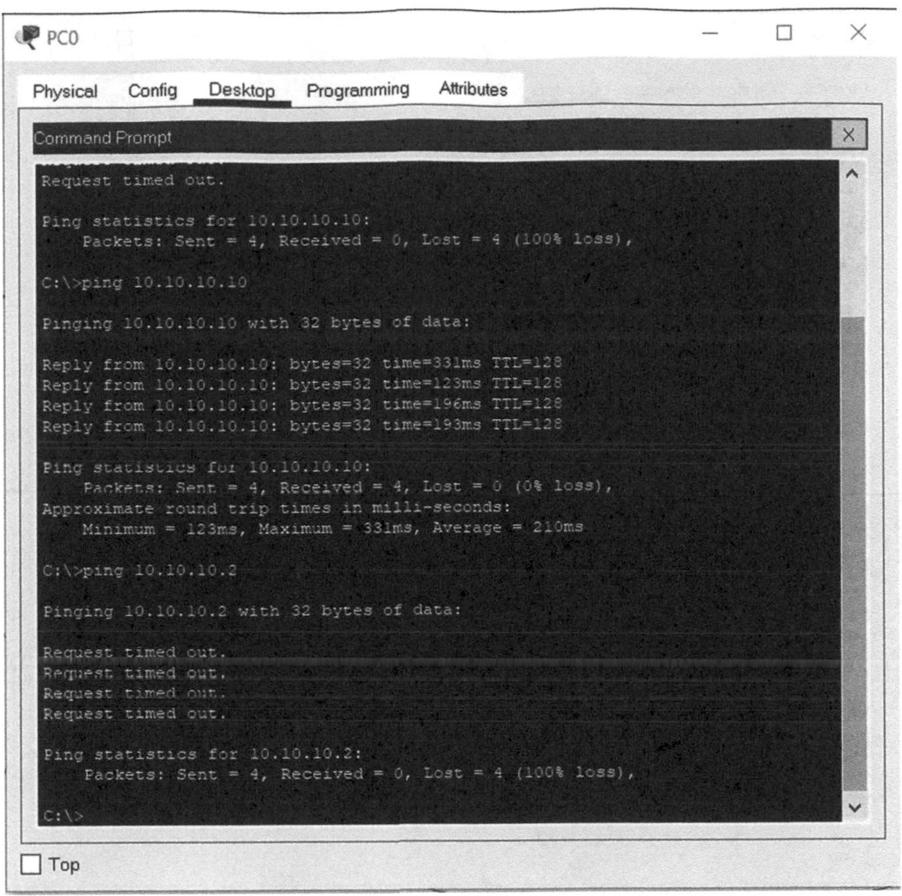

FIGURE 8.6
Configuration of pc0.

that is self-coordinating and auto associated in a de-centralized framework. Each gadget in MANETS moves uninhibitedly, starting with one area and then onto the next toward any path. They can make an organization with their neighbors' shrewd gadgets and forwarded information gadget. This structure can get to and convey Cloud administrations to the MANET clients through their savvy gadgets in the IoT system in calculations, information, and assets the executives perform. The shrewd gadgets can move starting with one area and then onto the next inside the scope of the MANETS organization. Different MANETs can associate with a similar Cloud; they can utilize Cloud administration continuously. For associating the shrewd gadget of MANET to Cloud there needs to be a mix of versatile applications. My principal commitment in this examination interfaces another system for giving secure correspondence on the web of shrewd gadgets utilizing MANETs concepts in 5G. The exploration system utilizes a right, productive reproduction of an ideal investigation and can be executed in the structure of the Internet of Things in 5G (Figure 8.1).

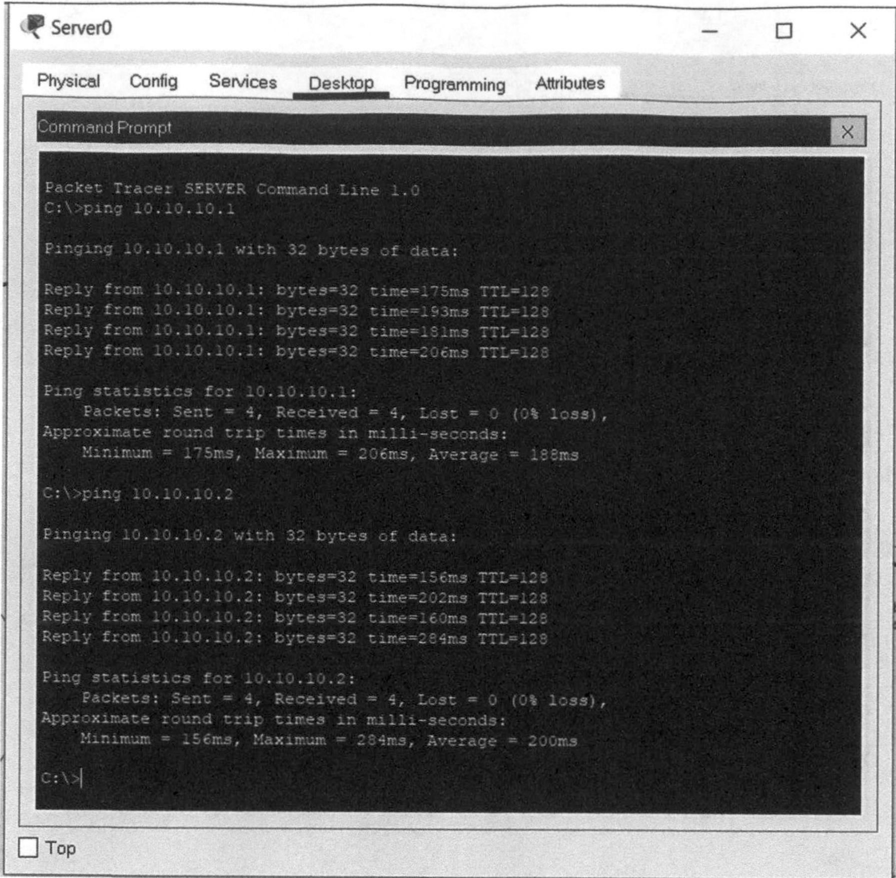

FIGURE 8.7
Configuration of server0.

8.6 Stimulation and Result

The proposed technique is assessed on the data set and the accuracy of this framework is subject to how effectively the model discovers the ubiquity data from the data set. Cloud service provider provide various application in field of art, business, data storage, backup service, education, social networking, agriculture etc. It tends to be imagined that the strategy endeavors to look through the prevalence of the information and for additional perception, the right proportion of the technique is estimated. Consequently, the proposed method is surveyed on the information data (for example Facebook data set) and afterward, the pre-handling unit utilizes the model channel alongside trading missing qualities administrator for setting up the total and significant data set and such significant data set is given to the following level to highlight extraction. The concentrate administrator removes information from the prepared data set and the yield of the

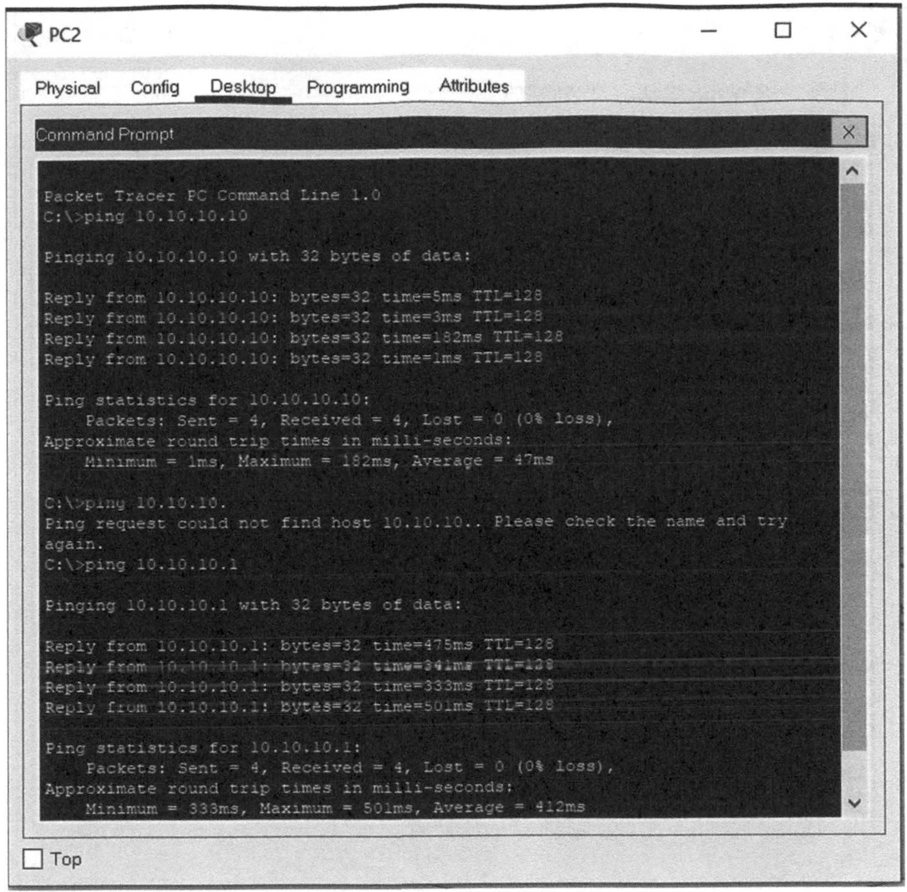

FIGURE 8.8
Configuration of pc2.

concentrate mode is a property vector or highlight vector and it passes to the determination unit. The yield of the concentrate mode is given to the element determination to the choice of highlights. The separated component is given to the SVM unit to group and the yield of the SVM arrangement method is given to the forecast model.

Figure 8.2 shows the design of the Cloud method and how it is constructed and executed.

Figure 8.3 shows the simulation result using the Cloud.

Figure 8.4 indicates the time of the last device, and the device packet is transferred using the Cloud and protocol.

Figure 8.5 shows the configuration of pc1.

Figure 8.6 shows the configuration of pc0.

Figure 8.7 shows the configuration of server0.

Figure 8.8 shows the configuration of pc2.

Figure 8.9 shows the configuration of pc3.

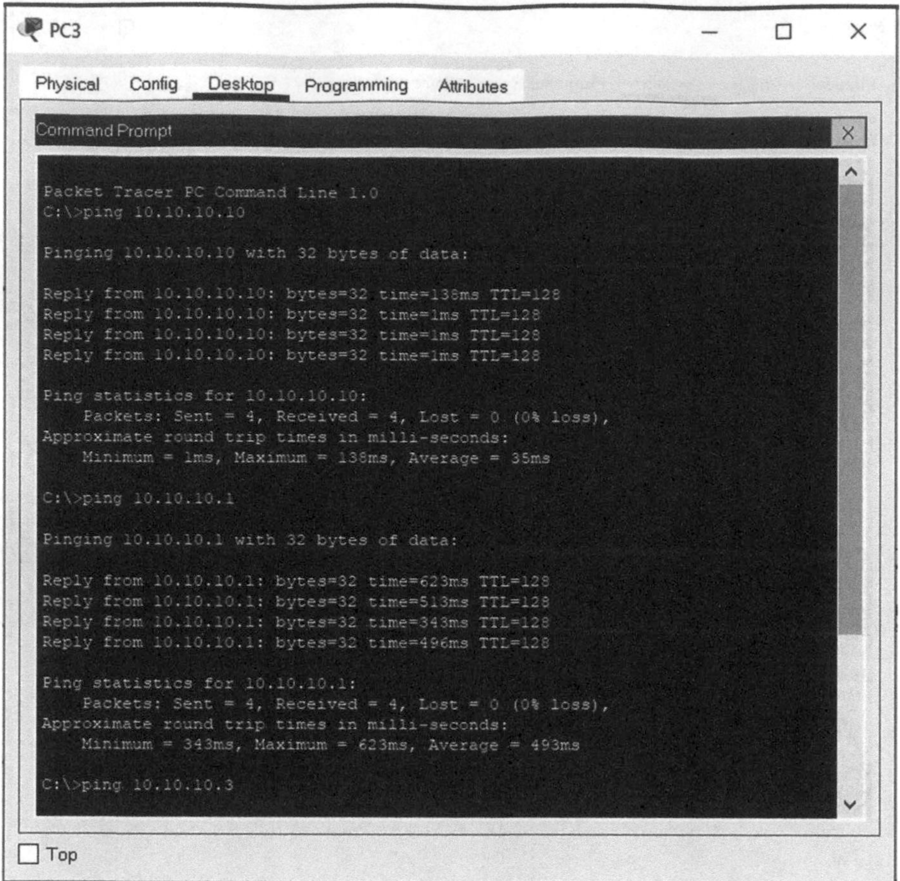

FIGURE 8.9
Configuration of pc3.

8.7 Result and Discussion

Cloud service in MANET modeling for gadget-to-gadget communication is useful and improves the capabilities of the smart gadget used in agricultural facilities and healthcare facilities. The Cloud environment offers various Cloud organization tools that assist in the supervision to control all kinds of Cloud events such as data integration and resource development. A gadget to-gadget network will improve the general exhibition, extend inclusion, and limit the energy utilization of versatile correspondences conveyed straightforwardly. Savvy gadget to keen gadget correspondence in the Cloud MANET structure of the web of things is a procedure that finds it is associated to close-by shrewd gadgets without a concentrated system, using protocol improve the performance.

Table 8.1 and Figure 8.10 show the execution time of previously proposed methods along with the new proposed framework, and the results show that the suggested framework takes minimum time for execution using Cloud and related protocol.

TABLE 8.1
Classification Using Execution Time Using the Cloud

Protocols	Nodes	Time (Sec)
ICMP	10.10.10.3	20.399
CDP	10.10.10.1	32.07
DTP	10.10.10.10	15.233
STP	10.10.10.2	27.393
ARP	10.10.10.4	34.109

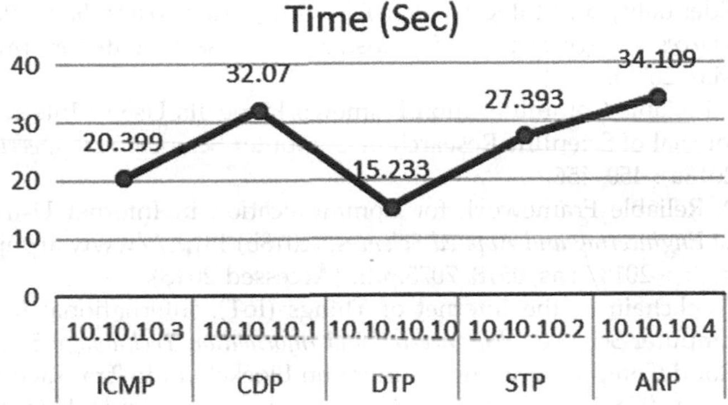

FIGURE 8.10
Analysis of execution time using the Cloud.

8.8 Conclusion

Optimal clustering schemes for Cloud management and operation over a mobile ad-hoc network is very useful for packet transfer from sender to receiver with the help of the Cloud. These management tools also provide administrative tools that provide control over platforms. Some important management applications are toggle and outright. It is useful in many faculties like agriculture and health care so that the data transfer rate is fast with minimum time. The Cloud-MANET versatility model can assume an essential part of 5G and improve effectiveness and speed of correspondence in the Clouds and MANETs. Cloud worldview depends on circulated engineering; it's acquired a few dangers and weaknesses that are identified with conveyed processing. Correspondence security dangers and difficulties depend on the back of the bait of the Cloud's calculation. Cloud MANET versatility model was created and tried. One gadget starts administration of MANET just as associated with the Cloud and begins to share association and trade data.

8.9 Future Scope

It is useful to improve the data transfer for the purposes of agricultural and medical facilities. As a further improvement, the model will be executed on nonstop evident data and the conjecture accuracy of the model. In the future it could be very useful for art, business, data storage and backup, education, management, social, entertainment, etc.

References

Abu-Sharkh, Osama M. "Adaptive Device-to-Device Communication Using Wi-Fi Direct in Smart Cities." *Wireless Networks* (2017). 10.1007/s11276-016-1278-z (Accessed October 2017).

Airehrour, David and Jairo Gutierrez. "An Analysis of Secure MANET Routing Features to Maintain Confidentiality and Integrity in IoT Routing." *Conference: International Conference on Information Resources Management*. (2015) https://www.researchgate.net/publication/277078202 (Accessed May 2015).

Allam, Tanweer. "A Reliable Communication Framework and Its Use in Internet of Things (IoT). International Journal of Scientific Research in Computer Science." *Engineering and Information Technology* 3 (2018a): 450–456.

Allam, Tanweer. "A Reliable Framework for Communication in Internet Using IEEE 802.15.4." *ARPN Journal of Engineering and Applied Sciences*. (2018b) http://www.arpnjournals.org/jeas/research_papers/rp_2018/jeas_0518_7075.pdf. (Accessed 2018).

Allam, Tanweer. "Blockchain in the Internet of Things (IoT). International Journal of Scientific Research in Computer Science." *Engineering and Information Technology* 5 (2019): 151–157.

Allam, Tanweer. "Cloud Computing in the Information Blockchain in Transactions on Sustainable Digital Innovation (ITSDI'20)" (2020). https://papers.ssrn.com/sol3/papers.cfm?abstract_id=3639063 (Accessed April 2020).

Allam, Tanweer. "Middleware Implementation in Cloud MANE Internet of Smart Devices." *International Journal of Computer Science and Network Security* 17 (2017): 87–94.

Allam, Tanweer. "Tactile Internet Development of Smart Cities." *International Journal of Electronics and Information Engineering* 13 (2019): 1–10.

9

A Novel Hybrid Method for Cloud Security Using Efficient IDS for Agricultural Weather Forecasting Systems

Rakshanda K. Borikar, Swati S. Sherekar, and Vilas M. Thakare

P. G. Department of Computer Science and Engineering, Sant Gadge Baba Amravati, Maharashtra, India University, Amravati, Maharashtra, India

CONTENTS

9.1 Introduction

Nowadays, the organization is moving their computing services towards the cloud. Cloud computing is a network of networks over the web; hence there are more probabilities of interruption are more with the data of intruder assaults. Cloud computing is disseminated in nature; consequently, the probabilities of interruption are more greater. On the development and additional breaking down, the working module over current Cloud security through intrusion detection system structure, suggests a current issue a weak, high false-negative rate, low recognition rate, and an absence over a standard base

DOI: 10.1201/9781003203926-9

programmed expansion for existing location instruments. Combining the important information on data mining innovation, to plan one enhanced network on Cloud security through intrusion detection systems structure dependent on data mining, collective misuse recognition, and irregularity recognition (Zhao et al., 2013). Because of the rapid development of an online network, the number of organization strikes has arisen, prompting the basics of a network IDS to get for an organization. Though, mixed gets too enormous traffic volumes, a few examples recognizable proof procedures have been brought into the exploration in local area (So and Mongkonchai, 2014). Data mining is an interaction of finding and extricating different models, examples, synopses, and got values from a given assortment of information. It includes the utilization of modern information investigation apparatuses to find beforehand ambiguous, genuine examples and connections in huge informational indexes. It is commonly drilled in a wide scope of profiling rehearses, profiling, like showcasing, observation, extortion recognition, and logical advancement (Elaziz et al., 2014). Cloud security through intrusion detection systems gives the capacity to distinguish security breaks in a framework (Ng et al., 2015). The subsequent cautions from abuse discovery-based IDSs are entirely dependable because of their low false alert rate. Be that as it may, they are weak against uncertain attacks. Then again, anomaly-based identification can deal with ambiguous attacks that include a deviation from ordinary conduct; however, they trigger a lot of false alarms (Bouteraa et al., 2018).

A Cloud Security through Intrusion Detection System expects a huge part to accomplish higher security in distinguishing malicious activities for quite a long while. Existing irregularity recognition is oftentimes connected with high incorrect alerts, by unobtrusive precision besides identification percentage and once it cannot recognize a wide range of assaults effectively (Muda and Udzir, 2011). As of late, different sorts of information mining strategies stayed are functional in Cloud security through intrusion detection. Dual significant ideal models are aimed at preparing information in mining-built interruption location of frameworks: abuse recognition and inconsistency discovery (Wang et al., 2011). In oddity identification, the k-means grouping procedure remains utilized towards distinguishing the original intrusion through grouping the organization association's information towards in gathering the greatest intrusion together in at least single groups (Elbasiony and Fahmy, 2013). Abuse identification distinguishes interruption, dependent on known examples, while abnormality recognition centers around obscure examples. K-means is a common grouping procedure that takes continue demonstrated is aimed at applications in Cloud security through an intrusion detection system (Eslamnezhad and Varjani, 2014). Cloud security through intrusion detection can likewise be viewed as a characterization disadvantage. In this examination the utilization of the K-means procedure and classification and regression trees (CART) algorithm (Aung and Min, 2018) is discussed.

Principal Component Analysis is an ordinary quantifiable methodology aimed at information assessment and pre-dealing that takes stayed broadly functional functionality in different turfs of examination. PCA is proposed to change the data in a reduced construction and keep most of the principal distinctions present in the hidden data. Complementing data, preventative technologies like firewalls, sturdy authentication, and user privilege. IDSs turned into a significant pieces of big business IT security management (Hadri et al., 2016). Network Cloud Security through Intrusion Detection Systems

take reliably stayed planned towards help intrusion detection systems helps and progresses the suggestion safety matter via the workplace of assessment, recognizing, surveying, and reporting any unapproved and ill-conceived network associations and exercises (Tahir et al., 2016). A Cloud Security through Intrusion Detection Systems has as of now pulled in the consideration of a significant segment of the world, determined their turn of events, and improving address addressed a high need for association and investigators and science focuses (Ariafar and Kiani, 2017). Intrusion is one of the most dangerous to parts of the Internet. Safety matters needed to remain at a tremendous disadvantage. A lot of procedures and techniques are have been invented to manage the requirements of intrusion detection systems like are low precision, high outburst rate, and time-consuming (Gadal and Mokhtar, 2017). Cloud security through intrusion detection techniques screens either network or alternative frameworks for malicious or strange practices. Supplementing protection advancements like firewalls, tough confirmation, and client advantages can be utilized for IDS (Salo et al., 2018).

A new fuzzy class-affiliation rule mining technique dependent on hereditary organization programming (GNP) for recognizing network interruptions. GNP is a developmental improvement procedure that uses coordinated diagram constructions rather than threads in patrimonial scheming or trees in patrimonial software design, which stimulates upgrading the portrayal capacity with minimized projects got from the reusability of hubs in a chart assembly (Mabu and Chen, 2010). Assailants might present Trojans to steal casualty's a user's login examples or else issue a huge size set of preliminaries with the help of a word referring to gain clients' passwords. At the point when effective they are effective, they may then sign in to the framework and access clients' records or adjust or obliterate framework locations. Luckily, most present host-based safety frameworks and organization-based intrusion detection systems that can find a professed interruption continuously (Leu and Tasi, 2015). Oddity location frameworks screen action to make a main concern of for routineness. Abnormality location frameworks have accomplishments in uncovering new assaults, similar to "zero" day assaults, yet have high false-positive rates (Goeschel, 2016). An interruption recognition framework is utilized to notice undesirable activities on network frameworks and individual PCs. The alert incorporates data about the assault-type and the objective of the assault. The substance of the caution relies upon the idea of the information and the sort of approach; for example, inconsistency-based essentially distinguishes the association stream of the identified assault while much of the data's ascents with the alert and with employments of mark-based methodology (Hussein, 2016). To distinguish an interruption by contrasting its mark and assault, it is saved in a data set of assault marks. The most notable is Principal Component Analysis which is utilized in the primary thought behind this procedure is to keep simply the important data which that call ordinarily in this setting of head parts (PCs) (Hadir and Chugdali, 2018). Intrusion Detection gathers the data and breaking down breaks it down for extraordinary or surprising occasions. Interruption recognition is the way toward checking and breaking down the occasions that happen in a PC framework to distinguish indications of safety issues (Shirbhate et al., 2011).

This chapter evaluates five different techniques, such as improved data mining, data mining classification, sequential data mining approaches, data mining techniques, and contemporary comparative study. This chapter proposes Cloud security through an intrusion detection model by applying the apriori algorithm to accomplish programmed allowance on the association rule base and supervised algorithm support vector machine selected towards the improvement of the quality of detection. The proposed method provides security in a Cloud environment by detecting attacks with high accuracy and detection rate, in less execution time, and with a low false alarm rate.

9.2 Background

Several methods on data mining representations stayed were completed towards an advanced flexibility arrangement in current earlier years such models are: recent years.

The misuse of discovery and anomaly identification to develop a hybrid IDS dependent on exploitation recognition and inconsistency identification. The creator chooses the K-means Clustering in bunching examination and the apriori algorithm over affiliation rule mining and improves it. Put on an enhanced Kmeans clustering toward accomplishing typical conduct modules and information detachment structure, and at that point use the improved apriori algorithm to accomplish a programmed expansion over a standard base. At last, by the trial, check the capacity of the two calculations (Zhao et al., 2013).

The assurance is to examine different notable data mining procedures on arrangement systems for Cloud security through intrusion detection systems over the two quality kdd data set for agricultural activities and ongoing http botnet bouts on Weka devices. An acknowledgment system was likewise investigated in three phases: dataset preparing, information filtering feature preference, and classification (So and Mongkonchai, 2014).

The author learned and executed various sequential data mining methods and afterward proposed another improved method. The presented technique builds the exactness of the cycle and the variety of distinguished examples. The paper recommends the structure for information base interruption discovery dependent on the altered technique. The literature utilizes a sensible immense database for figuring out the exhibition and the precision. The improved module projected module depends on enlightening the presentation of any of the apriori-based algorithm from the precision perspective, through perspective by applying a few adjustments. The changes proposed are principally in two zones, which are the cycle of the output of the exchanges and the way toward creating the applicants set (Elaziz et al., 2014).

The strategy is utilized to distinguish attacks that have not been characterized at this point. The standard of anything that is broken in the house is viewed as an attack and will be an overall inconsistency that will want to distinguish the definition recently given. The solution gives an instrument that runs information mining devices across a log record to recognize designs that might be viewed as an unapproved movement. After the example is affirmed by the proprietor of the framework as an attack, the attack example will be put away in a marked data set. The instrument presently utilizes the idea of grouping record sections that are recurrent on different occasions and distinguishes a savage power secret key breaking and DoS attacks on a framework in the Ubuntu stage (Ng et al., 2015).

The author presents relative research of data mining methods for the IDS. In particular, study the general exhibitions of those strategies just as the effect of preparing information size on their outcomes. The creator utilizes ISCX2012 as a benchmark for experimentation. A reasonable agricultural dataset that addresses at a specific level of the present organization traffic. The investigation shows that moderately old strategies beat a portion of the methods profoundly utilized really by the local area. Concerning the effect of preparing dataset size, the examined techniques respond uniquely in contrast to one another when the creator adds more information to the preparation dataset. Additionally, the outcomes feature the significance of attack traffic in the preparation data set. Additionally, they unequivocally recommend the utilization of Random Forest for the interruption location because of its direct exhibition connection with the preparation data set's size (Bouteraa et al., 2018). This paper introduces some data mining techniques, i.e., improved data mining, data mining classification, sequential data mining approaches, data mining techniques, and contemporary comparative study.

A chapter is ordered as follows:

This chapter is ordered as follows. Section I is the introduction and Section II discusses the background. Section III discusses previous work done and Section IV discusses existing procedures. Section V discusses analysis attributes and parameters and how these are affected by data mining methods. Section VI gives the proposed method and Section VII gives the stimulation and possible results. Section VIII discusses results and discussion. Section IX discusses conclusion of the appraisal chapter. Finally, Section X gives future scope.

9.3 Previous Work Done

In the study literature, many flexibility representations take remained studied towards the offer of various data mining techniques arrangements and enhanced the presentation in terms of accuracy and detection rate.

ZHAO Yanjun et al. (2013) have joined bad-use recognition and inconsist recognition to build a hybrid IDS dependent on bad-use recognition and inconsistence recognition. In the module, choose the K-means clustering in a bunching study and an apriori process over the affiliation rule mining and enhanced it. Put on the enhanced kmeans clustering toward accomplishing usual action modules and data detachment segment, at that point using the enhanced apriori algorithm toward accomplishing programmed allowance over a standard base. Through an analysis to confirm the capacity of both procedures.

Chakchai So and Mongkonchai (2014) has proposed method to examine different well-realized information mining strategies on grouping systems for Cloud security through intrusion detection system above the pair quality kdd data set for agricultural activities and late http botnet bouts on ongoing Weka instruments. An acknowledgment strategy was likewise investigated in four phases: dataset constructions, information pre-preparing, feature preference, and grouping.

Pakinam Elamein Elaziz et al. (2014) have examined and executed diverse consecutive information mining procedures and, afterward, proposed another upgraded process. The presented technique expands the exactness of the system and the numeral detection figures.

Jonathon Ng et al. (2015) have proposed a strategy that is utilized to identify attacks that have not been characterized at this point. The standard of anything that is broken in the house is viewed as an attack will be an overall anomaly that will want to distinguish the definition recently given. The arrangement gives an instrument that runs data mining devices against a record to distinguish designs that might be viewed as an unapproved action. Afterwards, the example is checked by the proprietor of the framework as an attack. The attack example will be put away in a mark database. The instrument acquires extra examples and becomes viable as time passes by and develops.

Imad Bouteraa et al. (2018) have introduced a detection of data mining methods for Cloud security through intrusion recognition. In particular, they study the general exhibitions of those techniques just as the effect of preparing information size on their outcomes. A reasonable agricultural data set addresses a specific level in the present organization traffic. The examination shows that moderately old strategies go around a portion of the methods profoundly utilized really by the local area. Concerning the effect of preparing the data set size, the researched strategies respond uniquely in contrast to one another when the creator adds more information to the preparation dataset. The outcomes feature the significance of attack traffic in the agricultural preparation dataset.

9.4 Existing Methodologies

Many data mining techniques have been executed over previous years. Various procedures remain are applied over various data mining representations that are improved data mining, data mining classification, sequential data mining approaches, data mining techniques, and contemporary comparative study.

A. ***Improved data mining:***
   To set up the ordinary behavior class, utilizing intrusion identification framework dependent on misuse, for example, snort to gather the organization typical conduct information as the pre-preparing information. Utilizing It utilizes the network sniffer to gather a network information parcel. Separating the information bundle, and the information field is put away in which comparing the comparing information structure. Normalizing structure the information to get ready for sifting the typical conduct. Utilizing conduct, and utilizes the group examination algorithm to bunch the put-away information and preclude a little piece of the typical information. Utilizing the alliance instructions procedure in information which withdrawal towards the kind an alliance study towards finding an innovative regulation and add it to the regulation base (Zhao et al., 2013).
B. ***Data mining classification:***
   Before performing mining, characterization utilizing Weka apparatuses; a customary kdd is needed towards change over a reasonable organization was picked. Quality Selection: Since there are such a large number of unimportant ascribes likely, prompting low arrangement accuracy and exact estimation intricacy, this choice level is utilized to sort out the reasonable credits spread on the data improvement to isolate the data set in that each improvement will be registered for every information measurement. There are six principal characterization models implanted into the new Weka apparatuses, in particular, neural networks and naive Bayes and SVM.
C. ***Sequential data mining approaches:***
   Here the first stage is called reinstatement, in which the proper successive algorithm is chosen dependent on the data set highlights and changed. The subsequent stage is called periodic development and location, in which a concurred fixed period gets is filtered. The third stage is called activity. That activity

is a manual organization activity. The data set manager should check the rundown shipped off him/her and affirm if these principles could cause an intrusion (Elaziz et al., 2014).

D. ***Data mining techniques:***
The initial phase in planning and executing a data mining apparatus for intrusion recognition was to analyzed and parse the network log documents. The initial step follows to remove the date and time, extract information until the main colon, Extract information inside the enclosure, and Decode the leftover data. The program adds another segment when a piece of the line is partly founded on uncommon characters along these lines as the header has the segment data. The separated information is added to the body of the record. The current form of the apparatus has carried out a bunching algorithm that matches associations that seem on various occasions. This empowers us to identify conceivable secret word speculating or DoS attacks (Ng et al., 2015).

E. ***Contemporary comparative study:***
The XML form of ISCX2012 (labeled_flows_xml.zip). In any case, before beginning analyses, some pre-handling steps are needed to get a steadier dataset that fits the examined techniques just as the area of organization interruption detection. 1) Feature's choice and extraction: ISCX2012 addresses the caught network traffic in 12 XML documents. Those records don't completely have the equivalent attributes. 2) Data change and standardization: Some of the examined information mining methods require numeric highlights. Specifically, ANN- and SVM-based strategies. Along these lines, map each conceivable estimation of appName to a special whole number beginning from 1 to 107. 3) Data inspecting: ISCX2012 contains 2.5 million occasions, which is generally enormous concerning experimentation's targets. Hence, examined the first data set is examined to size generally equivalent to the size of KDD99 10%. The decreased data set contains all the attack associations from the first one and 27,590 typical occurrences from every day of the first dataset. data set. For experimentations, the creator drives two equivalent size sub data sets by delineated apportioning. to be specific, 100%Training and Testing. The author utilizes the previous information for preparing and the last for testing (Bouteraa et al., 2018).

9.5 Analysis of Methods

The cycle of age rule is used when setting the least help degree; it produces the two successive arrangements of the help degree. The standard that fulfils the least certainty degree, is the incessant set produced simply in the solid guideline (Zhao et al., 2013). J48 can achieve 100% incorrectness for Teardrop and Ipsweep; IBK precision is near and with higher exactness for the Port sweep (So and Mongkonchai, 2014). It was seen that the huge expansion in the accuracy is after applying the subsequent alterations designs in a two-manner bearing on eliminating the rehashed designs, and the precision rate (Elaziz et al., 2014). The program can distinguish if an example exists in the ordinary record before being viewed as an attack. At that point, the program will identify if the attacks are now in the information base of attack designs and will sound an alarm if there is;

TABLE 9.1

Comparisons Between Different Data Mining Techniques

Methods and Techniques	Characteristics	
	Advantages	*Limitations*
Improved data mining	Predictive Analysis	Privacy Security
Data mining classification	High accuracy and simple	Expensive
Sequential data mining approaches	Flexibility when selecting parameters.	Security
Datamining techniques	Simple to implement, Lightweight	Privacy Issues, security issues
Contemporary comparative study	Lower Costs and Improve Revenue	Violates User Privacy

otherwise, it will provoke the client to add to the data set (Ng et al., 2015). The attacks occasions address just the testing dataset. Hence, if a model can catch a critical part of typical personal conduct standards, its precision will be high, paying little heed to its abilities against attack conduct. Besides OCSVM, different strategies got have amazing exactness precise midpoints with practically ideal correctness for RF and SVM (Bouteraa et al., 2018, Table 9.1).

9.6 Proposed Methodology

The innovative inconsistency in Cloud security through the intrusion detection technique remains projected to create over the apriori algorithm and support vector machine towards perceiving inconsistency there cognition. The planned method goals are to create an appropriate figure of detectors with exact recognition accuracy in the Cloud environment for agricultural activities. The 'Weka tool' is used to implement the proposed method. The core impression is created utilizing a frequent itemset mining. It is an iterative approach to discover the most frequent itemset. In the classification phase, the supervised algorithm support vector machine was designated toward the improvement of excellent detection over Cloud security. A proposed method provides security in a Cloud environment by detecting attacks with high accuracy and detection rate, in less execution time, and with a low false alarm rate.

Basic steps of an algorithm-

Step 1. Agricultural training dataset are loaded

Step 2. Data Pre-processing

Step 3. Association Rule phase: Applying the Apriori algorithm, mining the continuous agricultural data sets in the informational collection to frame the association rule, and put away in the standard base.

Step 4. In the Last phase, classification is done by using a supervised algorithm, i.e., SVM is utilized to categorize the agricultural dataset as standard or anomaly.

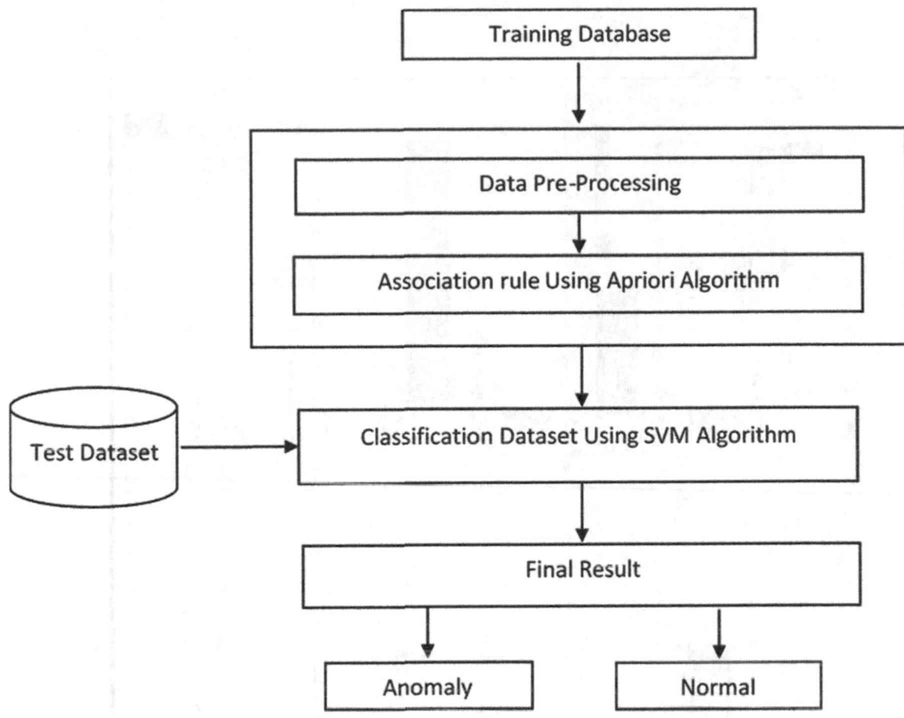

FIGURE 9.1
The Proposed Method.

Step 5. Outcome is obtained.

Diagrammatic representation of the proposed method is shown as follows (Figure 9.1).

9.7 Stimulation and Result

The investigational outcomes represent a direction over the accuracy in the proposed method is satisfactory and its magnitude is proportional to the reliability and accuracy. The results got from this proposed strategy and approaches beat extra through are the encouraging detection percentage and decreased false alarm percentage and give high accuracy in Cloud computing for agricultural activities.

In Figure 9.2, the KDD NSL standard agricultural data sets are uploaded in the Weka tool. Pre-processing is done with a numeric to nominal filter which that converts numeric attributes to nominal attributes.

In Figure 9.3, the Apriori algorithm is applied to the pre-processed data.

In Figure 9.4, the SVM classification is applied and indicates the normal and anomaly data sets.

In Figure 9.5, it appears the results of the apriori Algorithm

In Figure 9.6 it appears shows the results of the SVM Classification.

FIGURE 9.2
Datasets Uploaded.

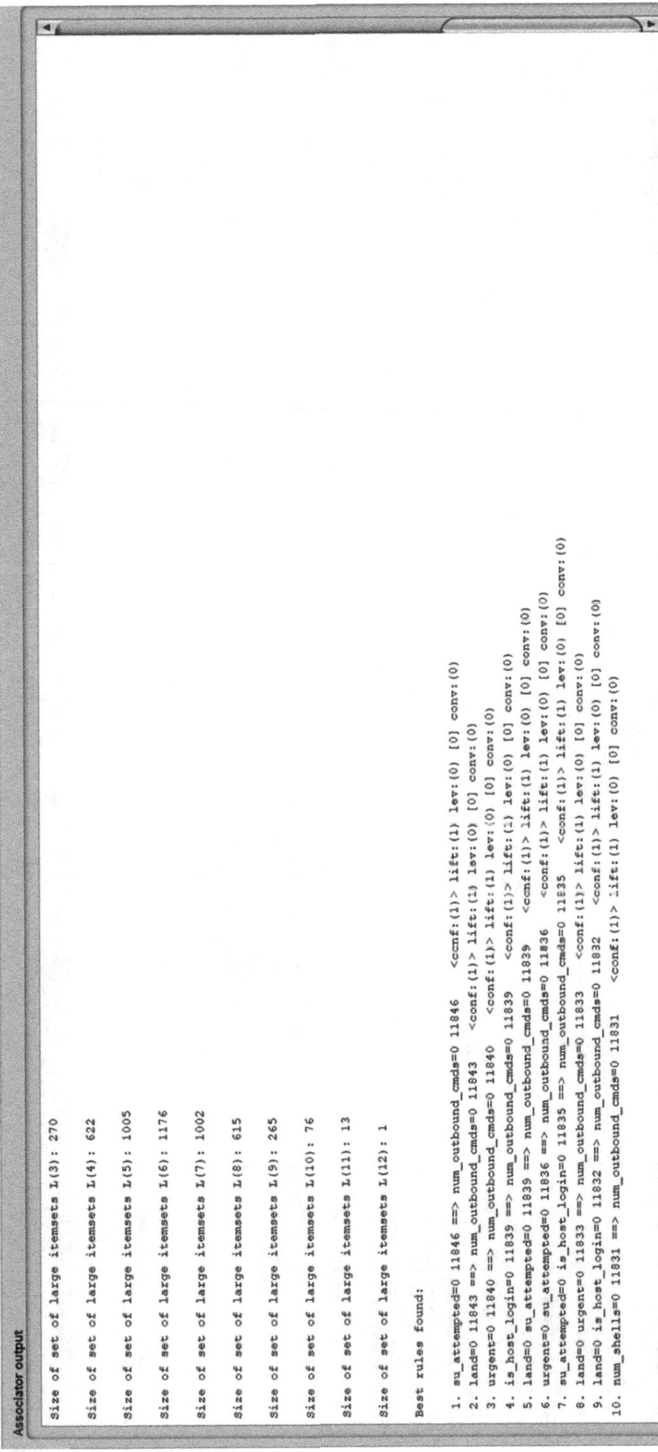

FIGURE 9.3
Association Rule Using Apriori Algorithm.

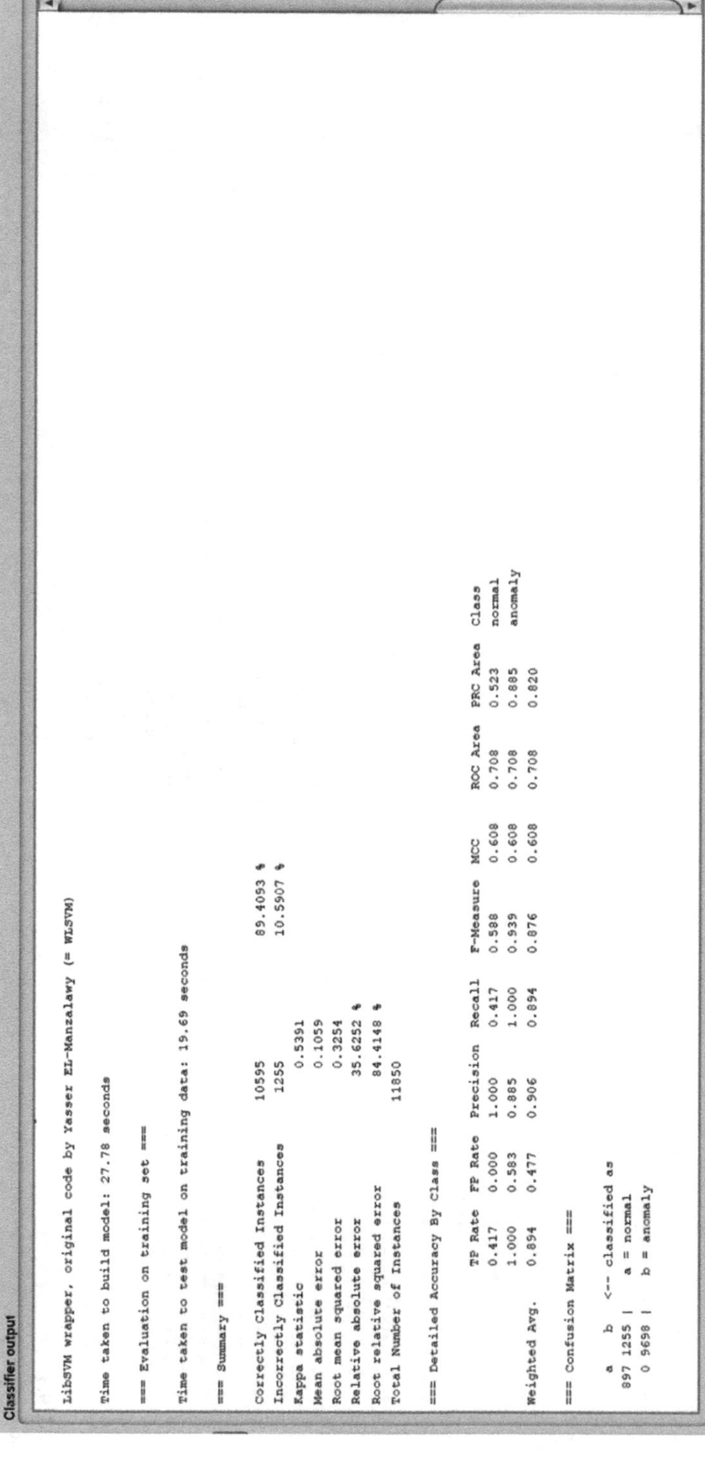

FIGURE 9.4
SVM Classification.

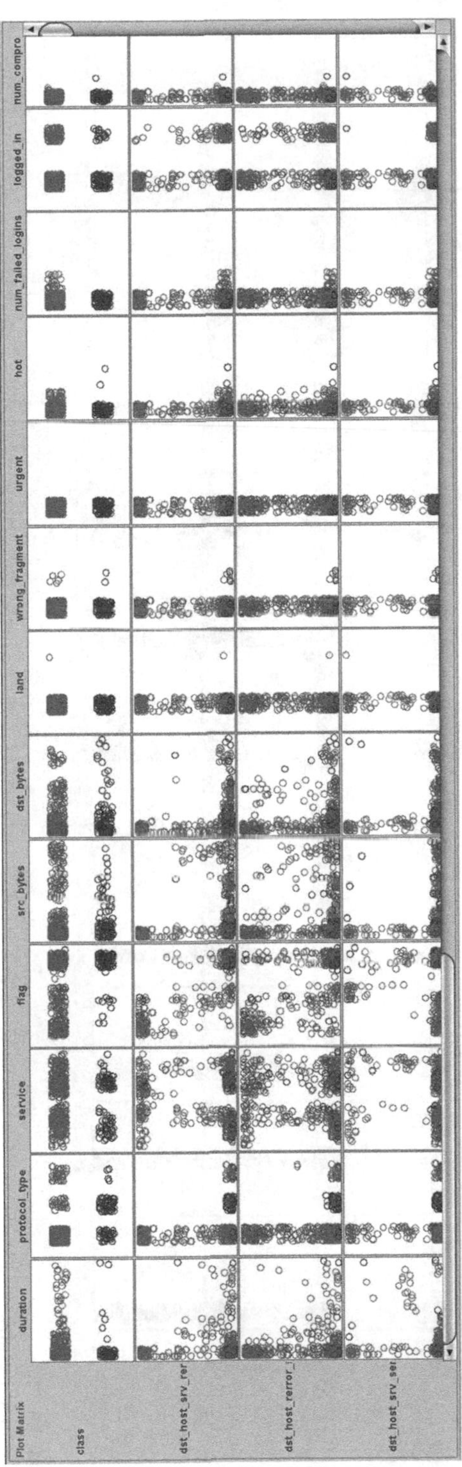

FIGURE 9.5
Apriori Algorithm Results Apriori Algorithm Results.

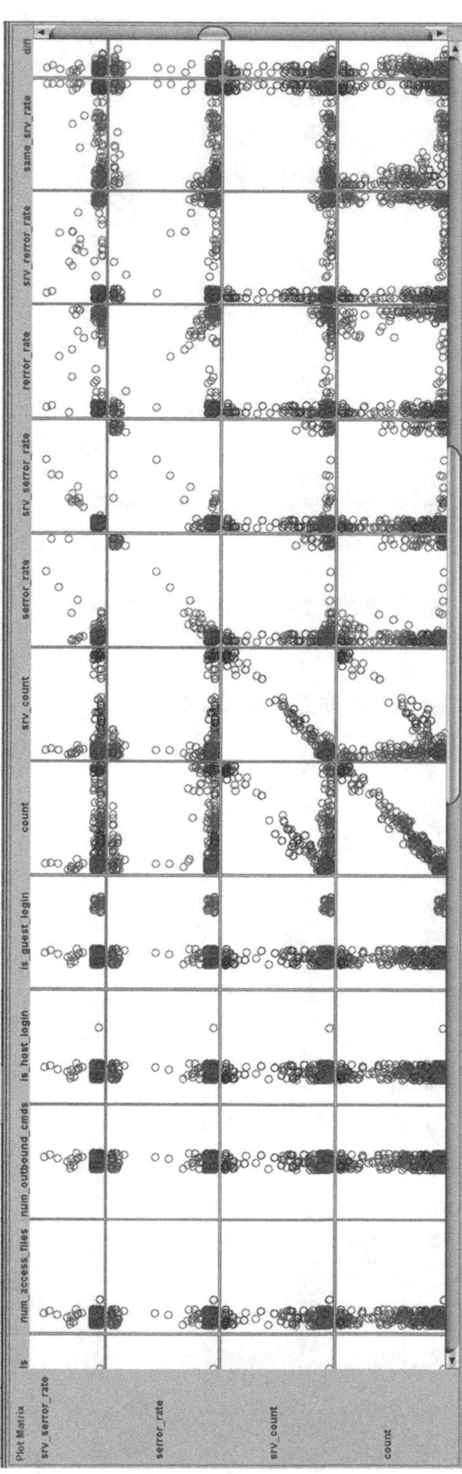

FIGURE 9.6
Classification Results.

TABLE 9.2

Execution Time of Methods

Sr.no.	Name of methods	Execution time(sec)time (sec)
[1]	Data mining classification models	36.3
[2]	Anomaly and signature-based algorithm	24.6
[3]	Framework base on random forests and weighted k-means	42.7
[4]	Improved k-means algorithm	55.2
[5]	Proposed Method	12.7

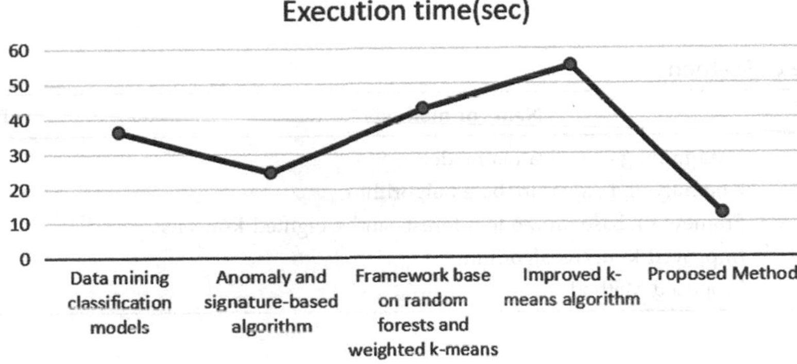

FIGURE 9.7
Analysis of Execution Time

9.8 Results and Discussion

Table 9.2 and Figure 9.7 show the outcomes of the observation on the presented structure. The outcomes appear show that the presented structure takes less time for execution.

Table 9.3 and Figure 9.8 show the outcomes of observation on the presented hybrid structure. The outcomes appear show that the presented hybrid structure obtains exact accuracy.

Table 9.4 and Figure 9.9 show the outcomes of the assessment on the proposed structure. The outcomes appear show that the presented hybrid structure obtains very exact recognition rates.

Table 9.5 and Figure 9.10 show the outcomes of the proposed method that achieves very low false-positive rates.

9.9 Conclusion

Cloud computing is a "network" of "networks", thus, the odds as for intrusion detection is additional thorough information of intruder's attacks for weather forecasting. Various IDS approaches are used to secure malicious attacks on customary organizations over

TABLE 9.3
Accuracy of Methods

Sr.no.	Name of methods	Accuracy
[1]	Data mining classification models	1.87
[2]	Anomaly and signature-based algorithm	0.93
[3]	Framework base on random forests and weighted k-means	2.82
[4]	Improved k-means algorithm	1.6
[5]	Proposed Method	0.833

TABLE 9.4
Detection Rate of Method

Sr.no.	Name of methods	Detection rate
[1]	Data mining classification models	0.003
[2]	Anomaly and signature-based algorithm	0.56
[3]	Framework base on random forests and weighted k-means	0.043
[4]	Improved k-means algorithm	0.76
[5]	Proposed Method	1.00

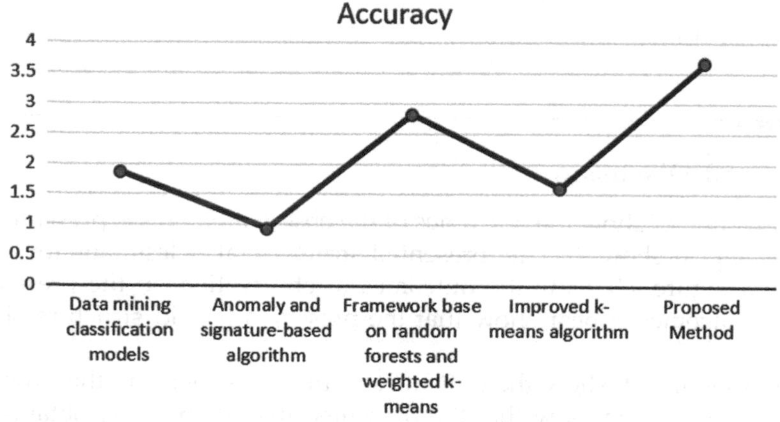

FIGURE 9.8
Analysis of Accuracy.

Cloud environments for agricultural activities. For Cloud processing, marvellous organization access proportion, giving up the controller over information and applications towards support provider and conveyed attacks weakness, a proficient, reliable, and information upfront IDS is essential. In this chapter, a multi-strung Cloud IDS technique is projected to be managed through outsider observing assistance for superior enhanced productivity and straightforwardness for the agricultural clients. The proposed method has several applications; the Cloud can store zone-specific weather, the weather forecast for specification a specific time, emerging agricultural security threads, and as well as effective information sharing for agricultural activities.

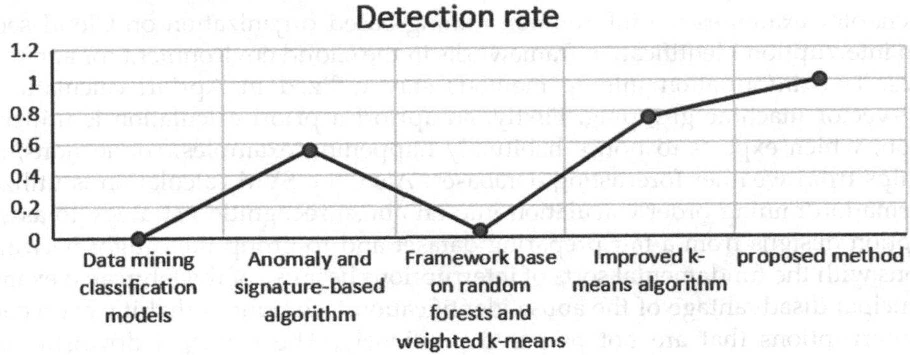

FIGURE 9.9
Analysis of Detection Rate.

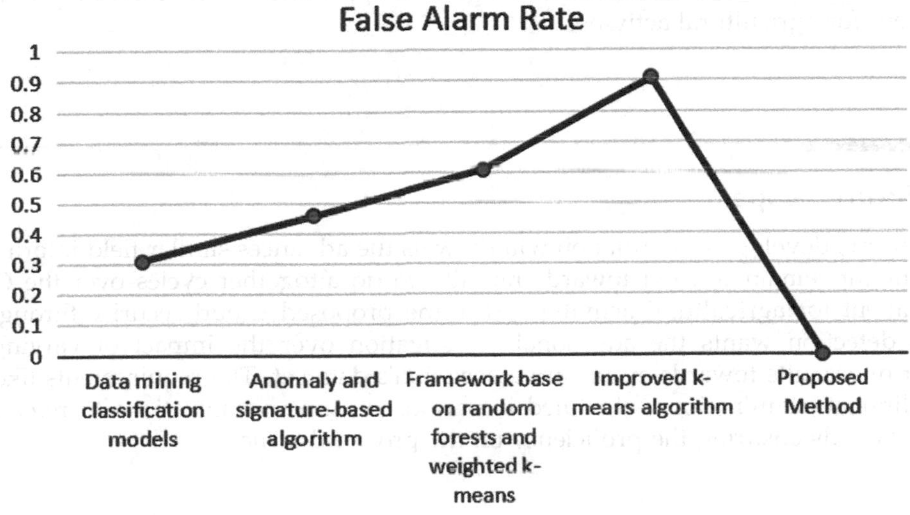

FIGURE 9.10
Analysis of False Alarm Rate.

TABLE 9.5
False Alarm Rate

Sr.no.	Name of methods	False alarm rate
[1]	Data mining classification models	0.31
[2]	Anomaly and signature-based algorithm	0.46
[3]	Framework base on random forests and weighted k-means	0.61
[4]	Improved k-means algorithm	0.91
[5]	Proposed Method	0.00

This chapter examines the information mining-based organization on Cloud security through interruption identification frameworks in the Cloud environment for agricultural activities. Two information mining methods stay utilized in Apriori calculation and support vector machine grouping. Firstly, an apriori a priori calculation is utilized for affiliation, which expects to notice habitually happening examples, connections, or relationships from weather forecasting databases. Also, the SVM calculation is utilized as an information mining order calculation into an abuse recognition strategy to assemble interruption designs from a fair preparing dataset and to group the caught network associations with the fundamental sorts of interruptions because of the fabricated examples. The principal disadvantage of the abuse identification technique is that it can't recognize novel interruptions that are not prepared previously. The principal downside of the abnormality identification strategy gives a high false alarm rate. A proposed strategy remains assessed over NSL-KDD data sets. An outcome over the Cloud security through an intrusion detection system accomplishes discovery rates and false-positive false positive rates better related on the way over present approaches over cloud the Cloud environment for agricultural activities.

9.10 Future Scope

In the future, developed information withdrawals the advances similar field information which might remain utilized towards rapidity to do altogether cycles over the Cloud environment for agricultural activities. Also, the proposed Cloud security through intrusion detection wants the additional investigation over the impact of varying the number of assaults towards an unsure association's data set. The requirements likewise are additional examinations scheduled in various genuine organizations to remain expected towards ensuring the proficiency on the projected structure.

References

Ariafar, E. and R. Kiani. "Intrusion Detection System on Optimized Framework Based on Data Mining Techniques." *4th* (2017). https://ieeexplore.ieee.org/document/8324903 (Accessed 26 March 2018).

Aung, Yi and Myat Min. "Hybrid Intrusion Detection System using K-means and Regression Trees Algorithm." *IEEE 16th International Conferences on Software Engineering Research, Management and Applications* (2018) https://ieeexplore.ieee.org/document/8477203 (Accessed 01 October 2018).

Bouteraa, Imad, Makhlouf Derdour and Ahmed Ahmim. "Intrusion Detection Using Data Mining: A Contemporary Comparative Study." 3rd *International Conferences on Pattern Analysis and Intelligent Systems* (2018). https://ieeexplore.ieee.org/document/8598494 (Accessed 03 January 2019).

Elaziz, Pakinam Elamein Abd, Mohamed Sobh and Hoda K. Mohamed. "Database Intrusion Detection Using Sequential Data Mining Approaches." *9th International Conferences on ComputerSoftware Engineering & Systems International Conferences on ComputerSoftware Engineering & Systems* (2014). https://ieeexplore.ieee.org/document/7030937 (Accessed 5 February 2014).

Elbasiony, Reda M. and Mahmoud M. Fahmy. "A Hybrid Network Intrusion Detection Framework Based on Random Forest and Weighted-means." *Ain Shams Engineering Journal* 4 (2013): 753–762.

Eslamnezhad, Mohsen and Ali Yazdian Varjani. "Intrusion Detection Based on Minmax K-means Clustering." *7th International Symposium on Telecommunication International Symposium on Telecommunication* (2014). https://ieeexplore.ieee.org/document/7000814 (Accessed 08 January 2015).

Gadal, Saad Mohamed Ali Mohamed and Rania A. Mokhtar. "Hybrid Method Utilizes an Anomaly Detection Technique of Data Mining Techniques." *International Conferences on Communication, Control, Computing and Electronics Engineering* (2017). https://www.researchgate.net/publication/314194900 (Accessed January 2017).

Goeschel, Kathleen. "Reducing False Positives in Intrusion Detection Systems Using Data-Mining Techniques Utilizing Support Vector Machine, Decision Trees, and Naïve Bayes for Off-Line Analysis." *Southeast Con2016* (2016). https://ieeexplore.ieee.org/document/7506774 (Accessed 11 July 2016).

Hadir, Amal and Khalid Chugdali. "A Network Intrusion Detection Based on Improved Nonlinear Fuzzy Robust PCA." *IEEE 5th International Conferences on emerging Trends in Computer Sciences and Information Technology* (2018). https://ieeexplore.ieee.org/document/8596643 (Accessed 31 December 2018).

Hadri, Amal, Kalid Chougdali and Rajae Touahni. "Intrusion Detection System Using PCA and Fuzzy PCA Techniques." *International Conferences on Advanced Communication Systems and Information Security* (2016). https://ieeexplore.ieee.org/document/7843930 (Accessed 09 February 2017).

Hussein, Safwan Mawlood. "Performance Evaluation of Intrusion Detection System Using Anomaly and Signature-based Algorithms to Reduction False Alarm rat and Detect Unknown Attacks." *International Conferences on Communication, Control, Computing Computational Science and Computational Intelligences* (2016). https://ieeexplore.ieee.org/document/7881496 (Accessed 20 March 2017).

Leu, Fang-Yei and Kun-Lin Tasi. "An Internal Intrusion Detection Systems by Using Fata Mining and Forensic Techniques." *IEEE Systems Journal* 11 (2015):427–438.

Mabu, Shingo and Ci Chen. "An Intrusion Detection Model Base on Fuzzy Class-Association-Rule Mining Using Generic Network." *IEEE Transactions on Systems, Man, and Cybernetic* 41 (2010): 130–139.

Muda, Z., W. Yassin, M. N. Sulaiman and N. I. Udzir. "Intrusion Detection based on K-means Clustering and Naive Bayes Classification." *7th International Conferences Information Technology in Asia* (2011): 1–6, doi: 10.1109/CITA.2011.5999520. https://ieeexplore.ieee.org/document/5999520 (Accessed 30 August 2011).

Ng, Jonathon, Deepti Joshi and Shankar M. Banik. "Applying Data Mining Techniques to Intrusion Detection." *12th International Conferences on Information Technology-New Generations* (2015). https://ieeexplore.ieee.org/document/7113585 (Accessed 01 June 2015).

So, Chakchai and Nutankarn Mongkonchai. "An Evaluation of Data mining Classification Models for Network Intrusion Detection." *4th International Conferences on Digital Information and Communication Technology and Its Applications International Conferences on Digital Information and Communication Technology and Its Applications* (2014). https://ieeexplore.ieee.org/document/6821663 (Accessed 29 May 2014).

Salo, Fadi, Mohammadnoor Injadat and Ali Bou Nassif. "Data Mining Techniques in Intrusion Detection Systems: A Systematic Literature Review." *IEEE Access* 6 (2018): 56046–56058.

Shirbhate, S. V., Vilas M. Thakare, Sweatha S. S. Sherekar. "Data Mining Applications for Network Intrusion Detection Systems." *National Conferences on Emerging Trends in Computer Science and Information Technology* (2011). https://www.researchgate.net/profile/SShirbhate/publication/265144790 (Accessed 2011).

Tahir, Hatim Mohamad, Abas Md Said and Norliza Katuk. "Oving K-means Clustering Using Discretization Techniques in Network Intrusion Detection System." *3rd International Conferences on Computer and Information Sciences International Conferences on Computer and Information Sciences* (2016). https://ieeexplore.ieee.org/document/7783222 (Accessed 15 December 2016).

Wang, Shenghui. "Intrusion Detection with Unlabeled Data Mining Using Clustering." *2nd International Conferences on Innovation in Bio-inspired Computing and Application* (2011). https://academiccommons.columbia.edu/doi/10.7916/D8MP5904 (Accessed 03 May 2011).

Zhao, Yanjun, Mingjun Wei and Jing Wang. "Realization of Intrusion Detection Systems Based on the Improved Data Mining Technology." *8th International Conferences on Computer Science & Education* (2013). https://ieeexplore.ieee.org/document/6554056 (Accessed 15 July 2013).

Section III

Cloud for Healthcare

10

Cloud Model for Real-Time Healthcare Services

Urmila Shrawankar and Girish Talmale

Department of Computer Science and Engineering, G H Raisoni College of Engineering, Nagpur, India

CONTENTS

10.1 Introduction

The real-time applications for healthcare have grown in interest in recent years. The Cloud computing model is used to store and analyze the healthcare data in an efficient and cost-effective way (Sisu et al., 2014). Cloud service providers such as Amazon provide virtual machines on lease for computing. The virtual machine allocation is done using provisioning policies, requirement, time, etc. (Li et al., 2018). The Cloud computing model is extensively used in providing real-time medical services such as a hospital data management system that stores all hospital patients' data, which is further analyzed to improve healthcare service, as represented in Figure 10.1 (Ning et al., 2019). The

DOI: 10.1201/9781003203926-10

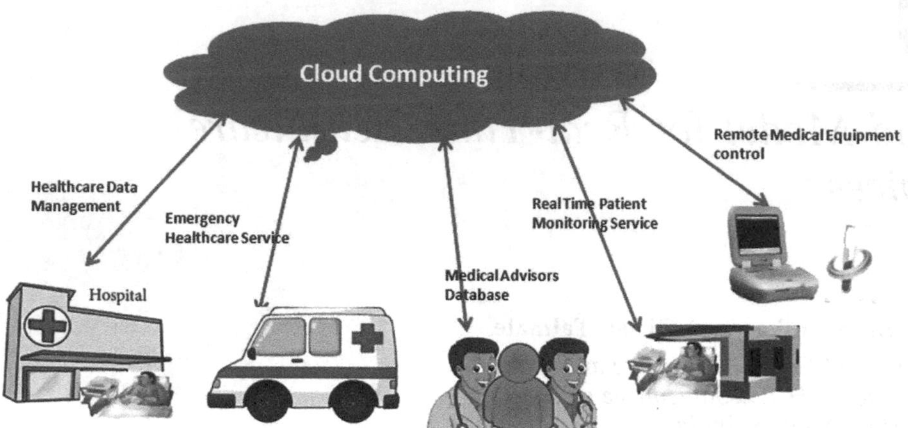

FIGURE 10.1
Real-time Cloud computing service in healthcare.

emergency healthcare service is provided using a Cloud computing model in case of emergency. The medical advisors database, real-time patient monitoring, and equipment control service are also provided using a Cloud computing model.

The healthcare services are heavily dependent upon the data collected through the various healthcare sensor and medical equipment. The storage and computation of these healthcare data is done on Cloud computing due to limited storage and computation power of these devices. These smart healthcare devices range from small devices such as temperature sensors to large medical equipment such as MRI scanners.

The main technology used in implementation of Cloud computing model is virtualization. The Cloud computing model is used to maximize the resource utilization but on other hand it compromise deadline and service quality (Chen et al., 2019). The virtualization creates the various dedicated virtual machines to handle these computing and storage requirement. The hypervisor, which is also called a virtual machine manager, is used to separate this virtual machine from the physical machine (Silva et al., 2020). The healthcare applications are time sensitive and to run this application on the Cloud environment depends upon various parameters like processing nodes, nature of tasks, and deadline of tasks. In this paper we are proposing the cluster-based real-time scheduling techniques for the allocation of virtual machines for time-sensitive healthcare applications such as remote patient monitoring systems, remote surgeries, etc., to ensure the timely execution of various real-time tasks (Mubarakali, 2020). This paper proposed the model of virtual machine allocations to process these smart healthcare tasks within the deadline and achieve high system utilization (Zanjal and Talmale, 2016). The smart healthcare system includes many embedded sensors like ECG sensors, temperature sensors, motion sensors, etc. (Talmale and Urmila, 2020). These smart devices used in healthcare applications generate periodic jobs and the proposed system is used to process these jobs on the Cloud to satisfy heavy computation and resource requirements (Taher et al., 2019). The proposed system allocates virtual machines using cluster-based real-time scheduling to these jobs to ensure the timely executions of these jobs.

10.1.1 Objectives of Research

The main objectives of this research work are as follows:

- To provide the overview of Cloud computing service for real-time healthcare service.
- To discuss the different benefits, challenges, and issues of Cloud computing in healthcare.
- To present the real-time virtual machine scheduling framework for Cloud computing.
- To discuss various case studies for healthcare Cloud providers.

10.1.2 Organization

The chapter organization is as follows: Section 1 gives the details about the background of related work completed. Section 3 presents the system model for real-time scheduling framework on the Cloud environment. Section 4 presents the real-time task allocation and scheduling techniques. Results are described in Section 5.

10.2 Related Work

The real-time computation demand increases due to smart applications such as healthcare. The real-time system used the Cloud environment to address this high computational demand (Ibarz et al., 2020). Running this smart real-time healthcare system on the Cloud environment and the allocation of resources is the main research area in recent years due to the following reasons like service reliability, maximizing utilization, timely response, etc. Apache spark provides real-time computation of large-scale healthcare data. Google Tensor Flow also used real-time scheduling techniques for their GPU architecture (Bhattacharya et al., 2019).

Cloud computing is the best computing platform for efficient computing and storage smart real-time application of healthcare applications (Rizk et al., 2020). The virtual machines must be assigned in an efficient way to real-time healthcare system applications (Mirobi and Arockiam, 2019). The real-time application tasks are executed on the remote Cloud computing platform (Stavrinides and Helen, 2019). The comparison of virtual machine scheduling proposed on Cloud computing platform (Khan et al., 2020). The dynamic distributed virtual machine scheduling techniques are proposed for efficient sharing of resources (Dhule and Shrawankar, 2020). The Ecalyptus is using round-robin scheduling of virtual machines (Zheng et al., 2019). The OpenNebula is used to schedule the virtual machine using rank algorithms for physical machines (Jain et al., 2019).

The real-time scheduling used for the multiprocessing nodes are categories into two main types. In partition-based scheduling, the tasks sets are assigned to dedicate processing nodes and scheduled using existing global scheduling techniques (Han et al., 2018). The advantage of partition-based scheduling approach is the task allocation done in the existing mature uniprocessing scheduling used. The tasks are not allowed to migrate among the cores so the migration overhead is zero. The drawbacks of partition-based scheduling techniques are task assignment in NP-Hard problems, low system utilization, and high response time. Another scheduling technique is global scheduling, in which the tasks are maintained in the common queue and scheduled to available processing nodes. The advantage of global scheduling techniques is high system utilization and low response time. The limitations of global scheduling techniques are high migration and preemption overheads (Bertout et al., 2020). The interesting contribution given is using fixed priority scheduling techniques (Choi et al., 2019). The power aware virtual machine allocation is done in the past (Ajmera and Tewari, 2018).

10.3 Different Cloud Computing Uses in Real-Time Healthcare Services

Cloud computing is extensively used in the healthcare sector. Some of the applications of Cloud computing healthcare services are as follows (Figure 10.2):

1. Healthcare Data Storage and Analytics:
   The healthcare sector produces huge amounts of patient data which are further analyzed to find the meaningful information about the disease pattern, drug discovery, and many more.
2. Artificial Intelligence and Machine Learning:
   Nowadays, intelligence techniques are being used in healthcare data for complex analytics and future predications using machine learning techniques, which

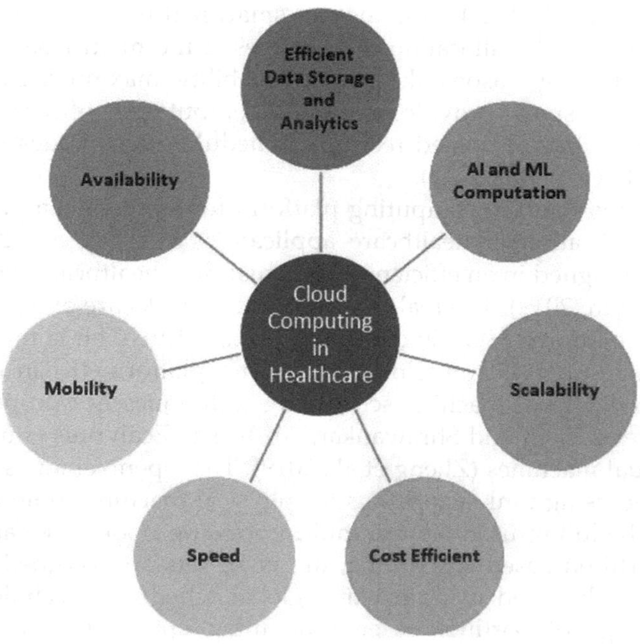

FIGURE 10.2
Benefits of Cloud computing in healthcare.

demand high computational requirement that can be efficiently addressed by using Cloud computing.

3. Scalability:
Cloud computing provides the feature of scalability for healthcare professionals to increase or decrease the requirement of Cloud storage and computation requirement. In the case of a pandemic like COVID-19, the demand of Cloud storage can be increased easily.
4. Cost Efficiency:
Cloud computing offers low-cost data storage and computational facility which helps the healthcare service provider by saving their money in purchasing and maintaining the huge computing and computational machines.
5. Speed:
Cloud computing provides fast access to huge healthcare data for the Cloud.
6. Mobility:
Cloud computing provides the facility's healthcare professionals access to patients' data from anywhere, from any device, which helps them to provide better treatment to their patients.
7. Availability:
Cloud computing service provider provides 24/7 service with an uptime of 99.9%, which helps healthcare practitioners access healthcare data anytime from the Cloud.

10.4 Cloud Computing in Healthcare Applications

Cloud computing in healthcare applications are described as follows.

10.4.1 Healthcare Data Management, Data Sharing, and Access in the Cloud

Cloud computing data storage services provide the real-time data storage and management services to the healthcare organization that help in efficient patient care management and monitoring. The patient data is available from anywhere, which will provide real-time access which helps the healthcare practitioner to manage the visit and reduce their daily hectic schedule. Cloud computing offers cost-efficient information management and access to the entire emergency care unit, ICU, testing labs, and nursing homes. Cloud computing provides real-time access of this healthcare information and will further improve the quality of healthcare services, increase the decision making, and create a faster response in case of emergency. In the healthcare service, the Cloud resources are categorized into three types such as compute Cloud, storage Cloud, and data Cloud. The compute Cloud is related to the hardware and software, such as a processor and operating system. The storage Cloud provide a huge database to store the patient data such as different healthcare reports and images that will be further used by other hospital and government organizations and medical research centers.

10.4.2 Preventive Medical Care Using Cloud Computing

Cloud-based preventive medical care is the new emerging application of Cloud computing in the healthcare sector in which IoT, wearable devices, and mobile devices send your health-related information on the Cloud; if there is any uncertain change in the health parameter then the real-time alert will be sent from the Cloud to persons, their relatives, doctors, and healthcare workers to take the corrective actions. Cloud-based preventive healthcare provides low-cost expert medical service to rural area people.

10.5 Issues and Challenges in Using Cloud Computing in Healthcare

Cloud computing provides various benefits in the healthcare section, but there are some issues and challenges that need to be addressed to provide more efficient Cloud service for healthcare. Some of the challenges are as follows and shown in Figure 10.3:

1. **HIPAA Compliance:** The HIPAA is the act related to the data protection and security of healthcare data. Giant Cloud providers may provide this HIPAA compliance, but it is very difficult for the smaller Cloud provider to follow this act.
2. **GDPR Compliance:** GDPR is another act for protecting personal information that may be followed by a major giant such as Microsoft but for a small Cloud provider it's very difficult to follow this act.
3. **Security and Privacy:** Cloud security is one of the challenges in using the Cloud for healthcare services. The Cloud stores sensitive data that may get hacked so more research is required in providing secure data storage. The privacy of patients' critical healthcare data must be ensured by the Cloud service providers.
4. **Portability:** Portability is one of the important issues in using Cloud computing in healthcare applications. It is very difficult to switch from one Cloud provider to another in case of performance issues. Moving healthcare data onto the Cloud also requires information about the Cloud data center.
5. **Ownership of Data:** Healthcare data can be easily stored and accessed using the Cloud, but to remove the data from the Cloud is not an easy task. Cloud service providers must ensure that the healthcare data must be easily removed from the Cloud storage when demanded by the healthcare organization.
6. **Reliability and Availability:** Cloud computing services for healthcare must be reliable and available 24/7. To ensure reliability and availability in Cloud computing is a challenge as in spite of redundancy, the Cloud faces the problem of outages.

10.6 Real-Time Virtual Machine Scheduling Framework of the Cloud Environment

Each virtual machine is mapped with a single CPU and then the tasks set are assigned to the virtual machine in such a way that the total utilization must be less or equal to one (Figure 10.4).

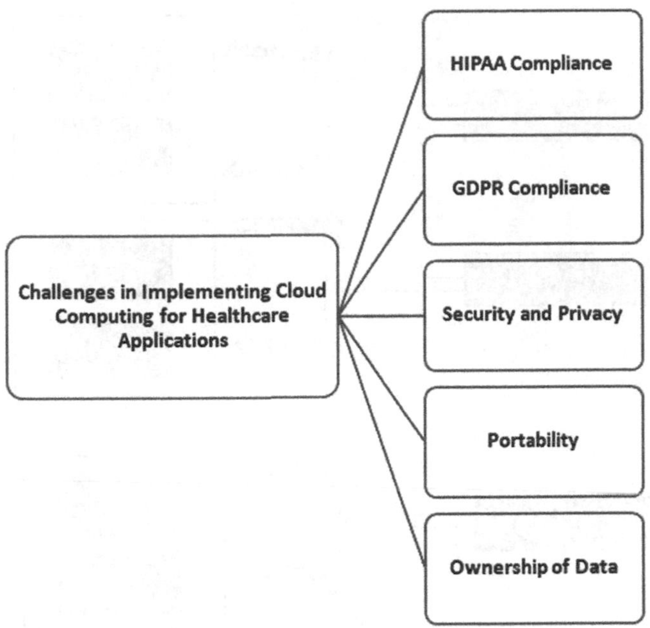

FIGURE 10.3
Cloud computing implementation challenges in healthcare.

Figure 10.4 shows the allocation of tasks using cluster-based real-time scheduling techniques. The tasks sets are divided into disjoint sets and assigned to clusters that consist of a set of virtual machines. Each cluster consists of two virtual machines and each virtual machine maps to one CPU. The tasks set assigned to clusters are allowed to migrate among the virtual machines of that cluster only. For example the tasks t1, t2, and t3 can migrate among the virtual machines vm1 and vm2 of cluster 1, which reduces the migration overheads of real-time tasks and solves problems of tasks assignment.

The cluster scheduling is divided into two steps.

Tasks Assignment: In this step, the tasks are assigned to clusters and group of virtual machines allocated to the cluster. The efficient tasks assignment techniques improve the Cloud resource utilization. The tasks assignment techniques can be static and dynamic. In static tasks assignments, the task workloads are assigned permanently to the cluster of virtual machines and never change. In dynamic tasks assignment, task workloads are assigned to clusters of virtual machines' runtime as it arises. The hard deadline task workloads are assigned using static tasks assignments. The dynamic tasks assignment techniques give efficient resource utilization techniques.

Tasks Scheduling: Once the task assignment is done, the order of execution of the tasks is decided using real-time scheduling. The real-time scheduling algorithm decides the order of execution of tasks on virtual machines of the cluster. The task scheduling on virtual machines is based on priority-based scheduling approach so that the hard deadline tasks must be complete to execute on time. The priority-based task scheduling is static and dynamic real-time scheduling. In the static priority real-time task scheduling, priority of the tasks is assigned statically and never changes, whereas in dynamic priority scheduling the scheduling decision is taken during runtime based on the current priority of the tasks.

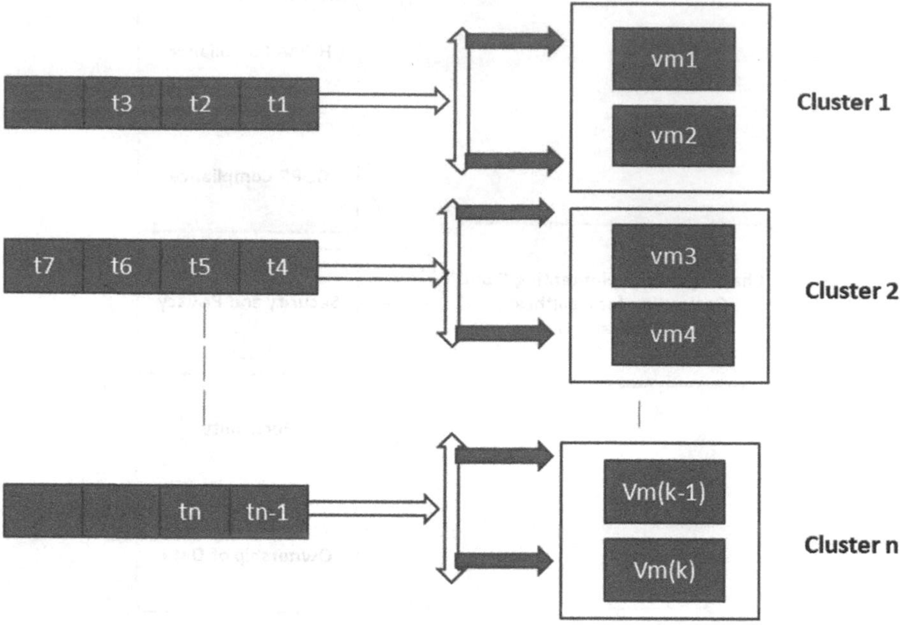

FIGURE 10.4
Task allocation using cluster scheduling.

10.6.1 Real-Time Healthcare Sensing and Actuation in the Cloud Environment

The different healthcare parameters are sensed using sensors such as ECGs, glucose meters, oximeters, temperatures, etc. The real-time scheduler running on a processing unit processes the sensory data in real time and decides the priority of data to be processed and transfers the information on the Cloud. The Cloud environments process the sensory data using high-performance computing of Cloud environments and in case of emergency situations that if any health parameter goes out of threshold value; in that case the real-time actuation is performed to ensure the timely action to save lives of patients. The machine learning tasks are performed on the patients' data to predict the probability of occurrence of any disease.

10.6.2 Real-Time Patients and Physician Interactions

The real-time patients and physician interactions are done using real-time communication in case of an emergency. If the patients or patient's relatives observed any abrupt changes in the patient's health, the patient's data is transferred and real-time alerts are generated in the Cloud to inform the physician to take corrective actions to save the life of the patient. Real-time communication ensures the quality of service in the communication. The real-time communication ensures the transmission of patients' data within the time frame so that the real-time response is achieved. The quality of service parameter ensures the parameters such as bandwidth, transmission delay, delay jitter, rate of loss, etc.

10.7 Case Study of Different Healthcare Cloud Providers

The different healthcare organizations use Cloud computing services and their case studies are as follows.

1. San Diego uses AWS to implement AI

The San Diego healthcare organization of U.S. researchers developed an image recognition model during the COVID-19 pandemic. This is a machine learning model that is used to detect pneumonia and acts as one of the major indicators to detect COVID cases. San Diego uses an AWS Cloud computing platform to execute the machine learning model on huge patient databases.

2. Cleveland Clinic and Rush University Healthcare Center uses Google Cloud's Apigee

The Cleveland Clinic uses Google Cloud Apigee for their healthcare service. Google Clouds Apigee is used to process a patient's electronic medical record. It provides a secure, scalable application programming interface to provide advanced analytics and machine learning–based predictive models. It gives detailed insights into a patient's electronic data, which helps to deliver improved healthcare service to the patient.

University Healthcare Center uses Google Cloud's Apigee to improve the patient's healthcare and experience. It is used to optimize the schedule, reduce wait time in the ICU, identify the increased cost, reduce readmission time, and for cyber security service.

3. SILVERLINE uses Salesforce Healthcare Cloud

SILVERLINE uses Salesforce Cloud service for customer relation management service for all their stackholders. Salesforce Cloud provides the healthcare Cloud CRM, which is used to build customer relationships, empower employees, and give patients correct information in real time. It provides an easy way to access information about patients and an entire history of the patient's health to the healthcare practitioner.

4. Northwest Community Healthcare Corp. uses IBM Watson Health Cloud

Northwest Community Healthcare Corp. uses IBM Watson Health Cloud for real-time, evidence-based decision making for healthcare-related problems. It helps the physicians, healthcare providers, insurers, and medical researchers to get more detailed information on people's health. It provides healthcare services such as accelerated improvement analytics of patients' data, clinical data analysis, empowers patients with efficient healthcare solutions, improves clinical care and workflow, and healthcare consultancy services.

5. GE Healthcare uses Microsoft Cloud

GE Healthcare uses Microsoft Cloud to manage their large-scale healthcare data, helps to improve patients' healthcare experience, increases operational efficiency, provides security and interoperability to healthcare data, and implements complex workflow mechanisms. Microsoft Cloud helps to combine the patient's data, clinical data, and operational data to predict the risk and improve the patient's health. It provides protection to healthcare data and privacy and security to manage patients and health-related data.

10.8 Conclusions

Real-time systems are now used in healthcare applications for the timely execution of healthcare tasks such as remote patient monitoring, remote surgery, etc. These tasks are executed on the devices that have limited recourse such as computation power and storage. The Cloud computing environment is used for efficient resource management and ensures real-time response for healthcare applications. This chapter presents the efficient resource utilization for smart healthcare applications on the Cloud environment. The cluster-based task allocation and scheduling techniques are developed to assign tasks to groups of virtual machines to increase system utilization and ensure execution of tasks within a deadline. The simulation result shows that the proposed real-time scheduling techniques improve system utilization and ensure task execution within the deadline on virtualized Cloud environments for smart healthcare applications. In the future, the proposed scheduling can be extended for synchronization and mixed criticality of task sets.

Acknowledgment

The authors want to acknowledge the support of Rajiv Gandhi Science and Technology Commission, Government of Maharashtra scheme for S&T Applications through University System at Rashtrasant Tukadoji Maharaj Nagpur University Nagpur (MH), INDIA RTMNU/IIL/RGSTC/P/2021/795.

References

Ajmera, Kashav and Tribhuwan Kumar Tewari. "Greening the Cloud Through Power-Aware Virtual Machine Allocation." *2018 Eleventh International Conference on Contemporary Computing (IC3)* (2018): 1–6.

Bertout, Antoine, Joel Goossens, Emmanuel Grolleau and Xavier Poczekajlo. "Workload Assignment for Global Real-time Scheduling on Unrelated Multicore Platforms." Proceedings of the *28th International Conference on Real-Time Networks and Systems* (2020).

Bhattacharya, Sukriti, Christian Braun and Ulrich Leopold. "A Tensor Based Framework for Large Scale Spatio-Temporal Raster Data Processing." *ISPRS - International Archives of the Photogrammetry, Remote Sensing and Spatial Information Sciences* (2019): 3–9.

Chen, Weiwei, Dong Wang and Keqin Li. "Multi-User Multi-Task Computation Offloading in Green Mobile Edge Cloud Computing." *IEEE Transactions on Services Computing* 12 (2019): 726–738.

Choi, Hyunjong, Hyoseung Kim and Qi Zhu. "Job-Class-Level Fixed Priority Scheduling of Weakly-Hard Real-Time Systems." *2019 IEEE Real-Time and Embedded Technology and Applications Symposium (RTAS)* (2019): 241–253.

Dhule, Chetan and Urmila Shrawankar. "POF-SVLM: Pareto Optimized Framework for Seamless VM Live Migration." *Computing* 102 (2020): 1–25.

Han, Jian-Jun, Xin Tao, Dakai Zhu, Hakan Aydin, Zili Shao and Laurence T. Yang. "Multicore Mixed-Criticality Systems: Partitioned Scheduling and Utilization Bound." *IEEE Transactions on Computer-Aided Design of Integrated Circuits and Systems* 37 (2018): 21–34.

Ibarz, Jean, Michale Lauer, Matthieu Roy, Jean-Charles Fabre and Olivier Flébus. "Optimizing Vehicle-to-Cloud Data Transfers using Soft Real-Time Scheduling Concepts." Proceedings of the *28th International Conference on Real-Time Networks and Systems* (2020): n. pag.

Jain, Suhani, Krishna Dhoot, Ajinkya Rede, Nandan Adeshara and Sunil Mhamane. "Optimization of Resources in Cloud Computing Using Virtual Machine Consolidation." *2019 International Conference on Smart Systems and Inventive Technology (ICSSIT)* (2019): 1285–1288.

Khan, Hamayun, M. Usman Hashmi, Irfan Ud. Din, Kashif Janjua, Akmal Sikandar, Muhammad Waqas Qazi and Zia Hameed. "An Efficient Scheduling Based Cloud Computing Technique Using Virtual Machine Resource Allocation for Efficient Resource Utilization of Servers." *2020 International Conference on Engineering and Emerging Technologies (ICEET)* (2020): 1–7.

Li, Xiang, Peter Garraghan, Xiaohong Jiang, Zhaohui Wu and Jie Xu. "Holistic Virtual Machine Scheduling in Cloud Datacenters towards Minimizing Total Energy." *IEEE Transactions on Parallel and Distributed Systems* 29 (2018): 1317–1331.

Mirobi, G. Justy and L. Arockiam. "Dynamic Virtual Machine Scheduling Approach for Minimizing the Response Time Using Distance Aware Virtual Machine Scheduler in Cloud Computing." *2019 International Conference on Smart Systems and Inventive Technology (ICSSIT)* (2019): 564–569.

Mubarakali, Azath. "Healthcare Services Monitoring in Cloud Using Secure and Robust Healthcare-Based BLOCKCHAIN (SRHB) Approach." *Mobile Networks and Applications* 25 (2020): 1–8.

Ning, Zhaolong, Xiangjie Kong, Feng Xia, W. Hou and Xiaojie Wang. "Green and Sustainable Cloud of Things: Enabling Collaborative Edge Computing." *IEEE Communications Magazine* 57 (2019): 72–78.

Rizk, Dalia, H. Hosny, El-Sayed El-Horbaty and A. Salem. "A Study on Cloud Computing Architectures for Smart Healthcare Services." *IDDM* 2753 (2020).

Silva, Wellington Francisco de, Roberta Spolon, Renata Spolon Lobato, Aleardo Manacero Júnior and Marcos Antônio Cavenaghi Humber. "Particle Swarm Algorithm Parameters Analysis for Scheduling Virtual Machines in Cloud Computing." *2020 15th Iberian Conference on Information Systems and Technologies (CISTI)* (2020): 1–6.

Stavrinides, Georgios L. and Helen Karatza. "An Energy-Efficient, QoS-aware and Cost-effective Scheduling Approach for Real-time Workflow Applications in Cloud Computing Systems Utilizing DVFS and Approximate Computations." *Future Gener. Comput. Syst.* 96 (2019): 216–226.

Taher, Nada Chendeb, Imane Mallat, N. Agoulmine and Nour El-Mawass. "An IoT-Cloud Based Solution for Real-Time and Batch Processing of Big Data: Application in Healthcare." *2019 3rd International Conference on Bio-engineering for Smart Technologies (BioSMART)* (2019): 1–8.

Talmale, Girish and Urmila Shrawankar. "Real Time on Bed Medical Services: A Technological Gift to the Society." *Bioscience Biotechnology Research Communications* 13 (2020): 133–137.

Xi, Sisu, Meng Xu, Chenyang Lu, Linh T. X. Phan, Christoper Gill, Oleg Sokolsky and Insup. Lee. "Real-time Multi-core Virtual Machine Scheduling in Xen." *2014 International Conference on Embedded Software (EMSOFT)* (2014): 1–10.

Zanjal, Samir V. and Girish R. Talmale. "Medicine Reminder and Monitoring System for Secure Health Using IOT." *Procedia Computer Science* 78 (2016): 471–476.

Zheng, Jianchao, Yueming Cai, Yuan Wu and Xuemin Shen. "Dynamic Computation Offloading for Mobile Cloud Computing: A Stochastic Game-Theoretic Approach." *IEEE Transactions on Mobile Computing* 18 (2019): 771–786.

11

Cloud Computing-Based Smart Healthcare System

Varsha Ratnaparkhe and Sumedha Borde
Government College of Engineering,
Aurangabad, Maharashtra, India

CONTENTS

11.1 Introduction

The electroencephalogram (EEG) signal shows the electrical activity of the human brain. EEG signals are extremely stochastic in nature, containing important information about the brain state. Various brain disorders can be detected by examining and processing EEG signals. Discriminative biomarkers can be identified. Based on these, a sleep disorder and alcoholic disorder brain pattern can be automatically detected. Different fractal dimension algorithms have been used in analyzing the EEG of cognitive and sleep disorder subjects.

DOI: 10.1201/9781003203926-11

The current scenario of the COVID-19 pandemic has a major effect on global healthcare and its associated fields. Tele-health management and remote monitoring systems in healthcare are most demanding nowadays. They include applications of electronically supported Information technology, microsystems, high levels of automation, personalized therapy, and artificial intelligence (AI)–based devices that are enabled with the Internet of Medical Things. Cloud computing has a bright potential. It can lead to new developments in diverse application domains. It provides a strong technical support for remote healthcare systems. Experts and medical researchers believe that Cloud computing technology can improve the level of healthcare services.

With this increasingly challenging pandemic situation, common people have fallen into depression. Depression is a common but serious mood disorder universally. There are millions of people suffering from depression worldwide. However, if the person has the symptoms for a minimum of two weeks, it is considered major. Various types of depressive disorders are diagnosed nowadays. The depression symptoms include change in sleep pattern, alcohol or drug abuse, fatigue, sluggishness, anxiety, irritability, etc., which sometimes may lead to suicide.

Generally sleep pattern and depression are linked. Insomnia, or sleep disorder, is one of the common signs of depression. The sleep and depression relationship is complex as both are interdependent and induce each other. The chance of people with depressive psychology to become alcoholic are more and they have a tendency to be suicidal or self-harm (Mahmoud et al., 2018). Chemistry of the brain is impacted due to alcohol and causes an increase in depression. Quality of also life worsens.

Healthcare systems, if applied in combination with Cloud computing, have a tremendous potential to improve the number of healthcare-related functions such as depression, post-hospitalization care, telemedicine and stroke detection, and fall detection. Virtual medication and immediate access causes improve these health-related conditions. Thus, Cloud computing is one of the most recent revolutionary technologies worldwide. These days many doctors and hospitals are moving towards these Cloud-based systems in order to provide better healthcare systems to their patients.

In the literature, with the outbreak of COVID-19, the life of each and every person is affecting globally. IoT-based hospital systems discussed by Uslu et al. (2020) can help to prevent the spread of the epidemic on a local and global level by avoiding physical contacts. On paper (Potluri et al., 2020), FOG computing is discussed, which is designed to support a distributed and decentralized computing platform by decreasing the burden on Cloud computing. A paper (Mahmoud et al., 2018) discusses the research heading towards the combination of Cloud computing and Internet of Things. Comparison and evaluation of various Cloud services offered by various Cloud service providers is done in Barton et al. (2017). A new technology called mobile Cloud computing for mobile web services is discussed in Hanen et al. (2016), which is now the heart of healthcare transformation and offers various new kinds of services and facilities for patients and caregivers. The study of Cloud computing–based smart, convenient, safe, and inexpensive healthcare system is discussed in Zhiquiang et al. (2015). Early-stage diagnosis of depression is very important and curable. Various EEG features are found by showing discrimination between alcoholic disorders, sleep disorders, and normal ones. Depression-level prediction is discussed in Mallikarjun and Suresh (2014). Features are extracted by calculating log power spectral density from the EEG bands of three different electrodes, namely C3, F3, and O1. These features are extracted from 16 healthy subjects and 92 pathological recordings by the authors. The obtained results are delivered to a neural network pattern recognition tool and ANFIS toolbox integrated in MATLAB to recognize alcoholic subjects from controls and sleep disorder subjects. Detection of alcoholism is done by mean synchronization and vertex strength of various 64 electrodes along with fractal dimension by Negar Ahmadi et al. (2017). In this paper, five features are extracted from two different groups; one is alcoholic subjects and the other is control subjects. EEG signals are broken down into five sub-frequency bands. Out of a total of 64 electrodes, most information-carrying electrodes are found by applying the principle component analysis (PCA). By investigating diverse features from respective frequency sub-bands, five classification features are preferred. The alcoholic subjects have weakened brain state synchronization. The synchronization of brain activity is reviewed by using a mean synchronization feature. Another feature, the vertex strength, is nothing but the sum of weights of links connected to the vertex. With these discriminated features, fractal dimension, energy, and entropy are also calculated in this paper. The study of detection of depression is intended to equate two EEG signal analysis methods: spectral asymmetry index (SASI) and HFD in Bachmann et al. (2013). The SASI method is a linear method based on the calculation of the spectral asymmetry of two EEG frequency bands as higher and lower than the alpha band and nonlinear Higuchi's fractal dimension method determines fractal dimension in time domains. It is reported that the HFD method gives good results. The database of EEG signals of 17 depressive subjects and 17 control subjects are used for implementation. A variety of algorithms is used in work reported in Esteller et al. (2001) for computation of fractal dimension. In this work Higuchi, Katz, and Petrosian's fractal dimension algorithms are used for both synthetic data and EEG data recorded throughout epileptic seizures. Synthetic data is produced by computer simulation, and it is used as a backup for test data sets of production or operational data for validation. The consequences of different window size, number of overlapping points, and signal-to-noise ratio are calculated for every method. This work reveals that selection of the fractal dimension algorithm is essential for particular applications.

In Kalauzi et al. (2012), FD of the signal is calculated from amplitude based in the FFT spectrum. Earlier signal FD was expressed as a fractal weighted average of FD values of its Fourier components. Due to non-linearity and non-stationary properties of an EEG signal, getting useful information by simply observing these signals is very difficult. Therefore, advanced signal processing techniques are used to extract important features for diagnosis of various diseases using advanced signal processing techniques. As per the work discussed in Puthankattil Subha et al. (2010), the effect of different consequences on an EEG signal and various signal processing methods are used to excerpt the hidden information from the signal. There are various techniques for non-linear dynamics, for example Lyapunov exponents, correlation dimension, Hurst exponent (H), different entropies, phase space, and recurrent plots.

Along with the Higuchi and Katz, in Paramnathan and Uthayakumar (2008), the size measure relationship (SMR) method is used to detect brain disorders by examining the behavior of EEG signals. In the medical field, the complexity measure of non-linear patterns like EEG signals is well executed by fractal dimension techniques. After evaluating the performance with two well-known algorithms, namely Higuchi and Katz, the authors found some problems in deciding the initial and final length of the scaling factors. A newly developed algorithm is based on the size measure relationship (SMR) method. The SMR algorithm detects brain disorders and discovers the impacted portions of the brain by examining the signals' behavior.

The algorithms for finding the FD of the EEG signals are originated by Higuchi (1988) and Katz (1988). These algorithms have a high time complexity with the maximum number of steps for comparisons. Besides the rest of non-linear methods, the fractal dimensions have been used in the analysis of EEG signal presenting non-stationary and transient features. From the analysis of electroencephalographic signals, HFD depends on the state of the brain and so it shifts due to various brain pathologies, like epileptic seizures, stages of sleep, and alcoholism (Klonowski, 2004). The important part of this work is introducing effective algorithms for FD calculations of an EEG signal with minimum complexity and less time. Higuchi's fractal dimension is a perfect method for analyzing fractal dimensions of biomedical signals (Accardo et al., 1997).

The analysis of magneto encephalogram (MEG) activity from 20 Alzheimer's disease (AD) subjects and 21 elderly control subjects using HFD is reported in Tim et al. (2004). The MEG is a record of magnetic fields, measured outside the head, and developed by electrical activity within the brain. The main aim of this work is to evaluate fractal dimensions for the assessment of a quiet stance center of pressure (COP). Using this analysis method, more information about control strategies used for postural stability can be gained for AD patients.

Santiago Fernandez Fraga et al. aimed to analyze an EEG database using Higuchi, Katz, and multiresolution box counting methods (MRBC), displaying the relationship between the fractal dimension methods and physiological condition of the brain event-related potentials. After comparing the results obtained by all the three methods, it is observed that the deviation of FD in Higuchi and MRBC is less, out of which Higuchi is considered as a good preference for BCI systems implementation (Fraga and Mondragon, 2017). Madhavi Rangswamy et al. examined the differences in beta (12–28 Hz) band power in the offspring of male alcoholics from majorly impacted alcoholic families in Rangaswamy et al. (2004). Here, authors have explored the gender difference in formulation of this potential risk marker for alcoholism. Two groups of closed eyes EEG of 171 high risk (HR) subjects who were offspring of male alcoholics and 204 low risk (LR) subjects with no family history of alcoholism were compared for absolute beta power in three bands: beta1 (12–16 Hz), beta2 (16–20 Hz), and beta3 (20–28 Hz). Their results suggest that increased EEG beta power can be believed as a probable indication of risk for developing alcoholism. Drowsiness is the form in which a person's attentiveness is contracted, becoming one of the important reasons of accidents. Catching such a state of the human brain is very important nowadays. For drowsiness detection in brainwaves, fractal dimension is calculated using three different methods *viz.* Higuchi, Katz, and Petrosian, along with the logarithm of energy, intrinsic dimension, and some statistical parameters like mean, standard deviation, and variance in Pavithra et al. (2014). The support vector machine (SVM) classifier is used for 15 normal and 15 drowsy subjects' EEG signals. The fractal dimension determines complexity and dimensionality of an EEG signal. At present, various FD algorithms are used for EEG signal analysis for cognitive disorders like epilepsy, sleep disorder, and alcoholic disorder (Goh et al., 2005).

From a number of non-linear algorithms, HFD is chosen as a main tool for diagnosis of epilepsy along with independent component analysis (ICA) and averaging filter at preprocessing step contributes convincing results in Khoa et al. (2012). In EEG signal processing, especially in HFD, noise is a severe problem. Therefore for pre-processing, a robust algorithm is chosen as an independent component analysis (ICA) and averaging filter to reduce noise.

Alcohol causes a wide scope of effects on the central nervous system. Frontal lobe changes in alcoholism were identified by using various types of databases. In this review, various effects are studied in detail (Moselhy et al., 2001). A mobile-based arrangement with wireless sensor technology is used to predict seizures automatically by using the information contained in EEG signals (Sareen et al., 2016).

FIGURE 11.1
Sierpinski triangle.

EEG is one of the very efficient tools for analyzing the brain dynamics. Therefore, it is most widely used to interpret the consequence of alcoholism on the brain and identify alcoholism from normal ones. To identify the risk of depression, it is endeavored to discriminate the subjects to be normal, alcoholic, or suffering a sleep disorder. The work is based on the EEG of the subjects. Brains behave like complex non-linear systems. Thus non-linear methods give more ideas than linear methods regarding EEG signal analysis. Proposed work is based on two methods of fractal dimensions: Higuchi and Katz, which are majorly used in biomedical signal processing and for analysis of pathological signals.

11.1.1 Fractal Dimension

A fractal is an unending pattern that repeats itself at various scales. This characteristic is called "self-similarity." A fractal is a formation of repetition of a simple process. Fractals are highly complex patterns. The fractals represented by the Sierpinski Triangle are shown in Figure 11.1, which is made by increasing the triangles repeatedly in a specific pattern.

A fractal dimension is a measure of self-similarity of the signals and its value is usually a non-integer and fractional number (Ahmadi et al., 2017). There are two approaches for FD calculation: time domain and phase space domain. In case of a time domain, FD of the original signal is directly calculated. Here the original signal is considered a geometric figure. Phase space domain calculates the FD of a signal in a state–space domain (Kalauzi et al., 2012). Considering signal as a geometric figure, the implementation of the time domain approach is discussed.

Geometric objects have a fractal dimension in the range of 1 to 2; for example, the famous Koch curve is qualified by the self-similarity property with a fractal dimension of 1.262 (Kalauzi et al., 2012). Their points are not lying on a one-dimensional curve or on a two-dimensional plane, but "somewhere in between." A more complex curve is one with a greater FD. This chapter projects the implementation of two methods for FD feature extraction as Higuchi's Fractal Dimension (HFD) and Katz's Fractal Dimension (KFD).

The main objective of this work is to prepare a Cloud-based smart healthcare system so as to help separate the sleep disorder subjects and normal subjects and the alcoholic

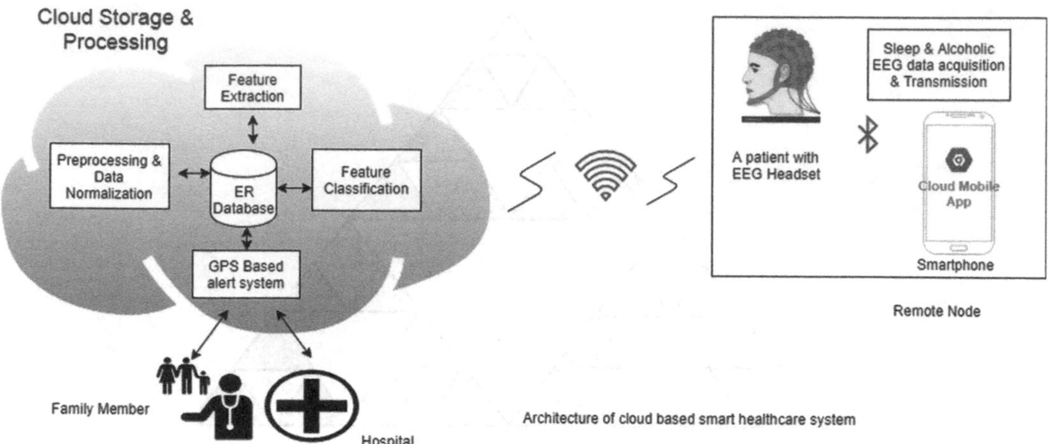

FIGURE 11.2
Architecture of Cloud-based smart healthcare system.

subjects and normal subjects based on fractal dimension calculation with minimum complexity and less time. The architecture of a Cloud-based smart healthcare system is shown in Figure 11.2. The real-time EEG data for sleep disorder and alcoholic disorder subjects can be uploaded on the hospital's Cloud. The Cloud-based smart healthcare system is trained with the preprocessing, normalization, feature extraction algorithms for finding various features that are given to the classifier automatically to detect whether the person is suffering from sleep disorder, alcoholic disorder, or is normal. Also, Cloud-based smart healthcare system is connected with GPS-based alert system.

11.2 Materials and Methods

11.2.1 EEG

An electroencephalogram (EEG) is a test used to measure the electrical activity in the human brain. To observe the brain signals, various electrodes are used. They are small metal discs attached with fragile wires (electrodes). They are located on the scalp, and then signals are given to the computer to show the results. Recognizable patterns are received to identify normal brain signals or seizures and other abnormal patterns. Medicos can diagnose based on these.

11.2.2 Data Set

The cyclic alternating pattern (CAP) is a periodic EEG activity appearing throughout non-rapid eye movement (NREM) sleep. It is described by cyclic sequences of cerebral activation (Phase A) followed by periods of deactivation (Phase B). Phase A period and following phase B period define a CAP cycle, and at least two CAP cycles are required to form a CAP sequence. For proposed work, the input signals of EEG are acquired from openly accessible databases. These CAP sleep signals for sleep disorder were found from physionet.org/physiobank/database. The CAP Sleep Database is a set of 108 polysomnographic transcriptions out of which for this work 21 subjects' data sets are considered.

Alcoholic and control subjects' signal data set of eight electrodes, sampled at 256 Hz (3.9-msec epoch) per second is taken for a total of 20 subjects, is received from http://kdd.ics.uci.edu/database (Mallikarjun and Suresh, 2014). It is an openly accessible database. Figure 11.3 shows a sample data set of sleep disorder, alcoholic disorder, and normal subjects. For measuring the EEG signals, a set of eight electrodes is located on the scalp, as shown in Figure 11.4. All of these electrodes are located as per the International 10–20 system. The data is collected from the electrodes FP2, FP1, F4, F3, C4, P4, AF8, and AF7. Table 11.1 shows various category-wise information of a data set.

The indicators of eight electrodes are shown in Table 11.2 as per the 10–20 electrode system. The samples are gathered from eight different channels with a sampling rate of 256 Hz. Data is normalized before applying for feature extraction. For pre-processing bandpass filter with a frequency band of 0–30 Hz is used.

For each subject, eight values of HFD and KFD are calculated for eight different electrodes' signals. In the following section, these algorithms are explained in brief.

11.2.3 Higuchi's Fractal Dimension Method

In 1988, Higuchi introduced this method to evaluate fractal dimension (Higuchi, 1988). This technique is considered the strongest of all the fractal dimension techniques and can be applied on a comparatively short section of data. It is based on length of the curve *L(k)*, which shows the time series by using a number of *k* samples, which is given in Equation 11.1 (Bachmann et al., 2013).

$$L(k) \sim k^{-FD} \tag{11.1}$$

With the help of following algorithm, the value of fractal dimension FD can be obtained.

Considering a time series, with regular interval: $X(1), X(2), X(3), \ldots X(N)$

Constructing a new time series, from this series, say X_k^m, written as:

$$X_k^m\text{: } X(m),\ X(m+k),\ X(m+2k), \ldots X\left(m + \left[\frac{N-m}{k}\right].k\right)(m = 1, 2, \ldots, k)$$

where m is initial time, k indicates interval time (delay), and the term in '[]' indicates integer part. For time interval equal to k we get k sets of new time series and N length of the signal.

For example, $k = 3$ and $N = 100$, three time series obtained as:

$$X_3^1;\ X(1),\ X(4),\ X(7), \ldots X(97),\ X(100),$$

$$X_3^2;\ X(2),\ X(5),\ X(8), \ldots X(98),$$

$$X_3^3;\ X(3),\ X(6), X(9), \ldots X(99).$$

Length of the curve X_k^m can be defined as shown in Equation 11.2 as:

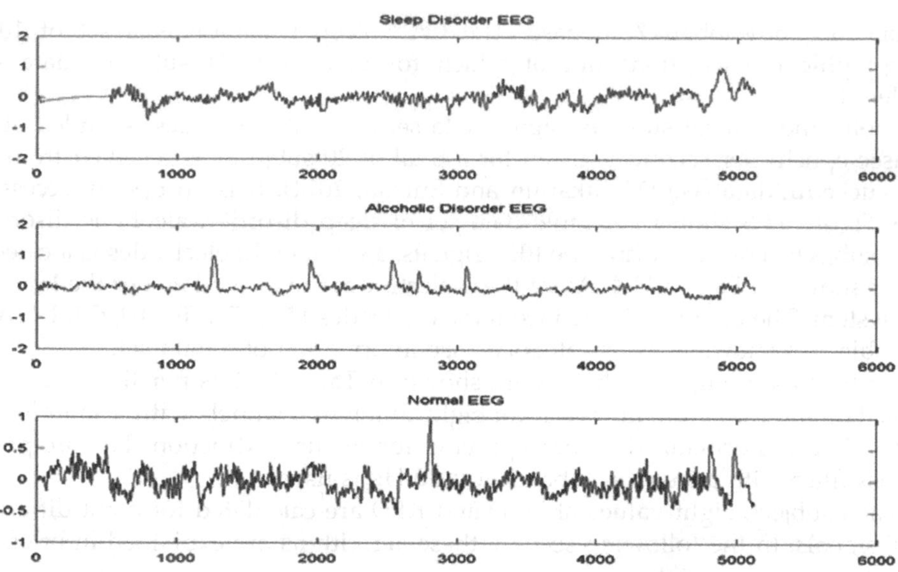

FIGURE 11.3
Sample data set of sleep disorder, alcoholic disorder, and normal subjects.

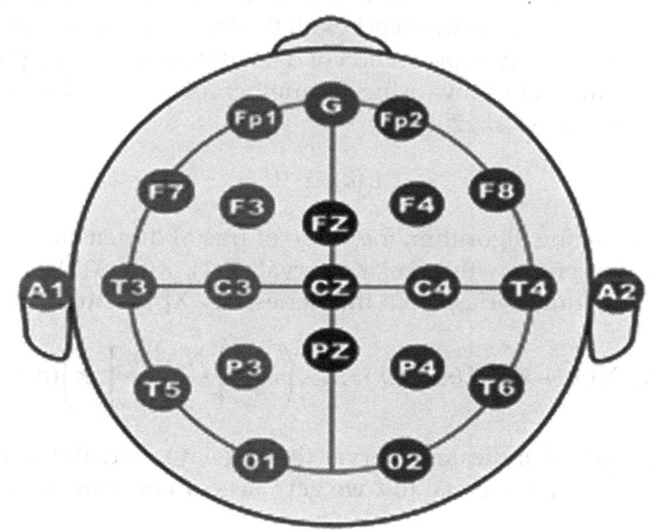

FIGURE 11.4
Placements of electrodes and labels in 10–20 system.

$$L_m(k) = \frac{\left\{\left(\sum_{i=1}^{\left[\frac{N-m}{k}\right]} |X(m+ik) - X(m+(i-1).k)|\right)\frac{N-1}{\left[\frac{N-m}{k}\right].k}\right\}}{k} \tag{11.2}$$

where N indicates total length of the sequence and X and $\frac{N-1}{\left[\frac{N-m}{k}\right].k}$ is a normalization factor.

TABLE 11.1

Category-Wise Information of Data Set

Sr. No.	Category	Subject Details	Electrodes
1	Sleep Disorder Subjects	12 Male 09Female Total = 21	FP2-F4, F4-C4, C4-P4, P4-O2, F8-T4, FP1-F3, F3-C3, F7-T3
2	Alcoholic Subjects	20	FP2-F4, F4-C4, C4-P4, P4-O2, F8-T4, FP1-F3, F3-C3, F7-T3
3	Normal Subjects	20	FP2-F4, F4-C4, C4-P4, P4-O2, F8-T4, FP1-F3, F3-C3, F7-T3

TABLE 11.2

The Indicators of Eight Electrodes

Position of electrode	Name of electrode
Left Temporal Lobe	FP1, AF7,O1
Right Temporal Lobe	FP2, AF8
Coronal Contour (T7-CZ-T8)	C3
Frontal Lobe	F3, F4

Now average value over k sets of $L_m(k)$ can be written as per Equation 11.3,

$$L(k) = \sum_{m=1}^{k} L_m(k) \tag{11.3}$$

The total average length for k sets, $L(k)$ is proportional to k^{-D}, where D is Higuchi's fractal dimension, i.e., $L(k)\ \alpha\ k^{-D}$, then the curve is fractal with the dimension D (Bachmann et al., 2013).

Selection of the value of K_{max} depends on the value of HFD and signal length N. Here, $L(k)$ is plotted against $(1/k)$ on a double logarithmic scale. By plotting the points with k =1,2, …, K_{max}, a straight line is obtained with a slope as FD of X. In this way, HFD is nothing but the slope of a line that fits the pair of points $\{\ln[L(k)],\ln(1/k)\}$. For the perfect value of K_{max}, HFD values are plotted against K_{max} values. The point where the FD becomes stable is considered as a saturation point and the same value of K_{max} can be chosen. In our case, K_{max} = 10 is considered (Klonowski, 2004; Accardo et al., 1997; Tim et al., 2004; Gomez et al., 2009).

11.2.4 Katz's Fractal Dimension Method

Calculation of Katz's fractal dimension is directly from the original signal (Katz, 1988).

The fractal dimension (FD) of a curve can be specified as indicated in Equation 11.4,

$$D = \frac{log(L)}{log(d)} \tag{11.4}$$

where L indicates the total length of the EEG signal and d is the Euclidean distance between the first point in the series and the point that provides the farthest distance from the first point.

In Equation 11.4, D is a Hausdorff dimension and taking utmost distance, d, the algorithm uses maximum enlargement for FD calculation. Fractal dimensions calculated by this method are dependent on the units of measurement used. To solve this problem, Katz algorithm intended normalization as stated in Equation 11.5 as Goh et al. (2005).

$$FD = \frac{\log(L/a)}{\log(d/a)} \tag{11.5}$$

where a indicates the average number of steps in the series.

Considering, $n = L/a$ and Equation (11.5) can be written as,

$$FD = \frac{log\,(n)}{\log(d/l) + \log(n)} \tag{11.6}$$

Equation 11.6 resumes Katz's approach to compute the FD of a waveform.

11.2.5 Classifier

From the total data set, 70% of the data set is used for training and the remaining 30% of the data set is used for testing. In proposed work, in one case a database of sleep disorders and normal subjects is used, whereas in another case a database of alcoholic and normal subjects is used. In classification, class labels are assigned to each sample. Classification can be achieved by defining the discriminant function and partitioning the feature. Depending upon the nature of discriminant function, there are two types of classifiers: linear and non-linear. Linear classifiers classify data into labels based on a linear combination of input features. Therefore, these classifiers separate data using a line or plane or a hyperplane. They can only be used to classify data that is linearly separable. There are various linear classifiers like minimum distance, support vector machine, and logistic regression; a normal density-based linear classifier is called a linear discriminant classifier (LDC). A support vector machine selects the weight vector that best minimizes hinge loss in the presence of regularization. Hard margin SVM assumes strictly separable data while soft margin SVM assumes almost linearly separable data. A logistic regression algorithm assumed that data set is linearly separable. Logistic regression has a strong geometric basis. To reduce the effect of outliers, it uses a sigmoid function for squashing. In nonlinear classifiers like KNN, decision tree, multilayer perceptron, random forest, and quadratic discriminant classifier (QDC), class boundaries that cannot be separated well with linear hyperplanes then these non-linear classifiers perform well. K Nearest Neighbors (KNN) is a distance-based algorithm that needs scaled features. KNN finds out the k nearest neighbors of a query point and does the majority vote to decide the final class label. In a decision tree, a selection of features for building a tree is done based on information gain. Features with the highest information gain are placed at a higher position in the tree. LDC is preferred for its robustness and accuracy. QDC uses quadratic decision surface to separate measurements of two or more classes. In this paper, LDC and QDC are used for classification. To measure the performance of the features, accuracy is the evaluation parameter used.

11.2.6 Cloud Platform

Currently, the most promising services for the Cloud platform are Microsoft Azure, Google GAE, Amazon EC2, Ali Cloud, and Baidu Cloud (Zhiquiang et al., 2015). Here, Ali Cloud platform can be selected as the dependence of medical Cloud platform for forming a remote healthcare system. In this platform, users can purchase Cloud service as per the requirement of the business. Users can configure the server, publish websites, and use other remote applications.

11.2.7 Data Access Interface

Healthcare data generated by a healthcare system requires persistent storage in the Cloud. It also needs input data manipulation, data querying, updating, and deleting. Currently, mobile device operating systems are Android and iOS. The application development done on these systems cannot be directly accessed by the Ali RDS database. Web service technology based database operations can be done to solve the problem. As web service technology is explored using conventional standards like XML and HTTP, cross-platform data communication is possible.

11.2.8 Client Development

a. Web Client Development: Rich Internet Applications (RIA) is a recent network application. It has very good interface functions to deploy rapidly and widely used features of web applications.
b. Mobile Client Development: Various parameters can be measured with the help of a mobile phone, but existing smartphone measuring instruments have stand-alone applications. Physiological signals like EEG or ECG, oxygen, and temperature each need software and data acquisition hardware. Nowadays, mobile physiological signal measuring systems are developed with virtual instrument browser technology (Zhiquiang et al., 2015).

11.3 Results

11.3.1 HFD Method

Average values of HFD for a group of alcoholic subjects and normal subjects in various EEG channels are presented in Figure 11.5 and average values of HFD for a group of sleep disorder and normal subjects in various EEG channels are presented in Figure 11.6.

The increase in HFD with alcoholic disorder is observable in all EEG channels from Figure 11.5 and decrease in HFD values with sleep disorder except in channels FP2 and F4 is evident from Figure 11.6. Various values of HFD parameters calculated are represented in Table 11.3 and Table 11.4. The average value for all EEG channels for depression with alcoholic disorder (1.156) is higher than the value obtained in normal subjects (1.145). The increase in HFD value with depression with alcoholic disorder is 1.1%. Similarly, the average value for all EEG channels for depression with sleep disorder

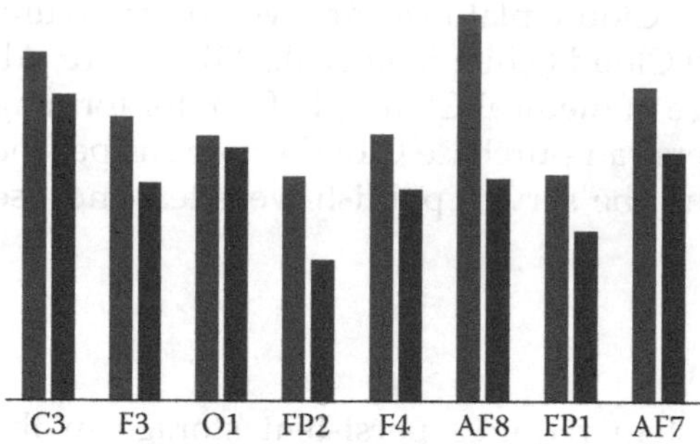

FIGURE 11.5
Average HFD values of alcoholic and normal subjects in various EEG channels.

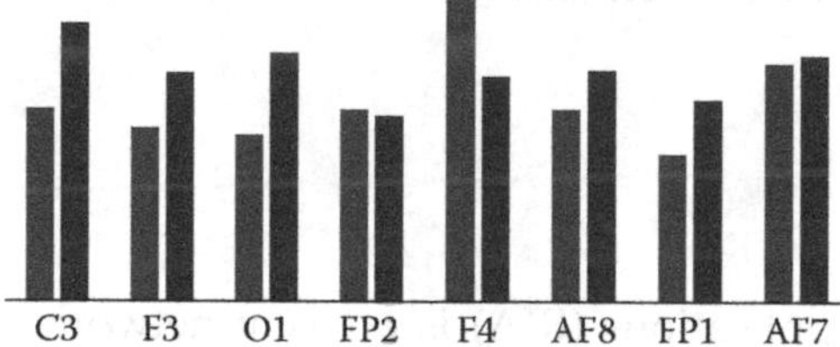

FIGURE 11.6
Average HFD values of sleep disorder and normal subjects in various EEG channels.

TABLE 11.3
Average Values of HFD Calculated for Alcoholic and Normal Subjects

FD EEG Channel	HFD Values Alcoholic	HFD Values Normal
C3	1.165	1.158
F3	1.155	1.144
O1	1.152	1.150
FP2	1.145	1.132
F4	1.152	1.143
AF8	1.171	1.145
FP1	1.146	1.137
AF7	1.160	1.149

(1.137) is lower than the value obtained in normal subjects (1.145). The decrease in HFD value with depression with sleep disorder is 0.8%. However, the style of increase with depression with alcoholic disorder and decrease with sleep disorder effects is a statistically important difference between depressive and normal groups in particularly frontal channels.

The measure of complexity of EEG signals is possible with values of HFD (Tim et al., 2004). Analysis of fractal dimension also has been used in many affairs in biomedical signal processing (Rangaswamy et al., 2004; Harne, 2014; Garner et al., 2018; Pavithra, 2014).

TABLE 11.4
Average Values of HFD Calculated for Sleep Disorder and Normal Subjects

FD EEG Channel	HFD Values Sleep Disorder	HFD Values Normal
C3	1.134	1.158
F3	1.129	1.144
O1	1.127	1.150
FP2	1.134	1.132
F4	1.166	1.143
AF8	1.134	1.145
FP1	1.121	1.137
AF7	1.147	1.149

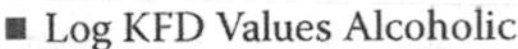

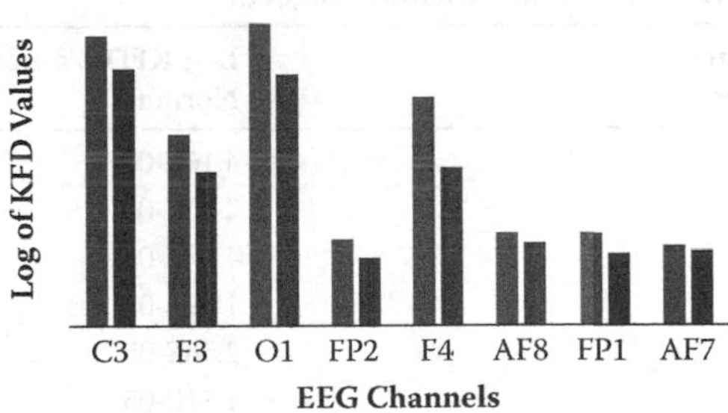

FIGURE 11.7
Average of log of KFD values for alcoholic and normal subjects.

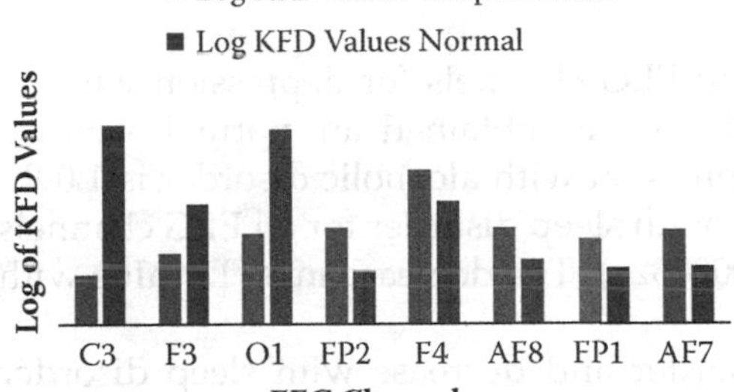

FIGURE 11.8
Average of log of KFD values for sleep disorder and normal subjects.

11.3.2 KFD Method

A log of KFD values averaged over a group of alcoholic subjects and normal subjects in various EEG channels is presented in Figure 11.7 and a log of KFD values averaged over a group of sleep disorder and normal subjects in various EEG channels is presented in Figure 11.8.

The increase of KFD with alcoholic disorder and sleep disorder is evident in all EEG channels from Figure 11.7 and Figure 11.8 except in channels C3, F3, and O1 in a sleep disorder case. Various numerical values of calculated KFD parameters are shown in

TABLE 11.5

Calculated Average of Log of KFD Values for Alcoholic and Normal Subjects

FD EEG Channel	Log KFD Values Alcoholic	Log KFD Values Normal
C3	4.70E-05	4.16E-05
F3	3.10E-05	2.50E-05
O1	4.90E-05	4.07E-05
FP2	1.40E-05	1.10E-05
F4	3.70E-05	2.56E-05
AF8	1.50E-05	1.34E-05
FP1	1.50E-05	1.17E-05
AF7	1.30E-05	1.21E-05

TABLE 11.6

Calculated Average of Log of KFD Values for Sleep Disorder and Normal Subjects

FD EEG Channel	Log KFD Values Sleep Disorder	Log KFD Values Normal
C3	1.03E-05	4.16E-05
F3	1.47E-05	2.50E-05
O1	1.89E-05	4.07E-05
FP2	2.01E-05	1.09E-05
F4	3.21E-05	2.56E-05
AF8	1.99E-05	1.34E-05
FP1	1.76E-05	1.17E-05
AF7	1.97E-05	1.21E-05

Table 11.5 and Table 11.6. Average values for all EEG channels for depression with alcoholic disorder (1.000063) is higher than the value obtained in normal subjects (1.0000521). The increase in KFD value with depression with alcoholic disorder is 1.09E-05%. Similarly, the averaged value of depression with sleep disorder for all EEG channels (1.0000442) is lower than in normal subjects (1.0000521). The decrease in KFD value with depression with sleep disorder is 7.9E-04%.

An increase in depression with alcoholic disorder and decrease with sleep disorder effects is a statistically important deviation between depressive and normal groups in frontal electrodes.

11.4 Discussion

The signals included for this work are from eight different electrodes as, C3, F3, O1, FP2, F4, AF8, FP1, and AF7. The healthy subjects considered for the analysis did not exhibit any neurological disorders. The pathological cases include 19 recordings of subjects

TABLE 11.7

Accuracy for LDC and QDC for Various Combinations

	Accuracy (HFD) %		Accuracy (KFD) %	
Specification	**LDC**	**QDC**	**LDC**	**QDC**
Sleep disorder and normal subject	90	68.18	80	70.77
Alcoholic disorder and normal subject	62	52.85	45	51.67
Sleep disorder and alcoholic disorder	90	68.18	88	65.45
Three-class classification	57.33	41.81	66.67	62.45

TABLE 11.8

Comparative Study for Computational Time Required for Classifiers

	LDC	QDC
Classification Time (Seconds)	2.0353	0.4755

diagnosed with NFLE (nocturnal frontal lobe epilepsy) and with bruxism. The 20 recordings are of alcoholic subjects.

Tables 11.3 and 11.4 are the result of HFD values for alcoholic disorder and sleep disorder with control subjects, respectively. Similarly, Tables 11.5 and 11.6 are the result of KFD values for alcoholic disorder and sleep disorder with control subjects, respectively. The results obtained from these are applied to LDC and QDC classifiers to classify the subjects with various disorders.

The results exhibited in Figures 11.5–11.8 and also in Tables 11.3–11.6 prove that both EEG analysis methods HFD and KFD, evidently distinguish particular depression characteristics in EEG signals. Both methods presented the best effects in frontal EEG electrodes. Both the values, HFD and KFD, show an increase in depression.

HFD indicates a 1.1% increase in alcoholics, whereas a 0.8% increase in sleep disorder and KFD indicates a 1.09E-05% increase in alcoholics and a 7.9E-04% decrease in sleep disorder. In spite of a relatively minor increase of HFD and KFD values, the changes are statistically important in frontal EEG electrodes.

In both methods, HFD and KFD for alcoholic disorder and normal subjects, there is a clear distinction of depressive subjects for all the channels, whereas for sleep disorder and normal subjects, distinction is clear except in C3, F3, and O1 channels. All the changes observed in both the methods and for both combinations are found in the frontal lobe effectively. The frontal lobe is densely connected to different cortical and subcortical areas of the brain. From neuropsychological studies, a specific loss in alcoholism suggests frontal lobe dysfunction (Goh et al., 2005).

From Table 11.7, the fractal dimension results obtained with an EEG show that the HFD values are most accurate and consistent than KFD. Accuracy in the case of sleep disorder subjects and normal subjects for HFD is 90% and that of KFD is 80% with LDC classifier, whereas for alcoholic and normal subjects it gives 62% in HFD and 51.67% in KFD. Percentage accuracy obtained for sleep disorder and alcoholic disorder is 90% with HFD and 88% with KFD using LDC. Percentage accuracy with three class classifiers is less for both HFD and KFD. Accuracy for sleep disorder and control subjects is found to be 88.32% for the same data set with a PSD calculation using the Welch method and with an ANFIS neural network classifier in (Mallikarjun and Suresh, 2014). Similarly by using the same features and classifier, the accuracy for alcoholic and normal subjects is 91.7%. For drowsiness detection in Pavithra et al. (2014), the accuracy for 15 alert and 15 drowsy signals is 80% using the SVM classifier. In Bachmann et al. (2013), HFD offered a detection rate of 94% in the depressive group and 76% in the control group. From Table 11.7 it is observed that results are improved in the case of HFD and KFD in proposed work due to EEG data taken from eight electrodes with 5,120 samples per electrode.

In Table 11.8, comparative study for computational time required for classifiers is shown. Computational time for QDC is less compared to LDC, but accuracy in the case of LDC is better. Hence, LDC is computationally more efficient than QDC in this work.

Higuchi's method gives a more accurate estimation of FD of a signal. With reference to Esteller et al. (2001), KFD requires a maximum number of floating point operations (flops), approximately twice the flops of Higuchi. However, it is computationally faster for small data samples. For a record of 2,000 points or more, the run times for Katz and Higuchi are the same. For 8,000 data points, Higuchi's performance improves and becomes only 13% slower than the fastest Petrosian's algorithm.

Similar alterations in HFD and KFD values can be caused due to other brain disorders also. Hence, interdisorder discrimination is hard in HFD and KFD methods. A selection of fractal dimension algorithm is necessary for a particular operation.

Three-class classification gives less accuracy. The limitation of both methods is a more complex distinction between sleep, alcoholic, and normal subjects due to a comparatively small difference in HFD and KFD values. Thus, fractal dimension analysis gives additional information compared with conventional spectral measures, which gives rise to identify different physiological states by directly examining the EEG.

There is a solid connection between sleep and depression. More than 70% of depressed patients have symptoms of insomnia. The symptoms cause enormous suffering, with a great impact on the quality of life. Nocturnal frontal lobe epilepsy (NFLE) has been depicted as a distinguishable symptom of sleep-related disturbances. NFLE seizures predominate in males. Bruxism is a consideration in which a person grinds or clenches teeth at night, which is called sleep bruxism. Regular dental care helps to know the signs and symptoms of bruxism (Mallikarjun and Suresh, 2014). In alcoholism, we found that anyone who feels depressed can think of drinking or drinking too much feels depressed.

11.5 Conclusion

With this algorithmic approach, perfectly implemented on the Cloud, a ready reference for suggestive diagnosis can be helpful for medicos. Cloud-based systems can flourish as practices grow. Technology infrastructure and medical devices are expensive to deploy in the healthcare industries. With more timely and relevant data, the healthcare industry can make remarkable improvement in patients' care. However, one can't totally rely on such automatic diagnostic systems, as patient's clinical examination, test reports, and medical expertise are the key markers for perfect diagnosis.

In both the methods HFD and KFD, differentiation of depressive features in eight different channels of EEG is observed and can be classified from control groups. Being simple, both of the methods have fast algorithms for calculations. In this study, it is noticed that fractal analysis allows the easy identification of two different situations. In the first case, FD values for depressive subjects with an alcoholic disorder are higher than in control subjects.

In the second case, FD values for depressive subjects with sleep disorder are lower than in control subjects with some exceptions. From proposed work, neuronal dysfunction in depressive subjects is affiliated with increased dimensional complexity in EEG signals.

Brain dynamic examinations by EEG signal analysis and calculating fractal dimension of brain signals are applied to identify various brain disorders. The proposed methods in this paper are simple and fast to calculate.

11.6 Future Scope

Sleep disorder and alcoholism are miscellaneous problems and hence forecasting of both plays a very important role to prevent it. Therefore, further results of both the techniques on independent and greater databases are needed to be done. In the future plan, interfacing of real-time EEG signals from wearable EEG caps can be done with the Cloud of Things (CoT) technology. For perfect detection, machine learning and deep learning classification algorithms are implemented. For these types of implementations, data from a number of electrodes will give better results.

References

Accardo, A., M. Affinito, M. Carrozzi and F. Bouquet. "Use of the Fractal Dimension for the Analysis of Electroencephalographic Time Series." *Biological Cybernetics* 77 (1997): 339–350. 10.1007/s004220050394.

Ahmadi, Negar, Yulong Pei and Mykola Pechenizkiy. "Detection of Alcoholism Based on EEG Signals and Functional Brain Network Features Extraction." *IEEE 30th International Symposium on Computer Based Medical Systems* (2017): 2372–9198/17. 10.1109/CBMS.2017.46.

Bachmann, Maie, Jaanus Lass, Anna Suhhova and Hiie Hinrikus. "Spectral Asymmetry and Higuchi's Fractal Dimension Measures of Depression Electroencephalogram." *Hindawi Publishing Corporation, Computational and Mathematical Methods in Medicine* 2013 (2013), Article ID251638, 8 pages. 10.1155/2013/251638.

Barton, John, Frank Chin, et al. Impact of Cloud Computing on Healthcare Version 2.0. Cloud Standards Customer Council (2017).

Esteller, Rosana, George Vachtsevanos, Javier Echauz, Brian Litt. "A Comparison of Waveform Fractal Dimension Algorithm." *IEEE Transactions on Circuits And Systems-I: Fundamental Theory And Applications* 48, no. 2 (2001). 10.1109/81.904882.

Fraga, Santiago Fernandez and Jaime Rangel Mondragon. "Comparison of Higuchi, Katz and Multiresolution Box-Counting Fractal Dimension Algorithms for EEG Waveform Signal Based on Event Related Potentials." *Revista EIA, ISSN 1794-1237* Jan-Jun 2017 (2017): 73–83. DOI: 10.24050/reia.v14i27.864.

Garner, David M., Naiara Maria de Souza and Luiz Carlos M. Vanderlei. "Heart Rate Variability Analysis: Higuchi and Katz's Fractal Dimensions in Subjects with Type 1 Diabetes Mellitus." *Romanian Journal of Diabetes Nutrition & Metabolic Diseases* 25, no. 3 (2018): 289–295. 10.2478/rjdnmd-2018-0034.

Goh, Cindy, Brahim Hamadicharef, Goeff T. Henderson and Emmanuel C. Ifeachor. "Comparison of Fractal Dimension Algorithms for The Computation Of EEG Biomarkers For Dementia". *CIMED2005 Proceedings* ISBN:O-86341-520-2@2005 IEE (2005).

Goldberger, Ary L., Luis A. Nunes Amaral, Leon Glass, Jeffrey M. Hausdorff, Plamen Ch. Ivanov, Roger G. Mark, George B. Moody, Joseph E. Mietus, Chung-Kang Peng and H. Eugene Stanley "PhysioBank, PhysioToolkit, and PhysioNet: Components of a New Research Resource for Complex Physiologic Signals." *Circulation [Online]* 101 (23) (2000): e215–e220.

Gomez, Carlos, Angela Mediavilla, Roberto Hornero, et al. "Use of Higuchi's Fractal Dimension for the Analysis of MEG Recording from Alzheimer's Disease Patients." *Medical Engineering & Physics* 31 (2009): 306–313. DOI: 10.1016/j.medengphy.2008.06.010.

Hanen, Jemal, Zied Kechaou and Mounir Ben Ayed. "An Enhanced Healthcare System in Mobile Cloud Computing Environment."*Vietnam Journal of Computer Science* 3 (2016): 267–277. 10. 1007/s40595-016-0076-y.

Harne, Bhavana P. "Higuchi Fractal Dimension Analysis of EEG Signal Before and After OM Chanting to Observe Overall Effect on Brain." *International Journal of Electrical & Computer Engineering* 4, no. 4 (2014): 585–592 10.11591/ijece.v4i4.5800.

Higuchi, T. "Approach to an Irregular Time Series on the Basis of the Fractal Theory." *Physica D* 31, no. 2 (1988): 277–283. 10.1016/0167-2789(88)90081-4.

Kalauzi, Aleksander, Tijana Bojic and Aleksandra Vuckovic. "Modeling the Relationship Between Higuchi's Bractal Dimension and Fourier Spectra of Physiological Signals." *International Federation for Medical and Biological Engineering Springer* 50 (2012): 689–699. 10.1007/s11517-012-0913-9.

Katz, M. "Fractals and the Analysis of Waveforms." *Computers in Biology & Medicine* 18, no. 3 (1988): 145–156. 10.1016/0010-4825(88)90041-8.

Khoa,Truong Quang Dang, Vo Quang Ha and Vo Van Toi. "Higuchi Fractal Properties of Onset Epilepsy Electroencephalogram." *Computational and Mathematical Methods in Medicine Hindawi Publishing Corporation* 2012 (2012) Article ID461426, 6, 2012. 10.1155/2012/461426.

Klonowski, W., E. Olejarczyk and R. Stepien. "Epileptic Seizures in Economic Organism." *Physica A* 342 (2004): 701–707 *ELSEVIER*. 10.1016/j.physa.2004.05.045.

Mahmoud, Mukhtar Mohamed Edris, Joel J. P. Rodrigues, et al. "Enabling Technologies on Cloud of Things for Smart Healthcare." *IEEE Access, Special Section on Cyber Threats and Countermeasures in the Healthcare Sector*(2018). DOI: 10.1109/ACCESS.2018.2845399.

Mallikarjun, H. M. and H. N. Suresh. "Depression Level Prediction Using EEG Signal Processing." *International Conference on Contemporary Computing & Informatics (IC3I)* (2014): 978-1-4799-6629-5/14. 10.1109/IC3I.2014.7019674.

Moselhy, Hamdy F., George Georgiou and Ashraf Khan. "Frontal Lobe Changes in Alcoholism: A Review of the Literature." *Alcohol & Alcoholism* 36, no. 5 (2001): 357–368. 10.1093/alcalc/36.5.357.

Paramnathan, P. and R. Uthayakumar. "Application of Fractal Theory in Analysis of Human Electroencephalographic Signals." *Elsevier, Computers in Biology and Medicine* 38 (2008): 372–378. 10.1016/j.compbiomed.2007.12.004.

Pavithra, M., B. NiranjanKrupa, Arun Sasidharan and Bindu M. Kutty. "Fractal Dimension for Drowsiness Detection in Brainwaves." *IEEE International Conference on Contemporary Computing and Informatics (IC3I)* (2014), 978-1-4799-6629-5. 10.1109/IC3I.2014.7019676.

Potluri, Sirisha, Achyuth Sarkar, Elham Tahsin Yasin and Sachi Nandan Mohanty . "IOT Enabled Cloud Based Healthcare System Using FOG Computing: A Case Study." *Journal of Critical Reviews* 7, no. 6 (2020). 10.31838/jcr.07.06.186.

Puthankattil Subha, Dharmapalan, Paul K. Joseph, U. Rajendra Acharya, Choo Min Lim. "EEG Signal Analysis: A Survey." *Springer Science + Business Media Journal of Medical Systems* 34 (2010): 195–212. Dec 2008. DOI 10.1007/s10916-008-9231-z.

Rangaswamy, Madhavi, Bernice Porjesz, et al. "Resting EEG in Offspring of Male Alcoholics: Beta Frequencies." *International Journal of Psychophysiology Elsevier* 51 (2004): 239–251. 10.1016/j.ijpsycho.2003.09.003.

Sareen, Sanjay, Sandeep K. Sood and Sunil Kumar Gupta. "An Automatic Prediction of Epileptic Seizures Using Cloud Computing and Wireless Sensor Networks." *Springer Journal of Medical Systems* 40 (2016): 226 10.1007/s10916-016-0579-1.

Tim, L. A., Doyle, Eric L. Dugan, Brendan Humphries and Robert U. Newton. "Discriminating Between Elderly and Young Using a Fractal Dimension Analysis of Centre of Pressure." *International Journal of Medical Sciences* 1, no. 1 (2004): 11–20. DOI: 10.7150/ijms.1.11.

Uslu, Banu Calis, Ertug Okay and Erkan Dursun. "Analysis of Factors Affecting IoT-Based Smart Hospital Design." *Journal of Cloud Computing: Advances, Systems and Applications* 9 (2020): 67. 10.1186/s13677-020-00215-5.

Zhiquiang, Gao, He Lingsong, Tian Hang and Ling Cong. "A Cloud Based Mobile Healthcare Service System." *IEEE* 3rd*ICSIMA Malaysia* (2015), 978-1-4673-7255-8/15 (C) 2015 IEEE. DOI: 10.1109/ICSIMA.2015.7559009.

12

Rehearsal of Cloud and IoT Devices in the Healthcare System

Bhargavi S. Chinchmalatpure
Bharatiya Mahavidyalaya, Amravati, India

CONTENTS

DOI: 10.1201/9781003203926-12

12.1 Introduction

Cloud computing is quickly becoming a necessity in the medical field. It helps to share real-time patient health information to medical providers in urgent cases. For this purpose, the Cloud concept is used. For example, a feasible Cloud strategy for a healthcare facility could be using a public Cloud infrastructure to allow public access to generic health information or retrieve medical resources. The public Cloud is also used by hospitals and health clinics for remote storage of their own medical data (Luarasi et al., 2013). On the contrary, a private Cloud could be implemented to connect healthcare providers to securely transfer electronic documents and share health information about patients. Figure 12.1 shows the basic workings of a Cloud-based healthcare system.

Microsoft Cloud for Healthcare brings together trusted capabilities to customers and partners that enhances patient engagement, empowers health team collaboration, and improves clinical and operational data insights to improve decision making and operational efficiencies (Dawoud and Turgay Altilar, 2017). Microsoft Cloud for Healthcare

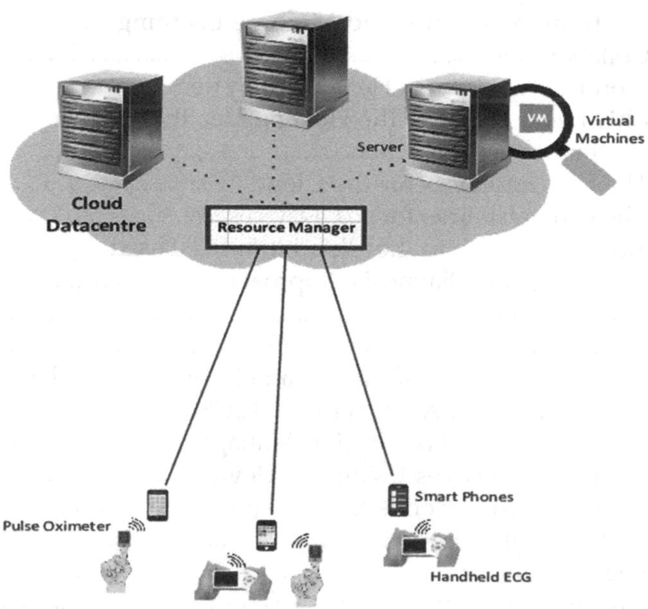

FIGURE 12.1
Vital healthcare system (Dawoud and Turgay Altilar, 2017).

makes it faster and easier to provide more efficient care and help ensure the end-to-end security, compliance, and interoperability of health data.

Although there are risks to data security for private Clouds, certain preventative measures such as utilizing a virtual private network (VPN), can be taken to address possible security threats when one has remote access into the Cloud. A secure, private Cloud environment using policy-based control of computing resources is a solution for Cloud consumers to avoid serious vulnerabilities (Lakshmanachari et al., 2017). However, it still requires specific requirements to only allow authorized personnel to have access to the data either hosted internally or externally.

IoT is a promising field that is revolutionizing the society by integrating the advances in wireless networking with miniaturized micro and nano sensors, devices, actuators, and embedded microprocessors/controllers to meet the demands of a wide range of applications existing in the world. The concept of the wireless senor networks is purely based on sensing, processing, and transceiving (Spacer et al., 2020). These three parameters provide numerous applications. Based on the different types of applications, smart nodes, smart sensors, and their communication, networking, and construction varies in IoT environments. The IoT environment is incomplete without the Cloud to access sensed data for further processing and decision making in an efficient manner (Elhoseny et al., 2018).

Cloud computing provides various services to users on the basis of their different model. Figure 12.2 describes the Cloud-based services in an efficient manner. First, in Software as a Service (SaaS), the Cloud can offer healthcare organizations on-demand hosted services, providing quick access to business applications and fulfilling customer relationship management (CRM).

As an Infrastructure as a Service (IaaS), Cloud solutions can offer on-demand computing and large storage for medical facilities (Zhiqiang et al., 2015). Lastly, in a Platform as a Service (PaaS), the Cloud can offer a security-enhanced environment for web-based services and the deployment of Cloud applications.

Transforming healthcare via the Cloud is about more than just the delivery of medical information from multiple computers at anytime, anywhere, and on any mobile device. It's also about the benefits of being able to connect medical centers and Cloud users for the purpose of sharing patients' health data over the Internet. Cloud computing is continually transforming healthcare in the modern age.

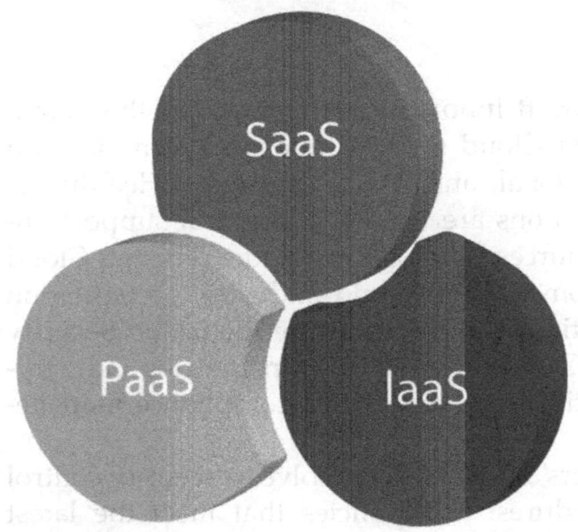

FIGURE 12.2
Cloud service models (Zhiqiang et al., 2015).

12.2 Efficient Services Provided for Healthcare Systems

Microsoft Cloud for Healthcare harnesses the power of the Microsoft Cloud by bringing together capabilities from Microsoft Azure, Dynamics 365, Microsoft Power Platform, and Microsoft 365 to transform the healthcare journey through more secure and connected patient experiences. Microsoft Azure, Microsoft Dynamics 365, Microsoft 365, and Microsoft Power Platform are subscription-based online services hosted by Microsoft Corporation within Microsoft-managed datacenters (Santos et al., 2018). These online services are designed to provide performance, scalability, security, management capabilities, and service levels required for mission-critical applications and systems used by business organizations. Cloud computing opportunities are plenty and, with the proper safeguards, healthcare providers can use the Cloud systems for the following:

- Drive revenue growth through personalized patient experiences.
- Through data transparency they can improve clinical productivity.
- The system provides streamline operations and deliver care beyond the hospital.

In medical fields such as Health Information Technology for Economic and Clinical Health Act (HITECH) and enforced by the American Recovery and Reinvestment Act of 2009 (ARRA) wants to legacy systems to include electronic health records (EHRs), a digital format of paper medical records to the hospitals. Such a transformation in healthcare has provided both administration personnel, physicians, and nurses with timely access to medical records when needed. EHRs helped simplify operations to make the process much more efficient and patient-centric than in the olden days. Adopting Cloud computing and Internet of Things solutions can make healthcare operations even more convenient and cost effective. They offer on-demand computing by using the latest in technology to deploy, access, and use networked information, applications, and resources. Unfortunately, it also has a complex infrastructure that may be challenging to understand.

Collaboration of IoT and Cloud computing is the best choice for their healthcare business, as it's often less costly than having multiple computers in various medical rooms each needing proper hardware, updated software, and network accessibility to upload, store, and retrieve patient or other medical data (Stergiou et al., 2018).

12.2.1 Microsoft Cloud Services

Various big and small organizations use Microsoft Innovative Architects for their company to leverage a growing suite of integrated Cloud services and make smarter and more informed decisions through a trusted, global, and hybrid platform. Healthcare-specific configurations, connectors, and applications are used for technical support, including unlimited 24/7 access to technical resources. Microsoft provides Trusted Cloud initiative for service delivery, contractual commitments, and industry accreditation (Radanliev et al., 2018). The Trusted Cloud Initiative is a program of the Cloud Security Alliance (CSA) industry group created to help Cloud service providers develop industry-recommended, secure and interoperable identity, and access and compliance management configurations and practices.

Microsoft's approach to securing our customers' information involves a security control framework of technologies, operational procedures, and policies that meet the latest global standards and can quickly adapt to security trends and industry-specific needs. provide a set of customer-managed tools that adapt to the organization and its security needs. The Security and Compliance center can track user and administrator activities, malware threats, data loss incidents, and more (Nizeti et al., 2020). The Reports dashboard is used for up-to-date reports related to the security and compliance features in the organization. Microsoft Azure Active Directory (Azure AD) reports can be used to stay informed on unusual or suspicious sign-in activities.

12.2.2 Information Security Management (SMS)

Microsoft-managed Cloud infrastructure to simulate real-world breaches, conduct continuous security monitoring, and practice security incident response to validate and improve the security of online services. Security policy defines the information security rules and requirements for the service environment. Microsoft performs periodic information security management system (ISMS) reviews and results are reviewed with management. This process involves monitoring ongoing effectiveness and improvement of the ISMS control environment by reviewing security issues, audit results, and monitoring status, and by planning and tracking necessary corrective actions (Kundalwal et al., 2018).

These controls include:

- Physical and logical network boundaries with strictly enforced change control policies.
- Segregation of duties requiring a business need to access an environment.
- Highly restricted physical and logical access to the Cloud environment.
- Strict controls based on Security Development Lifecycle (SDL) and Operational Security Assurance (OSA) that define coding practices, quality testing, and code promotion.
- Ongoing security, privacy, and secure coding practices awareness and training.
- Continuous logging and audit of system access.
- Regular compliance audits to ensure control effectiveness.

System hardening is enforced through group policy, with centralized software updating. For auditing and analysis, event logs (such as security and AppLocker) are collected from management workstations and saved to a central location. In addition, dedicated jump-boxes on the Microsoft network that require two-factor authentication are used to connect to a production network.

Microsoft focuses on:

1. Platform security
    - Infrastructure and processes of our datacenters.
    - Strong encryption technologies (at rest and in transit).
2. Secure access and sharing
    - Restrict access of information to approved people, devices, apps, locations, and data classification.
    - Enforce who can share information and with who.

3. Awareness and insights
   - Complete understanding of how individuals are using SharePoint and OneDrive.
   - Analyze usage to measure return on investment.
   - Identify potentially suspicious activity.
4. Information governance
   - Classify what constitutes sensitive data and enforce how it can be used.
   - Protection in the event of litigation.
   - Retain business-critical files when people leave your organization.
5. Compliance and trust
   - Ensure that service operations are secure, compliant, trustworthy, and transparent.

12.3 Need of Cloud Computing for Healthcare

In an industry where a significant amount of data is generated daily, the democratization of data and its remote accessibility free up providers and patients, breaking down geographical access restrictions to healthcare. Remote access and communication open up many possibilities and allow for greater patient safety. Virtual appointments and consults allow people to speak with healthcare professionals in the comfort of their own homes, which is beneficial for patients who have difficulty traveling while cutting down on the traffic in hospitals and clinics. Fewer people in a facility means better infection control (Frustaci et al., 2018). When doctors want an expert opinion, they can share patient data and discuss it with specialists online. Patients also benefit from better access to their own data, which provides transparency and reduces the need for calls and visits.

12.4 Benefits of Cloud Computing for Healthcare

Cloud computing technology provides so many benefits for the healthcare industry. They can use the Cloud concept to store and secure organizational data as well as patient data in large amounts with low cost and maintenance. Some benefits of Cloud computing technology are described here.

12.4.1 Security

If healthcare providers use Cloud servers to store data, it's beneficial for them. Many times equipment fails and medical institutions may lose all their data and applications; in such cases, the Cloud helps increase the security of healthcare. Cloud computing not only allows its users to access the information remotely, as it includes automation of backups and disaster recovery options but in the case of a breach, healthcare providers don't lose any data and can minimize the downtime for their staff. Most Cloud providers nowadays offer security, risk management, and monitoring services to protect their users from unauthorized access and breaches (Luo et al., 2018).

12.4.2 Cost

Since Cloud computing runs under a subscription model, healthcare providers can save up money from purchasing expensive systems and equipment. Plus, by adopting a Cloud server, healthcare institutions can also reduce costs by using the Cloud provider's resources.

12.4.3 Scalability

Unlike conventional self-hosted models, Cloud computing gives healthcare providers the flexibility to increase or decrease their data storage depending on the patients' flow (Kraemer et al., 2017). Healthcare institutions can adapt their technology to peak seasons. For example, the flu season, where the volume of patients increases without wasting time and money with the latest hardware purchases or software updates.

12.4.4 Data Storage

Healthcare providers have to deal with electronic medical records, patient portals, mobile apps, and big data analytics. That's a lot of data to manage and analyze, and not all in-house equipment can store it. Cloud computing allows healthcare institutions to store all that data while avoiding extra costs of maintaining physical servers.

12.4.5 Artificial Intelligence and Machine Learning

If there's one field where AI can be intimidating, it's in healthcare. But with tight schedules of medical professionals and now more than ever, as the world continues to fight a global pandemic and with the complexity and rise of data, AI and machine learning capabilities can be a crucial solution to support clinical decisions and, consequently, a faster time-to-treatment (Gia et al., 2017). As more and more Cloud platforms integrate AI and ML into their services, Cloud computing can support the transition of artificial intelligence into mainstream healthcare operations and help users manage massive amounts of data.

12.4.5 Collaboration

With healthcare organizations moving towards value-based care payment methods, the collaboration between doctors, departments, and even institutions are essential. Medical providers can transfer data between each other through a Cloud computing server, boosting cooperation for better treatment.

12.5 Risks of Cloud Computing in Healthcare System

Cloud computing provides various benefits to an organization, but there are some risks to use Cloud concepts in the healthcare industry. Such as some unauthorized person may use patient data illegally for their use because of security issues arises in this. Risks of the Cloud are explained here:

- Lack of security and privacy are the two primary concerns healthcare providers face when choosing a Cloud solution.
- In order to overcome these concerns, healthcare businesses must choose a reliable Cloud provider who acts in complete accordance with the provisions set forth in the Health Insurance Portability and Accountability Act (HIPAA) of 1996.
- With massive data breaches increasingly reported in recent years, there is a growing uneasiness amongst patients who fear that hospitals and doctors that use a Cloud service provider will complicate privacy of their data (McMahon et al., 2017). There are also concerns of allowing multiple users to share EHRs among facilities.
- In addition to patient privacy, data breaches cost healthcare organizations millions and millions of dollars each year. In fact, two of the most recent cost of a data breach studies from the Ponemon Institute show that stolen healthcare records cost twice the global average. The average cost per stolen record was $380 in 2017 (global average was $141).
- Such costs can be devastating for healthcare businesses.

12.6 Benefit of Microsoft Cloud in the Healing Healthcare System

By using Cloud technology in the healthcare field provides many benefits to doctors and patients worldwide. They can use all systems in a real-time manner but using this they face so many problems. To overcome these healthcare facilities that ultimately decide on a private, public, or hybrid Cloud solution can choose for a virtualization platform at VMware or Microsoft (Kraemer et al., 2016). At Innovative Architects, they chose Microsoft's secure Cloud platform, which uses Windows Server with Hyper-V and the System Center. This scalable solution is best able to meet most growing business's needs, helping easily power Cloud applications and supply Cloud-based computing and services.

The Microsoft Azure Cloud computing system, in particular, can provide on-demand simple access to healthcare applications and data. Using a PaaS environment, Microsoft provides a service to supply providers with networks, servers, and storage. Microsoft Azure complies with the data protection and privacy laws set forth in HIPAA and the HITECH Act. This system also meets Cloud Security Alliance (CSA) as well as Governance, Risk and Compliance (GRC) criteria. Either implement Azure's.NET Services to integrate public Cloud-based applications, or turn to SQL Server-based data services to properly secure the entire infrastructure.

Regardless of what Cloud service platform users choose or which provider delivers the best service, the delivery of computing and service must permit sharing of proprietary data resources to help physicians and healthcare providers do their jobs effectively and efficiently. Both the Cloud platform and Cloud provider must also ensure all of your digital medical data remains secure and private (Mukherjee et al., 2018). So long as these conditions are met, there will be less and less resistance to Cloud computing adoption in the healthcare industry.

12.7 Healthcare's Future is in the Cloud

As the pandemic swept away old constraints, digital health innovators rushed in to find a solution. In the face of a major crisis, providers and technologists worked tirelessly to make healthcare better, pushing change to save lives. Innovation and entrepreneurship don't come without risk, but they also can provide enormous benefits. Collecting and sharing data via the Cloud will enable a healthcare system fit for the 21st century. Until now, healthcare providers have been reticent to embrace the same kind of IT modernization (Ngu et al., 2016). Concerns about security, legal compliance, and potential downtime when dealing with the most sensitive personal data in life and death situations are all legitimate, but can all be addressed. Secure and reliable virtual access to healthcare professionals and data has become table stakes for us to meet our 21st century challenges and goals (da Silva and da Fonseca, 2019).

12.7.1 The Circumstances for the Cloud

Easy access to and sharing of data is an essential foundation for building a healthcare system that works for today's on-demand needs. Hybrid Cloud deployment among healthcare providers is expected to reach just 37% this year, up from 30% in 2022. Most hospitals still rely on outdated software systems that have been repeatedly patched. Building atop shaky foundations like this leads to major inefficiency and frequent errors (Saha et al., 2019). Healthcare professionals lose a great deal of time that could be better spent on patient care to these inflexible and unreliable systems. The Cloud provides unprecedented scaling, data integration, and access advantages. Doctors with access to complete information on a patient's electronic health record (EHR), prescriptions, test results, and imaging are better equipped to find the right diagnosis and identify the best course of treatment. Data-driven decisions, based on huge information sets, can help healthcare professionals and researchers to spot patterns, uncover insights, and deliver a higher standard of care.

12.7.2 The Circumstances for IoT Devices

By using IoT devices and products, remote health monitoring is done efficiently. The prediction of different symptoms and prevention of potentially life hazardous states and diseases could generally be enabled. Assistance to the elderly could also be ensured by monitoring a patient's general health condition and nutrition status that would be supported via IoT devices. Rehabilitation after a serious disease could also be efficiently supported with IoT technologies, especially in cases of home rehabilitation circumstances (Puliafito et al., 2017). Usage of IoT devices in healthcare will bring innovation with it and provide efficient and less error-prone interactions to the healthcare stakeholders. The intelligent devices will be able to provide faster processing for the repetitive tasks that the healthcare employees had manually done (Suguna et al., 2018). IoT enables healthcare professionals to be more watchful and connect with the patients proactively. Data collected from IoT devices can help physicians identify the best treatment process for patients and reach the expected outcomes.

12.8 Classification Techniques in the Cloud and IoT-Based Health Monitoring and Diagnosis Approach

Healthcare organizations struggle to deliver high-quality patient outcomes at an affordable cost. One key to reaching that goal is integrating health, social, and wellness services and that means embracing openness, cross-organizational data sharing, and Cloud-native technologies such as Internet of Things (IoT) and artificial intelligence (AI), while ensuring the utmost protection of personal data. Driving this transformation and innovation requires moving away from traditional, on-premises solutions where data is locked away and adopting a Cloud-first approach that enables rapid deployment of services for the continuum of patient care. There are many techniques used by authors to provide better work in the healthcare field based on Cloud and IoT technology. Some techniques are discussed here.

12.8.1 DXC Technology

DXC technology work on to transform care models and meet the industry's highest security and compliance requirements. Healthcare Cloud enables customers to securely and quickly embrace the benefits of an intelligent Cloud platform reducing complexity and risk, while allowing approved parties to securely access applications and data 24×7. Cloud-managed service tailored. The platform helps shift next-generation healthcare from reactive treatment to proactive care and wellness models that leverage precision medicine techniques (Chandra et al., 2017). Healthcare data is increasingly being digitized today and the data collected today coming in from all modern devices, has reached a significant volume all over the world. Privacy of healthcare is an important aspect governed by Healthcare Acts (e.g., HIPAA) and hence the data needs to be secured from falling into the wrong hands or from being breached by malicious insiders. It is important to secure existing healthcare big data environments due to increasing threats of breaches and leaks from confidential data and increased adoption of Cloud technologies. Figure 12.3 explains some application based on big data.

Healthcare data in big data environments today face several challenges. Sharing of healthcare data can be leveraged by Cloud technologies. Healthcare data from different vendors can be merged to analyze insights into medical treatment and diagnosis. Sharing the data via Cloud-based environments raises concerns in environments where security practices related to healthcare are not in place. Healthcare data centers today are required to follow HIPAA certification and the guidelines and rules laid out by HIPAA. Also, an inflow of a large volume of data from various sources results in a requirement of handling the extra burden for storage, processing power, and high-speed networking. The latest information technologies can be used in the healthcare field to overcome worldwide health problems such as uneven distribution of medical resources, the growing chronic diseases, and the increasing medical expenses. A big health application system is based on the healthcare IoT applications and big data (Wang et al., 2017).

12.8.2 Flexible Multi-Level Architecture

A flexible multi-level architecture using the fog approach, a computing paradigm in which heterogeneous devices at the edge of the network collect data, compute a task with minimal latency, and produce physical actions meaningful for the user, leveraging upon context and location awareness. The interaction layer collects data and receives

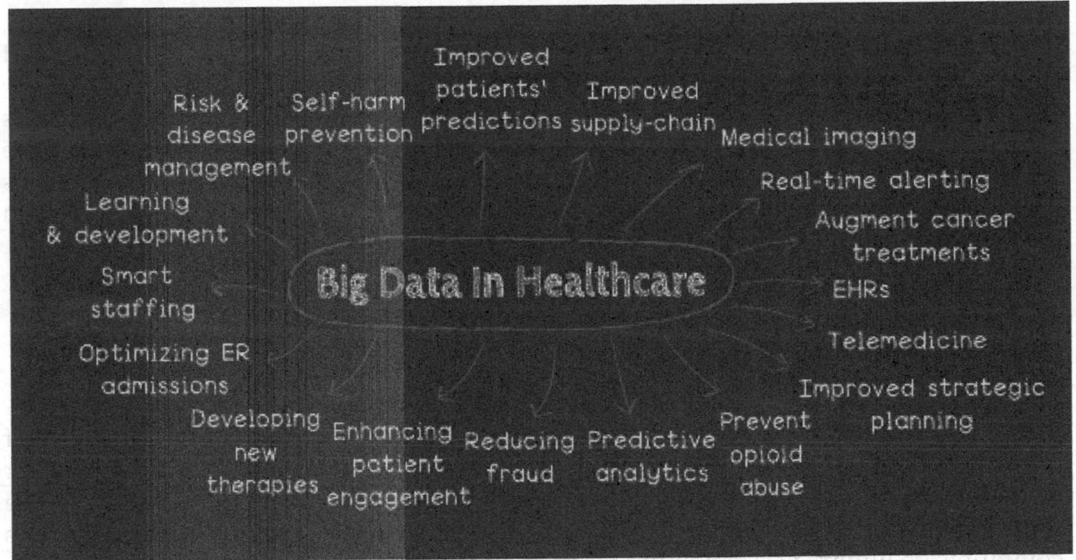

FIGURE 12.3
Applications of big data (Wang et al., 2017).

commands. The mesh layer aggregates data, transfers commands, and handles the security of lower nodes. The Fog node processes data to act on the ambient and possibly transfer information to the Cloud.

This architecture provides lower usage of bandwidth, prominent in all the situations in which a connection could be limited, for example elderly houses, rural areas, and emergency vehicles. By the use of this architecture its Minimized latency, higher context awareness and easier manageability, its also increased reliability and security, with flexible policies for data transfer and encryption. The separation of big data analytics and tailored action items directly empowers the final user.

The lower layer is built upon three elements: sensors that produces data, actuators that consume it in form of commands to generate a physical outcome, and the human-in-the-loop that can produce and consume data, and act upon it. The communication is handled from the mesh layer, which implements a first security level, authenticating the nodes. This architecture provides reconfiguration of the hardware tailored on the specific application, it gives high performance in data manipulation and signal processing, low power, comparable with other board computers like Raspberry PI or Beagle Board. FPGA-based nodes could represent a major driver for the implementation of Fog technologies in the future, with major benefits in terms of energy consumption, cost reduction, and system reactivity (Cerina).

12.8.3 Dynamic Cloud Platform for an eHealth System Based on a Cloud SOA Architecture (DCCSOA)

A novel Cloud computing platform based on a service-oriented Cloud architecture is proposed by the author. The proposed platform can be run on the top of heterogeneous Cloud computing systems that allows a Cloud vendor to customize and standardize services with minimal modifications. The platform uses a template layer which is divided into FTaaS that allows Cloud vendors to define a standard, generic, and uniform service, and BTaaS that allows defined services at BTaaS to bind to the Cloud vendor value-added services. The evaluation shows that the platform is scalable and the methods which are run on the platform have not introduced additional overheads. The experimental results show that the proposed platform have not introduced additional overheads. A template allows an eHealth system to use heterogeneous Cloud computing systems. It provides flexibility, customizability, and standardization for eHealth services that needs to be run on the Cloud computing (Bahrami and Singhal, 2017).

12.8.4 Cloud Based 8E-Prescription Management System for Healthcare Services Using IoT Devices

The system includes five types of users which are admin, doctors, pharmacists, receptionists, and patients. Doctor interacts with the Android interface provided in the form of an Android application. Four of the remaining users interact with the system using our web application, as each of the users has its own role in the different processes to be followed in the daily routine of healthcare systems. All of the stakeholder requests communicate with the system either through a web interface or a smartphone interface; also, the streaming analytics for the IoT devices as well. The backend, database, and IoT platform are deployed onto Amazon Cloud. The service receives a request to generate a token via communicating through the MQTT protocol.

The streaming analytics is responsible to stream the data to our hospital management database, which then generates a token receipt for the patient via an authenticated channel. Another use case is that the patient can take an offline appointment from the doctor. The receptionist can call the patients in a specific sequence, generated by the system. By the use of this architecture, the doctor prescribes one patient. He has the option to call the next patient and he can retrieve the historical information of the patient instantly on the Android tablet or a smartphone device. The doctor can prescribe the patient via checking him up via the IoT devices registered in the clinic, e.g., the blood pressure IoT device, temperature device (Mehmo et al., 2019). This process makes sure the automation of data inputs into the prescription instantly when the doctor uses the device with the patient. This reduces the effort for a doctor to focus more on the patient's health rather than consuming his/her time on entering the patient data manually. Although healthcare systems have been improved but a lot of systems still use the process of scanning the prescriptions manually and convert them into e-prescriptions. This provides an easier way for the users to interact with the system smartly. Architecture (Figure 12.4) provides a direction to the automation and possibilities inside the healthcare industry via the use of multiple IoT devices.

12.8.5 Android-Based Mobile Data Acquisition (DAQ)

This research paper proposes the Android-based mobile data acquisition (DAQ) solution, which collects personalized health information of the end user, stores, analyzes, and visualizes it on the smart devices and optionally sends it towards to the datacenter for further processing. The smart mobile device is capable of collecting information from a large set of various wireless such as Bluetooth, Wi-Fi, Cloud, and GPRS and wired (USB) sensors. Embedded sensors of the mobile device provide additional useful status information such as user location, magnetic or noise level, acceleration, temperature, etc. The user interface is suitable for different skilled users, highly configurable, and provides diary functionality to store information. The software enables correlation analysis between the various sensor data sets.

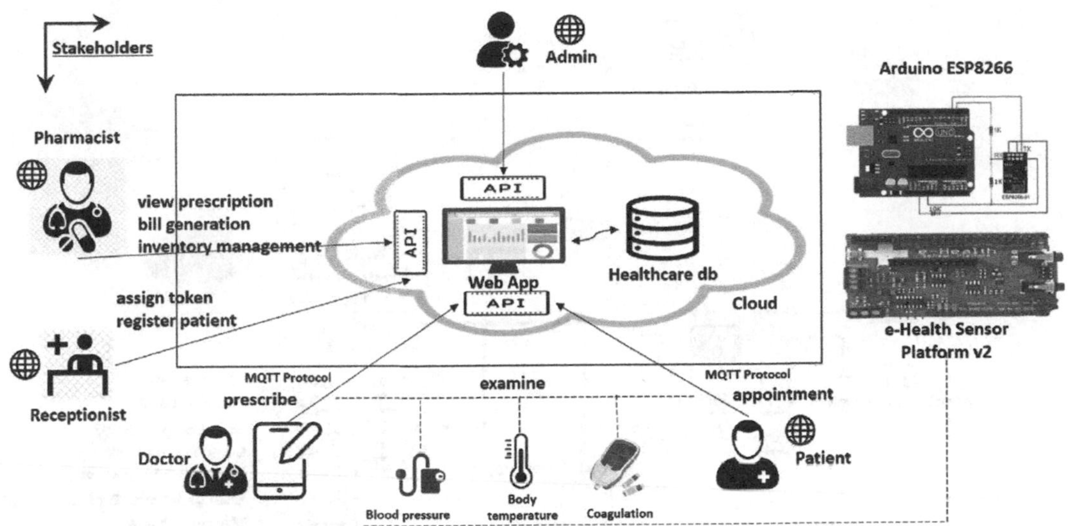

FIGURE 12.4
Cloud-based e-prescription management system for healthcare services using IoT devices (Mehmo et al., 2019).

The components of the proposed system (Figure 12.5) area, including the data processing layer, a data integration layer, a Cloud computing layer, and a network structure product provide services all over the world via the Internet; monitoring different objects in real time is becoming even more difficult. The Cloud of the Internet of Things is a concept combining technologies connected via the Internet to provide services in different places and environments in real time. The system depends on convenient and cost-effective solutions to deal with the data generated by the Internet of things. This current designed system provides low complexity, low power consumptions, and is highly portable for healthcare monitoring of patients and it can eliminate the need of utilization of expensive facilities. The doctor can easily access the patient's information anywhere with the help of an Android web server (Alamelu and Mythili, 2017).

In this paper, the author presents an architecture and an application based on the use of Android smartphones and Cloud computing that can be used in emergency situations. The application can be used especially by elderly people living alone or in assisted living centers. The application enables the retrieval of data remotely from the doctors' database. Taking into consideration the emergency situation, we consider that the patient can send only voice messages. Then the message is converted in text, which is sent as a request into a servlet connected to the doctor's database. Furthermore, the testing shows its applicability in health emergency situations.

12.8.6 WSN Architecture with IoT

IoT is a promising field that is revolutionizing the society by integrating the advances in wireless networking with miniaturized micro and nano sensors, devices, actuators, and embedded microprocessors or controllers to meet the demands of a wide range of applications existing in the world. The IoT environment is incomplete without the Cloud to access sensed data for further processing and decision making in an efficient manner.

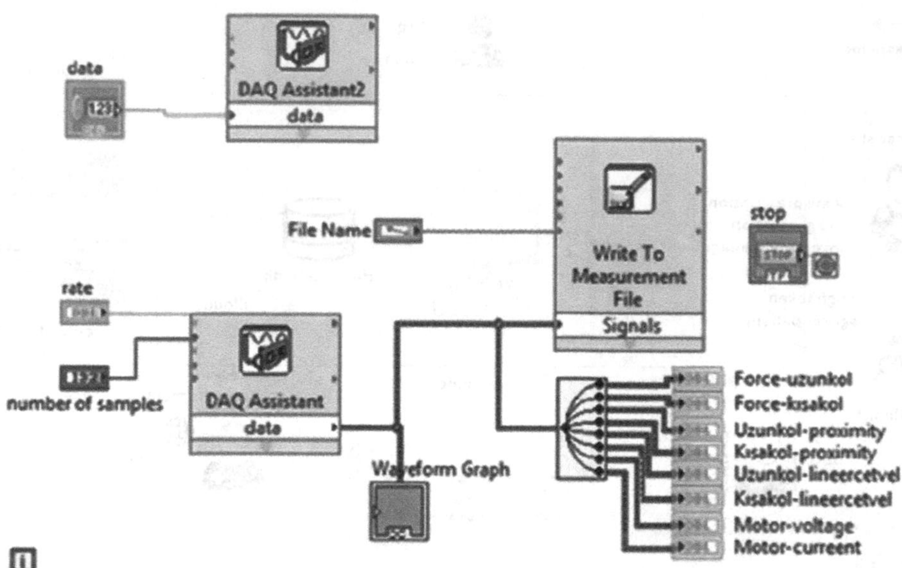

FIGURE 12.5
DAQ system (Alamelu and Mythili, 2017).

The IoHT architecture comprises WSN nodes, networks, communication protocols with supporting hardware, and storage with Cloud databases. The WSN has a source node and sink node wherein these nodes are bridged by a connecting gateway wirelessly. The figure shown in Figure 12.6 is the general architecture of the WSN in an IoT platform. The complete architecture of the WSN relies on its protocol and its layer model. The layer model comprises a physical data link, network, transport, and application layer and the entire model has a plane to manage the task, mobility, and power. In the proposed architecture, the sensor nodes are based on the healthcare application of the WSN-based IoT; further, a Cloud computing platform is defined. The Cloud can be a virtual sink node that can collect the sensor data from the source node of the healthcare system. The migration or the assistance of the computation should be aided with the implementation of the mobile agents for the Cloud to reduce energy consumption in the entire network. The source nodes in a network acquire the data from the environment based on the manner of the deployment and further the Cloud as a sink node handles the remaining data logging, storage, and computation with the help of the mobile agents (Awaisi et al., 2020). The results demonstrate that the proposed IoHT could be evaluated for its performance in the context of energy.

12.8.7 Fog Computing

Fog computing does not supersede Cloud computing but extends the properties of the Cloud at the edge of the network. Fog is a Cloud that is near to the ground. A profusion of benefits is offered by fog computing to diminish the challenges and issues of Cloud computing. Reduced network latency is one of the vital benefits of fog computing as compared to device-to-Cloud architecture. Figure 12.7 explains the Cloud computing concept collaborated with Fog computing and gives a better result to medical practitioners. Fog computing is an architectural style in which network components between

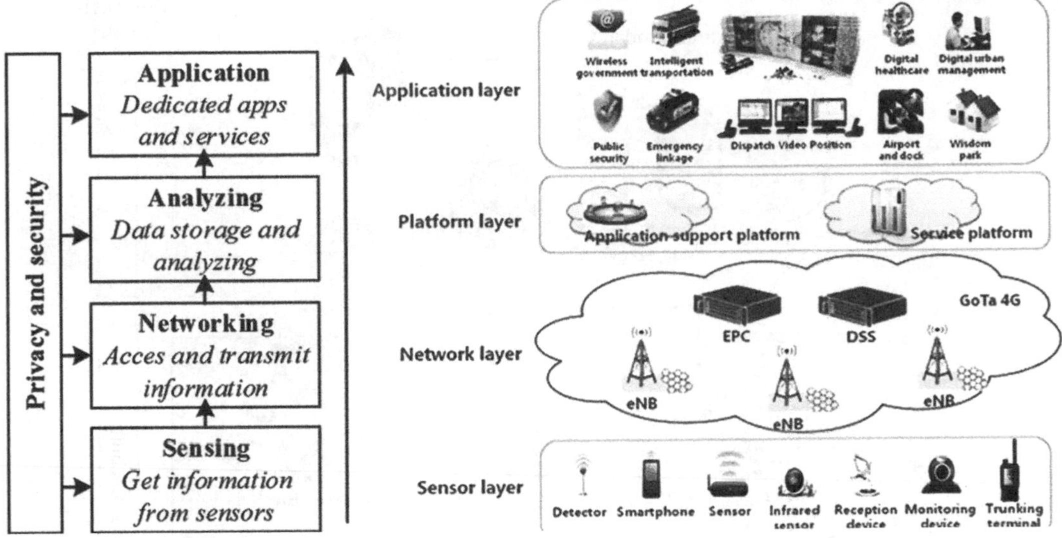

FIGURE 12.6
Architecture of WSN-based IoT (Awaisi et al., 2020).

devices and the Cloud execute application-specific logic. Fog computing provides healthcare informatics, and explores, classifies, and discusses different applications. Fog computing tasks can be executed, and provide trade-offs with respect to requirements relevant to healthcare. There is a significant number of computing tasks in healthcare that require or can benefit from Fog computing principles. In this architecture, processing on higher network tiers is required due to constraints in wireless devices and the need to aggregate data, and privacy concerns and dependability prevent computation tasks to be completely moved to the Cloud. These findings substantiate the need for a coherent approach towards Fog computing in healthcare (John and Shenoy, 2014). Fog computing decreases the volume of the data to be sent on the Cloud data center for analysis and processing. The reduction in the volume of the data sent to the Cloud data center leads to less network bandwidth usage. There are many potential benefits of Fog computing like energy efficiency and scalability (John and Shenoy, 2014).

12.8.8 Hospital Information Systems (HIS)

The healthcare industry has come a long way from more than just Hospital Information Systems (HIS) and Electronic Medical Records (EMRs) to computer-assisted surgeries and remote patient care, since the advent of information technology into the healthcare domain. With the advances in information technology, healthcare in all kinds of markets is becoming more digital, more collaborative, more patient-centric, and more data driven. Figure 12.8 shows the basic architecture of the Hospital Information Systems (HIS) model.

It aims toward accessing information anytime, anywhere. In this paper, the HIS system is described. This system is capable of offering various healthcare services that utilize Cloud computing. The health Cloud provides various services that can be used to manage and process medical data using a Cloud infrastructure in a secure, reliable, and economical way. Cloud computing can help the healthcare industry align its IT needs based

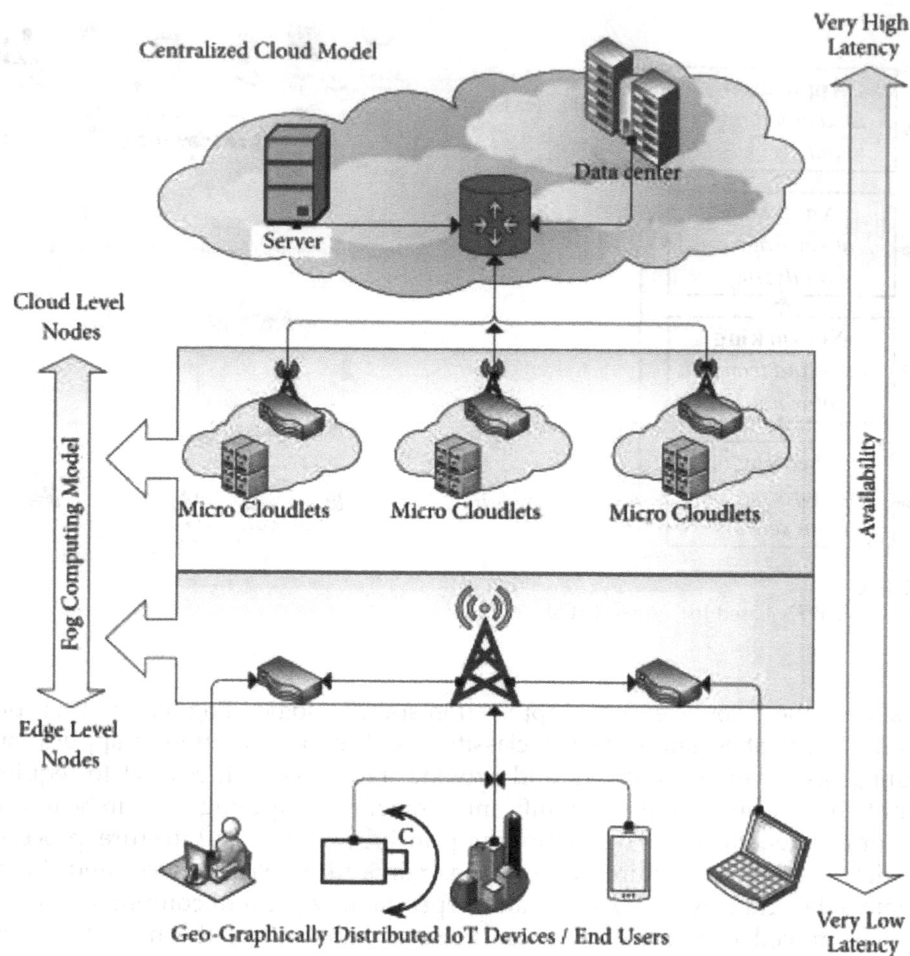

FIGURE 12.7
Cloud with Fog computing (Awaisi et al., 2020).

on a real-time requirement, rather than on a calculated guess. The health Cloud is an innovative way to bring down operational and management costs and provides affordable healthcare services in developing economies (Dhanaliya and Devani, 2016). The security of healthcare data, however, is a concern as certain regulatory bodies do not prefer patient data to be stored on public Cloud storage solutions.

12.8.9 E-Health Internet of Things (IoT)

In this paper, the author presents an e-healthcare system by using Cloud computing and web services. The use of Cloud computing made remote monitoring and controlling possible. IoT devices used in the medical field provide the facility to patients for more comfort. Figure 12.9 explains how the devices provide facilities to users at home.

It provides an automatic update of a measured parameter of patients as well as sends alert mail by using SMTP (Simple Mail Transfer Protocol) (George, 2018). An e-healthcare

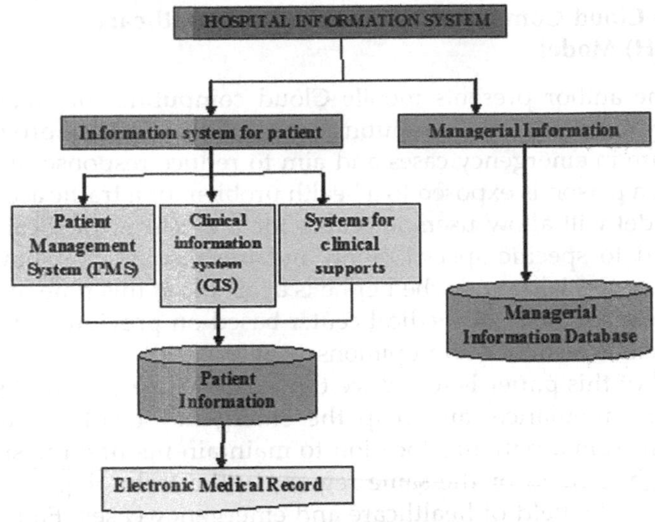

FIGURE 12.8
Hospital information systems (HIS) (John and Shenoy, 2014).

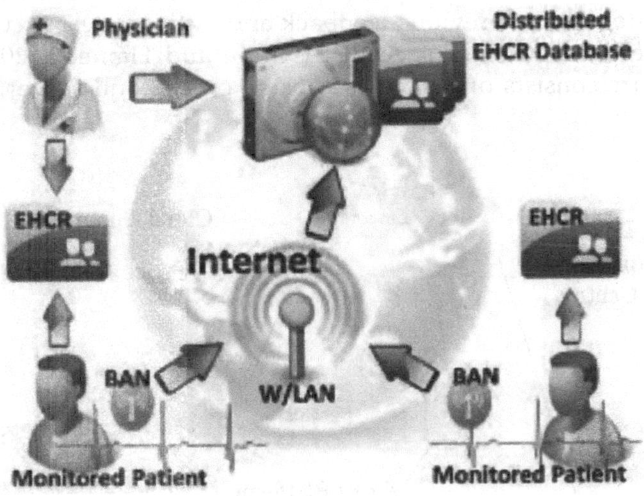

FIGURE 12.9
Internet of Things in healthcare (George).

system using Cloud computing and web services provide better solutions over a traditional method. Critical conditions can be avoided by frequently checking the sensor data on a web page. Here only one blood pressure sensor is attached. The system can be improved by attaching more.

Healthcare costs are reduced and the quality of service provided is improved on a greater scale with this proposed health monitoring IoT-based system with Fog computing. The main advantage of using IoT in medical healthcare is to decrease barriers in monitoring important health parameters along with avoiding unnecessary health costs. It improves the efficiency of the system by providing better medical support promptly (George, 2018).

12.8.10 Mobile Cloud Computing for Emergency Healthcare (MCCEH) Model

In this paper, the author presents mobile Cloud computing for emergency healthcare (MCCEH) model using a Cloud computing server (Figure 12.10), providing services related to healthcare in emergency cases and aim to reduce response time to save the patient's life. When a person is exposed to a health problem or a traffic accident is occurring, the MCCEH model will allow users to search for the nearest medical center or nearest specialists related to specific specialization and the results will show the availability timetable for every specialist and whether he is available at this time or not. The user will be able to choose a specialist or medical center based on previous experiences and may able to read previous feedback and opinions.

The main goal of this paper is to reduce the wasted time during the traditional way of requesting an ambulance, and help the emergency health cases to request the nearest specialist from a patient's location to maintain his life; the specialist could be in the same neighborhood or the same region. In the technological era, some efforts should be made in the field of healthcare and emergency cases. Figure 12.5 shows the MCCEH model architecture. It consists mainly of a web application and mobile application connected to a Cloud server. The process will start from a mobile application and search for the nearest medical center or specialist; it will get the data from the Cloud server. In addition, the user could be able to sort the results by availability time, specialization category, or previous feedback and voting rates. It could help the user to choose the better experience specialist (Nirabi and Hameed, 2018). The MCCEH model architecture consists of a database hosted on a Cloud server, mobile, and web application.

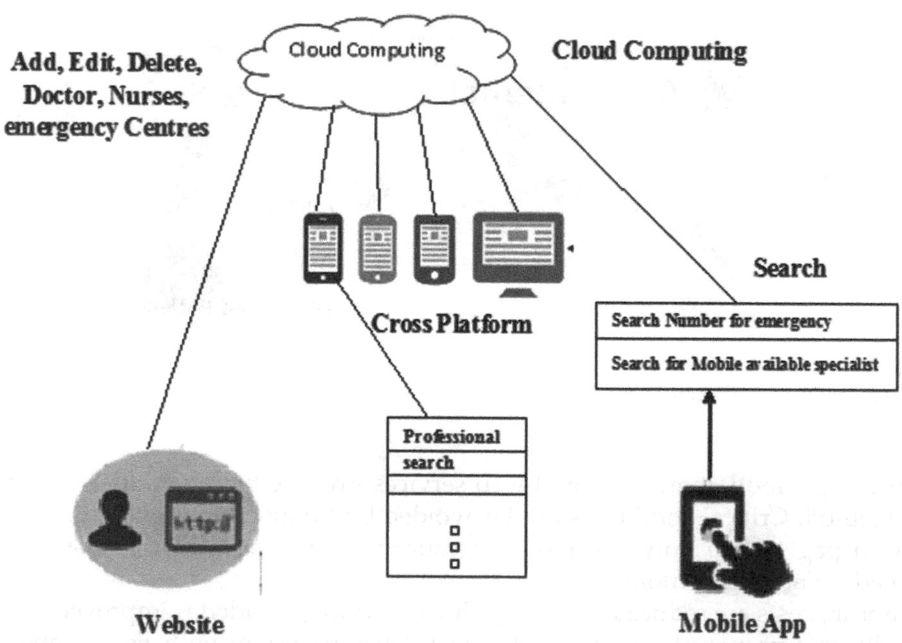

FIGURE 12.10
MCCEH model architecture (Nirabi and Hameed, 2018).

12.8.11 Cloud-Based Intelligent Healthcare Monitoring System (CIHMS)

Cloud-based healthcare is the integration of Cloud computing and health monitoring. The computing device enables the delivery of accurate medical information anytime anywhere by means of the Internet. A Cloud-based healthcare system consists of a computing device and number of sensors mounted on a patient's body. In this paper, the author used a Cloud-based Intelligent Healthcare Monitoring System (CIHMS), shown in Figure 12.11, which can provide medical feedback/assistance to the patient through the Cloud (if data already available) or hospital. The suitable sensor is/are to be used to obtain adequate data related to the patient's disease. The paper discusses the simulation of primary healthcare system on the intranet. It also discussed the multidisciplinary endeavor such as the Cloud for healthcare systems that provide greater benefits for patients and hospitals (Khyamling et al., 2014).

This paper surveys the classification technique on the Cloud and IoT-based health monitoring and diagnosis approach from the healthcare data acquired from any repository or by using sensors that collect real-time data and store them in tables for reference to the severity of the disease by any professional.

12.8.12 Remote Healthcare Service

In this paper, the author presents a Cloud computing–based remote healthcare service system. This system (Figure 12.12) mainly consists of three parts: portable medical devices, intelligent terminals such as phones, tablets, etc., and Cloud services platform. Portable medical acquisition devices transmit physiological signals to the intelligent terminal via wireless methods (Bluetooth/Wi-Fi).

Monitoring software in smart terminal responses for data display, storage, and push the measurement results to the Cloud service platform. The Cloud services platform is a special website developed using a Cloud server, Cloud storage, and Cloud push technology,

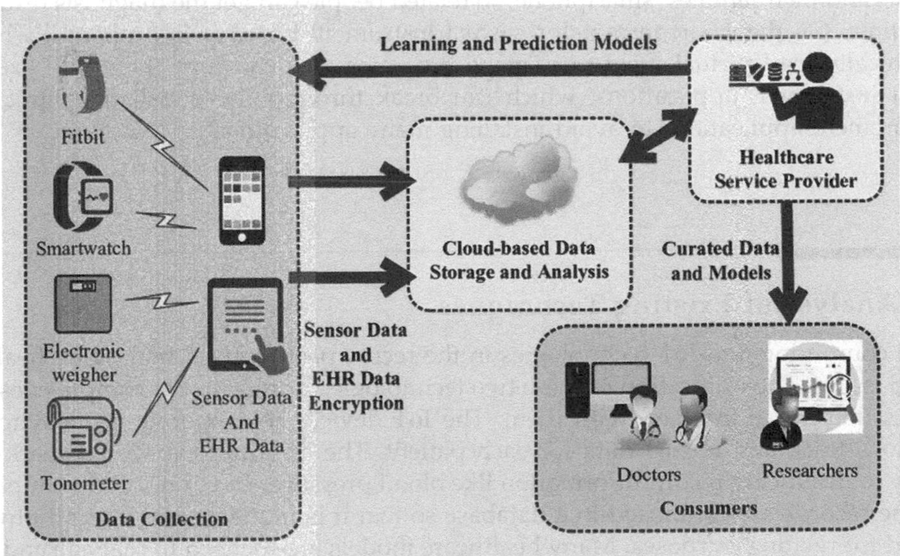

FIGURE 12.11
Cloud-based Intelligent Healthcare Monitoring System (CIHMS) (Khyamling et al., 2014).

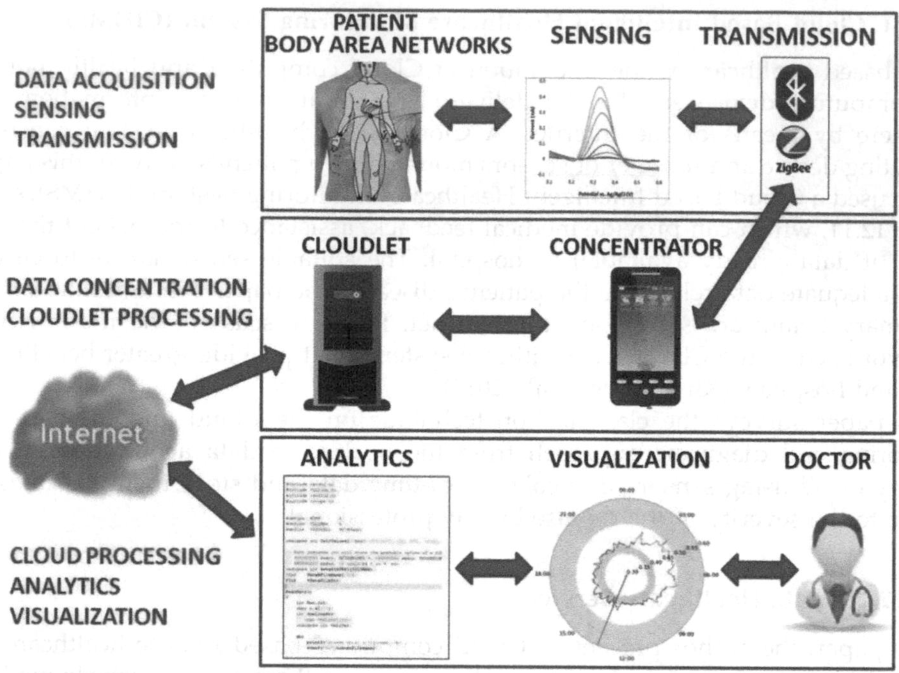

FIGURE 12.12
Remote healthcare service.

which is the core of the whole system. Users can view and maintain their health data record anytime and anywhere and only need an Internet equipment. Physicians can view their patient's health status the same way. If necessary, the doctor can also push the diagnosis to patients and their families' smartphone, so related people can get the diagnosis result at the same time. On the smart terminal, a virtual instrument browser is proposed, which can dynamically load virtual instrument page programs and can turn them into executable virtual instrument applications, which can break through the installation limitation of measurement applications to avoid installing many applications on the phone.

12.9 Analysisof Existing Techniques

Cloud computing and IoT technologies in the recent past focused mainly on healthcare-related issues. The unification of these two technologies brings up the completeness of the devices that are authorized with them. The IoT devices that operate on healthcare applications track and record data for each patient. The applications of information technology to healthcare record information like blood pressure, ECG rate, body temperature, etc. The records are composed in a database so that it is made referable to all physicians around for relating purposes. Many healthcare models are focused to manage and reduce responding time using Cloud computing and a cross platform. By adding a video streaming call, it may help to get an initial diagnosis and give some tips that help the patient. However, the use of the Cloud arises new risks on healthcare IT, such as security, malicious intrusions privacy risks, breach exposures of private information, and identity disclosures resulting from data mining and advanced analytics, lack of transparency into the Cloud environment, lack of support for regulations and service levels, possibility of Cloud supplier bankruptcy, etc. Network issues include outages, low bandwidth, unproven Cloud providers, and no end-to-end monitoring, incompatibility of Cloud with customer architecture and service management processes, and compatibility of the Cloud with a customer model and charging mechanisms.

The Internet of Things (IoT) is playing a pivotal role in bringing comfort and ease in human lives by connecting billions of devices across the globe. Currently, IoT and Cloud-based solutions are available to process and analyze patient data, but Cloud computing causes large end-to-end delays and network usage problems while processing huge amounts of data. Efficiency and security are still a challenge in IoT-based healthcare systems. Fog computing is introduced to overcome the issues of Cloud computing by providing computing and storage services at the edge of the network. With the help of new and upcoming developments in the IoT world, we can find out new use cases for the same to cater to the need of accessible and affordable healthcare. Concurrently, there's a constant development in the IoT automation and machine-to-machine communication, which is an integral contribution to the betterment of any new device-to-device processing and connectivity solutions for healthcare that is driven by the Internet of Things. A Cloud computation IoT framework is analyzed in an equipped manner to find accurate solutions to healthcare problems in a reliable manner. In this, different Cloud and IoT-based e-health systems scenarios are discussed and analyzed. These scenarios discussed the authentication and data processing in the different parts of the system. On the basis of existing technology, there is more work needed to solve some issues and security problem related to Cloud and IoT devices.

12.10 Conclusion

All countries need enhanced healthcare system for economical, technological, and social development. Development of healthcare systems necessitates a large number of manpower, especially when a patient needs continuous monitoring. Power of information and communication technology provides efficient and effective solutions to the healthcare system. Using the Internet of Things (IoT) condition of a patient can be monitored and controlled remotely. A robust partner ecosystem extends the value of the platform with additional solutions to address the most pressing challenges that each industry is facing today. Healthcare organizations can align to their clinical and operational needs, and then deploy quickly to empower their digital transformation and design a healthier future for their patients as happened with Microsoft Cloud for Healthcare.

Although the pandemic impacts are still unfolding in the healthcare and technology sectors, the upcoming years are very promising for the global healthcare Cloud computing market. As social distancing became the new norm, healthcare providers had to rethink the doctor-patient interactions, and trends that were previously slowly developing, like telehealth, have been sped up exponentially. Despite the challenges, Cloud computing promises too many advantages to patients, physicians, start-ups, and the wider healthcare industry.

12.11 Future Scope

Innovation and development in IoT have established new ways to analyze patient data in healthcare systems. New terminology such as artificial intelligence and machine learning will be introduced with IoT for the healthcare system to provide a first-aid treatment to patients. However, more focus is needed on security and privacy-preserving of users' data.

References

Alamelu, J. V. and A. Mythili. "Design of IoT based Generic Health Care System", 978-1-5386-1716-8, https://ieeexplore.ieee.org/xpl/conhome/8169966/proceeding, Vellore, India (2017).

Awaisi, Kamran Sattar, Shahid Hussain, Mansoor Ahmed, Arif Ali Khan and Ghufran Ahmed. "Leveraging IoT and Fog Computing in Healthcare Systems." *IEEE Internet of Things Magazine*, 2576-3180 (2020): 52–56.

Bahrami, Mehdi and Mukesh Singhal. "A Dynamic Cloud Computing Platform for eHealth Systems." 978-1-4673-8325-7. *17th International Conference on E-health Networking, Application & Services (HealthCom)*, IEEE (2017): 435–438. https://doi.org/10.1109/HealthCom.2015.7454539

Bruno Volckaert, Jose Santos, Tim Wauters. "Fog Computing: Enabling the Management and Orchestration of Smart City Applications in 5G Networks." *Entropy* 20, no. 1 (2018): 1–4.

Cerina, Luca, Sara Notargiacomo, Matteo Greco, Luca Paccani and Marco Domenico Santambrogio. "A Fog-Computing architecture for Preventive Healthcare and Assisted Living in Smart Ambients", 978-1-5386-3906-1. *2017 IEEE 3rd International Forum on Research and Technologies for Society and Industry (RTSI)* Modena, Italy, IEEE. https://doi.org/10.1109/RTSI41551.2017

Chandra, Sudipta, Soumya Ray and R.T. Goswami. "Big Data Security in Healthcare Survey on Frameworks and Algorithms." *2017 IEEE 7th International Advance Computing Conference (IACC)* (2017): 89–94. DOI: 10.1109/IACC.2017.25

da Silva, Rodrigo A. C. and Nelson L. S. da Fonseca. "On the Location of Fog Nodes in Fog-Cloud Infrastructures". *Sensors* 19 (2019): 2445.

Dawoud, Mohanad and D. Turgay Altilar "Cloud-Based E-Health Systems: Security and Privacy Challenges and Solutions." *2nd International Conference on Computer Science,* IEEE (2017): 861–865, https://doi.org/10.1109/UBMK.2017.8093549

Dhanaliya, Unnati and Anupam Devani, "Implementation of E-Health Care System using Web Services and Cloud Computing." IEEE, 978-1-5090-0396-9 (2016): 1034–1036.

Elhoseny, Mohamed, Gustavo Ramírez-González, Osama M. Abuelnasr, Shihab A. Shawkat, Arunkumar N. and Ahmed Farouk. "Secure Medical Data Transmission Model for IoT-Based Healthcare Systems". *IEEE* 6 (2018): 20596–20608.

Frustaci, Mario, Pasquale Pace, Gianluca Aloi and Giancarlo Fortino. "Evaluating Critical Security Issues of The Iot World: Present and Future Challenges". *IEEE Internet of Things Journal* 5, no. 4 (August 2018): 2483–2495.

George, A., H. Dhanasekaran, J.P. Chittiappa, L.A. Challagundla, S.S. Nikkam and O. Abuzaghleh. "Internet of Things in Health Care Using Fog Computing." *2018 7th International Conference on Computer and Communication Engineering (ICCCE)* (2018): 1–6.

Gia, Tuan Nguyen, Victor Kathan Sarkerv, Mingzhe Jiang, et al., "Low-Cost Fog-Assisted Health-Care IoT System with Energy-Efficient Sensor Nodes". In *Wireless Communications and Mobile Computing Conference (IWCMC) IEEE* (2017): 1765–1770.

John, Nimmy and Sanath Shenoy. "Health Cloud – Healthcare As A Service(HaaS) A Step Towards Redefining Healthcare Services for the Future." *IEEE* (2014): 1963–1966.

Khyamling, A. Parane, C. Patil Naveenkumar, R. Poojara Shivananda and S. Kamble Tejaskumar. "Cloud based Intelligent Healthcare Monitoring System." *2014 International Conference on Issues and Challenges in Intelligent Computing Techniques (ICICT)*, IEEE, Ghaziabad, India (2014): 697–701.

Kraemer, Frank Alexander, Anders Eivind Braten, Nattachart Tamkittikhun and David Palma. "Fog Computing in Healthcare–A Review and Discussion". *IEEE Access* (2017).

Kraemer, Frank Alexander, Anders Eivind Braten, Nattachart Tamkittikhun and David Palma. "Fog Computing in Healthcare—A Review and Discussion", 2169-3536. *IEEE* (2016): 1–16.

Kundalwal, Mayank Kumar, Ashish Singh and Kakali Chatterjee. "A Privacy Framework in Cloud Computing for Healthcare Data." *IEEE International Conference on Advances in Computing, Communication Control and Networking (ICACCCN)*, Greater Noida (UP), India (2018): 58–63.

Lakshmanachari, S., C. Srihari, A. Sudhakar and Paparao Nalajala. "Design and Implementation of Cloud based Patient Health Care Monitoring Systems using IoT". *IEEE International Conference on Energy, Communication, Data Analytics and Soft Computing (ICECDS-2017)*, 978-1-5386-1887-5 (2017): 3713–3717.

Luarasi, Tamara, Mimoza Durresi and Arjan Durresi. "Healthcare Based on Cloud Computing". IEEE (2013): 113–118.

Luo, Entao, Md ZakirulAlam Bhuiyan, Guojun Wang, Md Arafatur Rahman, Jie Wu and Mohammed Atiquzzaman. "Privacy Protector: Privacy-Protected Patient Data Collection in IoT-Based Healthcare Systems". *IEEE Communications Magazine* 56(2018): 163–168, IEEE, 0163-6804/18.

McMahon, Emma, Ryan Williams, Malaka El, Sagar Samtani, Mark Patton and Hsinchun Chen. "Assessing Medical Device Vulnerabilities on the Internet of Things". *IEEE International Conference onIntelligence and Security Informatics (ISI)* (2017): 176–178.

Mehmo, Asif, Faisal Mehmood and Wang-Cheol Song. "Cloud Based E-Prescription Management System for Healthcare Services Using IoT Devices", 978-1-7281-0893-3. *IEEE Conference Publication*, Jeju, South Korea (2019): 1380–1387.

Mukherjee, M., et al., "Survey of Fog Computing: Fundamental, Network Applications, and Research Challenges." *IEEE Communications Surveys and Tutorials* 20, no. 3 (2018): 1826–1857.

Ngu, Anne H., Mario Gutierrez, Vangelis Metsis, Surya Nepal and Quan Z. Sheng. "IoT Middleware: A Survey on Issues and Enabling Technologies". *IEEE Internet of Things Journal* 4, no. 1 (2016).

Nirabi, Ali and Shihab A. Hameed. "Mobile Cloud Computing For Emergency Healthcare Model:Framework". *2018 7th International Conference on Computer and Communication Engineering (ICCCE), IEEE*, Kuala Lumpur, Malaysia (2018): 375–379.

Puliafito, Carlo, Enzo Mingozzi and Giuseppe Anastasi. "Fog Computing for the Internet of Mobile Things: Issues and Challenges". In *Smart Computing (SMARTCOMP), IEEE International Conference on* (2017): 1–6.

Radanliev, Petar, Dave De Roure, Stacy Cannady, Rafael Mantilla Montalvo, Razvan Nicolescu and Michael Huth. "*Economic Impact of Iot Cyber Risk – Analysing Past and Present to Predict the Future Developments in Iot Risk Analysis and Iot Cyber Insurance*". *Conference at London on Living in the Internet of Things: Cybersecurity of the IoT*, 978-1-78561-843-7 (2018).

Saha, Rahul , Gulshan Kumar, Mritunjay Kumar Rai, et al., "Privacy Ensured e-Healthcare for Fog-Enhanced IoT Based Applications". *IEEE Access* 7 (2019): 44536–44543.

Sandro, Nizeti, Petar Soli, Diego López-De-Ipina González-de-Artaza and Luigi Patrono. "Internet of Things (Iot): Opportunities, Issues and Challenges Towards A Smart and Sustainable Future". *Journal of Cleaner Production* 274 (2020): 122877.

Spacer, Sara Beitel, Mohammad Mubashir, Kedir Mamo, Besher Mohammed and Zamshed Ali. "Prioritizing Health Care Data Traffic in a Congested IoT Cloud Network". 978-1-7281-5178-6, *IEEE Conference Paper*, IEEE (2020). http://dx.doi.org/10.1109/WCNCW48565.2020.9124867

Stergiou, Christos, Kostas E. Psannis, Byung-Gyu Kim and Brij Gupta. "Secure Integration of IoT and Cloud Computing". *Future Generation Computer Systems* 73, no. Part 3 (January 2018): 964–975.

Suguna, M., M.G. Ramalakshmi, J. Cynthia and D. Prakash. "A Survey on Cloud and Internet of Things Based Healthcare Diagnosis." *IEEE* (2018): 1–4.

Wang, Yujun Ma, Jun Yang, Yiming Miao and Wei Li, Yulei. "Big Health Application System based on Health Internet of Things and Big Data", 2169-3536. *IEEE* 5 (2017): 7885–7897.

Zhiqiang, Gao, He Lingsong, Tian Hang and Ling Cong, "A Cloud Computing Based Mobile Healthcare Service System". *IEEE 3rd International Conference on Smart Instrumentation , Measurement and Application (ICSIMA 2015)*, Putrajaya, Malaysia 1 6 (2015).

13

Cloud-Based Diagnostic and Management Framework for Remote Health Monitoring

Bharati Dixit[1], Advait Brahme[2], Shaunak Choudhary[2], Manasi Agrawal[2], and Atharva Kukade[2]
[1]*MIT World Peace University, Pune, India*
[2]*MIT College of Engineering, Pune, India*

CONTENTS

DOI: 10.1201/9781003203926-13

13.1 Introduction

Healthcare system of any country must ensure the well-being of the patients and should enrich the quality of life of the citizens. India has a huge healthcare system that is divided as a public and private healthcare line to serve the citizens but has many differences with respect to the volume and level of healthcare systems in urban and rural areas. There are many health schemes and policies rolled out by the government to make the healthcare facilities accessible and affordable to the masses. India being the second-largest population where the ratio of the number of patients per doctor is high, remote health monitoring becomes very significant as far as outreach of healthcare facilities are concerned.

The technologies that can play a pivotal role are the Internet of Things to interface wearable and non-wearable sensors, Cloud computing for remote access and storage of huge data, security of data, big data concepts, and advanced communication technologies for quick response and so on.

Researchers and scientists across the globe have proposed many models and frameworks for diagnostics of health and monitoring the availability, affordability, and accessibility of healthcare systems to the masses. These models serve the objective of effective utilization of healthcare infrastructure and efficient allocation and monitoring of healthcare services. A variety of such models are discussed in the paper.

This chapter proposes various methodologies for the design and development of remote healthcare systems. These methodologies are based on Data Science and Artificial Intelligence (AI), Cloud Technologies and also suggest leveraging the non-wearable and wearable sensor-based medical data capturing techniques through the Internet of Things (IoT), in addition to the location tracking and Cloud-based secured data storage mechanism.

The technologies commonly used for designing these models are data science and artificial intelligence and Cloud technologies with the biggest benefit of accessibility of data at anytime from anywhere.

Cloud computing can be used in remote healthcare monitoring in different ways by exploiting the inherent features as huge data storage, data security, and privacy. Various Cloud services can handle real-time data of patients, making the overall operations faster and accessible from any location. Security features in Cloud services/platforms can ensure safety and privacy of data. Various applications on different devices can be developed for healthcare analytics, record management, and overall patient care (Clarke et al., 2015; Ghosh 2016).

Cloud computing is a rapidly growing area and finding a path in the domain of healthcare, ubiquitous and for on-demand resources virtually available on pay-per-use model as well. Considering the growing demand of use of Cloud technology, many authors have carried out research in this area and findings are made available for further research. The major healthcare domains explored by researchers are telemedicine, medical imaging, hospital management, etc. (Griebel et al., 2015) with the statistics is revealed in Figure 13.1. These are the statistics of around one and half years, and is growing rapidly.

By leveraging the technological advancements, an e-healthcare model is developed to cater to the needs of patients and access of medical facilities and services to all the needy ones. The model is designed after analyzing various other existing systems and applications. Some of the limitations observed for existing systems are overcome in the implemented model. The model is part of this chapter as a case study and offers various

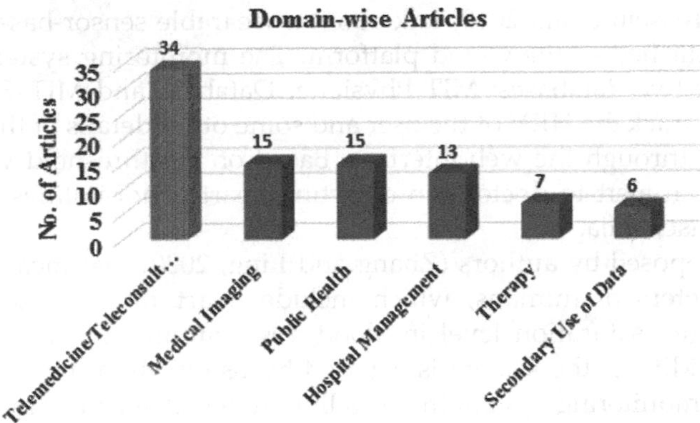

FIGURE 13.1
Use of Cloud computing in major health domains (Based on Lena Griebel et al., 2015).

features like disease prediction, virtual appointments with the doctor, finding the nearest clinic or hospital, and so on.

This chapter is further developed under different sections. Section II discusses the relevant work carried out by various researchers and diverse approaches for remote healthcare monitoring systems are presented in Section III. Section IV elaborates the implemented model of remote healthcare monitoring as an exemplary case study. This chapter concludes with the mention of the future scope in Section V. Acknowledgment and references are part of the chapter in the sections to follow.

13.2 Literature Review

Literature from renowned journals is referred to obtain know-how of the current state of the work in the area of healthcare systems and services. Some of the papers discussing related work carried out by various researchers are discussed in this section.

The authors (Albahri et al., 2019) proposed health monitoring with unique features like handling increasing numbers of users, monitoring of real-time data from remote patients, etc. are considered for designing the model. The model has the limitation that it cannot prioritize patients based on the urgency of treatment.

The researchers (Mathur et al., 2016) have proposed a cost effective wearable mobile sensor platform with the primary advantage that the system can be used in the absence of internet connectivity and works well on Android platforms. The authors have used Raspberry Pi, a low-cost microcontroller, and incorporated the use of solar energy to power the system. The system has a limitation that it records readings only during a small time period of movement, which may not always represent the accurate health status of the limb.

The paper discusses (Alizadeh et al., 2019) the use of electromagnetic radars instead of sensors or wearable devices to extract heart and respiratory rates in a bedroom setting. The system is functional with better accuracy for breathing and heart as compared to systems based on sensors. The system can be extended to track different vital organs or ECG patterns using frequency modulated continuous waves.

The authors (Hussein et al., 2018) talk about a wearable sensor-based heart rate monitoring system attached to the Cloud platform. The monitoring system is implemented and analyzed for two databases: MIT Physionet Database and MIT–St. Petersburg. The wearable devices track the HRV of the user and some other details of the user like gender, age, and address through the web interface. Based on the threshold values, the web interface can send an alert to doctors on detecting heart abnormalities like hypertension, arrhythmia, and ischemia.

A system is proposed by authors (Zhang and Ling, 2020) that measures six vital physiological parameters of humans, which include heart rate, blood pressure, electrocardiogram, oxygen saturation level in blood, respiration, and body temperature. The accuracy and validity of the system is ensured by using Mindray's iMEC10, which is a multi-parameter monitoring system that has limitations of speed of monitoring terminal.

The researchers (Ismail et al., 2020) developed a fully connected CNN structure–based regular pattern mining model that uses IoT devices to collect information regarding health conditions. The proposed model takes into consideration the parameters like blood pressure, body mass index, and blood sugar levels. Different raw data pre-processing methods can affect the performance of the CNN model.

The authors (Verma and Mishra, 2020) have proposed a system in which the vital data is measured using sensors and uses the Cloud for data storage. The proposed system is reliable, cost effective, and portable. The main aim of the system is to create an interface between people living in the rural areas and health practitioners.

The system developed by researchers (Gupta et al., 2018) needs the patient to carry the remote monitoring system device with themselves. Some of the sensors include temperature sensor, blood pressure sensor, ECG sensor, pulse oximeter, etc., to capture data and send to doctors. The authors have proposed the security of the system using blockchain technology. The system is scalable and cost effective.

A system is proposed (Bekiri et al., 2020) to automatically monitor the health using data collected from smart watches used by patients and doctors. Decision models using machine learning methods are built using the data. The system based on machine learning models have already designed, implemented, and validated on data of cardiovascular diseases. Remote servers have admin modules that can build automated decision models for disease prediction. The designed model provides better accuracy.

The research carried out (Jeddi and Bohr, 2020) has suggested the use of technologies like artificial intelligence and natural language processing to make patient monitoring more efficient and effective. The need of the system is justified as it can offer services to a growing number of people with chronic diseases. The use of wearable technologies and affordable software solutions demonstrate improved health outcomes and cost effectiveness.

The authors (Kuo et al., 2012) have studied data gathered from three different geographical locations and proposed possible solutions to Cloud-based data mining, which will help in migrating from traditional ways to Cloud-based solutions that can be leveraged in making the applications efficient, accessible, and secured in the domain of healthcare, agriculture, transportation, etc.

IT services are constantly being used in all aspects of the healthcare industry these days. Cloud storage seems to be a viable way to meet IT requirements in a cost-effective manner. As a result, the authors (Ermakova et al., 2013) have examined current research findings across topics to identify areas for potential research, such as the creation, validation, and enhancement of proposed solutions, as well as an assessment process.

The study (Kakria et al., 2015) has proposed an affordable and user-friendly data protection technique using a Cloud database system. Due to technological advancements, the spectrum of remote health monitoring systems has been greatly expanded. The proposed system by authors elaborates on data privacy aspects and enriches the solution.

The researchers (Kalid et al., 2017) have proposed a patient prioritization process. Focus is placed on the transparent problems and various aspects of using big data in the patient prioritization process. The approach proposes the decision making based on patient's data and prioritizing the patient's data.

The authors (Malasinge et al., 2017) have provided a review of different aspects of designing and deploying the remote healthcare system, right from data capturing until receiving a solution from doctors through a Cloud-based system. Different challenges at each level of the system are discussed.

The study of related literature highlight the need of remote health monitoring systems. The use of technological advancements in building more secure and efficient models and frameworks for diagnostic and remote health monitoring systems are elaborated in further sections. A smart doctor-patient system is implemented with the objective of remote health monitoring with added features of disease prediction.

13.3 Diverse Approaches for a Remote Healthcare Monitoring System

There are many facets of diagnostic and management of remote healthcare systems. Under this umbrella, many subsystems can be developed that can improve the healthcare system infrastructure and services. These subsystems can facilitate the expansion of the outreach of healthcare facilities to the masses and can improve quality of life. Cloud technologies is at the heart of any remote healthcare systems. This is because Cloud-based storage systems for data are preferred due to secure storage, cost efficiency, as well as easy to operate.

Different approaches are adopted by various researchers to design healthcare systems that can add value and make the system effective and efficient. Cloud-based storage is an integral part in some of these systems, while in other systems where Cloud computing is not used, it is recommended that the system can be made more efficient by using that approach. Some of the approaches are discussed in this section.

13.3.1 E-Health Monitoring System

This system is designed by Kotevski et al. (2016) with the objective of monitoring health parameters of patients remotely. The system is very useful for the people who cannot travel frequently and do not have access to medical facilities.

The available technologies of smart TV and mobile and web applications are integrated for designing this system. Patient data collection is done through mobile and web applications. Notifications and reminders of timely consumption of medicines can be given by smart TV application. This application improves the connectivity and accessibility of patient and doctor. The system can be made better with the help of feedback from all the stakeholders.

Web services are used to deploy the applications. The database of patient's vital health parameters is created using MS-SQL. Any net-enabled device can access the application. The general architecture is as presented in Figure 13.2.

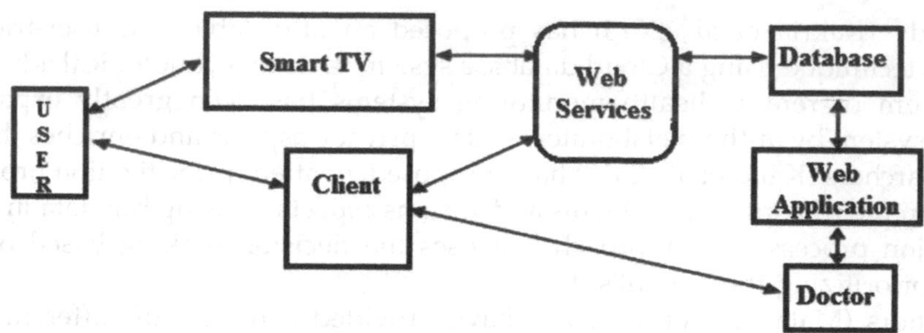

FIGURE 13.2
General architecture (Based on Kotevski et al., 2016).

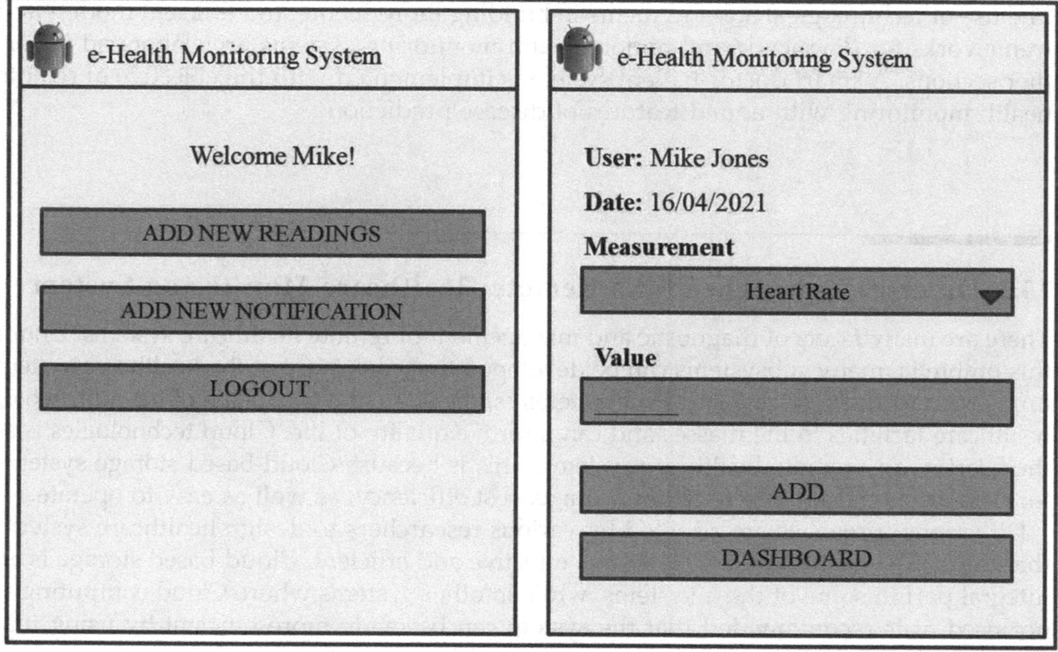

FIGURE 13.3
Patient interface (Adapted from Kotevski et al., 2016).

The patient's interface for the system is described below. Patients have their own profile and account through which they can view their prescriptions and any specific instructions given by the doctors. Patients can update the vital health parameters using the account of their own.

The usability aspects by elderly people are considered while designing a patient's interface. The interface needs minimal typing, large fonts, and clear directions as features of UI. The snapshot of the patient's interface and doctor's interface is as shown in Figures 13.3 and 13.4, respectively.

This cost-effective remote health monitoring system is easy to deploy and use, and provides better virtual connectivity between the doctor and patient. Also, by using Cloud

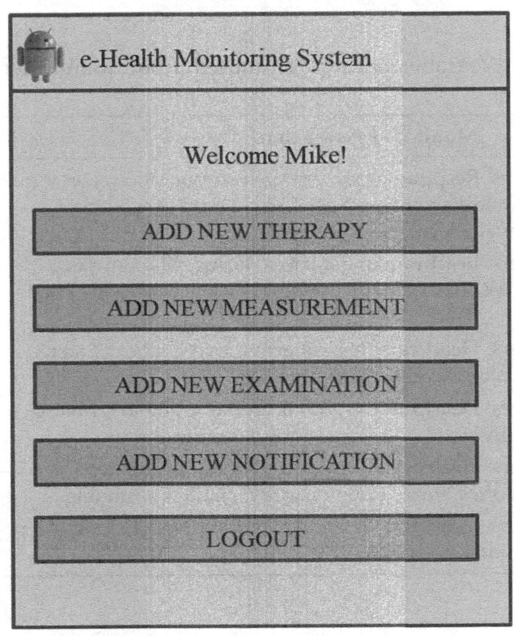

FIGURE 13.4
Doctor dashboard (Adapted from Kotevski et al., 2016).

computing, the data would be accessible from any place, at any given point of time, thus making the system more robust and user friendly.

13.3.2 Wearable Sensors-Based Remote Health Monitoring System

Energy-efficient and cost-effective remote health monitoring systems are designed using wearable sensors (Majumder et al., 2017). The system is designed after studying various cost-effective, non-invasive, and wearable sensor approaches for remote health monitoring. Before incorporating textile-based sensors in design, the compatibility of various communication technologies for remote health monitoring is studied.

Different products developed to support a variety of applications are tabulated in Table 13.1. These products are designed based on physiological parameters obtained through monitoring physical activities and through wearable sensors.

Overview of remote health monitoring systems designed to monitor cardiovascular measurements, knee joint monitoring, blood pressure, SpO2 level, and other physiological parameters is as presented in Figure 13.5. The general architecture of an ECG monitoring system and details of a cardiovascular monitoring system is as represented in Figures 13.6 and 13.7 and displays activity monitoring for a typical walking cycle as captured by the health monitoring system.

Comparative study of various activity monitoring systems is as tabulated in Table 13.2.

The system discussed is designed by using multiple sensors. All the sensors wearable on textile and communication protocols are chosen for effective communication of health data to respective processing modules. Various physiological parameters and physical activities are measured to further transfer the data to a health provider. The system highlights the need of an effective data handling algorithm to be deployed at the data collection node to handle large volumes of data. The algorithms should cater the data security and privacy as an important factor.

TABLE 13.1

Comparative Study of Products Designed Using Wearable Sensors (Adapted from Majumder et al., 2017)

Product Name	Monitored Parameters
Biometric Shirt by Hexoskin	Physiological parameters: Respiratory rate, oxygen consumption, Heart rate and its variabilityPhysical activities: No. of steps, pace of walking/running, distance travelled, calories burnt etc.
Fitness Tracker by Jawbone UP3	Physiological parameters: heart rate, parameters during different sleep stagesPhysical activities: No. of steps, running, distance covered, Food and liquid intake
Fusion Bio Fitness Tracker by Striiv	Physiological parameters: Heart ratePhysical activities: Number of steps, calories burned, distance travelled, sleep quality
Band 2 by Microsoft	Physiological parameters: Heart ratePhysical activities: Climbing, biking, running, Sleep quantity, food and liquid intake, calories burnt.
Fitness Tracker by Fitbit	Physiological parameters: Heart RatePhysical activities: No. of steps, food and liquid intake, calories burnt, sleep quantity, climbing, running
Fitness Tracker by Garmin vivosmart	Physiological parameters: Heart RatePhysical activities: No. of steps, sleep quantity, climbing, running, swimming

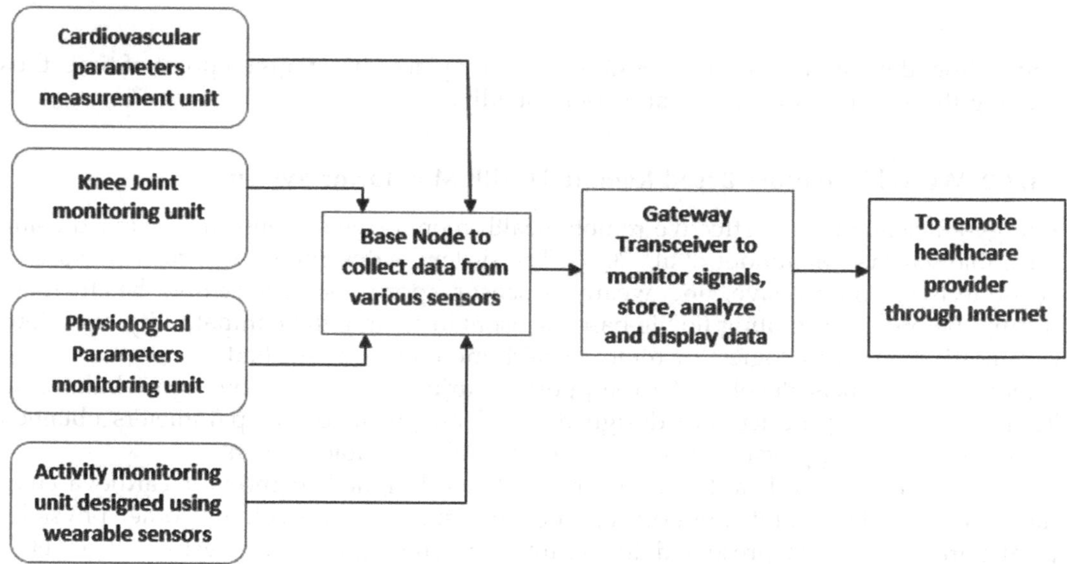

FIGURE 13.5
Overview of the remote health monitoring system (Based on Majumder et al., 2017).

13.3.3 Secured Remote Health Monitoring System

It is a Cloud-based system that explores different facets of Cloud technologies for access control and secure transmission of data for medical sensor networks. Various encryption and decryption algorithms are deployed to secure the data transmission over the network (Sathya and Pugalendhi, 2012). All the entities in the system are connected to the Cloud-based database, which is used for storage of all the data generated by the system.

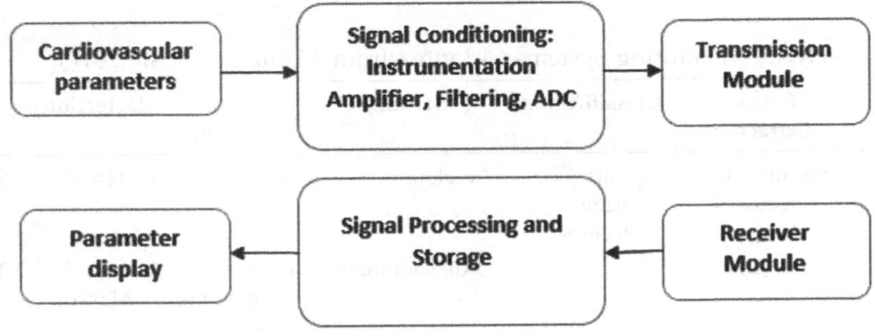

FIGURE 13.6
Cardiovascular system details (Based on Majumder et al., 2017).

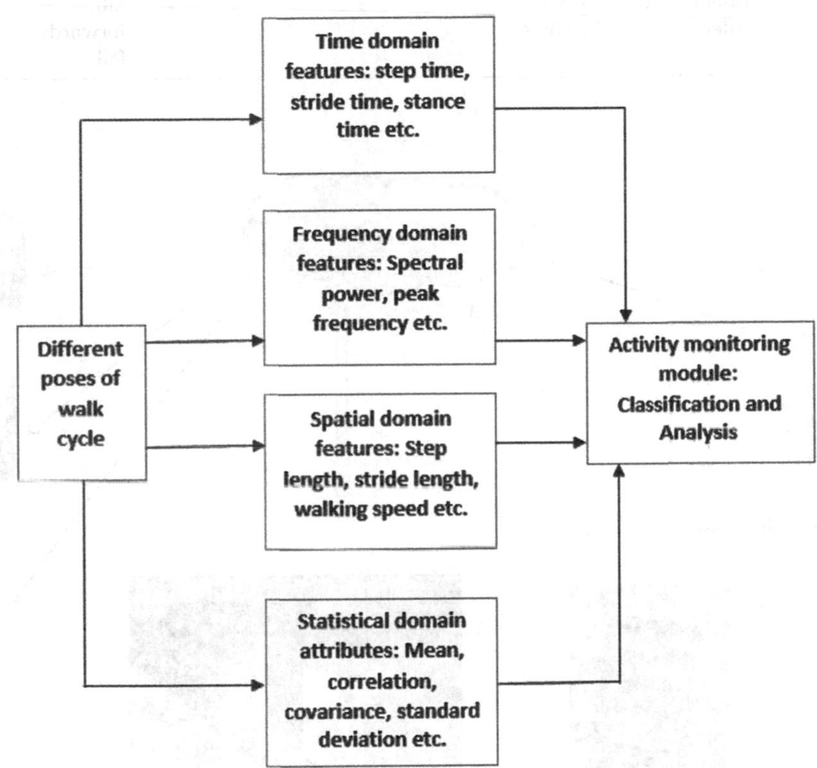

FIGURE 13.7
Activity monitoring for a typical walk cycle (Based on Majumder et al., 2017).

The system is designed using various body sensors and the security aspects of collected data is well taken care of in the system. An overview of the system is presented in Figure 13.8.

The system is designed using a combination of different encryption and deception algorithms for better results in terms of a secure system. Timing parameters of encryption

TABLE 13.2

Summary of Activity Monitoring Systems (Adapted from Majumder et al., 2017)

Proposition	Feature Extraction	Classification	Sensors	Sensor Placement	Detection	Percentage Accuracy
Recognition system for GAIT	Significant Features	Support Vector Machine	Accelerometer	Waist	Different walking speed	>99%.
Algorithm			development	Time-Frequency domain features	Hidden Markov	3-axis gyroscope
Chest	Walking, running	~95%				
Fall Detection system	Madgwick orientation filter	Support Vector Machine	Accelerometer	Waist	Backward fall, forward fall	90.37%–100%

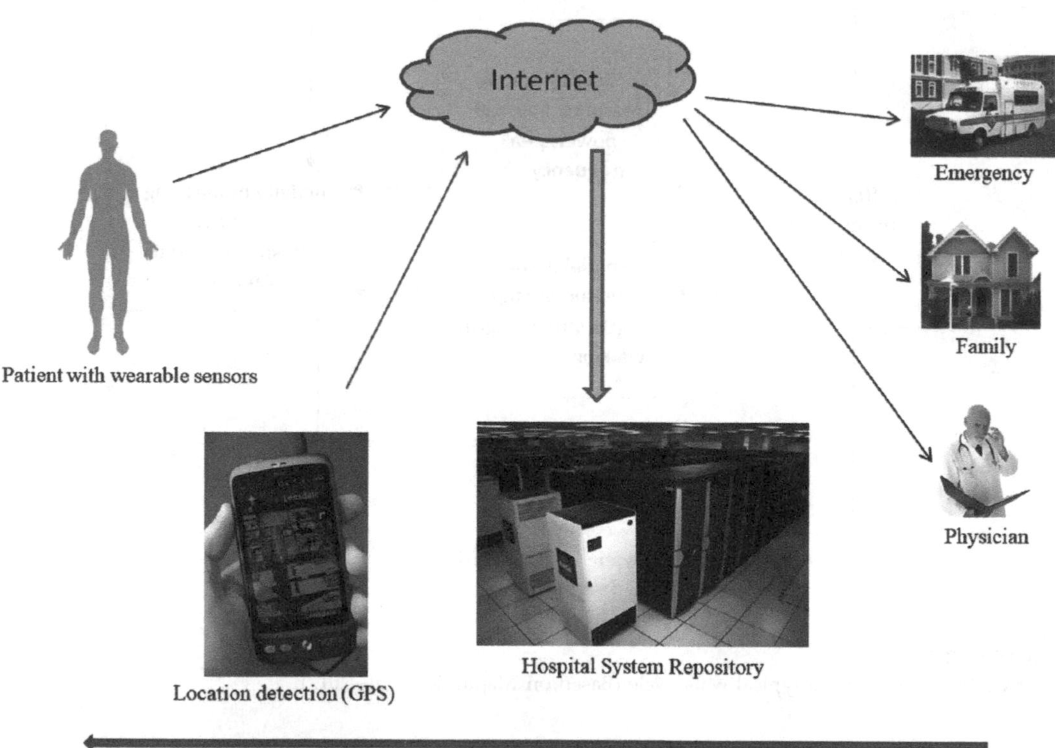

FIGURE 13.8
Overview of secured health monitoring system (Based on Sathya and Pugalendhi, 2012).

TABLE 13.3

Total Computation Time (Adapted from Sathya and Pugalendhi, 2012)

Algorithms	51 Kb	204 Kb	407 Kb	1,531 Kb	3,061 Kb	6,122 Kb	9,193 Kb
AES and MD5, s	7	10	15	19	25	35	42
CP-ABE and AES, s	12	15	18	30	33	42	56
Blowfish and CP-ABE, s – SHS	5	5.5	7.6	13	15.2	24	30

and decryption algorithms are compared. Total computation time for some of the algorithms is as suggested in Table 13.3.

Wireless data transmission is more vulnerable with respect to security aspects. The confidential medical data of patients is secured by using encryption and decryption algorithms. Public key algorithms are more computationally intensive so they are not suitable for small data transmission. The popular algorithms available are AES, DES, Blowfish, RC6, IDEA, etc. are considered and tested on time parameters with respect to message sizes varying from 50 Kb to 1 Mb. Most of the algorithms performed well and can be chosen depending upon the requirement of application.

13.3.4 Smart Technology for Healthcare Professionals – An Analysis

The power and usage of mobile devices has been extensively increased for the past 5 years. The use of smart technology has transformed every sector, specifically the healthcare sector. Hospital management, inclusive of doctors, patients, and nurses, are very much dependent on smart technology and mobile devices. Multiple applications and software are being developed specifically for clinical practices (Ventola, 2014). The chief aim of adopting mobile devices in the healthcare sector is to provide a more reliable communication channel for hospital management. Healthcare professionals need multiple resources and adopting mobile devices in healthcare will help in providing the following resources easily.

This system explores the use and need of technology for the healthcare sector. The healthcare professionals use mobile gadgets for various reasons. Some of them like maintaining health records, for drug references, to monitor patients, etc. Various advantages of mobile devices and apps like increased efficiency and accuracy, convenience, and improved productivity are explored in this system. The facts related to usage of digital gadgets are as tabulated in Table 13.4.

The other requirements of the systems are the availability of a decision support system, diagnostic aids, interfaces to communicate patient's health and medical records, integrated text messages and mailing facility, voice calling, and videoconferencing facility.

TABLE 13.4

Use of Digital Gadgets (Based on Ventola, 2014)

Device	Percentage Use
Laptops/Desktops	98%
Tablets	63%
Smartphones	56%

Various information management systems can also be used as required by the system. Some of the commonly used information management systems are iAnnotate PDF viewer, tools provided by Google suit, etc.

The predicted trends suggest that the use of digital gadgets will be popularly used in managing chronic diseases, whereas apps that can provide better communication systems between patients and physicians are also the need of the hour. It is recommended that the future direction data storage modules of similar applications can be deployed using Cloud computing for seamless operation of such mobile applications.

The limitations of the approach are reluctance in use of these tools by health professionals and usage of tools without evaluating the risks involved with it. A thorough, rigorous evaluation and validation of healthcare apps is necessary to safeguard the patient's data as well as a professional who is handling this data.

13.3.5 Disease Prediction as an Added Feature of an e-Healthcare Application

The system is based on the idea of preparing the data set of common symptoms of various diseases and predictions using machine learning algorithms. The e-health application developed using the data sets can be made accessible to users from anywhere in the world by incorporating Cloud computing. This can serve as an add-on feature of e-health applications for certain diseases where prediction can help users to be cautious about their health and adopt necessary changes in their lifestyle and plan the medical treatment as a preventive measure. One such disease prediction methodology is discussed in the section below.

The researchers have deployed probability-based machine learning on a database with 4,920 records and 41 diseases. Prediction was attempted using three different algorithms: decision tree, naive Bayes, and random forest (Grampurohit and Sagarnal, 2020). Performance comparison of three algorithm decision trees, random forest and naïve Bayes is as tabulated in Table 13.5. The results are obtained after an application of these algorithms on the data of 41 new patients, taking into consideration 95 symptoms.

The study concludes with a recommendation of the use of artificial intelligence in disease prediction as a future direction for increasing the volume of data and stored using modern technology like the Cloud for better accessibility, efficient storage, and preserving the privacy of confidential medical data.

13.3.6 Cloud Technology Supported Hospital File Management System

With the advent of ICT and Cloud technologies, it is possible to manage the medical records of patients with appropriate measures to maintain security of rapidly growing

TABLE 13.5

Performance Comparison of the Three Algorithms (Based on Grampurohit and Sagarnal, 2020)

Algorithm Used	Accuracy Score	Confusion matrix	
		Correctly classified	Incorrectly classified
Decision Tree	0.951219	39	2
Random Forest	0.951219	39	2
Naive Bayes	0.951219	39	2

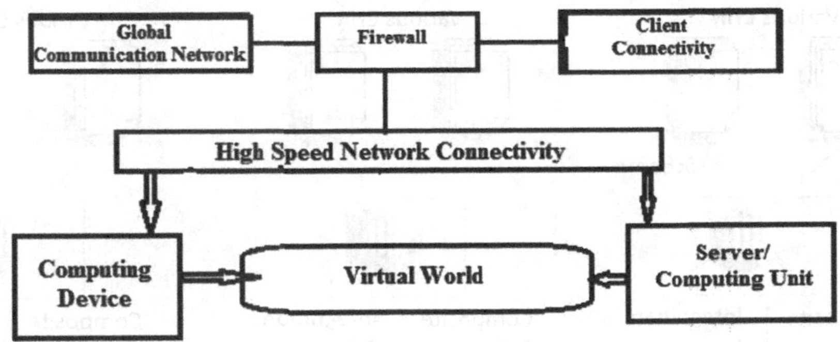

FIGURE 13.9
Overview of hospital file management system (Adapted from Naveen Ananda Kumar and Suresh, 2019).

records. Multispecialty hospital chains with many centers within and across the countries can exploit the benefit of the proposed hospital management system (Naveen Ananda Kumar and Suresh, 2019).

Various Cloud computing platforms, computing service stack, and need-based hiring of Cloud services are making space in hospital management systems. The architecture of HFMS provides registration of clients/patients in the HFMS system and the availability of all medical records along with medical history is available to doctors through HFMS. The architecture of HFMS is as shown in Figure 13.9.

Various challenges like stability of operation, availability and interoperability of data, and confidentiality of data leads to setting up a health Cloud – a solution can address the challenges to some extent by encrypting the EHR – electronic health record prior to storing on a Cloud server. Every challenge can be handled at a different level so a collaborative health informatics research model is proposed by authors, as shown in Figure 13.10. Cloud models can be mapped with security models and compliance models as elaborated in Figure 13.11.

To ensure the security of health data, it is recommended to store electronic records in a separate network, vulnerability checks, risk assessments, and audits must be in place. It is necessary to install firewalls and use antivirus software with adequate features can handle all the security aspects. All these measures enable the HFMS to be deployable to the service of the community.

13.4 Exemplary Design "Smart Doctor-Patient Diagnostic and Management System"

13.4.1 System at a Glance

The implemented system as "Smart Doctor – Patient Diagnostic and Management System" is discussed in this section. This system provides an application interface for patient record interoperability. To achieve this, the system supports data storage on the firebase database, which is a Cloud-hosted database (Greenhalgh et al., 2016; Singh et al., 2018; Marzencki et al., 2011) and supports easy-to-manage electronic records. Hence, tracking and monitoring of patients and their case sheets can be efficiently carried out without any use of paperwork. Using the SVM algorithm in machine learning, the application is designed to

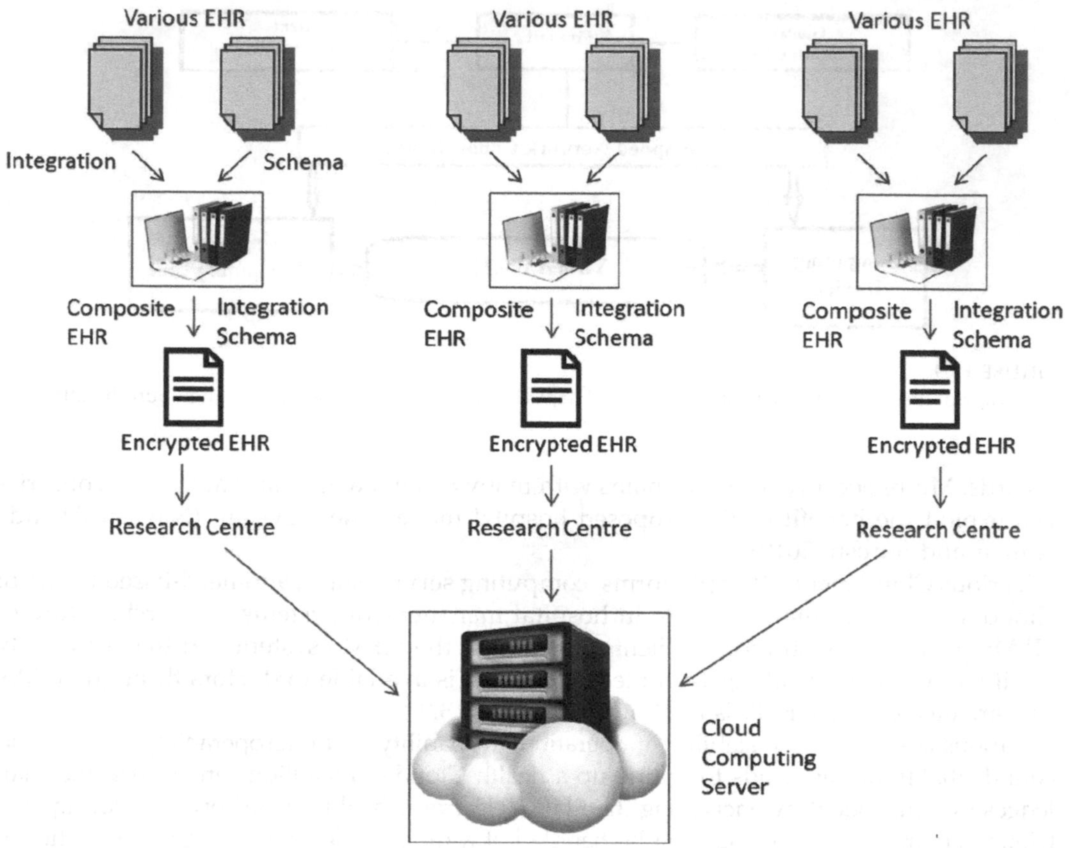

Various EHR Various EHR Various EHR

Integration Schema

Composite EHR Integration Schema

Encrypted EHR

Research Centre

Cloud Computing Server

FIGURE 13.10
Overview of hospital file management system (Based on Naveen Ananda Kumar and Suresh 2019).

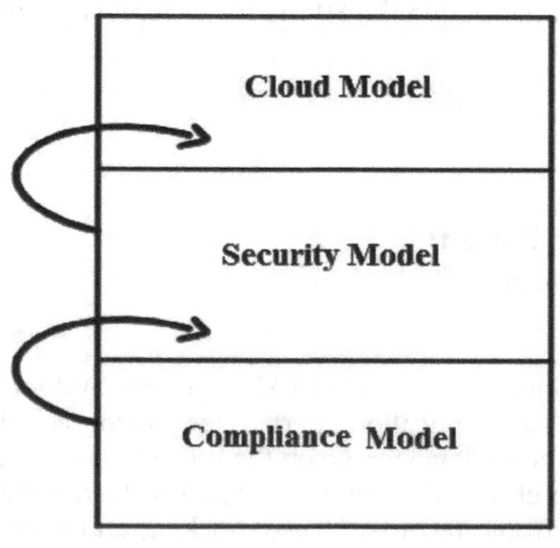

FIGURE 13.11
Synchronization and mapping of models (Adapted from Naveen Ananda Kumar and Suresh, 2019).

predict the disease(s) that a patient may be suffering from. This prediction is based on the history data and the symptoms the patient has developed. The application has a medical anomaly probability predictor. A lot of people these days are blindsided as they do not know what disease their symptoms point to. The application gives a probabilistic answer to this. In addition to this, the application is equipped with various other features like locating the nearest hospital/doctor's clinic, text-to-speech conversion, secure record of prescriptions and patient documents, etc. The application is safe and secure as access is given to patients and doctors only by using their unique login credentials, like the official registration number for doctors, or unique password for patients and so on.

13.4.2 Overview

"Smart Doctor – Patient Diagnostic and Management System" is an Android application targeted for connecting doctors and patients seamlessly, and making their communication simpler. In uncertain times like COVID-19 pandemic times, when people have restrictions moving out of their house, this application will help them not to miss their regular interactions with their doctor. Also, the SVM Machine Learning algorithm (Bratan and Clarke 2006; Majumdar et al., 2018; Ferrua et al., 2020) based disease prediction module is part of this application. Using this module, a patient can get an idea of what disease he may be suffering from, as per the symptoms faced. This module is only for giving the patient a rough idea, which will help him in deciding which doctor or specialist to visit. This system/application is not replacement of doctors, and strongly recommend taking medical advice before deriving conclusions. The application has a prescription module, where doctors can upload prescriptions for the patient, and patients receive the same on his mobile device. All these prescriptions and documents are stored remotely on the Cloud-hosted Firebase Database, thus ensuring its security and privacy. Doctors can log in after entering their official registration number. This adds a security layer, and keeps the authenticity of the application. Using "find a doctor feature," patients can locate the nearest hospital or doctor's clinic. The application is linked with Google Maps to make it more efficient. Another feature of the application is the text-to-speech conversion. In times where social distancing is becoming the norm, doctors and patients can sit at a safe distance from each other and still communicate smoothly. Whatever is typed on the mobile phone will be spoken on the speaker and be easily audible. All in all, the developed application is a one-stop solution to making the workings of the doctor–patient relationship more efficient and enhances the outreach of doctors and other medical facilities.

13.4.3 System Modules

The complete implementation of the system includes various modules or activities that the system performs. This section of the chapter throws light on the different features of the applications as an app/product and how they operate. The application is addressing the following functional requirements.

13.4.3.1 Disease Prediction

Sometimes when people have certain disease symptoms they are able to determine what they may exactly be suffering from. The disease prediction module helps in providing the insight. The user has to select the symptoms that they are suffering from. The app has incorporated most common symptoms the user can select by ticking the checkbox. Based on the symptoms provided by the user, the app shows three likely diseases that are most common with respect to the entered symptoms. The database includes the mapping of a number of diseases and their symptoms. This database has been developed using information from medical journals, medical websites and doctors, and is stored and retrieved from Google firebase Cloud. At the same time, the database is dynamic and gets continuously updated. Most importantly, this module does not give a 100% guarantee about any disease but surely shows the path to the user. It is strongly recommend that as per the predicted disease, the patient immediately take the advice from a relevant doctor. The functionality described next is in line with this approach.

13.4.3.2 Finding a Doctor

As mentioned previously, the app only suggests which disease a patient may have, and does not give a diagnosis. In this module, the patient will be able to find nearby doctors, clinics, and hospitals as per their requirements. The app is linked directly to Google Maps, so that when a user enters this module and searches with keywords like "hospital," Google Maps will be opened and show you the hospitals nearby the user's current location. To use this module, the user has to allow the application to access their current location.

13.4.3.3 Online Prescription

This feature is similar to sending a message. The doctor can write a prescription through the app on his mobile device. Once the doctor saves that prescription for a patient, it gets uploaded on the Google firebase Cloud. Patients can view the prescription after the doctor has uploaded one. The prescription also gets stored on the Google firebase Cloud, and the patient can refer to all his previous prescriptions. To maintain the authenticity and security, only the doctor will be able to add or edit a prescription. The patient can only view the prescription. This will prevent any malpractices that may otherwise take place.

13.4.3.4 Text-to-Speech Conversion

This is an additional feature to make the application more user friendly. Especially in patients who are senior citizens, they may face difficulties reading the contents of the prescription or other details from the screen of their phone. Using text to speech, the patients will be able to hear it instead of reading them. This would also be beneficial while ordering medicines, as many times people are not able to pronounce the names of certain medicines properly. This feature can also help in current COVID times to maintain social distancing.

13.4.3.5 Emergency Alert Button

This button is like an SOS button, helping people contact their close ones in the time of an emergency. The user will pre-enter the contact details of the people whom he would contact in an emergency. During the emergency, clicking on a single button will send an emergency message to those contacts.

13.4.3.6 Doctor Login with Registration Number

As per the security measure of the app, a doctor can only register with their official registration number. The registration number of the doctor is stored in the Google

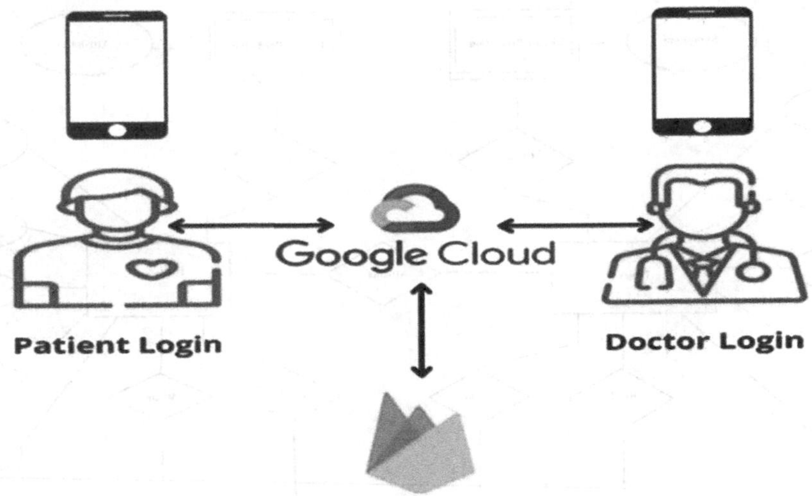

FIGURE 13.12
The system design.

firebase Cloud. If the registration number of the doctor matches with the one in our Cloud storage, only then is the signup approved. Thus, it is not possible for any other person to register himself as a doctor with the app.

13.4.4 System Design

We have modeled the application in a way that will be helpful in designing and shaping the further process. The system architecture and ER diagram are as depicted in Figures 13.12 and 13.13, respectively.

13.4.5 ER Diagram

An entity-relationship model, i.e., an ER diagram, shows interrelation between the various entities of a system. The ER diagram depicts the connectivity among different modules of the app. The two main entities of the system are the patient and the doctor. They are connected with each through the system, and have a number of different parameters and features as a part of the system. Most of these are the same for the patient and the doctor, while some specific ones are different. For example, a patient can only read a prescription, but a doctor can write, i.e., make changes in the prescription as well.

13.4.6 Algorithm Details

The SVM algorithm is used, which is abbreviated for Support Vector Machine Algorithm. SVM is a supervised learning model, and is associated with learning algorithms that analyze the data used for regression analysis and classification.

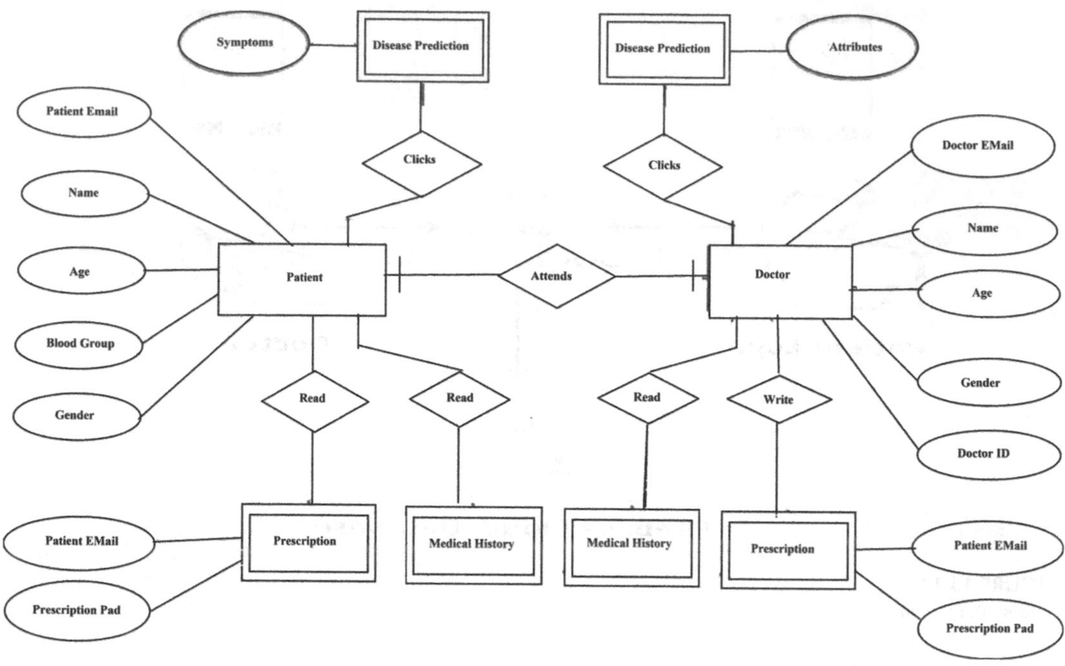

FIGURE 13.13
ER diagram.

The steps to build a classification model using SVM are:

1. Use around 60% samples for initial model building
2. Use 40% samples to test the model
3. For each feature, find the best decision of categorization
4. Calculate generalized value for each related feature
5. Order the feature to find significant features
6. Use preserved samples to retrain the model
7. Use each pair of features until the last step of training

The training of the model is complete when the error rate is at a minimum and stabilizes. Now the model can be used to perform classification of patients' records.

13.4.7 Dashboard for Patient and for Doctors

An Android application is developed to connect patients with doctors seamlessly. The dashboard for a patient with features like viewing patient profile, medical history of patient, common symptoms for diseases, the utility of find the doctor, and availability of prescription is designed.

The doctors who are registered on the application can create their profile. Along with the profile, the doctors can see the list of their patients, their medical history, earlier prescriptions, etc.

After the updates are given by patients through the app, the concerned doctor can advise the patient for common diseases with mild symptoms.

13.4.8 Concluding Remarks

The Smart Doctor – Patient Diagnostic and Management System has been developed in the form of an Android application. More features can be added to the existing application like booking appointment of doctors, uploading lab reports, etc. By using a hardware device like an NFC chip, application can be equipped with better security. This application can be used by both doctors and patients. With the support of Cloud technologies, hospitals can also use it to manage their entire database and have all records stored in a single database, which can be secured and made available on a single click from anywhere and anytime.

13.5 Conclusions and Future Work

Good healthcare systems and services are one of the basic needs of every individual. Providing all time access to affordable healthcare systems is a challenge for any nation, especially countries with very large populations.

Technology-enabled diagnostic and management services for remote healthcare systems can provide solutions to a large extent for these challenges. The outreach of existing healthcare infrastructure and services can be expanded with the support of technology.

Some of the prominent approaches adopted by various researchers are discussed at length. The effective solution provided by implementation of "Smart Doctor – Patient Diagnostic and Management System" is elaborated in depth.

All of these approaches and developed systems provide a viable and feasible solution to take a step forward towards deployment of models and frameworks for diagnostic and management of remote healthcare systems.

However, there is always room to explore selection and interface of sensors to capture health parameters effectively, efficient and secured algorithms, low-cost data storage, and availability of 24X7 Internet support and so on. These requirements can be sufficed by Cloud-based systems, however advancements in relevant technologies should be explored to make the systems better.

Acknowledgments

We acknowledge the contribution of all the researchers who devised and proposed various approaches of designing remote healthcare systems. This has laid a good foundation to improve upon the performance of the existing systems and design of new systems in line with advances in technology.

References

Alizadeh, M., G. Shaker, J. C. M. D. Almeida, P. P. Morita and S. Safavi-Naeini. "Remote Monitoring of Human Vital Signs Using mm-Wave FMCW Radar." *IEEE Access* 7 (2019): 54958–54968.

Bekiri, R., A. Djeffal and M. Hettiri. "A Remote Medical Monitoring System Based on Data Mining." *1st International Conference on Communications, Control Systems and Signal Processing (CCSSP), EL OUED*, Algeria (2020): 282–286.

Bratan, T. and M. Clarke. "Optimum Design of Remote Patient Monitoring Systems." *International Conference of the IEEE Engineering in Medicine and Biology Society*, New York, NY (2006): 6465–6468.

Clarke, M., P. Schluter, B. Reinhold and B. Reinhold. "Designing Robust and Reliable Timestamps for Remote Patient Monitoring." *IEEE Journal of Biomedical and Health Informatics* 19, no. 5 (2015): 1718–1723.

Ermakova, Tatiana, Jan Huenges, Koray Erek, Ruediger Zarnekow. "Cloud Computing in Healthcare – A Literature Review on Current State of Research." *Americas Conference on Information Systems, Chicago*, Illinois, USA (August 2013).

Ferrua, Marie, Minvielle, Etienna., Fourcade, Aude, et al., "How to Design a Remote Patient Monitoring System? A French Case Study." *BMC Health Services Research* 20 (2020): 434.

Ghosh, A. M., D. Halder and S. K. A. Hossain "Remote health monitoring system through IoT." *2016 5th International Conference on Informatics, Electronics and Vision (ICIEV)*, Dhaka (2016): 921–926.

Grampurohit, Sneha and Chetan Sagarnal. "Disease Prediction using Machine Learning Algorithms." *International Conference for Emerging Technology* (INCET), Belgaum, India (2020): 1–7.

Greenhalgh Trisha, Vijayaraghavan Shanti, Wherton Joe, et al., "Virtual Online Consultations: Advantages and Limitations (VOCAL) study." *BMJ Open* 6 2016): 282–286.

Griebel, Lena, Hans-Ulrich Prokosch, Felix Köpcke, Dennis Toddenroth, Jan Christoph, Ines Leb, Igor Engel and Martin Sedlmayr. "A Scoping Review of Cloud Computing in Healthcare." *BMC Medical Informatics and Decision Making* 15 (2015): 17, DOI: 10.1186/s12911-015-0145-7.

Gupta, Sarthak, Divyansh Dahiya and G. Raj. "Remote Health Monitoring System Using IoT." *International Conference on Advances in Computing and Communication Engineering* (ICACCE), Paris (2018):300–305.

Hussein, Ahamed Faeq, N. Arun Kumar, Marton. Burbano-Fernandez, Gustavo Ramírez-González, Enas Abdulhay and Victor Hugo C. De Albuquerque. "An Automated Remote Cloud-Based Heart Rate Variability MGustavoonitoring System." *IEEE Access* 6 (2018): 77055–77064.

Ismail, W. N., M. M. Hassan, H. A. Alsalamah and G. Fortino. "CNN-Based Health Model for Regular Health Factors Analysis in Internet-of-Medical Things Environment." *IEEE Access* 8 (2020): 52541–52549.

Jeddi, Zineb and Adam Bohr. "Remote Patient Monitoring Using Artificial Intelligence." *Artificial Intelligence in Healthcare*, Academic Press, (2020): 203–234.

Kakria, Priyanka, N. K. Tripathi, Peerapong Kitipawang. "A Real-Time Health Monitoring System for Remote Cardiac Patients Using Smartphone and Wearable Sensors." *International Journal of Telemedicine and Applications* vol. 2015, Article ID 373474, 11 pages.

Kalid, Naser, A. Zaidan, Bilal Bahaa, Omar Salman, Mashitoh Hashim and Muzammil Hussain. "Based Real Time Remote Health Monitoring Systems: A Review on Patients Prioritization and Related "Big Data" Using Body Sensors information and Communication Technology." *Journal of Medical Systems* 42, no. 2 (2017): 1–30.

Kotevski, Aleksandar, Natasa Koceska and Saso Koceski. E-health Monitoring System (2016): 259–265.

Kuo, Mu-Hsing, Feipei Lai, Sarangerel Dorjgochoo and Chinburen Jigjidsuren. "A Cloud Computing Based Platform for Sharing Healthcare Research Information." *International Conference on Collaboration Technologies and Systems (CTS) by IEEE* (2012).

Majumder, S., T. Mondal and M.J. Deen. "Wearable Sensors for Remote Health Monitoring." *Sensors* 17, no. 1 (January 2017): 130. DOI: 10.3390/s17010130.

Majumder, S., M. A. Rahman, M. S. Islam and D. Ghosh. "Design and Implementation of a Wireless Health Monitoring System for Remotely Located Patients." *4th International Conference on Electrical Engineering and Information & Communication Technology* (iCEEiCT), Dhaka, Bangladesh (2018): 86–91.

Malasinghe, L.P., N. Ramzan and K. Dahal. "Remote Patient Monitoring: A Comprehensive Study." *Journal of Ambient Intelligence and Humanized Computing* 10 (2017): 57–76.

Mathur, Neha, G. Paul, James Irvine, Mohamed Abuhelala, Arjan Buis and Ivan Glesk. "A Practical Design and Implementation of a Low Cost Platform for Remote Monitoring of Lower Limb Health of Amputees in the Developing World." *IEEE Access* 4 (2016): 7440–7451.

Marzencki, Marcin , Philip Lin, T. Cho, J. Guo, Brandon Ngai and Bozena Kaminska. "Remote Health, Activity, and Asset Monitoring with Wireless Sensor Networks." *IEEE 13th International Conference on e-Health Networking, Applications and Services*, Columbia, MO (2011): 98–101.

Naveen Ananda Kumar J. and Shivani Suresh. "A Proposal of Smart Hospital Management Using Hybrid Cloud, IoT, ML, and AI." *Proceedings of the Fourth International Conference on Communication and Electronics Systems (ICCES 2019) IEEE Conference* Record # 45898.

Sathya, Duraisamy and Ganeshkumar Pugalendhi. "Secured Remote Health Monitoring System." *Healthcare Technology Letters* 4, no. 6 (2012): 228–232.

Singh, Ajeet, Hari Shanker Joshi, Arun Singh, Medhavi Agarwal and Palveen Kaur. "Online Medical Consultation: A Review." *International Journal of Community Medicine and Public Health* 5, no. 4(2018): 1230–1232.

Verma, Priyanka and Rajan Mishra. "IoT based Smart Remote Health Monitoring System." *International Conference on Electrical and Electronics Engineering (ICE3)*, Gorakhpur, India (2020): 467–470.

Ventola C. Lee. "Mobile Devices and Apps for Healthcare Professionals: Uses and Benefits." *P T.* 39, no. 5 (2014): 356–364.

Zhang, Kai and Wenjie Ling. "Health Monitoring of Human Multiple Physiological Parameters Based on Wireless Remote Medical System." *IEEE Access* 8 (2020): 71146–71159.

14

Efficient Accessibility in Cloud Databases of Health Networks with Natural Neighbor Approach for RNN-DBSCAN

Rupali J. Wadnare, Swati S. Sherekar, and Vilas M. Thakare
Sant Gadge Baba Amrawati University, Amrawati, India

CONTENTS

14.1 Introduction

Clustering is a widely used data mining technique. The target of clustering is to cluster information as indicated by their likeness, so that it can be used in machine learning, pattern reorganization, etc. Different clustering algorithms are available. The density in density-based clustering algorithm depends upon the cut-off distance, which may lead to stoical error, and the density-based grouping isn't appropriate for multi-scale information (Zhu and Yang, 2016). The main aim of the clustering algorithm is to collect comparative articles in the same cluster and disparate in a different one. The clustering method can

DOI: 10.1201/9781003203926-14

identify clusters properly in arbitrary shape and automatically identify a number of clusters, and it is powerful to ambiguity is density-based algorithm (Bryant and Cios, 2017). The data that are more similar are put into one cluster and data with dissimilarity is put into another cluster. Different clustering techniques are available like k-means and DBSCAN, but their performance depends upon the parameter selection like *K*-means algorithm accuracy depends on initial parameter selection and number of clusters (Jiang et al., 2019). The finding cluster with descending density needs to characterize various clusters ahead of time. It likewise needs a manual determination of cluster center in the decision graph that may lead to data points may assign to the wrong cluster or multiple clusters (Liu et al., 2019). The most strong and robust clustering algorithm is density-based clustering, which means it can recognize a cluster with a different dimension and structure. In a density-based clustering, data points that have high density and relatively longer to each other are selected as a cluster center. The points with low density are assigned to the cluster using the assignment procedure. DPC and DBSCAN are parameter-dependent algorithms that need to get input from users like dc in DPC, which is cut-off distance, and €and MinPts in DBSCAN, which is the limit for determining the cluster points (Liu et al., 2020). Clustering is an exceptionally viable solo learning approach and it is broadly utilized in different fields including information mining design acknowledgment and picture investigation. Due to the evidence importance of clustering various, clustering algorithms have been proposed in the previous many years, which include partitioning methods, density-based clustering, and hierarchical clustering. The partition-based clustering is simple and effective but more fragile to noise. DBSCAN is a density-based clustering algorithm whose performance does not affect with the ambiguity, structure, and difference in data point densities but its performance totally depends upon the parameter cut-off distance, which it needs to select in advance. In a density-based clustering framework (DCF), a density partition needs to be repeated for large data sets and cluster with more overlap so it may be time consuming (Lu and Zhu, 2017). Recently density and distance-based clustering algorithms were invented in which time utilization is high yet center thought is novel. Inspired by their work, another KMDD technique for enormous spatial informational collections and high dimensional data sets is imagined.AS the *k*-means are request delicate to the data, the result of KMDD is not stable. In some cases core and noise are difficult to identify (Wang et al., 2017). Density Peak Clustering With Symmetric Neighborhood Graph (DPC-SNR) is suitable for larger data sets. Clustering of data sets can be done correctly. The cluster center can successfully identify the cluster center regardless of their distributions and dimensionality. The efficiency of the algorithm is depends upon the selection of parameter *k* (Wu et al., 2019). ICCK K-means is a method developed for the identification of a number of clusters spontaneously. It's vigorous, more steady, and gives excellent outcomes, yet the age of a distance framework causes a lot of time utilization (Li et al., 2019). The clustering algorithm is based on message passing (MPSC), which effectively deals with multi-scale data sets; however, it devours a great deal of time when managing huge scope information, very much like conventional otherworldly bunching (Wang et al., 2019). Clustering is a broadly utilized, unaided information mining procedure. In clustering, the main aim is to put similar data objects in one cluster and dissimilar in another cluster. The k-implies is the most famous clustering algorithm because of its effortlessness. But the execution of k-means clustering method depends upon variable selection. Parameter selection like cluster count and inceptive cluster center are key of k-means algorithm. Distance augmentation method and density method quadratic clustering method are for the most part utilized to initial cluster selection (Xiang et al., 2016). Clustering is widely used for information extraction. In Natural Language Processing (NLP), extracting information from text sources is an important task. Some language technology required text information for better performance. Topic modeling is important for some applications like NLP and information retrieval. It is an unsupervised methodology where a predetermined number of themes is separated from a specific arrangement of reports on measurable ideas (Alhawarat and Hegazi, 2017). For convenient use of social media sites, the user uses personalized tags and familiar words according to their own understanding. A tag is a keyword that gives more information about the object. Many developers take the advantage of tag information to build personalize tag recommendation systems for users. But there are many problems in a tagging system because of its free nature and lack of explicit meaning in the social tag. Different clustering techniques are used in tag development such as *K*-means and its improved version, hierarchical clustering, latent semantic analysis (LSA) with clustering. But this technique doesn't use semantic relations between the tags, hence less accurate and real clusters are found (Yang and Wang, 2017). The actionable knowledge extraction from text documents is a complex process and requires a lot of expertise. In-text mining needs to find previously unknown and implicit data from text documents which include a grouping of data with similar content, topic modeling and detection, clarification model, document summarizations, and document querying. It is a multi-step process that requires multiple algorithm implementation and parameters set by the user. It has a high computation cost and is time consuming because it needs the best joint analysis selection of techniquesWang 2017 (Cerquitelli et al., 2017). Day-to-day data available on crime is increased. It is not feasible to study that data manually to solve crime-related queries. Thus, natural language preparing strategies are most broadly utilized for handling and taking care of such unstructured information for criminal examination. Past strategies utilized in natural language handling are administered procedures and require a ton of human oversight from the criminal business (Das et al., 2019). Clustering is a widely used data mining ,technique; various clustering algorithms are available in literature like k-means, DBSCAN, K- and *K*-spectral clustering. Different clustering algorithms have different objectives so no one clustering algorithm gives accurate results on categorical data. To be more accurate, stable clustering results in cluster ensembles method to combine the results of different base clustering .results (Wang and Liu, 2018). Clustering is a widely used technique in data mining to discover patterns or extract knowledgeable information from data. Most of the available clustering algorithms work well when data is contained in an arbitrary shape or with low noise. But in actuality it is not possible to always have data contain a high percentage of data with low noise because intrinsic randomness or error in measurement (Zhang and Yuan, 2018) Clustering is the process in data mining to organize data according to the groups for knowledge extraction. A density-based algorithm is able to find a cluster accurately in data with a different size and shape and also robust to noise. Most of the density-based clustering algorithms fail to identify clusters properly in massive data because of computational complexity (Chen et al., 2019). In data mining, clustering aims to group data according to their objectives. Different clustering algorithms are available, but still a clustering algorithm does not give a proper cluster if data contains noise or prior knowledge of the data set is not available. It is also sensible to parameters and cannot identify clusters with different sizes and densities. A density-based clustering algorithm can identify a cluster with a different size and without prior knowledge of the data set. But it fails to identify the cluster with different densities (Zhou et al., 2019). As the data is increasing day by day in many applications like business cloud management and Cloud computing, a social media clustering algorithm is seeing more in demand.

DBSCAN is a density-based clustering algorithm widely used because it can identify a cluster with varying shape and size and also robust in noise. But a DBSCAN can suffer many problems in cluster identification. DBSCAN performance is dependent on parameter selection, which cause the DBSCAN to suffer for identifying cluster in heterogeneous density data sets (Cai and Wang, 2020). Anomaly detection is very important in a Cloud computing service provider as of the large data available. To provide any service accurately in the Cloud outlier detection is necessary. Clustering is recently the most used technique in anomaly detection because it does not require labeled data as it is an unsupervised technique. The author proposed a practical outlier detection technique by recognizing the potential trend and mitigate their negative impact on clustering result (Zhang et al., 2018). The author understands the *K*-Means clustering in the distributed computing. The MapReduce programming thoughts are applied to message clustering in hadoop stage, and improve text grouping preparing speed on the premise of guaranteeing the exactness of grouping. Examinations demonstrate that the distributed computing can fundamentally improve the clustering preparing speed (Xu et al., 2012).

This paper focused on five different techniques, such as natural neighbor. To identify the density of data object: RNN-DBSCAN method, DPC-KNN method, finding cluster with descending density, LP-SNG algorithm, and proposed efficient approach.

14.2 Background

The idea of a natural neighbor is presented by the author. Points with excessive density and distance are selected as the cluster center by utilizing the new characteristics density to develop a decision graph. Datum with high density and differences are selected as the cluster by using the new defined density construct decision graph. According to some rules, clusters are expanded by using MNN (Maximum Neighbour Graph). The points which are not satisfying the rule are clustered according to their neighbor cluster. This method calculates the density of data points without any parameter by using the NaN result. It is suitable for multi-scale data and more adaptive to a manifold data structure (Zhu and Yang, 2016).

Author proposed the RNN-DBSCAN approach to remove limitations of the DBSCAN. This approach reduces complexity as it required only one parameter *k*. In DBSCAN, it needs a symmetric distance measure, which leads to an inability to distinguish deterministic properties of clustering results but RNN-DBSCAN does not have such restriction. It identifies density locally due to this ability to determine dense regions and clusters with varying densities. It also describes a method to identify parameters automatically and the effect of *K* on the cluster is evaluated. Production of RNN-DBSCAN is measured by comparing other algorithms on multiple real, synthetic data where it outperformed others (Bryant and Cios, 2017).

The author proposed an approach DPC-KNN. In this paper, the author adds a new concept based on *K*-nearest neighbor for computing the interception if two data points δ and allocation process. This method also gives more accurate results for a non-spherical data set and varying cluster sizes. On experiment, it shows that the DPC-KNN gives a more efficient cluster than DPC and DBSCAN. It is also able to avoid the domino effect, which leads to DPC during the assignment procedure (Jiang et al., 2019).

Finding a cluster with a descending density method finds the density of data points using local density and Gaussian density. Then it arranges data points with descending density order and categorizes them by applying the GMM model selection. It proposed an algorithm for a traveling data set and merging them into a cluster on suspicion that boundary points that have tantamount density with cluster center ought to consider as inward data points. The effectiveness of the method is shown by qualitative and quantitative experiments on different data sets (Liu et al., 2019).

The author proposed a method for identifying clusters properly in a manifold or ring data set; it finds a local peak which is a high-density point at the local level. Local peaks are assigned to small clusters during the searching of local peaks and the outlier can easily remove them. Based on the similarity of the cluster on a symmetric hood graph, they are combined according to a graph-based scheme and lastly, an outlier is assigned to the nearest cluster. Comparison is done on various artificial and real data sets to prove their efficiency (Liu et al., 2020).

This paper focused on five different techniques as a natural neighbor to identify the density of data objects, RNN-DBSCAN method, DPC-KNN method, finding cluster with descending density, LP-SNG algorithm. The paper is organized as follows: **Segment I** Introduction. **Area II** talks about the background. **Area III** talks about past work. **Area IV** talks about existing procedures. **Area V** talks about characteristics and boundaries and how these are influenced by grouping strategies; **Section VI** is a proposed strategy, **Section VII** is the results, Segment **VIII** is the conclusion. At last, **Section IX** gives a future look.

14.3 Previous Work Done

Zhu and Yang (2016) present the NANDP approach in which the author introduces a new concept of natural neighbor that identifies the number of the cluster without any parameter selection. This algorithm is more effective on multi-scale data (Zhu and Yang, 2016).

Bryant and Cios (2017) had proposed RNN-DBSCAN technique. It reduces complexity of computation by using k and identifies clusters on multiple density data points by using the reverse nearest which is applied locally on data. An experimental result shows its superiority on OPTICS, IS-DBSCAN, and ISB-DBSCAN (Bryant and Cios, 2017).

Jianhua Jiang et al. (Jiang et al., 2019) invented the DPC-KNN method. It overcomes the drawback of DPC, which is not suitable for an aspherical data set like a spiral. It also improves the assignment process in clustering by including the concept of K-nearest neighbor in distance computation. It gives more efficient results than DPC and DBSCAN (Jiang et al., 2019).

Tong Liu et al. (Liu et al., 2019) had proposed a A-DPC approach, which uses only the concept of local density. This method arranges density in descending order and applies the GMM method for the categorization of density. It also proposed a new algorithm for data points traversal and merges them into clusters automatically (Liu et al., 2019).

Zhi Liu et al. (Liu et al., 2020) had proposed an LP-SNG approach to overcome a drawback on DPC, which cannot find clusters in a manifold data set and DPC-SNR, which cannot perform well on a data set with a different type. It uses RKNN to find local peaks and develop a cluster by using it comparably on a symmetric neighborhood graph. Lastly, persistence points are collected by the nearest cluster. This technique is most suitable for local data points than a global one (Liu et al., 2020).

14.4 Existing Methodologies

Many clustering plans have been executed throughout the most recent quite a few years. There are various systems that are carried out for various grouping models, i.e., Natural Neighbor to identify the density of data object, RNN-DBSCAN method, DPC-KNN method, A-DPC, LP-SNG algorithm.

14.4.1 Natural Neighbor to Identify the Density of Data Objects

The proposed technique utilizes another idea of regular to distinguish the density of information objects. To track down the regular neighbor, it utilizes the KD algorithm. After finding the natural neighbor value of k is fixed, according to the maximum of the natural neighbour which neighbor is used find the density of data object. The object with high densities and far is selected as the center. For extension of center, it uses some rule. The data object that satisfies the rule is assigning the cluster. The remaining objects are combining in the clusters of their that are nearest them (Zhu and Yang, 2016).

14.4.2 RNN-DBSCAN Method

This approach proposed a RNN-DBSCAN method to find the k-nearest hood and reverse nearest hood of data points. It categorizes data points is into a noise point, boundary point, and core point. The point is a core data point if its RNN value is greater than k and boundary point if less than k to find a cluster it uses reach ability rules. Direct reachability is restricted to the closest with its core perception. This concept is applicable only for core points, not for non-core points. It uses an arbitrary assignment process for non-core points to assign it to the cluster that is reachable from that point. Then it finds clusters and its density. A cluster is extended to include unselected observation and it becomes a super cluster if the core observation lies within a cut of distance (Bryant and Cios, 2017).

14.4.3 DPC-KNN Method

In a DPC algorithm, the cluster center is identified based on the two parameters that is local density ρ and distance δ; suitable cut-off distance is selected. This parameter are depends upon the distance between the points. Euclidean distance mathematical method is used to determine how far one point is with another. In DPC-KNN, the formula to calculate density of a local point is the same as DPC but distance is calculated on the base of k-nearest neighbor. Density and distance attributes of data points are used to build a decision graph. From the decision graph it selects a center by using the criteria having the highest density and relatively longer distance. To assign the cluster to the remaining point, it uses distance calculated based on an KNN algorithm. By combining the results, the final cluster is found. The mathematical model for DPC-KNN is defined as: For all data points Pi, apart from the point with high density and distance, density δi is calculated as: $\delta i = \min\{distance(Pl, Pt)\}$, $Pl \in Si$, $Pt \in Hi$ where Pl and Pt are two pints. Si is a collection of points which are nearest to the point pi and Hi is collection of points that having a highest density than point pi (Jiang et al., 2019).

14.4.4 A-DPC Method

This author proposed a new approach for finding A-DPC. It focus only the on the density of data points. It groups data points according to their density in descending order in cluster center, inter points, and boundary points. By applying a GMM-based model selection on density merges it into one-dimensional characteristic of densities. This method proposed an algorithm to travel all samples automatically and find a cluster based on the assumption that the cluster center should be inner points and low density points are boundary points. The number of points that have less distance from cut-off distance dc from current point i is represented as a local density pi of a current point (Liu et al., 2019).

14.4.5 LP-SNG Algorithm

The author proposed a method for identifying clusters properly in manifold or ring data set, to find a local peak which is high-density points at the local level. Local peaks are assigned to small clusters during the search of local peaks and the outlier can easily remove them. Based on the similarity of the cluster on a symmetric hood graph, they are combined according to a graph-based scheme and lastly, an outlier is assigned to the nearest cluster. Comparison is done on various artificial and real data sets to prove its efficiency (Liu et al., 2020).

14.5 Analysis of Method

Execution of the proposed calculation is contrasted with the density peak clustering algorithm and AP algorithm on different real and artificial data sets. It uses CE index and NMI index as criteria. According to the performance, Ap algorithm does not give proper cluster results compared with density peak and NANDP algorithm. It also shows that NANDP is more effective on manifold data as compared to cluster-DP because it describes distributed characteristics of data more effectively (Zhu and Yang, 2016). Correlation of RNN-DBSCAN is done on manufactured and genuine informational indexes regarding ARI and NMI execution to other density-based algorithms. Comparison of the performance of RNN-DBSCAN is comparable to DBSCAN and its complexity is less as compared to DBSCAN because it required only one parameter k (Bryant and Cios, 2017). The results show that DPC-KNN can identify a cluster center more easily on a decision graph than DPC. K-means and the DPC algorithm fail to identify clusters on irregular data set where DPC-KNN and DBSCAN can achieve good results. But the performance of the DPC-KNN is influenced by the value of K (Jiang et al., 2019). Subjective and quantitative correlations among DPC, DBSCAN, DPCHD, Fuzzy-DPC, and automatic DPC (A-DPC) is done with three internal criteria: Davies-Bouldinscore (DBI), Silhouette coefficient, and Calinski-harabasz score (CH). From experimental results it shows A-DPC can find a cluster automatically and robust to noise but density distribution among clusters (Liu et al., 2019). The proficiency of LP-SNG is tried by contrasting outcomes with different clustering techniques and k-implies on engineered genuine informational index including building informational collections. The LP-SNG gives a high score with respect to the Acc and NMI than other clustering algorithms on most of the data sets. Trial results show that it can distinguish clusters, paying little mind

TABLE 14.1

Comparisons Between Different Clustering Techniques

Clustering scheme	Advantages	Limitations
Natural Neighbor to Identify The Density Of Data Object	The proposed strategy figures the density with no parameter. It is straightforward and well mirrors the information.	It is time consuming because it needs to calculate neighbors of each data point. It cannot identify outliers.
RNN-DBSCAN method	It can identify the cluster with varying density data. Time complexity is reduced.	This approach execution depends upon the r parameter.
DPC-KNN method	The cluster center in the proposed method diagram is more striking than DPC.	The presentation of the DPC-KNN is impacted by the estimation of K.
A-DPC	It is powerful to ambiguity.	Delicate to unbalance appropriation of density between clusters
LP-SNG algorithm	It can identify an accurate cluster on the manifold or ring data sets.	It is not suitable for large size data sets as it requires more time to computer similarities between clusters and defining clusters with maximum similarity.

to their density and beat DPC-SNR, AP, DPCDPC, and DBSCAN techniques (Liu et al., 2020) (Table 14.1).

14.6 Proposed Methodology

This paper proposes a method of efficient accessibility in Cloud databases of health networks with a natural neighbor approach for RNN-DBSCAN. To calculate the density of data objects, it used MNN (Maximum Nearest Neighbor), which finds density without using any parameter. After calculating the density, data points are dividing into core, non-core, and noise points by using the value of k. On the off chance that the current perception is the center and is yet to appoint a group, it is doled out to the current cluster. This current cluster extended after applying an expansiveness decision tree to deal with un-clustered perceptions. Within the core observation, weakly connected components of a sub-graph are used to define clustering of core observations. Lastly, remaining un-clustered observations are used to produce extended clusters and assigned to the cluster whose distance is less than density of cluster. The remaining observations are considered as noise points.

Basic steps of algorithm:

Step 1. Define the data set and apply a KD tree to the data to find the natural neighbor.

Step 2. Find the value of k by applying a maximum of the natural neighbor method.

Step 3. Divide the data points into core, non-core, and noise data according the value of k.

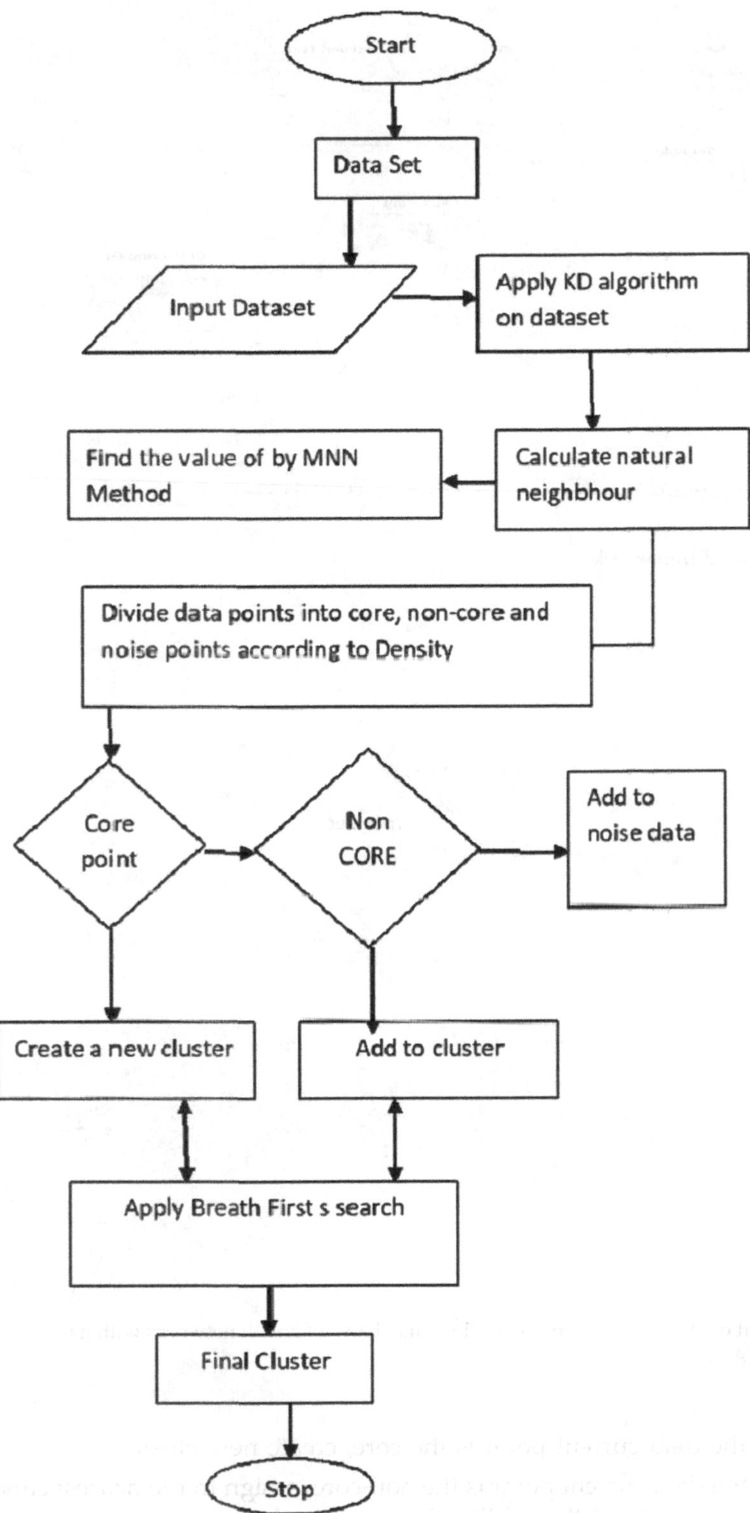

FIGURE 14.1
Flowchart of efficient accessibility in Cloud databases of health networks with natural neighbor approach for RNN-DBSCAN.

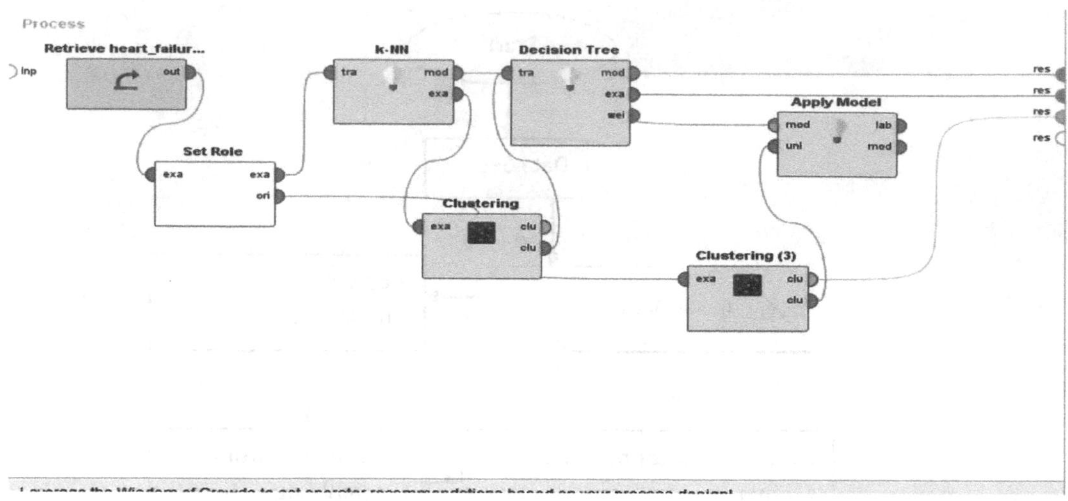

FIGURE14.2
Design of proposed framework.

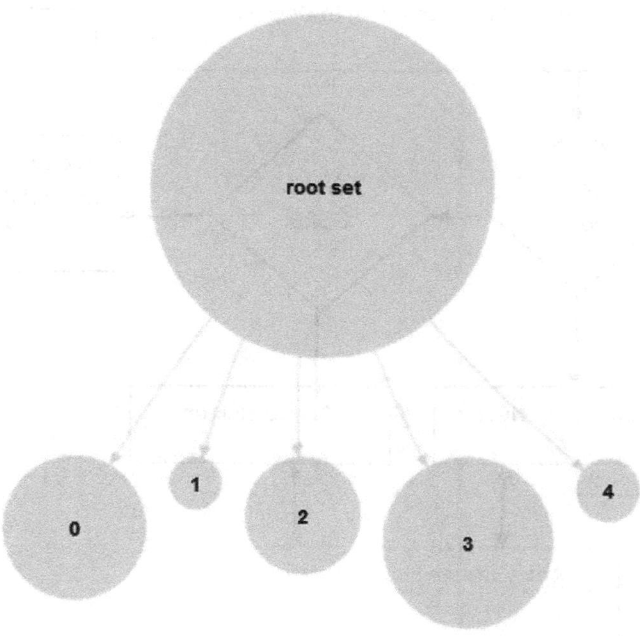

FIGURE14.3
Clustering result of efficient accessibility in Cloud databases of health networks with natural neighbor approach for RNN-DBSCAN.

Step 4. If the data current point is the core, create new cluster.

Step 5. If the data current point is the non-core, assign to the nearest cluster and if it is a noise point then collect in the noise data set.

Step 6. By applying breath first search merge the cluster to find the final cluster.

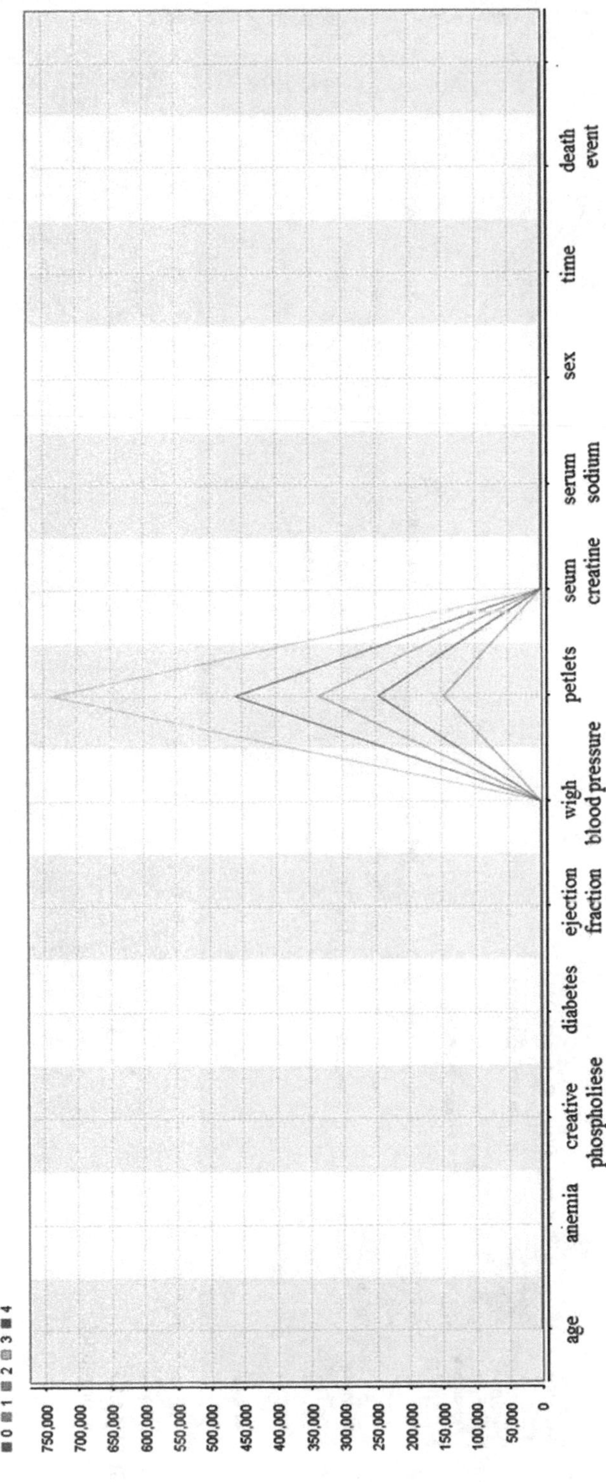

FIGURE14.4
Result in graph format.

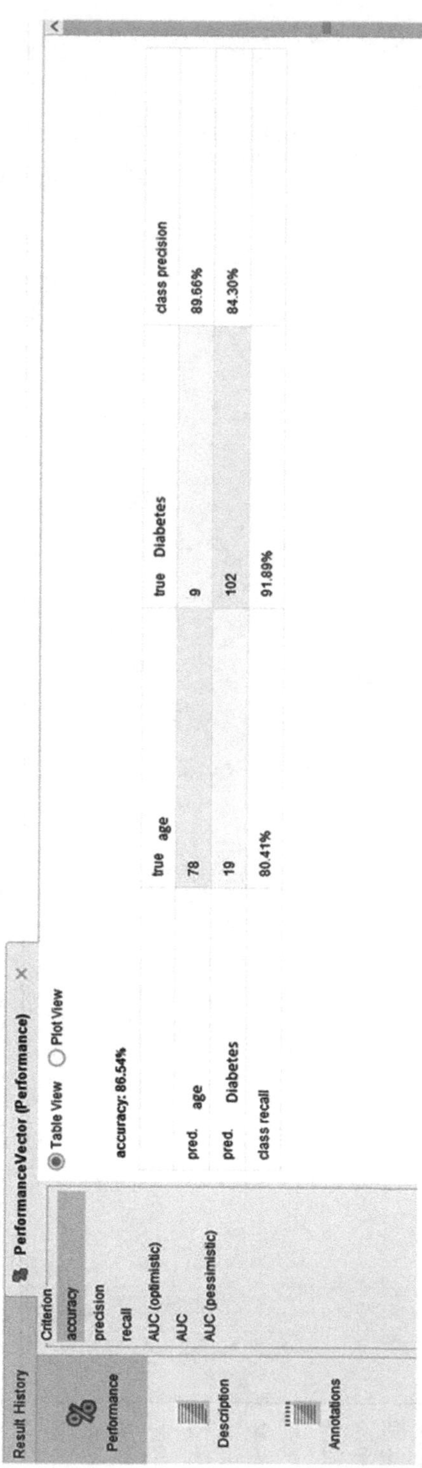

FIGURE 14.5
Accuracy of model.

precision: 84.30% (positive class: Mine)

	true age	true Diabetes	class precision
pred. age	78	9	89.66%
pred. Diabetes	19	102	84.30%
class recall	80.41%	91.89%	

FIGURE 14.6
Precision of model.

recall: 91.89%

	true age	true diabetes	class precision
pred age	78	9	89.66%
pred diabetes	19	102	84.30%
class recall	80.41%	91.89%	

FIGURE 14.7
Recall of model.

Figure 14.1 shows a diagrammatic representation of the proposed method is shown as follows.

14.7 Simulation and Results

Figure 14.2 shows the design of a proposed method constructed and executed (Figure 14.3).

The clustering result in the form of a graph is shown in Figure 14.4.

14.8 Results and Discussion

Evaluate the performance by testing the performance of the proposed model by calculating the accuracy precision and recall. It gives an accuracy of 86.54%, precision of 84.30%, and recall of 91.89% (Figures 14.5–14.7).

14.9 Conclusion

This paper focuses on the analysis of various clustering techniques and health services on Cloud computing, natural neighbor to identify the density of data object, RNN-DBSCAN method, DPC-KNN method, A-DPC method, and LP-SNG algorithm. But in the RNN-DBSCAN method, the performance depends upon the value of k. This paper proposes a method of efficient accessibility in Cloud databases of health networks with a natural neighbor approach for RNN-DBSCAN. This method identifies a cluster on the health data Cloud environment with less time with accuracy.

14.10 Future Scope

From observations of the proposed method, the future work will include a diagnosis of problems in health service on Cloud data with a clustering technique and try to reduce it.

References

Alhawarat, M. and M. Hegazi. "Revisiting K-Means and Topic Modeling, a Comparison Study to Cluster Arabic Documents." *IEEE Access* (2017): 42740–42750.

Bryant, Avory and Krzysztof Cios. "RNN-DBSCAN: A Density-based Clustering Algorithm using Reverse nearest Density Estimates." *IEEE Transactions on Knowledge and Data Engineering* (2017). https://ieeexplore.ieee.org/document/8240674.

Cai, Z. and J. Wang. "Adaptive Density-Based Spatial Clustering for Massive Data Analysis." *IEEE Access* (2020): 22346–22358.

Cerquitelli, T., E. Di, et al., "Data Miners' Little Helper: Data Transformation Activity Cues for Cluster Analysis on Document Collections." *ACM Reference Format* (2017): 1–6.

Chen, Y., X. Hu, W. Fan, et al., "Fast Density Peak Clustering for Large Scale Data Based on KNN." *Science Direct- Knowledge-Based Systems* 187 (2019): 1–7, China.

Das, P., A.K. Das, J. Nayak, et al., "A Graph based Clustering Approach for Relation Extraction from Crime Data". *IEEE Access* (2019): 101269–101282.

Jiang, Jianhua, Yujun Chen, Xianqi Meng, et al., "A Novel Density Peaks Clustering Algorithm Based on k Nearest Neighbors for Improving Assignment Process." *Science Direct* (2019): 702–713.

Li, Yating, Jianghui Cai, Haifeng Yang, et al., "A Novel Algorithm for Initial Cluster Center Selection". *IEEE Access* (2019): 74683–74693.

Liu, Tong, Hangyu Li and Xudong Zhao. "Clustering by Search in Descending Order and Automatic Find of Density." *IEEE Access* (2019): 133773–133790.

Liu, Z., C. Wu, Peng Qi, Lee Jia and Y. Xia. "Local Peaks-Based Clustering Algorithm in Symmetric Neighborhood Graph." *IEEE Access* (2020): 1600–1612.

Lu, Jianyun and Qingsheng Zhu. "An Effective Algorithm Based on Density Clustering Framework." *IEEE Access* (2017): 4991–5000.

Wang, L., S. Ding and H. Jia. "An Improvement of Spectral Clustering via Message Passing and Density Sensitive Similarity." *IEEE Access* (2019): 101054–101062.

Wang, Hongling and Gang Liu. "Two-Level-Oriented Selective Clustering Ensemble Based on Hybrid Multi-modal Metrics." *IEEE Access* (2018): 64159–64168.

Wang, Jang, Cheng Zhu, Yun Zhou, et al., "From Partition-Based Clustering to Density-Based Clustering: Fast Find Clusters With Diverse Shapes and Densities in Spatial Databases." *IEEE Access on Special Section on Advanced Data Analytics for Large-Scale Complex Data Environments* (2017): 1718–1729.

Wu, C., J. Lee, T. Isokawa, et al., "Efficient Clustering Method Based on Density Peaks With Symmetric Neighborhood Relationship." *IEEE Access* (2019): 60684–60693.

Xiang, C., H. Zhen and X.K. Li. "An Improved K-means Text Clustering Algorithm by Optimizing Initial Cluster Centers." *International Conference on Cloud Computing and Big Data* (2016). https://ieeexplore.ieee.org/document/7979917 (access November 2016).

Xu, Yunfeng, Zhang Yan and Rui Ma. "K-Means Algorithm Based on Cloud Computing." *Fifth International Symposium on Computational Intelligence and Design*, Hangzhou, China (2012). https://ieeexplore.ieee.org/abstract/document/6406015 (access March 2012)

Yang, J. and Jian Wang. "Tag Clustering Algorithm LMMSK: Improved K-means Algorithm Based on Latent Semantic." *Journal of Systems Engineering and Electronics* (2017): 374–384.

Zhang, T. and B. Yuan. "Density-Based Multi-scale Analysis for Clustering in Strong Noise Settings with Varying Densities Adaptive." *IEEE Access* (2018): 25861–25873.

Zhu, Qingsheng and Lijun Yang. "Natural Neighbor-based Clustering Algorithm with Density Peak." *International Joint Conference on Neural Network*, Vancouver, BC, Canada (2016). https://ieeexplore.ieee.org/abstract/document/7727185 (access July 2016)

Zhang, Xiao, Fanjing Meng and Jingmin Xu. "Perflinsight: A Robust Clustering Based Abnormal Behavior Detection System for Large Scale Cloud." *International Conference on Cloud Computing*, Nicosia, Cyprus (2018). https://ieeexplore.ieee.org/document/ 8457898 (access July 2018)

Zhou, X., H. Zhang, G. Ji and G. Tang. "A Multi-Density Clustering Algorithm Based on Similarity for Dataset With Density Variation." *IEEE Access* (2019): 186004–186016.

15

Blood Oxygen Level and Pulse Rate Monitoring Using IoT and Cloud-Based Data Storage

Latesh Malik, Ameya Shahu, Sohan Rathod, Pranay Kuthe, and Prachi Patil
Government College of Engineering,
Nagpur, India

CONTENTS

DOI: 10.1201/9781003203926-15

15.1 Introduction

15.1.1 Overview

Many people die due to human negligence. The patients living in rural areas face difficulties in accessing proper treatment. This system's central concept is to assist doctors by using IoT and Cloud-based data storage (Infrastructure as a Service) to monitor patients in real-time for speedy treatment and conditions post-hospitalization. Cloud-based historical data of patients assist doctors in decision making. The concept of this paper is to monitor the blood oxygen saturation and pulse rate of the patients and start the treatment quickly. The IoT-enabled patient monitoring system provides a real-time graphical user interface for patient monitoring.

It uses IoT to monitor the patients and Cloud-based database storage. In India, 50 lakh people die annually because of human negligence. Also, the doctor to population ratio is 1:1,800 (Deo, 2013), which indicates the doctor's pressure as he has to consult more patients, and it is very tedious for the patients to get the treatment. The IoT-enabled patient monitoring system has a user-friendly digital cross-platform interface. It has a Cloud-based storeroom. It permits patients to get a speedy treatment. Through the IoT-enabled patient monitoring system, patient monitoring can be done anytime. As data is stored in the Cloud, it also provides personal sensitive data security. It provides medical treatment by leveraging analytics. The main advantage of this system is that the user does not need any specialized hardware, and he or she can take measurements virtually anywhere and in almost any circumstances.

15.1.2 Problem Statement

To assist and reduce doctors' workload by developing a real-time graphical user interface can help the doctors monitor the patients. It also provides a feature to monitor and analyze biological parameters such as heart rate and a patient's blood oxygen level through IoT.

15.1.3 Background

Healthcare is a fundamental human right, but the pandemic's strain on the healthcare system has affected many people's primary health provision. Due to the fear of the spread of coronavirus, the healthcare providers avoid contact with the patient. In India, the doctor to population ratio is 1:1,800. The government doctor to population ratio is 1:10,189, while the nurse to population ratio is 1:483. The total number of deaths in India because of human negligence is 50 lacs; completely miserable (Deo, 2013). The number of enrolled clinical experts is 840,130. Notwithstanding the populace blast, the general specialist populace proportion is presently 1:1,800, reflecting numerous individuals. Essential Health Centers (EHCs) are the foundation of rustic well-being conveyance frameworks. The quantity of EHCs has expanded from 77 in the primary arrangement (1955) to 23,887 out of 2011, a 300-acre increment. An investigation by Harvard University a year ago showed that almost 5,000,000 passes happen in India yearly because of clinical blunders set off by an absence of pragmatic information among the specialists and medical attendants to deal with patients when brought to the clinic (Press Trust of India, 2018). The A.C.C.C. intends to prepare the clinical subject-matter experts and the specialists of different specializations, for example, careful, gynecology, muscular health, and crisis to presume and distinguish patients in danger of decay to reduce the death rate. As per the specialists, the loss of life might have been a lot lower if satisfactory clinical courses of action were accessible in medical clinics and the staff members were prepared well.

In India, in the well-being area, the advancement has been remarkable since freedom –newborn child death rate (I.M.R.) has dropped from 150 to 50, the maternal mortality proportion (MMR) declined tenfold from 2,000 to 200 for every 100,000 live births, and the future upon entering the world has gone up from 31 to 65 years. Sixty years prior, the all-out number of doctors was 47,524, with a doctor populace proportion of 1 to 6,300. Today, the quantity of enlisted clinical experts is 840,130 (a 17-overlap increment) (Deo, 2013).

The lack of essential specialists is anything but a public wonder. On the more splendid side, 30% of EHCs have two or more doctors, and an equivalent number gives 24 × 7 h administrations. The number of doctors at the EHCs have expanded from 20,308 to 26,329 (addition of 1,200 specialists each year) in 2006–2011 (Deo, 2013). On the off chance that the pattern proceeds, specialists' deficiency in the EHCs could be met in the following not many years inside the current framework without expanding clinical universities' numbers. It can't be denied as rustic well-being administrations are a long way from agreeable. However, a significant part of the ills of the provincial area are because of helpless administration and widespread defilement. Not very far in the past, the Uttar Pradesh government was blamed for misrepresentation to the tune of 10,000 crores in India's leader well-being program, the National Rural Health Mission. In any case, the specialists are hesitant to serve in towns.

15.2 Literature Review

Technology in healthcare is the need of the hour. There is much research going on to integrate modern-day technologies such as machine learning, artificial intelligence, IoT, etc., with healthcare. This paper is related to the IoT and Cloud-based data storage in healthcare and some of these papers below give the different concept of automated farming.

A paper published by R. Kumar and M. Pallikonda Rajasekaran discussed monitoring a patient's body temperature, respiration rate, heart beat, and body movement using a Raspberry Pi board. Raspberry Pi is most costly compared to node MCU (ESP 8266) (2020).

A health monitoring system with arduino-uno is developed by D. Shiva Rama Krishnan and team. This system uses Temperature and heartbeat sensors for tracking patients' health. Both the sensors are connected to the Arduino-uno. To track the patient's health, the microcontroller is in turn interfaced to a LCD display and wi-fi connection to send the data to the web-server(wireless sensing node). If there should be an occurrence of any unexpected changes in understanding pulse or internal heat level alarm is sent about the patient utilizing IoT (2020).

With advancement in wearable devices, it opens the door for many more technologies in this field. One such paper by AKM Jahangir Alam Majumder and team discussed the use of IoT in such low-energy consumption devices (Majumder et al., 2019).

The paper by Manisha Shelar and team presents the advancement of a microcontroller-based framework for remote heartbeat and temperature observing utilizing ZigBee. In

India numerous patients are passing on in light of cardiovascular failures and the explanation for that they are not getting convenient and legitimate assistance. To give them ideal and appropriate assistance first we need to constantly screen patient well-being. The fixed observing framework can be utilized just when the patient is sleeping and this framework is colossal and just accessible in the emergency clinics in ICU. The framework is created for home use by patients that are not in a basic condition but rather should be continually or occasionally observed by clinician or family (Shelar et al., 2013).

In a paper by Tuan NguyenGia and team, they presented the study of achievability of intrusive and persistent glucose observing (CGM) framework using IoT-based methodology. They planned an IoT-based framework engineering from a sensor gadget to a back-end framework for introducing continuous glucose, internal heat level, and relevant information (for example, natural temperature) in graphical and intelligible structures to end clients like patients and specialists. What's more, the nRF correspondence convention is altered for fitting the glucose checking framework and accomplishing an undeniable degree of energy effectiveness. Moreover, enhance energy utilization of the sensor gadget and plan energy collecting units for the gadget (Gia et al., 2017).

15.3 Problem with Existing System

15.3.1 Problems Faced by Doctors

The diagnosis of the patient solely depends upon the physician's intuition and patient records. Very few systems use clinical data for prediction purposes. The doctors get affected by third-party payer interference. Doctors find it difficult to maintain medical devices and also treat mental illness. Shortage of coordination and communication can not only cause frustration and confusion for doctors; it can also lead to readmissions.

15.3.2 Problems Faced by the Patient

The patient finds it difficult to pay the traveling cost. It incorporates a vast load of costs. Traveling is not considered safe in the pandemic time because of which people avoid visiting the hospitals. Patients feel a lack of accessible care. There is the danger of medical complications in the hospital. Then there are fears of human errors, like the patient can get the wrong drug or dosage.

15.4 Components and Sensors

15.4.1 Pulse Oximeter

Heartbeat oximeters are minimal expense, non-obtrusive clinical sensors used to quantify the oxygen immersion of hemoglobin in the blood continuously. It shows the level of blood that is stacked with oxygen. Oxygen saturation, commonly known as SpO2, measures the amount of oxygen-carrying hemoglobin in the blood relative to hemoglobin not carrying oxygen (Essay, 2014).

15.4.1.1 MAXIM MAX30100 Sensor

MAX30100 is an incorporated heartbeat oximeter and pulse screen sensor arrangement. It's an optical sensor that derives its readings from emitting two wavelengths of light from two LEDs – a red and an infrared one – then measuring the absorbance of pulsing blood through a photodetector – this particular LED. Color combination is optimized for reading the data through the tip of one's finger. It is completely configurable through programming registers, and the advanced yield information is put away in a 16-profound FIFO inside the gadget. It has an I2C digital interface to communicate with a host microcontroller (Essay, 2014).

15.4.1.2 Working of MAX30100 Sensor

MAX30100 has a working voltage of 1.8–5.5 V. The device has two LEDs, one producing red light, another infrared-radiating light. For beat rate, just infrared light is required. Both red light and infrared light are utilized to gauge oxygen levels in the blood (Saravanan, 2020). Working of MAX 30100 is shown in Figure 15.1.

MAX30100 uses a reflectance method to measure oxygen saturation in the blood. In the reflective approach, the LED and the photodetectors are placed on the same side, i.e., next to each other. There will be some fixed light reflection back to the sensor in the reflective method due to the finger. With each heartbeat, there will be an increase in the finger's blood volume, resulting in more light reflection back to the sensor.

Hence if we see the waveform of the received light signal, it will consist of peaks at each heartbeat. A fixed low-value reading is there in between the heartbeats. This value can be considered constant reflection. This difference of the rise subtracted from the continual reflection value is the reflection value due to blood flow at a heartbeat.

As shown in the graph, the absorbance rate of oxygenated hemoglobin to various light wavelengths is represented. You will see oxygenated hemoglobin (R.E.D. line) absorbs more infrared light than red light. Also, the deoxygenated hemoglobin (blue line) absorbs more red light as compared to infrared light. The blood's oxygen content can be easily calculated by comparing how much red light (R) is absorbed compared to infra-red (IR) light (Saravanan, 2020) as shown in Figure 15.2.

Depending on the amount of oxygenated hemoglobin or deoxygenated hemoglobin, the red light ratio absorbed against Infra-red light (R/IR) absorbed will change. Typically R/IR ratio of 0.5 equates to approximately 100% SpO2, a percentage of 1.0 to about 82% SpO2, while a ratio of 2.0 equates to 0% SpO2 (2017).

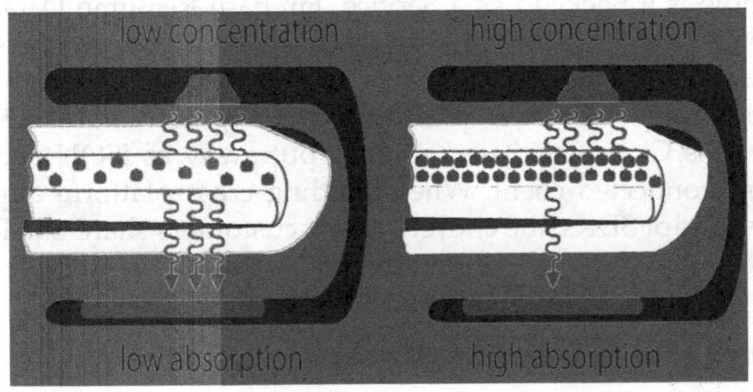

FIGURE 15.1
Absorption of red light by blood.

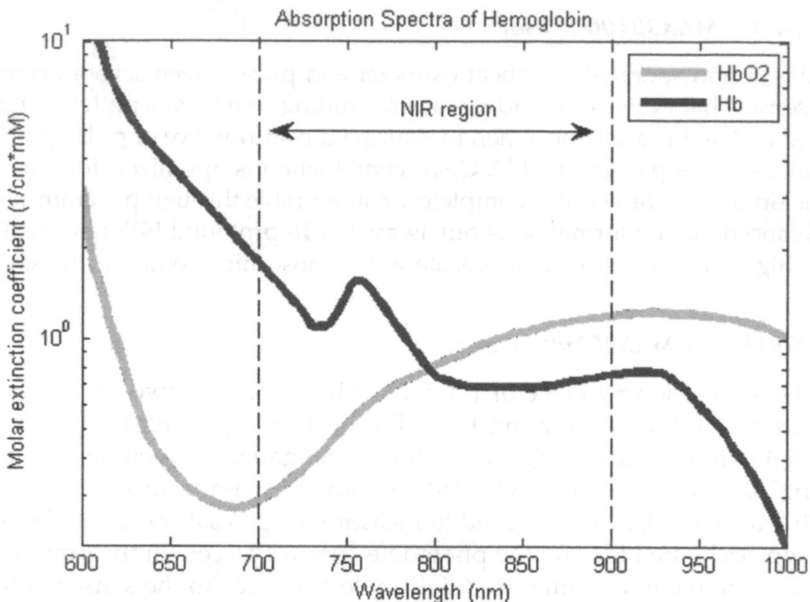

FIGURE 15.2
Amount of red light absorbed by oxygenated hemoglobin vs. deoxygenated hemoglobin.

At the point when the heart siphons blood, there is an expansion in oxygenated blood due to having more blood. As the heart unwinds, the volume of oxygenated blood additionally diminishes. By knowing the time between the increment and diminishing of oxygenated blood, the beat rate is resolved. In the end, oxygenated blood retains more infrared light and passes more red light, while deoxygenated blood assimilates red light and gives more infrared light. The essential capacity of the MAXIM MAX30100: it peruses the ingestion levels for both light sources and stores them in a support that can be perused through I2C. Block diagram of MAX30100 is shown in Figure 15.3.

15.4.2 Firebase Realtime Database

Firebase as a whole is a Backend as a Service. Firebase Realtime Database is one of the services provided by Firebase, which is an IaaS. It stores also, synchronizes information with our NoSQL Cloud data set. Information is matched up across all customers in real time and remains available when the application goes disconnected. The Firebase Realtime Database is Cloud-facilitated. Data is put away as JSON and synchronized in real time to every connected client. When building cross-platform applications for iOS, Android, and JavaScript SDKs, the entirety of our customers share one Realtime Database case and naturally get refreshes with the freshest information (2020).

15.4.2.1 Structure of Firebase Realtime Database

All Firebase Realtime Database data is stored as JSON objects. The database is in the format of a Cloud-hosted JSON tree. Unlike a SQL database, there are no tables or

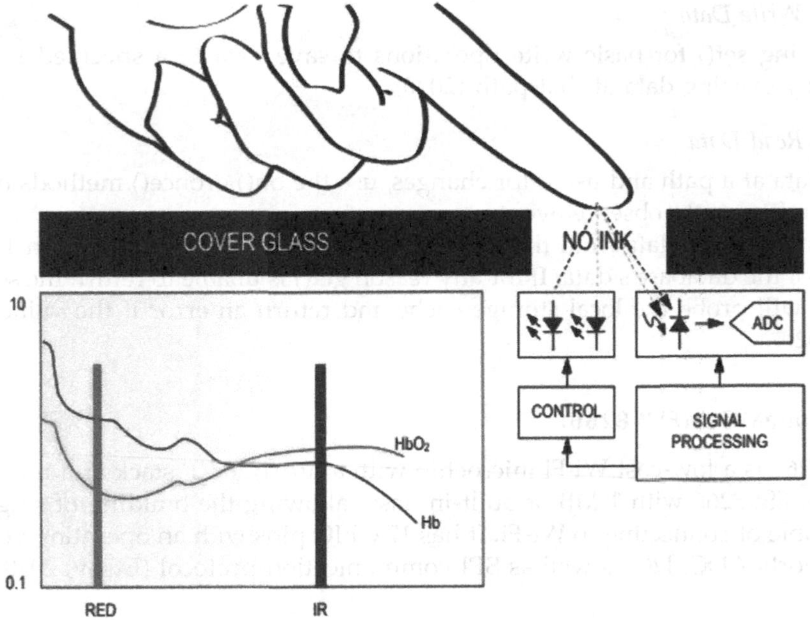

FIGURE 15.3
Architecture.

records. When data is added to the JSON tree, it becomes a node in the existing JSON structure with an associated key. As we are providing keys to each input in the database, such as user IDs or semantic names, or they can be provided by using push() (2020).

15.4.2.2 Configuration of Firebase Realtime Database

A Firebase account is required to use Firebase Realtime Database. After successful login and signup to the firebase console, navigate to the Realtime Database section. It will prompt the selection of existing projects or create new projects in the firebase. Post-project creation and mode selection is there. There are two modes in Firebase Realtime Database – Test mode and Locked mode. In Test mode, anyone can edit data in the real-time database. Locked mode denies all reads and writes from mobile and web clients. Only authenticated application servers can access the database. In the next step, it is required to select the nearest region depending on the application's audience. Depending on your choice of region, the database namespace will be of the form <databaseName>.firebaseio.com or <databaseName>.<region>.firebasedatabase.app. This URI will help to access databases from the interface. After the final setup, URI and authentication keys need to be inserted into the SDK object for connection (2020).

15.4.2.3 Read and Write Data on Firebase Realtime Database

To read or write data from the database, the data is required to initiate the instance of the firebase. The Database.Reference class is provided in the standard development kit of firebase (2020).

15.4.2.3.1 Write Data

We are using set() for basic write operations to save data to a specified reference, replacing any existing data at that path (2020).

15.4.2.3.2 Read Data

To read data at a path and listen for changes, use the on() oronce() methods of firebase – database reference to observe events.

As we require the data from the real-time database, we use the get() function to get a snapshot of the database's data. If for any reason get() is unable to return the server value, the client will probe the local storage cache and return an error if the value is still not found (2020).

15.4.3 NodeMCU (ESP 8266)

The ESP8266 is a low-cost Wi-Fi microchip with a full TCP/IP stack and microcontroller capability. ESP8266 with 1 MB of built-in flash, allowing the building of single-chip devices capable of connecting to Wi-Fi. It has 17 GPIO pins with an operating voltage of 3.3 V. It supports ADC, I2C as well as SPI communication protocol (Essay, 2020).

15.5 System Architecture

The architecture of the system is divided into two parts: sensor and microcontroller configuration and interface application. The user interface will request data, reports, or files to Cloud-based storage on the first-time load. After Interface is fully loaded, it will receive updates from Firebase Realtime Database. Google Firebase. MAX30100 sensor sends data to ESP8266 using I2C protocol.

Further, ESP8266 maintains an established connection after proper authentication with Firebase Realtime Database through the Internet. ESP8266 is connected to Wi-Fi for Internet access. It is the job of the microcontroller ESP8266 to send updates to the Firebase Realtime Database. User interface will authenticate a user. Authentication will be performed on the Firebase. After a successful authentication sensor, data can be accessible to doctors. Also, data will be updated in real time at the interface. Complete system architecture is in Figure 15.4.

15.6 Implementation

Broadly, the implementation of Cloud-based patient monitoring systems is divided into two parts: Patient monitoring and user interface development. Patient monitoring allows doctors to observe the bio parameter – pulse rate and blood oxygen level of a patient remotely through IoT. As doctors are naive users of technology hence, the patient monitoring system has a user-friendly interface. Development in individual module until this report are as follows.

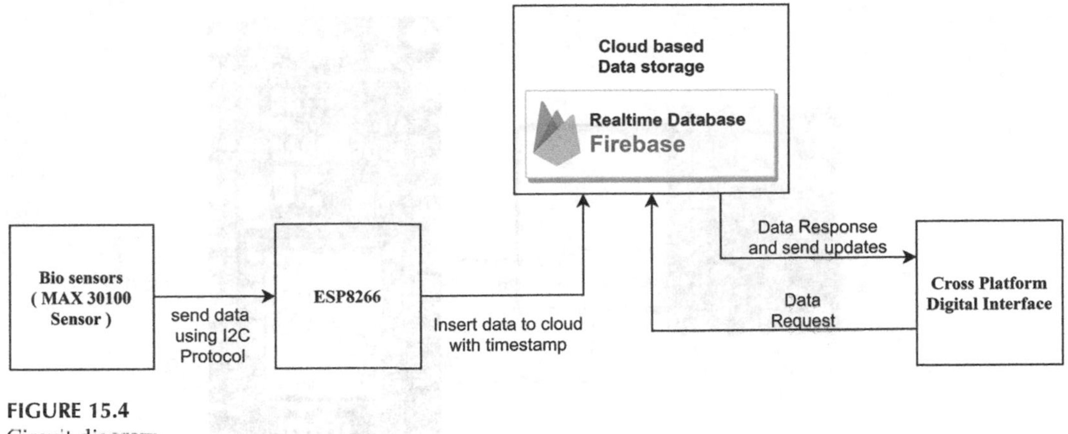

FIGURE 15.4
Circuit diagram.

15.6.1 Patient Monitoring

The patient monitoring system has a remote patient monitoring service that can also store data of patients. This data is only available to the doctor of the respective patient. Currently, the blood oxygen level and heart rate of a patient can be monitored through this system.

MAXIM MAX 30100 biosensor is used to measure the blood oxygen level and heart rate of a patient. Through the I2C communication protocol, data stored in the buffer of MAX30100 is transferred to the microcontroller. In this system, ESP8266 is a microcontroller that collects data from MAX30100, and forwards it to Cloud data storage. ESP8266 has an onboard Wi-Fi module as well as a support I2C protocol (Essay, 2020).

15.6.1.1 Connection Between MAX30100 and ESP8266

The Vin pin of MAX30100 is connected with the 3V3 output pin of ESP8266. S.C.L. pin both modules connected. This signal acts as a clock for MAX30100. Communication between MAX30100 and ESP8266 is through S.D.A. The GND pin of MAX30100 is associated with the ground of ESP 8266. FIFO buffers in the MAX30100 need to be updated as soon as possible to avoid overflow. ESP8266 has also triggered this (Fahad, 2021). Figure 15.5 shows the connection between ESP8266 and MAX30100.

15.6.1.2 Communication Between ESP8266 and Cloud Data Storage

ESP8266 reads data from MAX30100, and after every 5 seconds, it forwards data to Cloud data storage. Google Cloud Firebase Realtime Database is used to store data in real-time. Microcontroller maintains its connection with Google Cloud Firebase Realtime Database through WebSocket. Connection between a ESP8266 and Firebase Realtime database is authenticated using client secret key provided by the firebase console (Dkhairnar, and Instructables, 2017). Google Cloud Firebase Realtime Database stores data in real time and sends updates to all the authenticated clients. It stores data in the form of a JSON tree (2020). JSON sent by the microcontroller appends to that JSON tree. JSON sent by microcontroller has the following format:

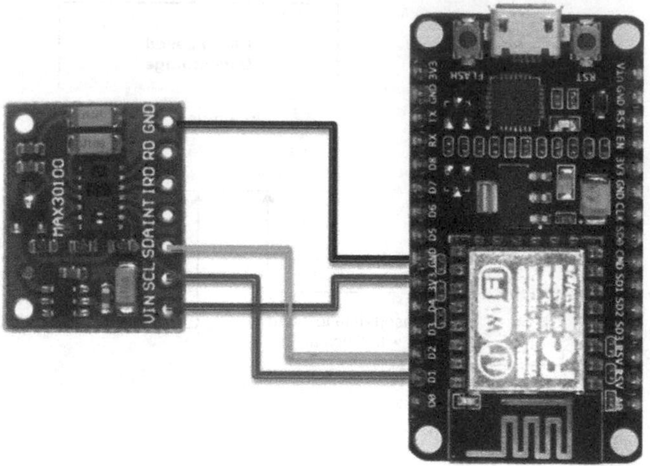

FIGURE 15.5
Circuit diagram.

{
"SpO2": value,
"heartRate": value
}

It is essential to have intervals between updating the JSON tree much much greater than the buffer writing time of MAX30100 because if both times are comparable, the buffer will overflow, and it will halt the MAX30100 sensor.

As soon as ESP8266 appends the new JSON, the latest reading is updated on the user interface. Dataflow of the system is as shown in the system architecture diagram.

15.6.1.3 Data Storage in the Cloud and Its Data Structure

The Firebase Local Emulator Suite is a bunch of cutting-edge devices for engineers hoping to fabricate and test applications locally utilizing Cloud Firestore, Realtime Database, Authentication, Cloud Functions, Pub/Sub, and Firebase Hosting. It provides a rich user interface to help get running and prototyping quickly. Local development with Local Emulator Suite can be a good fit for prototyping, development, and continuous integration workflows (2020).

Firstly, user authentication is an essential factor. The Firebase Realtime data set is Cloud-facilitated. Information is put away as a JSON tree and synchronized continuously to each associated customer. When building cross-stage applications with our iOS, Android, and JavaScript SDKs, the entirety of the customers share one Realtime Database occurrence and consequently get refreshes with the freshest information. When integrated with Firebase Authentication data can be secured and only available to authorized users. The Realtime Database is a NoSQL data set and, accordingly, has various enhancements and usefulness contrasted with a social information base (2020). The Realtime Database API is planned uniquely to permit tasks that can execute rapidly. This empowers us to assemble a huge constant encounter that can serve a huge number of clients without settling on responsiveness. Along these lines, it is vital for consider how clients need to get to information and afterward structure it in like manner.

Data Structure is in the form of JSON tree structure which looks like this:

```
{
"Project Name": {
"sensors":{
"SpO2":{
//unique key are created automatically
//as the new data is been added to the database
"unique key": "95"
},
"PulseRate":{
//unique key is created which is used to identify each instance
//in firebase realtime database as the new data is been added to the database
"unique key": "78"
}
}
}
}
```

The JSON tree in the firebase realtime database starts with a key as a project name, which is created during configuration. Further, branches of key are user defined. In this project, a subtree is created which has a key as "sensors," it will store subtrees that will consist of data from ESP8266. "Sensors" has two subtree "SpO2" and "PulseRate." ESP8266 appends data to these subtrees. "SpO2" stores the value of oxygen level, whereas "PluseRate" stores the value of pulse rate data received from ESP8266.

15.6.2 User Interface

A user interface is designed to establish end-to-end communication between all the system components. Front-end is developed using a React JS framework, which is an open source framework of javascript backed by Facebook (2020). It is converted to a progressive web app that can be accessible on any platform that can run on a browser. It maintains an active WebSocket connection with Firebase Realtime Database. Any changes in blood oxygen level and heart rate are reflected on the user interface such that doctors can monitor it from a remote location. User interface will not be accessible without authentication. Authentication is also supported by firebase.

In the project, the application is built with JSX components. Application has a component of firebase in which all the authentication is provided, which later on can be accessed to retrieve data and display it on screen. In the front end, a circular progress bar is also used to show the data. Further, Firebase data is accessed in the main component, using the firebase real-time database. From one end, the sensors and the data are retrieved and stored in the real-time database, and the application gets the data and keeps on updating the data, which gets displayed on the screen (Linnyk, 2020).

15.7 Data Analysis and Results

The following images in Figure 15.6 and Figure 15.7 show the results of the patient monitoring module. When we put the finger under the scanner of the pulse-oximeter sensor (MAX-30100), it detects the oxygen level in the body and shows accurate results. User interface is shown Figure 15.8.

15.8 Future Scope

Various sensors can be installed, which can help in running multiple tasks at a time. Development of digitized hospitals: A monotonous waiting room with long queues desperately waiting to visit the doctor as soon as possible. And on the other hand, the gloomy faces of the patients there with their painful cries. Well, this was the situation of hospitals a few years back. Now, things are changing with the speed of technology. Advanced healthcare facilities, mobile healthcare applications, and an all-new concept

FIGURE 15.6
Actual implementation images.

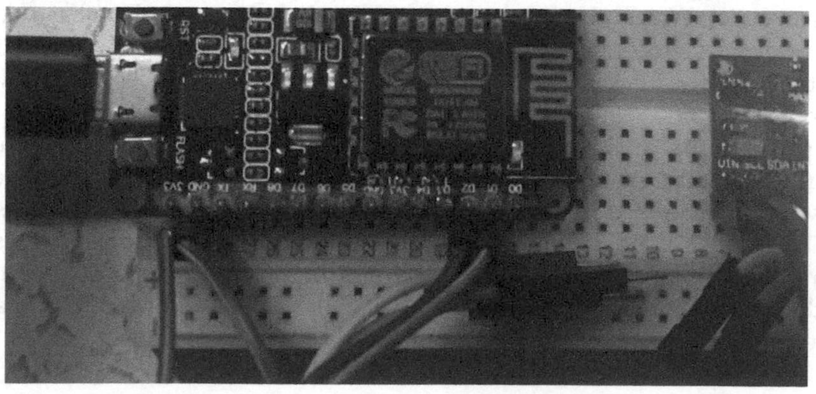

FIGURE 15.7
Actual implementation images.

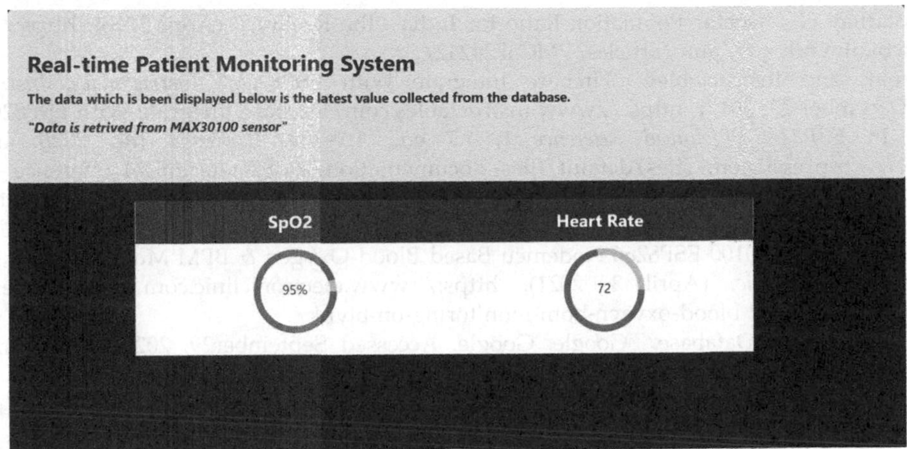

FIGURE 15.8
Real-time update on user interface.

IoT are turning the healthcare domain's whole face. It would be more beneficial for patients by providing remote dialogist reports.

15.9 Conclusion

If there is a disease in the human body, it can be recognized only in the hospital. The Internet of Things is considered a feasible solution for any remote value tracking, especially in health monitoring. Through Medicaid, the patients can check their medical status by monitoring their pulse rate and heart rate anywhere. The records are correctly saved, which helps to identify the current health condition of the person. It also provides aid that will reduce the risk of danger. The person's situation is monitored periodically. If there are changes in the patient's body, they are detected, and proper action can be taken against them, reducing the patient's death. Hence, the IoT-enabled patient monitoring system is helpful not only for the patients but also for the doctors. The doctors can get a second opinion in case of any confusion.

References

"An IoT Based Patient Monitoring System Using Raspberry Pi." IEEE Xplore. Accessed September15, 2020. https://ieeexplore.ieee.org/abstract/document/7725378.

"An IoT Based Patient Health Monitoring System." IEEE Xplore. Accessed September15, 2020. https://ieeexplore.ieee.org/abstract/document/8441708.

"Build Documentation | Firebase." Google. Google. Accessed November25, 2020. https://firebase.google.com/docs/build.

Deo, Madhav G. "'Doctor Population Ratio for India - the Reality,'" (April 2013). https://www.ncbi.nlm.nih.gov/pmc/articles/PMC3724242/.

Dkhairnar, and Instructables. "Firebase Integrate With ESP8266." *Instructables. Instructables* (December 27, 2017). https://www.instructables.com/Firebase-Integrate-With-ESP8266/.

Essay. In *ESP8266 Technical Reference* 1, 1.7 ed., 1:1–104. Espressif Inc, 2020. https://www.espressif.com/sites/default/files/documentation/esp8266-technical_reference_en.pdf.

Essay. In *MAX30100 Pulse Oximeter and Heart-Rate Sensor IC for Wearable Health*, 1–28. Maxim Integrated Products, Inc., 2014. https://datasheets.maximintegrated.com/en/ds/MAX30100.pdf.

Fahad, Engr. "Max30100 ESP8266 Nodemcu Based Blood Oxygen & BPM Monitoring on Blynk." *Electronic Clinic*, (April 2, 2021). https://www.electroniclinic.com/max30100-esp8266-nodemcu-based-blood-oxygen-bpm-monitoring-on-blynk/.

"Firebase Realtime Database." Google. Google. Accessed September29, 2020. https://firebase.google.com/docs/database.

"Getting Started." React. Accessed September30, 2020. https://reactjs.org/docs/getting-started.html.

Gia, Tuan Nguyen, Mai Ali, Imed Ben Dhaou, Amir M. Rahmani, Tomi Westerlund, Pasi Liljeberg, and Hannu Tenhunen. "IoT-Based Continuous Glucose Monitoring System: A Feasibility Study." Procedia Computer Science. Elsevier (June 12, 2017). https://www.sciencedirect.com/science/article/pii/S1877050917310281.

"Iowa Head and Neck Protocols." *Pulse Oximetry Basic Principles and Interpretation | Iowa Head and Neck Protocols* (March 10, 2017). https://medicine.uiowa.edu/iowaprotocols/pulse-oximetry-basic-principles-and-interpretation.

Konutgan, Mikael May 2 2018 · Article, and Mikael Konutgan. "Firebase Tutorial: Getting Started." raywenderlich.com. Accessed November25, 2020. https://www.raywenderlich.com/3-firebase-tutorial-getting-started#toc-anchor-002.

Linnyk, Yuriy. "All You Need Is React & Firebase." *Codementor*. Accessed September29, 2020. https://www.codementor.io/@yurio/all-you-need-is-react-firebase-4v7g9p4kf.

Majumder, A.K.M. Jahangir Alam, Yosuf Amr ElSaadany, Roger Young, and Donald R. Ucci. "An Energy Efficient Wearable Smart IoT System to Predict Cardiac Arrest." Advances in Human-Computer Interaction. Hindawi (February 12, 2019). https://www.hindawi.com/journals/ahci/2019/1507465/.

Press Trust of India. "India's Medical ERROR Deaths, Nearly 5 MN a Year, Can Be Cut by 50%: Expert," (October 28, 2018). https://www.business-standard.com/article/current-affairs/india-s-medical-error-deaths-nearly-5-mn-a-year-can-be-cut-by-50-expert-118102800193_1.html#:~:text=A%20study%20by%20the%20Harvard,when%20brought%20to%20the%20hospital.

Saravanan. "MAX 30100 Heart-Rate Sensor Module." alselectro. Accessed October28, 2020. http://www.alselectro.com/max30100-pulse-oximeter-spo2-and-heart-rate-sensor-module.html.

Shelar, Manisha, Jaykaran Singh and Mukesh Tiwari. "Wireless Patient Health Monitoring System." *International Journal of Computer Applications Volume* 62, no. 6 (2013). https://citeseerx.ist.psu.edu/viewdoc/download?doi=10.1.1.303.3601&rep=rep1&type=pdf.

16

Parkinson Disease Prediction Model and Deployment on AWS Cloud

Harshvardhan Tiwari[1], Shiji K. Shridhar[2], Preeti V. Patil[2], K. R. Sinchana[2], and G. Aishwarya[2]

[1]*Centre for Incubation, Innovation, Research and Consultancy, Jyothy Institute of Technology, Thathaguni, Bengaluru, India*
[2]*Department of Information Science and Engineering, Jyothy Institute of Technology, Thathaguni, Bengaluru, India*

CONTENTS

16.1 Introduction

Parkinson's disease (PD) is a brain disorder that occurs when the death of nerve cells in an area of the brain known as substantia nigra causes a loss of the dopamine (di-ortho-phenyl-alanine) chemical and as a result body movement is affected. Parkinson's disease is considered to be the second most common disease after Alzheimer's. PD is a nuerodegenerative disorder affecting 1% of the population over the age of 50.

DOI: 10.1201/9781003203926-16

Parkinson's disease was earlier named as "The Shaking Palsy" or "Paralysis agitans" by a British doctor named James Parkinson (1817) and then named as Parkinson's disease, honoring James Parkinson (National Collaborating Centre for Chronic Condition, 2006). Parkinson's disease (PD) is a chronic disorder which results in motor and non-motor symptoms. The motor symptoms caused are due to the loss of dompamine. The motor signs and symptoms of PD refer to those who have an effect on the body movement, even though the presence of non-motor signs and symptoms help neuronal loss in non-dopaminergic regions as well. Some of the motor symptoms experience a slight tremor (in hands, finger, and foot on one side of the body etc.), bradykinesia (slow movements), rigid muscles, etc., and some of the non-motor signs and symptoms depression, vision problems, hallucinations, and delusions. The signs and symptoms of PD gets worse over time. There are several environmental factors associated with Parkinson's disease. The factors that caused Parkinson's disease in a person are environmental factors; much research and evidence has shown that the environment has a major impact on the development of neurodegenerative diseases, mainly Alzheimer's and Parkinson's and also it's believed a combination of genetic changes. Loss of dopamine may be responsible for the condition. However the Parkinson's disease symptom is controlled by treating PD affected in the early stages. For this, early prediction of disease is important. The diagnosis of PD is based on the medical history. PD is usually an unusual disorder and it can cause a wide range of problems, but those symptoms differ greatly from one patient to another. Parkinson's disease usually begins at the age of 50 and above and the risk increases with age (3% population > 65 years old). In earlier research, the statistic shows that PD is more common in men above the age of 50 compared to women and 80% of PD patients are over 65 years old. More than 1 million people are living with PD worldwide. The number of PD cases worldwide increases day by day. More than 60,000 cases are found per year. Five Lakh–1 million people are suffering with Parkinson's disease above the age of 50 in America. Although much research is ongoing, it is said that to date there is no known cure or way to prevent Parkinson's disease but few symptoms such as walking, bradykinesia (slowed movement), tremors, and non-motor symptoms such as mood disorders, can be controlled or reduced by medical and non-medical therapies which may help to manage problems of people who are suffering with PD and in a few cases the neurologist advises surgical procedure. Levodopa, dopamine agonists, and MAO-B are medications that will help to reduce the symptoms in which Levodopa is the most effective medication compared to others. Researchers are developing new treatments for Parkinson's disease, treatments that give real hope for people suffering with the disease. The current studies involve fetal cell transplantation, the use of stem cells, and gene therapy. Although there's a large amount of studies on PD, we still have know idea what exactly causes PD. And we have few problems diagnosing it at times. Hence, diagnosing it at an earlier stage could help prevent or reduce the effects. Voice analysis is the first step to predict that the person will get the disease or not. For this prediction, the data will be collected from people who are suffering PD and also from healthy persons who are above 50 years of age. To distinguish with diseased and healthy people there is much research to be done. For the research, utilization of voice measurement is a powerful approach for estimating early stages of Parkinson's disease. In this study, different classification techniques have been used to distinguish healthy people and those with PD. Machine learning is used often for medical analysis due to its effective implementation and reliability.

In this experiment, results are indicated that may be useful to help prioritize scarce healthcare resources.

16.2 Related Work

There are many researches ongoing to classify PD and healthy people. To estimate early stages of Parkinson's disease, the machine learning techniques are utilized in much research.

In Little et al. (2008), the author proposed the paper "Suitability of Dysphonia Measurements for Telemonitoring of Parkinson's Disease." In this study, collected sustained vowel phonations from 31 people, with 23 with PD and 8 healthy people. Achieved accuracy of 91.4% using Support Vector Machine (SVM) for classification is obtained.

Das (2010) made use of different prediction techniques such as Neural Networks, DMnueural, Regression, and Decision Tree and then led to a comparison of classification score for diagnosis of PD. The Neural Networks classifier achieved the simplest results of 92.9%.

Murat Gök (2015) in the proposed paper "An ensemble of k-nearest neighbours algorithm for detection of Parkinson's disease" the accuracy achieved is 98.46% and applying rotation-forest ensemble k-nearest neighbour classifier algorithm area under receiver operating characteristic curve (0.99) scores.

Tiwari (2016) proposed the article "Machine learning based approaches for prediction of Parkinson's disease" using the Parkinson's data set from the UCI Machine Learning Repository. The data set consists of a variety of biomedical voice measurements from 31 people, 23 with Parkinson's disease (PD). Machine learning algorithms such as bagging, boosting, random forest, rotation forest, random subspace, support vector machine, multi-layer perceptron, and decision tree-based methods are used in the Parkinson's data set. Twenty features selected by selection algorithms with minimum redundancy and maximum relevance provide an overall accuracy of 90.3%, an accuracy of 90.2%, Mathews correlation coefficient values of 0.73, and ROC values of 0.96, which is better compared to all other machine learning methods used.

Swapna and Devi (2019) proposed the paper "Performance Analysis of Classification algorithms on Parkinson's data set with Voice Attributes" that used different classification methods carried out using Parkinson's data and the achieved an accuracy of 78.56% using Random Forest.

In this work, for predicting Parkinson's disease using a subject's voice samples the author approached deep neural network (DNN) and long short-term memory (LSTM) network-based model and various simulations were performed on the dataset to exhibit the efficency of the models along with their comparison to the conventional machine learning techniques (Danish Raza Rizvi, 2020). The results obtained the highest accuracy rate of 97.12% and 99.03% for DNN and LSTM respectively which strongly suggest their efficiency for the detection of PD.

In this the author used the Parkinson's Disease audio dataset taken from UCI Machine Learning Repository (Rodrigo Olivares, 2020). Using the bio-inspired optimization algorithm for adjusting the parameters of the Extreme Learning Machine is a real alternative for improving its performance. The results suggest that the classification process for Parkinson's Disease achieves a maximum accuracy of 96.74% and a minimum loss of 3.27%.

Senturk (2020) has proposed a method to predict early diagnosis of Parkinson's disease using machine learning algorithms on Parkinson's disease data set. This data set consists of 195 samples of biomedical voice measurement features from 31 people, where 23 with PD and 8 of them are healthy above the age of 50. They have used different classification algorithms such as Regression Trees, Artificial Neural Networks, and Support Vector Machines and achieved the high test accuracy rate (93.84%) for the Support Vector Machines classification algorithm compared to other classification algorithms. The significance of classifying this kind of clinical medical data is to potentially develop a predictive model to classify or recognize PD-affected subjects from normal controls. In this work, we are using the machine learning classification techniques KNN, SVM, Random Forest, and Logistic regression to develop the prediction models.

16.3 Description of Data Set

The first step for classification is collection of data. The voice measurements can be accessed online from the UCI Machine learning repository for research work and was created by Max Little of University of Oxford who recorded the speech signals for the analysis in collaboration with the National Centre for Voice and Speech, Denver, Colorado. This data set consists of 195 samples of biomedical voice measurement features from 31 people, where 23 with PD (16 males and seven females) and 8 of them healthy (five females, three males) above the age of 60. The data used is in the ASCII CSV format. The features consist of the patients name and three different fundamental frequencies: Minimum vocal fundamental frequency (MDVP:Flo(Hz), Maximum vocal fundamental frequency (MDVP:Fhi(Hz)), and Average vocal fundamental frequency (MDVP:Fo(Hz)), several measures of variation in fundamental frequency (Jitter and its type), several measures of variation of amplitude (shimmer and its type), NHR (Noise Harmonic Ratio), and HNR (Harmonic to Noise Ratio) two measures of ratio of noise to tonal components in the voice. Two nonlinear dynamic complexity measures RPDE (Recurrence period density entropy) and correlation dimension D2, DFA (Detrended fluctuation analysis) is a signal fractal scaling exponent, and three nonlinear measures of fundamental frequency variation (spread1, spread2, PPE). The main aim is to differentiate healthy people from those with PD, according to status column, which is set to 0 for healthy and 1 for PD. There are about six recordings per patient. The data set has about 75% of cases suffering from Parkinson's disease and 25% of cases are healthy (Figure 16.1, Table 16.1).

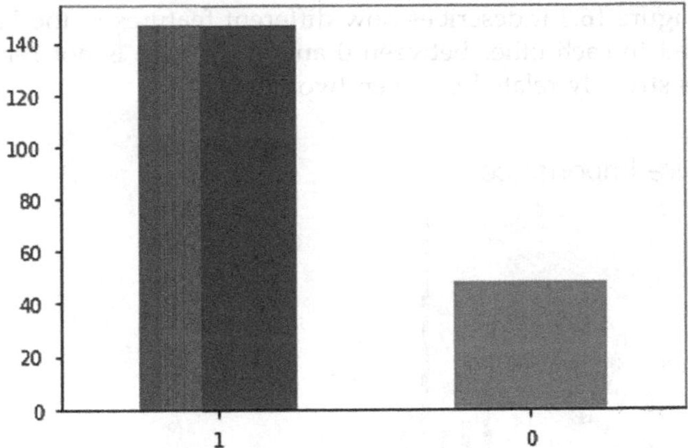

FIGURE 16.1
Show value counts for two categorical 0 for healthy and 1 for Parkinson's.

TABLE 16.1
UCI Parkinson's Disease Data Set

ATTRIBUTE	DESCRIPTION
MDVP:Fo (Hz)	Average vocal fundamental frequency
MDVP:Fhi (Hz)	Maximum vocal fundamental frequency
MDVP:Flo (Hz)	Minimum vocal fundamental frequency
MDVP:Jitter(%)MDVP:Jitter(Abs) MDVP.RAPMDVP:PPQJitter:DDP	Several measures of variation in fundamental frequency.
MDVP:ShimmerMDVP:Shimmer(dB) Shimmer:APQ3Shimmer:APQ5MDVP:APQShimmer:DDA	Several measures of variation in amplitude
PDE,D2	Two nonlinear dynamical complexity measures
NHR, HNR	Two measures of ratio of noise to tonal components in the voice
DFA	Signal fractal scaling exponent
Spread1, spread2,PPE	Three nonlinear measures of fundamental frequency variation.
Status	Health status of the subject (one) - Parkinson's, (zero) - healthy.

16.4 Feature Importance Analysis

Feature importance refers to a class of techniques for assigning scores to input features to a predictive model that indicates the relative importance of each feature when making a prediction (Figure 16.2). Feature important analysis provides insight into the data set and model. Most important scores are calculated by a classification model that has been fit on the data set. In Figure 16.3 it describes how different features in the Parkinson's disease data set correlated to each other between 0 and 1 where 0 is not related between two attribute and 1 is strongly related between two attributes.

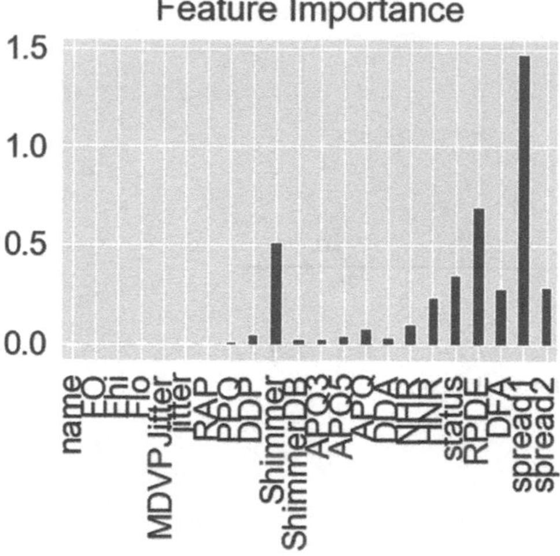

FIGURE 16.2
Feature important analysis.

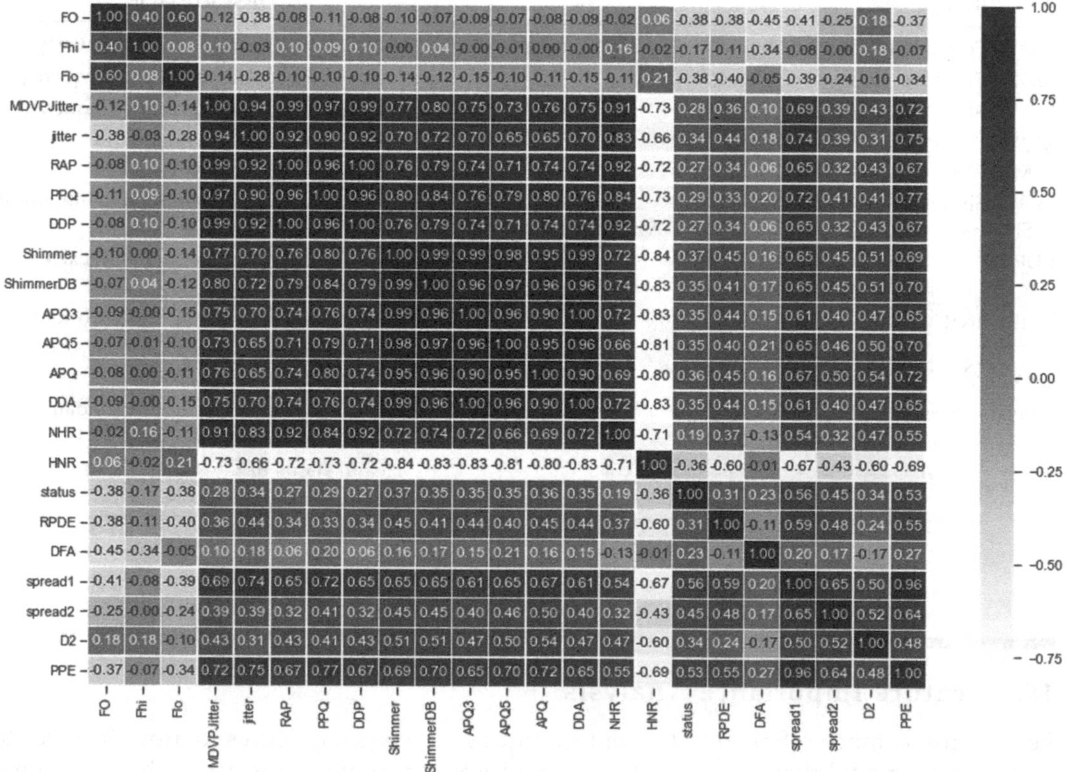

FIGURE 16.3
Correlation between features of Parkinson's disease.

16.5 Prediction Techniques

16.5.1 Logistic Regression

In machine learning, one of the most used classification techniques is logistic regression. It is the supervised learning technique. Logistic regression is a type of predictive model that can be used when the target variable is a categorical variable. Logistic regression performance as a machine learning model predicts the risk of major chronic diseases with low incidence and simple clinical predictors. Logistic regression measures the relationship between the categorical dependent variables by estimating the probabilities; the dependent variable must be binary in nature, e.g., 0 or 1.

16.5.2 Decision Tree

The decision tree algorithm is used for the classification as well as regression problems, which is a supervised learning algorithm. A decision tree is one of the predictive models used in statistics, data mining, and machine learning. The goal of a decision tree is to split a population of data into smaller segments. The decision node and leaf node are the two nodes in decision trees. Decision nodes are used to make any decision and have multiple branches, whereas leaf nodes are the output of those decisions and do not contain any further branches. The goal is to create a model that predicts the value of a target variable by learning simple decision rules inferred from the data features.

16.5.3 SVM (Support Vector Machine)

A support vector machine (SVM) is a supervised machine learning algorithm. It is a popular classification technique. The main agenda of SVM distinctly classifies the data points to find a hyper plane in an N-dimensional space (N-number of features). The SVM classifier is a frontier that best segregates the two classes (hyper plane/line). The aim of SVM is to divide the data set into classes to find a maximum marginal hyper plane (MMH). Its high generalization character allows it to be used in many fields of classification fruitfully.

16.5.4 KNN (K-Nearest Neighbor)

K-Nearest Neighbor can be used for both classification or regression challengers based on supervised learning techniques. It is mostly used in classification problems and it is one of the simplest machine learning algorithms. K is an important parameter in creating a KNN classifier. A KNN algorithm assumes the similarity between the new data and available data and put the new data into the category that is most similar to the available categories. The KNN algorithm stores all the available data and classifies a new data point based on the similarity. This means when new data appears then it can easily be classified into a well suited category by using KNN algorithm. A KNN algorithm is robust to noisy training data and it can be more effective if the training data is large.

STEPS

I. Load the data
II. Initialize the value of k.

III. Fitting the KNN algorithm to the training set.
IV. Euclidean distance is used. The distance between test data and each row of training data is calculated to predict a data. Sort the calculated distance based on the distance value and test the accuracy of the result.
V. Visualizing the test-set result.

16.5.5 Random Forest

A random forest is a supervised machine learning algorithm based on ensemble learning. To form a more powerful prediction model, different types of algorithms or the same algorithm can be joined multiple times. Random forest is one of the accurate learning algorithms. Random forest, like the name implies, consists of a large number of individual decision trees that operate as an ensemble.

16.6 Deploying Model on AWS Cloud

Amazon net offerings (AWS) is an Amazon cloud offering. AWS is a platform that may be a price effective, complete, and smooth to apply cloud computing (Amazon, 2020). A mixture of cloud computing offerings include infrastructure as a service (IaaS), platform as a service (PaaS), and packaged software program as a service (SaaS) blanketed on this platform of Amazon. AWS enables us to recognize the middle ML experiments and dietary supplements of the rest of the essential capabilities with smooth abstracted tools.

Amazon Sage-Maker is a totally controlled platform. Amazon Sage-Maker reduces this complexity via a way of means of making it less complicated to construct and set up a device getting to know ML models. The boundaries that usually gradual down builders who desires to use a machine getting to know could be eliminated via way of means of the Sage-Maker. For deploying the version, first we

I. Create a notebook instance.
II. Load the data and transform.
III. Upload the data set in s3 bucket.
IV. In this step, we use a training data set to train the ML model.
V. Evaluate the performance and accuracy of the ML model.

Amazon Sage-Maker makes use of the Jupyter Notebook and Python with boto to hook up with the s3 bucket, or it has its high-stage Python API for version constructing. The compatibility with cutting-edge deep getting to know libraries like TensorFlow, PyTorch, and MXNet reduces the version constructing time.

16.7 Result

In this work, different classification techniques for the prediction of Parkinson's disease using a reliable Parkinson data set from the UCI machine learning repository where 195 samples of features from 31 people, where 23 with PD (16 males and 7 females) and 8 of them are healthy (5 females, 3 males) above the age of 60. The collected data correctly classified was analyzed in various classification algorithms and Table 16.2 gives the result of all 23 attributes using five classification techniques: logistic regression, support vector machine (SVM), decision tree, K-Nearest Neighbor (KNN), and random forest. We can observe that we achieved the highest test accuracy rate of 94.87% using random forest.

Figure 16.4 shows the comparison of all predictive models on the Parkinson's data set.

Figure 16.5 shows the comparison between MDVP: Jitter(%) with status helps us to predict Parkinson's positive and Parkinson's negative.

Figure 16.6 shows Parkinson's function of NHR (Noise Harmonic Ratio) and HNR (Harmonic to Noise Ratio) shows PD positive and negative cases.

Different performance evaluation metrics are accuracy, recall, sensitivity, specificity, and F1-score.

TABLE 16.2

Result of 5 Classification Techniques on Parkinson's Data Set

	Logistic Regression	K-Nearest Neighbor (KNN)	Decision Tree	Random Forest	Support Vector Machine (SVM)
ACCURACY	0.897436	0.897436	0.871795	0.948718	0.846154

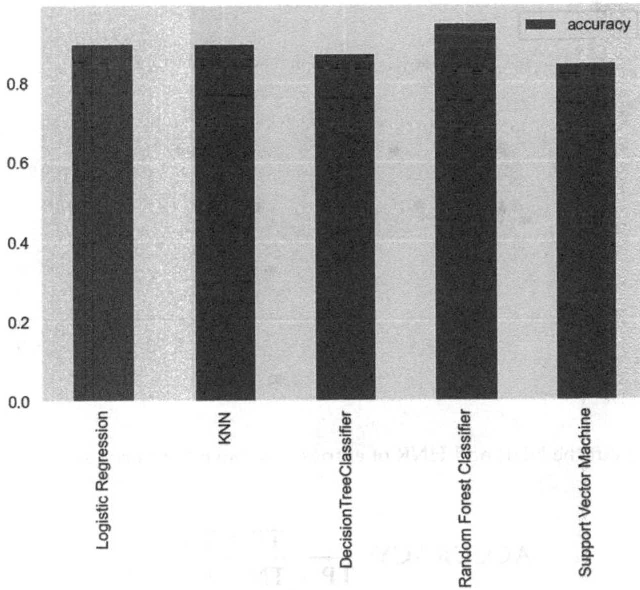

FIGURE 16.4
Accuracy of different predictive models on Parkinson's data set.

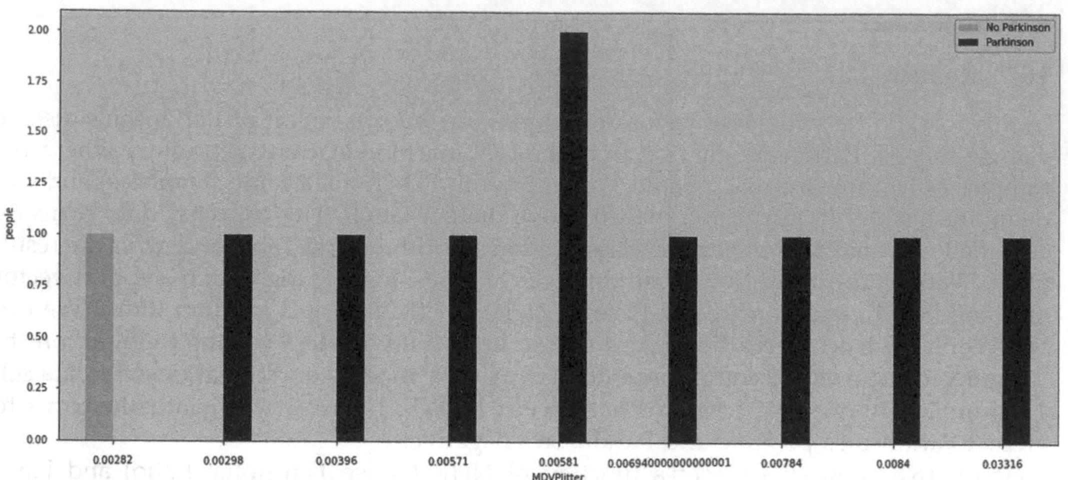

FIGURE 16.5
Plot to compare MDVP:JITTER(%) with status.

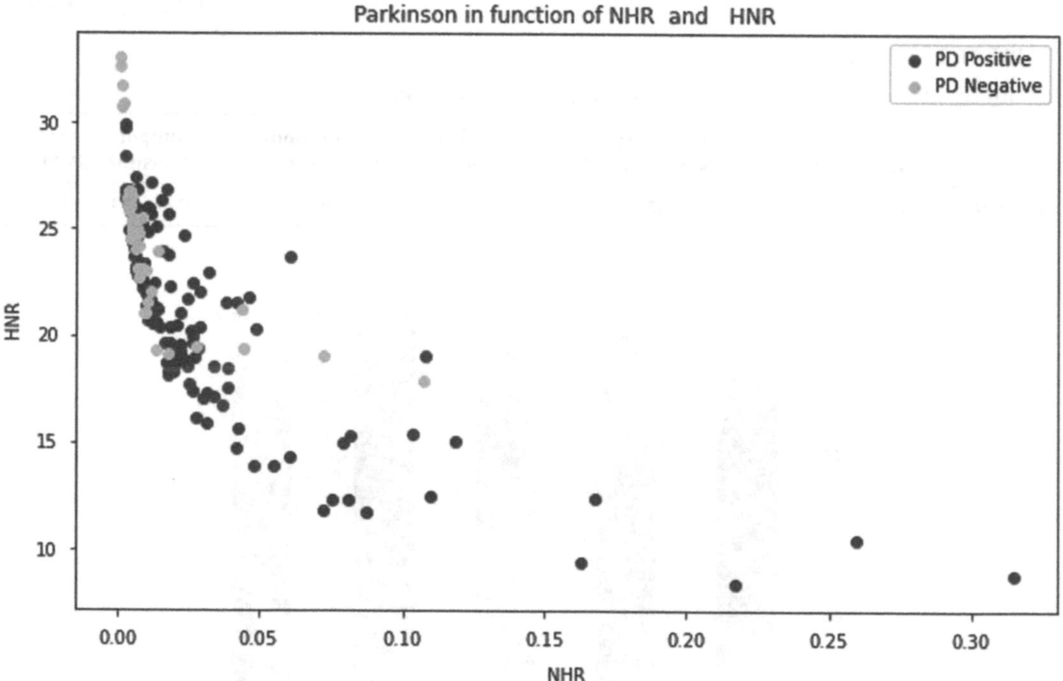

FIGURE 16.6
Scatter plot for finding out the NHR and HNR of entries who have Parkinson's.

$$\text{ACCURACY: } \frac{\text{TP} + \text{TN}}{\text{TP} + \text{TN} + \text{FP} + \text{FN}} \tag{16.1}$$

$$\textbf{PRECISION: } \frac{\textbf{TP}}{\textbf{TP + FP}} \tag{16.2}$$

$$\textbf{RECALL: } \frac{\textbf{TP}}{\textbf{TP + FN}} \tag{16.3}$$

$$\textbf{F1 - SCORE: } \frac{\textbf{2}_*\textbf{(RECALL}_*\textbf{PERCISION)}}{\textbf{RECALL + PRECISION}} \tag{16.4}$$

$$\text{It may also represented as: } \textbf{f1 - score} = \frac{\textbf{2}_*\textbf{TP}}{\textbf{2}_*\textbf{TP + FP + FN}} \tag{16.4}$$

Accuracy in Equation 16.1 was used as a performance metric. **Accuracy** is a success rate of the classification process. **Precision** in Equation 16.2 is defined as the ratio of correctly predicted positive samples to total number of positive prediction. **Recall** in Equation 16.3 is defined as the ratio of total predicted correct positive. **F1-Score** in Equation 16.4 conveys the balance between precision and recall. The following terms are associated with performance metrics: TP stands for number of true positive, TN stands for true negative, FP stands for false positive, and FN stands for false negative. TP refers to the number of PD patients classified correctly as PD, TN refers to a correctly classified person without PD, FP refers to the number of healthy people misclassified as a PD patient, and FN refers to those classified as a healthy person but actually belong to the PD class (Figure 16.7).

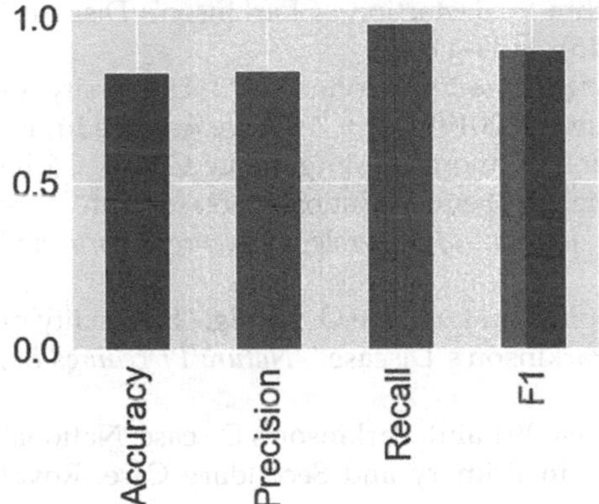

FIGURE 16.7
Confusion matrix: Accuracy, precision, recall, F1-score.

16.8 Conclusion

This paper deals with the application of five classification algorithms on the acquired data set. The classification techniques include logistic regression, support vector system (SVM), decision tree, K-Nearest Neighbor (KNN), and random forest and are used to expect the final results whether or not the character is healthy or a PD-affected person primarily based on voice parameters. Then the results lead to the comparison of one another. From the end result the belief acquired is that the ensemble techniques offer powerful outcomes in comparison with other base classification techniques. Accuracy achieved by the five classifiers lies within the range of 80–100%. Random forest classifier executed excessive accuracy in comparison to different techniques. It performs with impressive accuracy of 94.87%. This technique of estimating the stage of the disease will help in understanding the consequences of disease and to take precautionary measures for better treatment. Overall this study deploys a machine learning model for detecting Parkinson's disease using the Sage-Maker algorithm on AWS. There are several ways to enhance the technology as the diagnosis can be done via numerous means.

References

Amazon, A. W. S. "Amazon Web Services (AWS)-Cloud Computing Services." (2020).

Afza, M. Noor, Manoj Challa and J. Mungara "Speech Processing Algorithm for Detection of Parkinson's Disease." *International Journal of Engineering* 2, no. 4 (2013): 1798–1803.

Bind, Shubham, Arvind Kumar Tiwari, Anil Kumar Sahani, P. M. Koulibaly, F. Nobili, M. Paganiand K. Tatsch. "A Survey of Machine Learning Based Approaches for Parkinson Disease Prediction." *International Journal of Computer Science and Information Technologies* 6, no. 2 (2015): 1648–1655.

Das, R. "A Comparison of Multiple Classification Methods for Diagnosis of Parkinson's disease". *Expert Systems with Applications* 37, no. 2 (2010): 1568–1572.

Despotovic, V., T. Skovranek and C. Schommer. "Speech Based Estimation of Parkinson's Disease Using Gaussian Processes and Automatic Relevance Determination." *Neurocomputing* 401 (2020): 173–181.

Gök, M. "An Ensemble of *k*-nearest Neighbours Algorithm for Detection of Parkinson's Disease." *International Journal of Systems Science* 46, no. 6 (2015): 1108–1112.

Dua, Dheeru. and Casey Graffi. *UCI Machine Learning Repository*. Irvine, CA: University of California, School of Information and Computer Science (2019) http://archive.ics.uci.edu/ml

Moisan, Frédéric, Sofiane Kab, Fatima Mohamed, Marianne Canonico, Morgane Le Guern, Cécile Quintin and Alexis Elbaz. "Parkinson Disease Male-to-Female Ratios Increase with Age: French Nationwide Study and Meta-analysis." *Journal of Neurology, Neurosurgery and Psychiatry* 87, no. 9 (2016): 957.

Little, Max A., Patrick E. McSharry, E. Hunter, Jennifer Spielman Lorraine O. Ramig. "Suitability of Dysphonia Measurements for Telemonitoring of Parkinson's Disease." *Nature Precedings* 56, no. 4 (2008): 1015–1022.

National Collaborating Centre for Chronic Conditions (Great Britain). Parkinson's Disease: National Clinical Guideline for Diagnosis and Management in Primary and Secondary Care. Royal College of Physicians (2006).

Olanrewaju, R. F., N. S. Sahari, A. A. Musa and N. Hakiem. "Application of Neural Networks in Early Detection and Diagnosis of Parkinson's Disease." In *2014 International Conference on Cyber and IT Service Management (CITSM)* (2014, November): 78–82. IEEE.

Olivares, Rodrigo, Raberto Munoz, Ricardo Soto, Broderick Crawford, Diego Cárdenas, Aaron Ponce and Carlo Taramasco. "An Optimized Brain-Based Algorithm for Classifying Parkinson's Disease." *Applied Sciences* 10, no. 5 (2020): 1827.

Parisi, Luca, Narrendar RaviChandran and M. Lyne Manaog. "Feature-Driven Machine Learning to Improve Early Diagnosis of Parkinson's Disease." *Expert Systems with Applications* 110 (2018): 182–190

Parkinson, James . *An Essay on the Shaking Palsy*. London: Sherwood, Neely and Jones, 1817.

Rizvi, D. R., I. Nissar, S. Masood, M. Ahmed and F. Ahmad. "An LSTM Based Deep Learning Model for Voice-Based Detection of Parkinson's Disease." *International Journal of Advanced Science and Technology* 29, no. 5 (2020): 8.

Sadek, R. M., S. A. Mohammed, A. R. K. Abunbehan, A. K. H. A. Ghattas, M. R. Badawi, M. N. Mortaja,... and S. S. Abu-Naser. "Parkinson's Disease Prediction Using Artificial Neural Network" (2019).

Sajal, M. S. R., M.T. Ehsan, R. Vaidyanathan, S. Wa, K. A. Al Mamum and T. Aziz. "Telemonitoring Parkinson's Disease Using Machine Learning by Combining Tremor and Voice Analysis." *Brain Inf* 7 (2020): 12. 10.1186/s40708-020-00113-1

Senturk, Zehra Karapinar. "Early Diagnosis of Parkinson's Disease Using Machine Learning Algorithms." *Medical Hypotheses* 138 (2020): 109603.

Shahid, Afzal Hussain and Maheshwari Prasad Singh. "A Deep Learning Approach for Prediction of Parkinson's Disease Progression." *Biomedical Engineering Letters* 10, no. 2 (2020): 227–239.

Sriram, Tarigoppula V.S., M. V. Rao, G. S. Narayana, D. S. V. G. K. Kaladhar, and T. P. R. Vital. "Intelligent Parkinson's Disease Prediction Using Machine Learning Algorithms." *Int. J. Eng. Innov. Technol* 3 (2020): 212–215.

Swapna, T. and Y. S. Devi. "Performance Analysis of Classification Algorithms on Parkinson's Data set with Voice Attributes." *International Journal of Applied Engineering Research* 14, no. 2 (2019): 452–458.

Tiwari, A. K. "Machine Learning Based Approaches for Prediction of Parkinson's Disease." *Mach Learn Appl* 3, no. 2 (2016): 33–39.

Tsanas, Athanasios, Max A. Little, Patrick E. McSharry, Jennifer Spielman and Lorraine O. Ramig. "Novel Speech Signal Processing Algorithms for High-accuracy Classification of Parkinson's Disease." *IEEE Transactions on Biomedical Engineering* 59, no. 5 (2012): 1264–1271.

Wang, Wu, Junho Lee, Fouzi Harrou and Ying Sun. "Early Detection of Parkinson's Disease Using Deep Learning and Machine Learning." *IEEE Access* 8 (2020): 147635–147646.

Wroge, T. J., Y. Özkanca, C. Demiroglu, D. Si, D. C. Atkins and R. H. Ghomi. "Parkinson's Disease Diagnosis Using Machine Learning and Voice." In *2018 IEEE Signal Processing in Medicine and Biology Symposium (SPMB)* (2018, December): 1–7. IEEE.

17

Federated Learning for Brain Tumor Segmentation on the Cloud

Deep Gandhi, Jash Mehta, Nemil Shah, and Ramchandra Mangrulkar
Dwarkadas Jivanlal Sanghvi College of Engineering, Mumbai, India

CONTENTS

17.1 Introduction

Artificial intelligence, the term first adopted by John McCarthy (2018), is a technology that is much older than one would imagine. It has come a long way since the creation of the first AI program named "Logic Theorist" (Gugerty, 2006). With the help of) and Samuel (1959), Frank Rosenblatt created the perceptron (Rosenblatt, 1958) in 1957. A breakthrough in the field of deep learning came in the year 1967 when the first feed-forward, multilayer perceptron network (Ivakhnenko and Lapa, 1966) was developed.

DOI: 10.1201/9781003203926-17

Simultaneous, AI inchoated computer vision in the 1960s, which was revolutionized by the concept of neocognitron (Fukushima, 2004).

Recently, with advancements in big-data-driven AI like AlphaGo (Silver et al., 2016), which defeated top human Go players – AI technology has shown a huge potential in transforming almost all industries and assisting humans in all walks of life. AI algorithms require large data sets that feature millions of parameters that need to be learned to generalize well on the unseen data. Even though there has been a huge surge in the amount of data that is being collected from a plethora of sources, the quality of data is poor and limited data is available for computation due to it being stored in different locations. Transporting data across different organizations for collaboration and then fusing the data for analysis has posed a huge challenge in recent times.

With data protection and privacy laws such as GDPR (2019) being enforced by the European Union in 2018, finding a solution that sidesteps all these barriers and enables the availability of huge chunks of data, has been a pressing issue. Especially for the healthcare sector, where the data is very sensitive, there are numerous restrictions and privacy-related rules which have been laid down to preserve the privacy of patients.

At the same time, there has been a rise in awareness among people regarding the huge tech giants compromising on the privacy and security of their users. The Facebook-Cambridge Analytica data scandal (Granville, 2018), where private data of millions of Facebook users was acquired without their consent, fueled the need for a system where AI can be used to its utmost potential while keeping ethical, legal, economic, and technical challenges related to privacy in mind.

Current data processing models in AI often involve multiple parties collaborating through simple data transactions where one party transfers its data to the other party. Now the other party is responsible for cleaning and fusing the data before sending it to a third party for building models on the same data. These models can now be utilized by other parties or can be sold as a service.

However, this process might be in violation of the laws enforced by GDPR. This is what gave rise to a new approach known as federated learning, which is a possible solution to all the aforementioned problems.

Recently, Google proposed federated learning (McMahan et al., 2017; Shokri and Shmatikov, 2015), which is a machine learning paradigm that is employed to train a neural model based on decentralized data sets distributed across multiple locations in order to prevent data leakage. Since this process includes the local storage of raw data on the client's device and not exchanging or transferring it to different locations, it ensures that the privacy concerns are taken care of. The central model is improved with the help of focused updates from varied devices which are aggregated to achieve the learning objective. Central storage of data, even if it is anonymized, is prone to attacks and security can be compromised. However, decentralized computation in federated learning offers minimal security risks as the uploaded content is restricted to the weights of the model, keeping in mind the principle of data minimization (Anonymous, 2013).

One of the most common algorithms used in federated learning is the federated averaging algorithm (McMahan et al., 2017), which is used to update the central model using the updates from clients. According to this algorithm, each party has a decentralized local data set where n is the index of the participating party. Now, each party computes the average gradient on its local data with the help of the central model which is sent by the server to all the clients before the start of the training round. As the central server receives the update from the party, it aggregates the updates to obtain a new model. Now, for the next training round, an updated model is sent to all the parties and the process continues. There are several advantages of implementing federated learning. Apart from the security and privacy reasons, in some applications, it has shown an increase in the accuracy of the model in comparison to the traditional method of centrally training on the whole data (Hard et al., 2018). The requirement of large storage space for the central server is no longer a necessity since the data is stored locally with the respective party. This helps in increasing the accuracy to some extent since the data need not be truncated to meet the storage requirements. Moreover, fewer computational resources are needed at the central server since most of the computation is done on remote devices.

To explore the extent to which federated learning can be used for medical data, the problem of brain tumor segmentation is taken up in the chapter, which is a pressing problem in the field. About 24,000 cases of brain tumors were estimated in 2020 in the United States alone (2021). There are numerous methods used by doctors to diagnose brain tumors.

There are two primary types of brain tumors, namely meningioma and glioblastoma. Meningioma is easily segmented and localized; however, glioblastoma is very difficult to localize since they are diffused and have tentacle-like structures. According to a report, 85% to 90% of all primary central nervous system (CNS) tumors are identified to be brain tumors and the 5-year survival rate is only 36% (2021). Hence, brain tumor segmentation is a pressing problem in the medical field.

A horizontal federated learning framework for the task of brain tumor segmentation using the data set created by Bakas et al. (2017), and (Bakas et al., 2018) has been suggested in the chapter. The data set comprises scans from 19 different medical institutions, taken from different scanners to add robustness. The data set consists of four different types of MRIs. Hence, an aggregated ensemble of four different segmentation U-Net models is implemented and an average of the codes is considered for the formation of an MRI to detect the location of the tumor area. Dynamic U-Net, which is pre-trained on ResNet34, is used.

Data from various institutes is exchanged using the horizontal federated learning framework and trained on this model. Homomorphic encryption is used to preserve the privacy of the sensitive data and the FedProx algorithm is used for federated training. The possibility of malicious clients sending updates that may hamper the efficiency of the model is considered and appropriate measures are taken. A Cloud-based approach is proposed to ensure privacy and the models are deployed on the Cloud using the AWS suite.

17.2 Data Set and Preprocessing

17.2.1 Data Set

The data set used to solve this problem was created by Bakas et al. (2017), and Bakas et al. (2018) who collected multimodal scans from 19 institutions with different clinical protocols. To make the data more robust, the images were taken from various scanners at these institutions. The data set contains 57,195 unique data points available as NIfTI files. Each data point consists of native (T1), post-contrast T1-weighted (T1Gd), T2-weighted (T2), and T2 Fluid Attenuated Inversion Recovery (T2- FLAIR) volumes.

Each of the different types of images has the following specialties:

1. Native(T1): In the T1 image only the fat tissues are bright. T1 is considered to be the most anatomical image.
2. Post-contrast T1-weighted(T1Gd): Gadolinium enhances the arteries. 5–15 ml of Gd is injected intravenously before the image is taken. This might help to detect certain abnormalities.
3. T2-weighted (T2): In the T2 image, two tissues are bright: water and fat tissues. The cerebrospinal fluid is bright in T2 images due to its water content.
4. T2 Fluid Attenuated Inversion Recovery (T2-FLAIR): The T2-FLAIR image is quite similar to T2. In T2-FLAIR images, the CSF is not shown to be bright. This can be helpful in some cases, particularly those involving the central nervous system.

Utmost care has been taken by the data creators to manually segment the data, as it was rated by one to four raters, by following the same annotation protocol. All of these annotations were approved by experienced neuroradiologists. Annotations comprise the GD-enhancing tumor (ET-label 4), the peritumoral edema (ED – label 2),0 and the necrotic and non-enhancing tumor core (NCR/NET – label 1), as described both in the BraTS 2012–2013 TMI paper (Bakas et al., 2017) and in the latest BraTS summarizing paper (Bakas et al., 2018) as well as the absence of any tumor (label 0). The data was preprocessed in the following ways. It was first co-registered to the same anatomical template, interpolated to the same resolution (1 cubic mm), and skull-stripped. After preprocessing the data it was distributed.

The proposed architecture utilizes this data set for brain tumor segmentation by using each of the four images individually as the training set in similar neural network architecture. Further, these four neural networks are used to stack an ensemble neural network.

17.2.2 Data Set Preprocessing

After the initial data setup, the data was resized into a 224 * 224 pixels image, which is the requirement of the neural network used in this chapter. All these images are converted into arrays for computation. Then, the data is divided into training and validation sets. The data set is shuffled randomly and then 10% of the data set is placed into the validation set at some predetermined random seed to ensure that the data set remains deterministic at any given time. After this process is completed, data augmentation is performed on the data set. Data augmentation primarily serves two functions:

1. It introduces some randomness in the data set to make it more robust.
2. It also increases the size of the data set, which also helps to increase the accuracy of the model.

Data augmentation is one of the most important regularisation techniques in computer vision mentioned in Mikołajczyk and Grochowski (2018). In data augmentation, small random transformations are applied to the data that do not change the fundamental characteristics of the data but helps the model to generalize better. Random crop, zoom-in, and random rotation are some of the data augmentation techniques.

As the data set includes sensitive medical information, the methods used for the data set would ensure that all the biological characteristics displayed in the images remain intact. All the transforms in this data set must be applied to the tumor images as well as the annotation image to maintain the uniformity of the data. Some of the data augmentation techniques used include:

1. Padding: It adds pixels at each border of the image as specified by the users. The images are padded with the values at the border of the images.
2. Horizontal Flip: The images in the data set are flipped horizontally. This is particularly important to ensure that the model remains accurate even when the plane of vision changes.
3. Random Rotation: Even though horizontal flip is applied to the data set, rotating all the pixels of the image by a small amount helps to introduce randomness in the given data set. The images were rotated between –30 and 30.
4. Vertical Flip: The images of the data set are flipped vertically. It was decided that there is a probability of 0.25 whether the image will be randomly flipped or not. Like the horizontal flip, vertical flip also ensures that the model isn't sensitive to changes in the plane of vision.
5. Dihedral: First, the image is randomly flipped either horizontally or vertically. Then, the image is then rotated by a multiple of 90 degrees. So, dihedral data augmentation helps to rotate the image by any of the 8 dihedral angles.

After applying all these transformations, a databunch was created depending on the selected batch size. This batch size shouldn't be so small that it introduces noise in the data set and it shouldn't be so large that the system crashes due to the lack of sufficient computation resources such as GPU, RAM, etc. After the creation of the databunch, Imagenet stats are applied to these images. Imagenet stats are the exact statistical functions that were applied to the data for training state-of-the-art ResNet models.

Generally, the ImageNet statistics used are [0.485, 0.456, 0.406] as meanwhile [0.229, 0.224, 0.225] is used as standard deviation as these same statistics were used while training the architecture. Using these ImageNet stats facilitates the use of transfer learning thereby saving computational power.

17.3 Double Clustered Federated Learning System

Figure 17.1 depicts the proposed system known as the "Double Clustered Federated Learning System," which is explained in detail in the chapter further.

17.3.1 U-Net Architecture

It is identified that in order to perform the task of segmentation of the aforementioned data set images, it would be necessary to use a generative model, which would help in identifying the absolute dimensions of the tumors very clearly in the image. Thus, the prominent model that is being used for biomedical image segmentation for a long time is proposed. The use of U-Net is proposed in this chapter. The U-Net is explained in further detail below.

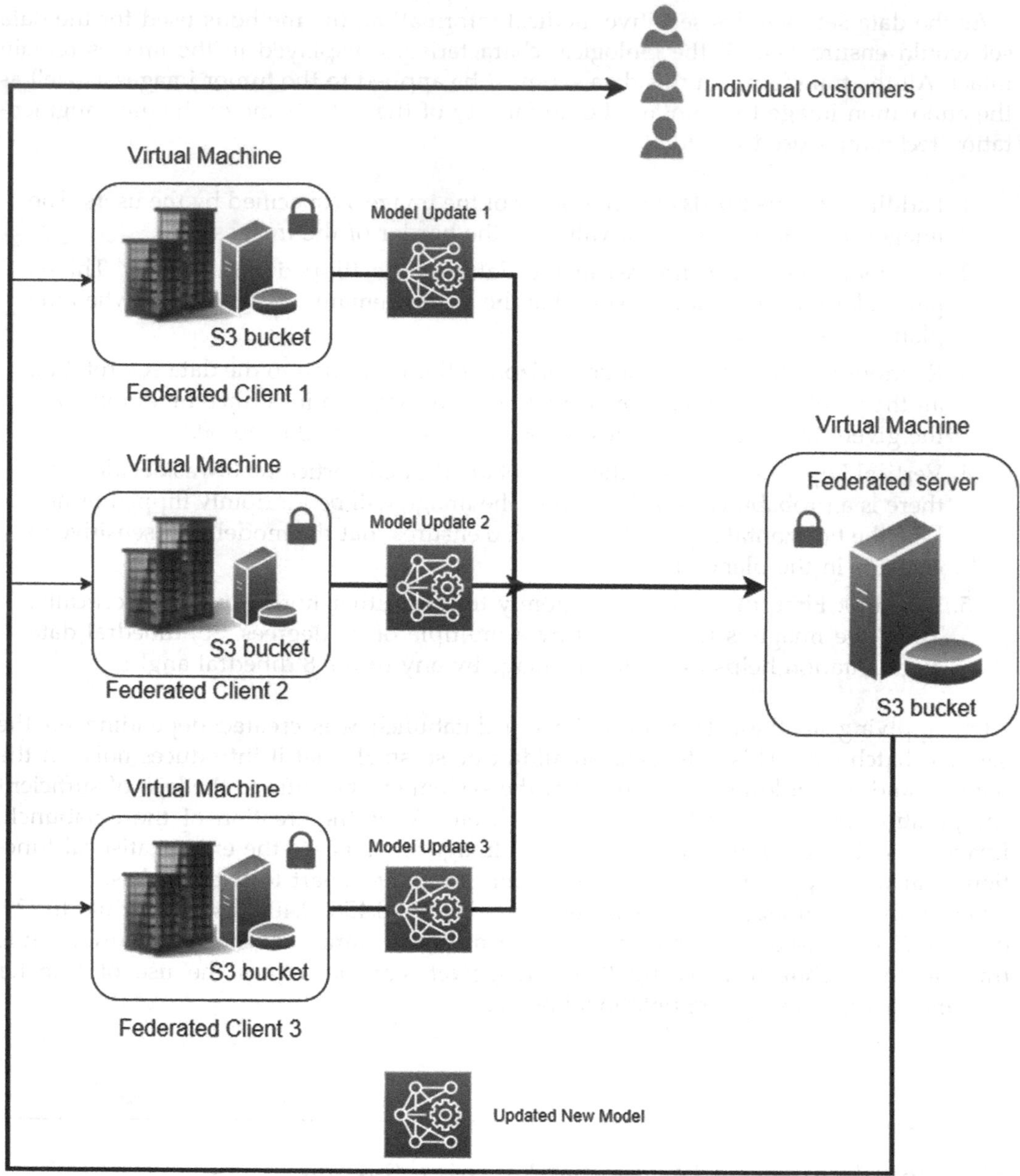

FIGURE 17.1
Double clustered federated learning system.

As proposed by Ronneberger et al. (2015), a U-Net was used for biomedical image segmentation right from 2015. Conventionally, it can be claimed that a U-Net can perform the classification of every pixel in an image file, and thus, it is useful for segmentation tasks and thus, the use of this architecture for the task of brain tumor segmentation is proposed. As it is evident from the name, a U-Net has a U-shaped architecture that consists of two phases: downsampling and upsampling. Downsampling is often

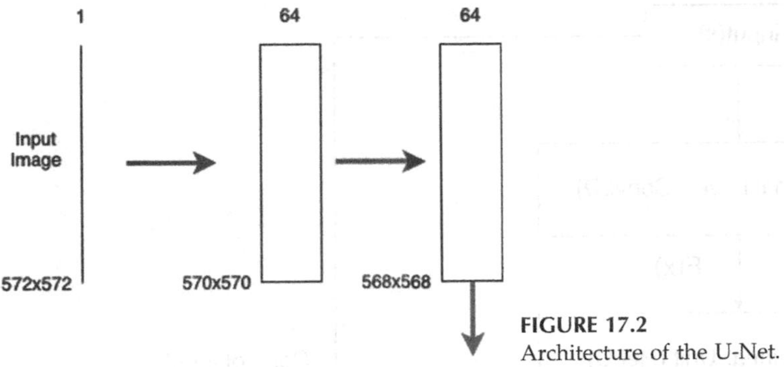

FIGURE 17.2
Architecture of the U-Net.

carried out with stride two convolutions and upsampling is carried out using stride 0.5 convolutions as an image has to be formed while upsampling.

17.3.1.1 Downsampling Stage of U-Net

As it can be observed in Figure 17.2, each stage of the U-Net consists of two convolutional layers and as the gray arrow indicates downsampling, the size of the image is halved due to the stride two configuration of the U-Net. The blue arrow indicates that a convolutional layer is applied to the image along with a ReLU. This process of Conv2D, ReLU, and Max Pooling is applied three times until the number of channels in the input vector becomes 1,024. After this, a convolutional layer and ReLU is applied twice to the vector, but Max Pooling is not applied to the same.

It is useful for the current problem to combine the transfer learning approach along with the downsampling path to get better results from pre-trained models. Thus, the downsampling is done with the help of a pre-trained model using transfer learning. Thus, a model known as ResNet is used which is trained on the Imagenet data set as proposed in He et al. (2016). This U-Net is also known as the Dynamic U-Net.

17.3.1.2 ResNet

As observed in He et al. (2016), it becomes difficult to train deeper neural networks due to a lot of factors such as the increasing number of parameters and the stacking of a lot of layers. It was also observed in He et al. (2016) that increasing model complexity with stride-1 convolutions doesn't help and thus building upon the works of Krizhevsky et al. (2012), the authors of He et al. (2016) propose a network with skip connections. This skip connection can be explained with the help of Figure 17.3.

Thus, as observed in Figure 17.3, the previous outputs are also preserved and thus, preventing the zeroing of gradients at any given point. The aid provided by these skip connections is also observed in Li et al. (2018) as the loss is toned down due to these connections.

Thus, Equation 17.1 for the Resblock can also be written as:

$$Output = x + Conv2(Conv1(x)) \quad \ldots \tag{17.1}$$

Thus, downsampling using this pre-trained ResNet34 model is performed. However, a separate approach is carried out while upsampling.

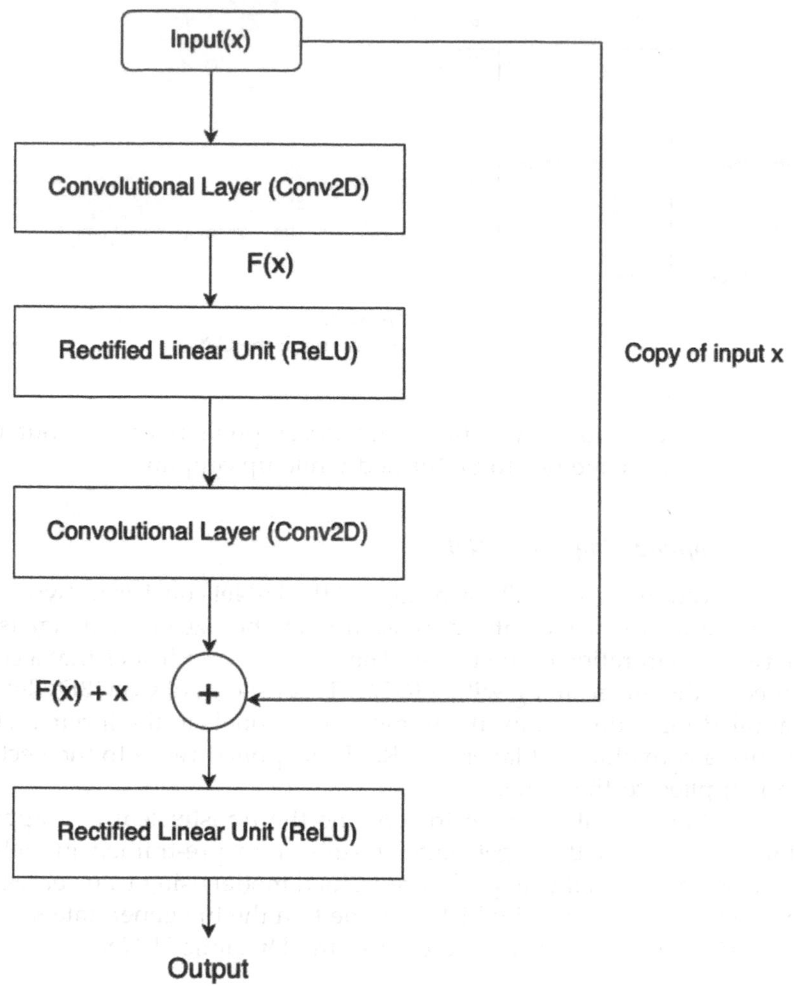

FIGURE 17.3
Resblock.

17.3.1.3 Upsampling in U-Net Architecture

Figure 17.4 shows the lowermost turning point of the U-Net after which the inferences come together to create a new image using the 0.5 stride convolutions. Here, for the upsampling part, a technique called Pixel Shuffle from Shi et al. (2016) is used. This method is effective in resampling the order of an input vector of size (N, C* r* r, H, W) to a vector of (N, C, H * r, W * r), where r is the upsampling factor, that is, since there is a convolutional step of 0.5, the upscale factor would be 2. C, H, W, and N is the size of the original input layer. For the upsampling layer, a specific initialization as proposed in Aitken et al. (2017) is used, which helps in dealing with various factors such as the checkerboard effects which may occur when upsampling an image. This ICNR initialization also helps in smoothening of loss and as proposed in Aitken et al. (2017), it has been observed that it is easier for the U-Net to generalize well and converge quickly rather than the random weights method which would have been to generate random initial weights and then converge to solutions.

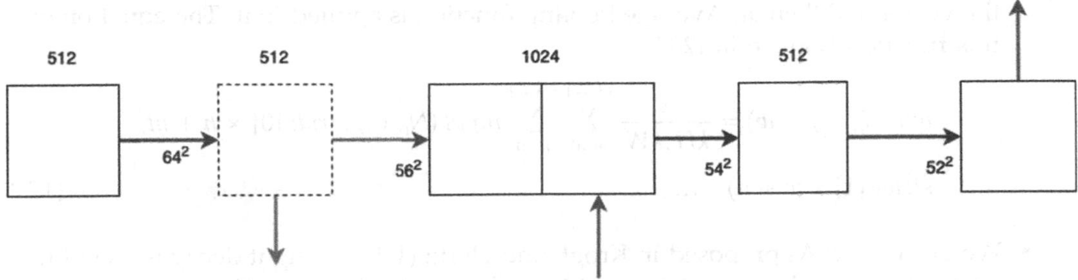

FIGURE 17.4
Flow of data through U-Net.

Thus, the usage of a Dynamic U-Net is proposed as the core model at the center of the proposed "Cloud-based Federated Learning Brain Tumour Segmentation System."

17.4 General Training

The training has to be carried out using the user data exchanged using the federated learning approach. However, before deploying the model, it is found that pre-training the model using the conventional training approach with the help of the aforementioned data set is useful. Since the data set consists of four different types of MRIs, an aggregated ensemble of four different segmentation U-Net models is proposed. Thus, an average of the codes is taken after every result to form the end MRI for the location of the tumor area. Hence, the conventional training approach is discussed initially and then, the federated way of fine-tuning the same model using the Cloud is explained.

17.4.1 Pre-Training the U-Net

As discussed earlier while explaining the architecture of the dynamic U-Net to be used, the pre-trained architecture used for the training of the U-Net is ResNet34. A ResNet34 refers to the depth of the layers in the architecture meaning that there are 34 layers in the model. Regarding the use of various hyperparameters to be used for training this dynamic U-Net, it is found that the following hyperparameters are the most useful for optimization:

- Blurring: According to Sugawara et al. (2018), it is observed that whenever images are generated, a checkerboard type effect is generated in them producing pixels in the form of checkerboards. Performing an ICNR initialization helps with this sub-pixel convolution as discussed in the architecture of U-Net. This effect is also reduced while upscaling using blurring. Thus, for upscaling using Pixel Shuffle and then performing border normalization, it is essential to apply a blurring effect over the H*W matrix as mentioned in Sugawara et al. (2018). To apply this hyper-parameter, a Replication Padding is created on all the sides of the vector and then an Average Pooling function is applied to it. The equation of this function is given in (2021):

$$out(N_i, C_j, h, w) = \frac{1}{kH_* kW} \sum_{m=0}^{kH-1} \sum_{n=0}^{kW-1} input(N_i, C_j, stride[0] \times h + m,$$

$$stride[1] \times w + n) \quad \ldots \tag{17.2}$$

- Weight Decay: As proposed in Krogh and Hertz (1991), weight decay is useful to prevent the weights from being set to null while backpropagation is performed. In the case of an increased number of parameters, while calculating the loss, the loss function calculates the sum of the squares of these exact parameters to determine the loss of the models. This square sum would be large and thus, the model would come to the conclusion to set the weights 0 as this would be one of the optimum solutions under huge loss conditions. To prevent this from happening, a term called *weight decay* is also multiplied to the present weights. The number used to multiply here is called weight decay. Thus, the loss Equation 17.3 would now look as:

$$Loss = MSE(y_h, y) + wd * sum(w^2) \quad \ldots \tag{17.3}$$

After this, during the gradient descent step, the weights are updated as given in Equation 17.4:

$$w_t = w_{t-1} - lr * \frac{d(Loss)}{dw} \quad \ldots \tag{17.4}$$

Now, for the other term in the loss equation, the gradient would be calculated as shown in Equation 17.5:

$$\frac{d(wd * w^2)}{dw} = 2 * wd * w \quad \ldots \tag{17.5}$$

Thus, in this way, a portion of the current weight is also subtracted from the current weight multiplying a constant called learning rate with the loss function. This helps in faster convergence of models without nullifying the weights of the models.

$$MSE = \frac{1}{n} \sum_{i=1}^{n} (y_i - y_h)^2 \quad \ldots \tag{17.6}$$

- Accuracy Metric: A mean squared error is used to keep track of the accuracy while generating the images. Equation 17.6 for the Mean Squared error is given as

This is essential to check if there are any discrepancies for image generation for a specific MRI. It can be checked using specific hooks and extraction of the end layers of the model and constructing a relevant heat map on the image. Thus, model convergence for every U-Net in the ensemble is checked using the same.

17.5 Federated Learning and Cloud Development

17.5.1 Federated Learning

There are primarily three types of federated learning, as explained in this paper Yang et al. (2019):

1. Horizontal federated learning: In horizontal federated learning, there is a huge overlap in the data features but the data samples are quite different from each other. This is analogous to the data that is horizontally partitioned inside the tabular view. Hence, it is known as horizontal federated learning. As all the data used in this chapter share the same feature space, horizontal federated learning has been used.
2. Vertical federated learning: When there is a large overlap in the data samples but the data features differ from each other, vertical federated learning is used. Vertical federated learning gets its name from the vertically partitioned data inside a tabular view.
3. Federated transfer learning: When there is little overlap in data features, as well as data samples, both horizontal and vertical federated learning prove ineffective. In such cases, federated transfer learning techniques are leveraged to bridge this gap between heterogeneous data.

In horizontal federated learning, K participants (clients or users or parties) train a machine learning model in collaboration with each other. The server plays an important role in the collaboration of various clients. The client performs the averaging of the horizontally partitioned data set by leveraging the FedAvg algorithm.

The FedAvg algorithm was first used for horizontally partitioned data sets. There are two types of gFedAvg algorithms:

1. Gradient Averaging: In gradient averaging, the participants share the gradients to the client who averages the gradients and then computes the model parameters and shares the parameters back to the clients for further computation. This is also known as synchronous stochastic gradient descent (SGD) or federated SGD (FedSGD). This process continues till model convergence or the maximum number of iterations are reached or for the maximum training time. Although gradient averaging guarantees convergence of the model, it is not used much as gradients need to be sent and received after every iteration which requires heavy communication and a strong and reliable connection. There is also a greater danger of Reconstruction attack as a malicious client can easily reconstruct the data from the gradients.
2. Model Averaging: Instead of sharing gradients at each iteration, local models can be trained by the clients. Then, the weights of these models are sent to the server for aggregation and the local model is updated by the aggregated model. This is known as model averaging. Model averaging is the same as gradient averaging if weights are updated at every iteration and all the local clients train the model with the same initial weights. Model averaging is more secure than gradient averaging. Although model convergence takes greater time in model averaging,

it is preferred over gradient averaging due to less reliance on reliable networks. This is shown by Equations 17.7 and 17.8 as follows:

$$\forall\ k,\ w_{t+1}^{k} \leftarrow \bar{w}_t - \eta g_k \quad \ldots \tag{17.7}$$

$$\bar{w}_{t+1} \leftarrow \sum_{k=1}^{K} \frac{n_k}{n} w_{t+1}^{k} \quad \ldots \tag{17.8}$$

Both model averaging and gradient averaging are considered a part of the FedAvg approach. This plain FedAvg algorithm introduced in McMahan et al. (2017) exposes plaintext results such as gradients from an optimization algorithm or the model weight to the client. A malicious client may reconstruct data from these results. Usually, some encryption techniques are used along with the vanilla federated learning to make the system more secure and reduce the possibility of various attacks.

Some of the methods to make the federated learning approach more secure are described below:

1. Secure Multi-Party Computation (MPC): The Secure Multi-Party Computation a.k.a. Secure Function Evaluation (SFE) as shown in Lindell (2020) allows the users to compute a private function from input by each party without revealing the input to other parties. Given a secret value x that is split into n shares so that a party Pi only knows xi, all parties can collaboratively compute so that party Pi learns nothing beyond the output value yi corresponding to its input. As any parties don't have information about the inputs of other parties, the FedAvg is secured against any attacks from the clients. The MPC can be carried out by three approaches namely Oblivious Transfer (OT), Secret Sharing (SS), and Threshold Homomorphic Encryption (THE). As both OT and THE modify the idea of Secret Sharing, it is the most widely used. In Secret Sharing (SS), a secret value is hidden by splitting it into random parts in such a way that each party has only one share and by extension, only a single part of the secret.
2. Homomorphic Encryption (HE): The modern homomorphic encryption first introduced in Sen (2019) is another approach to be used along with FedAvg to prevent any attacks. In homomorphic encryption, it is possible to perform operations over the cipher text without decrypting the ciphertext. Let $Enc_{enk}(\ldots)$ denote the encryption function with enk as the encryption key. Let M denote the plaintext space and C denote the ciphertext space. A secure cryptosystem is called homomorphic if it satisfies the condition mentioned in Equation 17.9, as follows:

$$\forall\ m_1, m_2 \in M,\ Enc_{enk}(m_1 \odot_M m_2) \leftarrow Enc_{enk}(m_1) \odot_c Enc_{enk}(m_2) \quad \ldots \tag{17.9}$$

For some operators $\odot_M$ in M and $\odot_c$ in C, where $\leftarrow$ indicates the left-hand side term is equal to or can be directly computed from the right-hand side term without any intermediate decryption.

There are three homomorphic schemes:

1. Partially Homomorphic: In partially homomorphic schemes, any addition or multiplication can be performed an unlimited number of times.
2. Somewhat Homomorphic: In somewhat homomorphic schemes both addition and multiplication can be computed a limited number of times.

3. Fully Homomorphic: In a fully homomorphic scheme, both addition and multiplication can be performed an unlimited number of times.

3. Differential Privacy: Differential privacy was originally used for secure analysis over sensitive data (Dwork, 2006). The key idea of differential privacy is that the outcome of a specific function should be insensitive to any particular record in the data set. Differential privacy is achieved by adding noise to the data set. A randomized mechanism M preserves (ε,δ)-differential privacy if given any two data sets D and D′ differing by only one record, and for all S Ì Range (M) and this is demonstrated in Equation 17.10.

$$Pr[M(D) \in S] \leq Pr[M(D') \in S]e^{\varepsilon} + \delta \quad \ldots \tag{17.10}$$

where ε is the privacy budget and δ is the failure probability. There are two ways of adding noise to a data set:

1. Addition of noise depending on the sensitivity of function: The sensitivity of a function is defined as the maximum change in the value of a function when a particular record is added or removed from the data set. Generally, a Laplacian or Gaussian noise is added to the data set to achieve differential privacy.
2. The Exponential Mechanism: The exponential mechanism is given a quality function q that scores the outcomes of calculation. The exponential mechanism samples the outcome from the probability distribution generated by quality function over the output. Higher scores lead to better differential privacy.

As homomorphic encryption allows arithmetic operations on encrypted data the privacy of users is preserved. Since there is no addition of noise in homomorphic encryption, there is no degradation in the accuracy of models. For these reasons, it was decided to use homomorphic encryption along with the FedProx algorithm.

17.5.1.1 FedProx

FedProx algorithm first introduced in Sahu et al. (2020) is similar to the FedAvg method. The main aim of FedProx algorithm is to minimize the loss as given by Equation 17.11:

$$\min_{w} f(w) = \sum_{k=1}^{N} p_k F_k(w) = E_k[F_k(w)] \quad \ldots \tag{17.11}$$

Here, N = number of devices, pk ≥ 0 and $\sum_k p_k = 1$

FedProx makes some simple yet important changes that guarantee the convergence of models.

These changes also result in significant empirical improvements. FedAvg algorithm only aggregates the parameters of models that have computed uniform amounts of work (the algorithm runs for the same number of epochs). However, it is unfair to assume that devices with different computational capabilities perform uniform work. FedProx allows the generalization of FedAvg by allowing the aggregation of partial amounts of work done by the clients according to their computational capabilities. As FedProx provides a better guarantee of convergence and allows aggregation of models from more users than FedAvg, it was beneficial to use FedProx to perform model averaging.

17.5.2 Federated Training

As discussed earlier in the chapter, the Cloud is utilized to conduct federated learning. However, it is also necessary to take care of various other factors along with the training strategies and Cloud node connections. Various client sampling and management techniques for conducting computationally efficient training is discussed in this part.

The approach proposed by Beutel et al. (2020) has been used to conduct training and thus, the factors to be considered are:

1. Fraction Fit: This determines the percentage of clients to consider in one cycle when a fit is carried out. It might not be useful to consider all the clients in the cluster when the application is deployed on a large scale. Thus, a fractional fit approach is considered for saving computational resources, and also, the clients chosen during this approach are completely random. Thus, it avoids any bias or overfit on a particular device. This method is to be used on the server-side.
2. Valid Clients: It would be useful to consider the approach similar to fraction fit even during the time of validation to save time as well as introduce randomness. Thus, this was also deployed to the server side to select a preset percentage of clients at random to conduct validation.
3. Parameter Initialization: While using the designated federated strategy, it would be useful if some parameters for the model are initialized on the server side and then the new models which are trained would receive the updated global weights with a contribution of these initialized parameters. Thus, the weights of the pre-trained U-Net are initialized on the server side so that if a selected model sends some weights which are way off, then after the federated fit, the model would not be disturbed completely due to the initialized weights being considered too.
4. Rounds: This is similar to the epochs of a model. Just like epochs, this determines the number of times the federated fit is carried out. Carrying out a federated fit more than once is necessary so that the fraction fit doesn't end up only fitting a fraction of the data. Thus, the total number of clients taking part in one complete cycle of the federated fit would be the product of the number of clients in a federated fit and the number of rounds the federated fit is carried out. The number of rounds should be determined by the server to establish consensus.
5. Thus, these approaches which are setup on the server side are used, and for the client end, regular endpoints are created for sending and receiving the parameters. Every client must be connected to the server as the gRPC client during the whole training process for training without any failures. These gRPC connections as discussed earlier are all established on the Cloud. A gRPC message limit has also been implemented to limit the message being sent only to the parameter size. This helps in preventing any anonymous attack leading to data transfer to the server too.

17.5.3 Cloud Deployment

This system of brain tumor segmentation on the Cloud is deployed using the AWS suite. To bring this process to fruition, the required resources from AWS for the whole federated training to take place are identified first.

The devices at the medical institutions taking part in the training process might not be computationally sufficient to train a large data set generated by these institutions. Thus, a virtual machine would be required to train these models whenever federated learning is about to take place, and also a central server would be required to complete it and share the updated weights among these models.

An EC2 instance is assigned to every client taking part in the federated training process and also a central instance for conducting the federated training using the FedProx algorithm. When the scheduled federated training is about to start, an EC2 instance is assigned to every training endpoint. However, it must be noted that only the clients sampled by the federated server are assigned an EC2 instance and undergo training instead of all the clients together. This helps cut costs and saves computation power too. These endpoints use the current model weights on their device to train the models on the EC2 instance.

When these clients are done training in a particular round of the federated training process, the updated local model weights are saved in an S3 bucket.

This S3 cluster is then called by the central EC2 instance which samples the updated local model weights and performs averaging using the FedProx algorithm. However, before undergoing the FedProx process, it is made sure that none of the participants try to poison the model by sending random weights and damaging all the learning that has been carried out. To prevent this, the central server first conducts validation of the weights sampled on the data set that is used for pre-training the models. These weights sent by the clients are only considered if they don't deter from the pre-training accuracy by more than 50%. Thus, model poisoning is prevented using this consensus protocol. It must be noted that all of these transfers to and fro the S3 bucket are of homomorphically encrypted weights and not the raw ones.

After carrying out the FedProx algorithm and completing all the rounds of the required training procedure, the central instance sends the updated weights to all the participants of the system – the ones who were involved in the training and the ones who weren't. This leads to all the endpoints receiving the updated weights and thus carry out meaningful inference work from the same.

17.6 Global Deployment

This section of the chapter deals with the actual deployment of the proposed system. It is generally the case that when the hoi polloi are considered as the end-user clients for this system, much training data cannot be generated from a single user endpoint since a common working person would not try segmentation of MRIs more than once in years. Thus, the inclusion of various medical institutions as the end-user clients for the same system is considered feasible. This results in the hospitals or any similar institutions improving their technology for tumor identification along with the patients' data never leaving the hospital servers. Thus, increasing a sense of trust between them and their clients.

It is proposed that the end-user clients who are not registered medical institutions could be given only inference privileges and thus, their local models would not be used while training and they'd only receive updated model weights. This results in two clusters being formed among the end users for the system.

One of these clusters which are the registered medical institutions would have a two-way relationship with the central server. This means that these end users would send their own weights after training and also receive the updated weights from the central server after undergoing the federated cycle. However, the other cluster which would consist of the non-training end users would only have a one-way relationship with the server. This means that they would only receive the updated weights from the server and not send any as training does not take place over these devices.

It is claimed here that this system could then also be used to form various super clusters based on geographical regions and then create sub-central servers for each of these super clusters. This would help the institutions in a particular geographical region to only use a model trained on the model using data from that region. Thus, this would be useful to even track any upcoming endemic related to such brain diseases.

Thus, a globally utilizable Cloud system for brain tumor segmentation is proposed without compromising on any sensitive medical data.

17.7 Conclusion

In this chapter, "Cloud-based Federated Learning Brain Tumour Segmentation System" has been proposed. An ensemble of four different segmentation U-Net models and leveraged Federated Learning using FedProx is utilized to enable collaboration between various medical institutes while preserving privacy. This approach helps us achieve high performance in the segmentation task.

However, this method is more beneficial due to the data not residing on the central server and hence preventing data leakage. Moreover, the model was pre-trained on a data set comprised of robust data, collected from 19 different medical institutions and is not necessarily independent and identically distributed. This demonstrates the flexibility of the architecture in performing reasonably well even with the given constraints. For future work, the Committee Consensus (Li et al., 2021) method can be implemented that can help in reducing the amount of consensus computing and solve the issue of malicious attacks.

References

Aitken, A., C. Ledig, L. Theis, Jose Caballero, Zehan Wang and W. Shi. "Checkerboard Artifact Free Sub-pixel Convolution: A Note on Sub-pixel Convolution, Resize Convolution and Convolution Resize." ArXiv abs/1707.02937 (2017).

"AvgPool2d." AvgPool2d \- PyTorch master documentation. Accessed March 23, 2021. https://pytorch.org/docs/master/generated/torch.nn.AvgPool2d.html.

"Artificial Intelligence (AI) Coined at Dartmouth," October 14, 2018. https://250.dartmouth.edu/highlights/artificial-intelligence-ai-coined-dartmouth.

Bakas, Spyridon, Hamed Akbari, Aristeidis Sotiras, Michel Bilello, Martin Rozycki, Justin S. Kirby, John B. Freymann, Keyvan Farahani and Christos Davatzikos. "Advancing The Cancer

Genome Atlas Glioma MRI Collections with Expert Segmentation Labels and Radiomic Features." *Scientific Data* 4 (2017): n. pag.

Bakas, Spyridon, M. Reyes, A. Jakab, S. Bauer, Markus Rempfler, A. Crimi, R. T. Shinohara, C. Berger, Sung Min Ha, M. Rozycki, Marcel Prastawa, E. Alberts, Jana Lipková, J. Freymann, J. Kirby, M. Bilello, H. Fathallah-Shaykh, R. Wiest, Jan Kirschke, B. Wiestler, R. Colen, A. Kotrotsou, Pamela LaMontagne, D. Marcus, Mikhail Milchenko, A. Nazeri, M. Weber, A. Mahajan, Ujjwal Baid, D. Kwon, Manu Agarwal, M. Alam, A. Albiol, Alex Varghese, T. Tuan, T. Arbel, A. Avery, B. Pranjal, S. Banerjee, Thomas Batchelder, N. Batmanghelich, E. Battistella, M. Bendszus, Eze Benson, J. Bernal, G. Biros, M. Cabezas, S. Chandra, Yi-Ju Chang, et al., "Identifying the Best Machine Learning Algorithms for Brain Tumor Segmentation, Progression Assessment, and Overall Survival Prediction in the BRATS Challenge." ArXiv abs/1811.02629 (2018).

Beutel, Daniel J., Taner Topal, Akhil Mathur, Xinchi Qiu, Titouan Parcollet and N. Lane. "Flower: A Friendly Federated Learning Research Framework." ArXiv abs/ 2007.14390 (2020).

"Brain Tumor." *Cancer.Net*. Accessed March 22, 2021. https://www.cancer.net/cancer-](http://www.cancer.net/cancer-)types/brain-tumor/statistics).

"Cancer of the Brain and Other Nervous System - Cancer Stat Facts." *SEER*. Accessed March22, 2021. https://seer.cancer.gov/statfacts/html/brain.html.

Dwork, C. "Differential Privacy." *International Colloquium on Automata, Languages, and Programming* (2006), Springer, Berlin, Heidelberg.

Fukushima, K. "Neocognitron: A Self-organizing Neural Network Model for a mechanism of Pattern Recognition Unaffected by Shift in Position." *Biological Cybernetics* 36 (2004): 193–202.

Granville, Kevin. "Facebook and Cambridge Analytica: What You Need to Know as Fallout Widens." *The New York Times. The New York Times*, March 19, 2018. https://[www.nytimes.com/2018/03/19/technology/facebook-cambridge-analytica-](http://www.nytimes.com/2018/03/19/technology/facebook-cambridge-analytica-explained.html.

Gugerty, Leo. "Newell and Simon's Logic Theorist: Historical Background and Impact on Cognitive Modeling." *Proceedings of the Human Factors and Ergonomics Society Annual Meeting* 50 (2006): 880–884.

Hard, Andrew, Kanishka Rao, Rajiv Mathews, Françoise Beaufays, Sean Augenstein, Hubert Eichner, Chloé Kiddon and Daniel Ramage. "Federated Learning for Mobile Keyboard Prediction." ArXiv abs/1811. 03604 (2018): n. pag.

He, Kaiming, X. Zhang, Shaoqing Ren and Jian Sun. "Deep Residual Learning for Image Recognition." *2016 IEEE Conference on Computer Vision and Pattern Recognition (CVPR)* (2016): 770–778.

Ivakhnenko, Alekseĭ Grigor'Evich and Valenti Grigorévich Lapa. *Cybernetic Predicting Devices*. CCM Information Corp, New York (1966).

Krizhevsky, A., Ilya Sutskever and Geoffrey E. Hinton. "ImageNet Classification with Deep Convolutional Neural Networks." *Communications of the ACM* 60 (2012): 84–90.

Krogh, Anders and John Hertz. "A Simple Weight Decay Can Improve Generalization." *Proceedings of the 4th International Conference on Neural Information Processing Systems, NIPS* (1991): 950–957.

Li, Hao, Zheng Xu, G. Taylor and T. Goldstein. "Visualizing the Loss Landscape of Neural Nets." *Proceedings of the 32nd International Conference on Neural Information Processing Systems, NeurIPS* (2018): 6391–6401.

Li, Yuzheng, Chuan Chen, N. Liu, Huawei Huang, Zibin Zheng and Qiang Yan. "A Blockchain-Based Decentralized Federated Learning Framework with Committee Consensus." *IEEE Network* 35 (2021): 234–241.

Lindell, Yehuda. "Secure Multiparty Computation (MPC)." *IACR Cryptol. ePrint Arch.* 2020 (2020): 300.

McMahan, H. Brendan, Eider Moore, Daniel Ramage, Seth Hampson and Blaise Agüera y Arcas. "Communication-Efficient Learning of Deep Networks from Decentralized Data." *Artificial Intelligence and Statistics,* AISTATS (2017): 1273–1282: PMLR.

Mikołajczyk, Agnieszka and Michał Grochowski. "Data Augmentation for Improving Deep Learning in Image Classification Problem." *2018 International Interdisciplinary PhD Workshop (IIPhDW)* (2018): 117–122.

Obama , Barack. "Consumer Data Privacy in a Networked World: A Framework for Protecting Privacy and Promoting Innovation in the Global Digital Economy." *Journal of Privacy and Confidentiality* 4 (2013).

"Official Legal Text." *General Data Protection Regulation (GDPR)*, 2019. https://gdpr-info.eu/.

Ronneberger, Olaf, Philipp Fischer and Thomas Brox. "U-Net: Convolutional Networks for Biomedical Image Segmentation." ArXiv abs/1505.04597 (2015).

Rosenblatt, Frank. "The Perceptron: A Probabilistic Model for Information Storage and Oganization in the Brain." *Psychological review* 65 6 (1958): 386–408.

Samuel, Arthur L. "Some Studies in Machine Learning Using the Game of Checkers." *IBM Journal of Research and Development* 3 (1959): 210–229.

Sahu, Anit Kumar, Tian Li, Maziar Sanjabi, M. Zaheer, Ameet Talwalkar and Virginia Smith. "Federated Optimization in Heterogeneous Networks." arXiv: Learning (2020).

Sen, Jaydip. "Chapter 1 Homomorphic Encryption — Theory and Application." (2019).

Shokri, Reza and Vitaly Shmatikov. "Privacy-Preserving Deep Learning." *2015 53rd Annual Allerton Conference on Communication, Control, and Computing (Allerton)* (2015): 909–910.

Shi, W., Jose Caballero, Ferenc Huszár, J. Totz, A. Aitken, R. Bishop, D. Rueckert and Zehan Wang. "Real-Time Single Image and Video Super-Resolution Using an Efficient Sub-Pixel Convolutional Neural Network." *2016 IEEE Conference on Computer Vision and Pattern Recognition (CVPR)* (2016): 1874–1883.

Silver, David, Aja Huang, Chris J. Maddison, Arthur Guez, Laurent Sifre, George van den Driessche, Julian Schrittwieser, Ioannis Antonoglou, Vedavyas Panneershelvam, Marc Lanctot, Sander Dieleman, Dominik Grewe, John Nham, Nal Kalchbrenner, Ilya Sutskever, Timothy Lillicrap, Madeleine Leach, Koray Kavukcuoglu, Thore Graepel and Demis Hassabis. "Mastering the Game of Go with Deep Neural Networks and Tree Search." *Nature* 529 (2016): 484–489.

Sugawara, Y., Sayaka Shiota and H. Kiya. "Super-Resolution Using Convolutional Neural Networks Without Any Checkerboard Artifacts." *2018 25th IEEE International Conference on Image Processing (ICIP)* (2018): 66–70.

Yang, Qiang, Yang Liu, Tianjian Chen and Yongxin Tong. "Federated Machine Learning: Concept and Applications." arXiv: Artificial Intelligence (2019).

18

Smart System for COVID-19 Susceptibility Test and Prediction of Risk along with Validation of Guidelines Conformity Using the Cloud

Rashmi Welekar, Manjiri Vairagade, Mohit Sawal, Shreya Rathi, Shrijeet Shivdekar, and Siddhi Belgamwar

Department of Computer Science and Engineering, Shri Ramdeobaba College of Engineering and Management, Nagpur, India

CONTENTS

18.1 Introduction

The spread of SARS-CoV-2 resulted in a worldwide epidemic (Welekar et al., 2020). The coronavirus, under the category of Public Health Emergency of International Concern (PHEIC), was declared as the pandemic by The World Health Organization on 11th March 2020 (Chatterjee et al., 2020). As of 14th August 2020, approximately 2.45 million cases were observed and total deaths cases were found to be around 48,040. The widespread influence of the coronavirus pandemic has ensured the government to implement safety measures and precautions to control the spread so as to reduce the severity of population from getting infected, due to the increase in fatality rate found to be 2% as of

DOI: 10.1201/9781003203926-18

April 2020 to 3.02% as of September 2020. Comprehensive testing proved to be an efficient method to control the transmission rate. Finding the chunk of the population at risk and testing them using various testing methods such as RT-PCR, serologic testing, lateral flow assay, etc. have shown potent identification of COVID-19 patients and tracing of contacts is also done (Chatterjee et al., 2020). However, the mainly responsible for further spread is the number of cases observed is the 14 days' incubation period. This incubation period speaks of the approximate time required for the prominent presence of symptoms to be visible in a COVID-19 positive patient. During these 14 days, ignorance of symptoms and irresponsibility towards precautions may usher the people in exposure with COVID-19 positive person being vulnerable to COVID infection. Such transmission is referred to as the asymptomatic transmission of the virus. People with heart condition, health issues like hypertension, blood pressure, diabetes, etc., need to ensure their extra safety as they are more prone to the infection, hence heightening their risk. Though the RT-PCR testing method is highly accurate, it has been non-affordable for those struggling with finances. The use of technology, Internet connectivity, and availability of large crowd using a smartphone can be put together to emerge with a solution to determine user susceptibility for coronavirus by monitoring oxygen saturation level in blood primarily known as SpO_2. Thus, in times of COVID-19, keeping track of oxygen level in blood has become especially important, because oxygen levels falling below a certain threshold indicates the positive presence of COVID-19, while the person carrying the virus being unaware of it. Many asymptomatic patients are found to have abnormally low blood-oxygen levels, or hypoxia without even registering, which makes it difficult to diagnose the infected individuals (Brouqui et al., 2020). The reason being low oxygen levels do not guaranteedly point out to any visual respiratory issues. This silent drop in the level of oxygen in the body of patients showing no symptoms can eventually cause congestive heart failure. Gauging oxygen saturation in the early stages of the disease is essential for patients with no symptoms. They do not understand that oxygen level is less. However, they might experiences things which cannot be clearly linked to deficiency of oxygen in the body. Generally, a healthy human's oxygen saturation level (SpO_2) is around 95% and above. When SpO_2 starts falling below 92% then it's a warning and not following preventive measures can lead to virus transmission. We aim to generate a system that will aid in monitoring the user's health status and give him the power to test himself against the virus, along with other facets, to validate his acquiescence against prescribed measures (Welekar et al., 2020). There is now increasing recognition of the potential of Cloud technologies, which provide data storage and computing resources managed by external service providers, to help improve safety, quality, and efficiency of healthcare. However, adoption of Cloud technology has been variable across healthcare organizations. It is hampered by concerns that the technology might not align with the existing methods of quality assurance and governance of privacy, data integrity, and service reliability (Alashhab et al., 2021). The benefit of Cloud-based services to individual organizations is that they allow fast implementation and upscaling across a range of settings, as they do not need the organization to purchase additional hardware and they can be implemented remotely (Cresswell et al., 2021). Services provided by the Cloud make it easier to deploy the applications.

18.2 Proposed Solution

With the help of aarogya setu app, which is an existing application in the said scenario, the following application is developed. The application primarily relies on SpO_2 measurement to predict the susceptibility of users as risk-averse or risk-negative. The WHO categorized coronavirus infections into three categories: 80% of infections are mild or asymptomatic, 15% that are severe and may require external oxygenation, and 5% are critical cases that require ventilation. Thus, the maximum care has to be taken to prevent infection transmission due to asymptomatic transmission. Patients with sugar and BP needs to be monitored specially for oxygen. SpO_2 is defined as the ratio of blood oxyhaemoglobin to total content of haemoglobin of the blood. The levels of SpO_2 indicate the fitness of respiratory mechanisms within an individual. The normal range of SpO_2 is between 95 and 99. It is important to monitor SpO_2 levels, as pointed out by a study conducted for 140 patients with COVID-19, out of which 36 patients (25.7%) died, and had SpO_2 levels less than 90%. Thus, in times of COVID-19, it is extremely important to monitor oxygen levels, as it's the indicator of contacting the disease, which the patient may not know of. The phenomenon in which asymptomatic patients suffer from exceptionally low oxygen levels (hypoxia) without any realization besides experiencing confusion, euphoria, or impaired psychomotor functioning has made the prognosis of the infected individuals even more difficult, as they do not point towards oxygen deprivation (Brouqui et al., 2020). This is extremely dangerous and may lead to an unexpected cardiac arrest. Normally, a person's oxygen saturation (SpO_2) is around 94–96% and becomes a cause for concern when it starts dropping below 92%. Thus, a device which measures the oxygen concentration levels is important in such times to determine timely susceptibility of each individual. Apart from this, our application also has a mask compliance feature, which notifies the user to give the proof of following government protocols in areas outside the home location. It also has a bluetooth feature to augment social distancing measures, to enable the user to make informed decisions during traveling so as to maintain social distancing guidelines and stay safe and to make the phenomenon of social distancing incentivizing in nature by providing a daily score to the users, with the aim to minimize it (Welekar et al., 2020). A machine learning model is trained to determine the risk status of the user depending upon the symptoms (Chatterjee et al., 2020). The app is built on Google Cloud and it offers real-time information and updates of the government guidelines about the COVID-19 pandemic.

18.3 Methodology

18.3.1 SpO_2 Level Measurement

The application majorly focuses on measuring SpO_2 to predict the risk of being affected. The signal has DC and AC components in a standard pulse oximeter. The DC component is subtracted while the AC component is amplified. The SpO_2 level in the blood can be found using to the formula given below:

$$spo2 = X - Y * ((std\_dev\_red/mean\_red)/(std\_dev\_blue/mean\_blue))$$

where $X(=100)$ and $Y(=25)$ were obtained by calibration (Welekar et al., 2020).

FIGURE 18.1
Position of the finger while capturing video.

Steps for measuring SpO_2:

1. A small video of 2–3 seconds is recorded on a smartphone by the user when he keeps his palm on the smartphone's camera with the flashlight on in such a way that the image produced on the screen is sufficiently bright red in color. The user can then start recording the clip (Kanva et al., 2014; Welekar et al., 2020).
2. Recording stops automatically after the allotted time and after that a new screen is launched in the app. The recorded video is used to extract the first 50 frames from the clip (Welekar et al., 2020).
3. The frames under consideration are processed individually. Each frame is normalized. The red and blue components are separated. The parameters were calculated for each image: mean of red and blue color component standard deviation of red and blue color component. The mean values are the DC values obtained and std_dev is the AC value. The SpO_2 level is measured using these values. The calculated average SpO2 value of all the 50 frames will be then displayed.

The physiological signals received by the mobile device are immediately sent to the Cloud server with the help of the Internet. A personal physiological database maintained in the Cloud server is used to determine the best personal physiological data. These values are used to set the danger levels of the physiological parameters for initial diagnosis. The extreme levels are set according to the personal physiological details of the user. When the physiological data crosses these designated extreme levels, it immediately warns the user to get the necessary medical aid (Welekar et al., 2020).

Finally, the user is provided with the following guidelines:

1. If the SpO_2 calculated is between 96 and 99, the user is healthy.
2. If the SpO_2 calculated < 92, it asks the user to try again. In case of persistent value, medical advice is suggested (Welekar et al., 2020; Figures 18.1–18.3).

18.3.2 COVID Risk Detection

To support the above results of $SpOp_2$ level measured in the body, a machine learning model is trained to apprise the user of his health status. The model is trained over an already existing data set present on Kaggle, which is a Google Cloud subsidiary. There

FIGURE 18.2
Frame extracted from video.

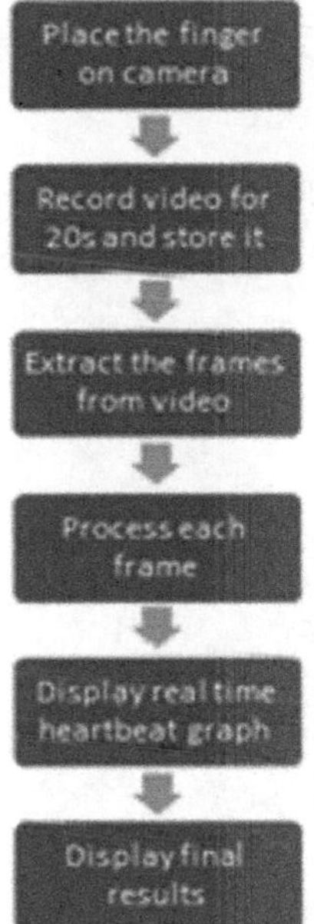

FIGURE 18.3
SpO_2 methodology.

are various data mining tools present to search through this data set. Different inputs like fever, cough, sore throat, fatigue, etc., are taken from the user. These parameters are given as input to model. The output suggests whether the user is safe or needs medical help. The output is in the form of text like "low risk," "moderate risk," "high risk." The application provides a dashboard connecting Cloud-based electronic health records to identify trends in symptoms and risk associated with it in the patients.

The algorithm used by the model is the multiple tree classifier. Input is given in the format of numbers and text like yes or no wherever necessary (Figures 18.4–18.9).

18.3.3 Mask Detection

1. Gain user location.
2. If location is found different from home location, ask the user to take the photo again.
3. The accepted image goes through a number of image processing techniques.

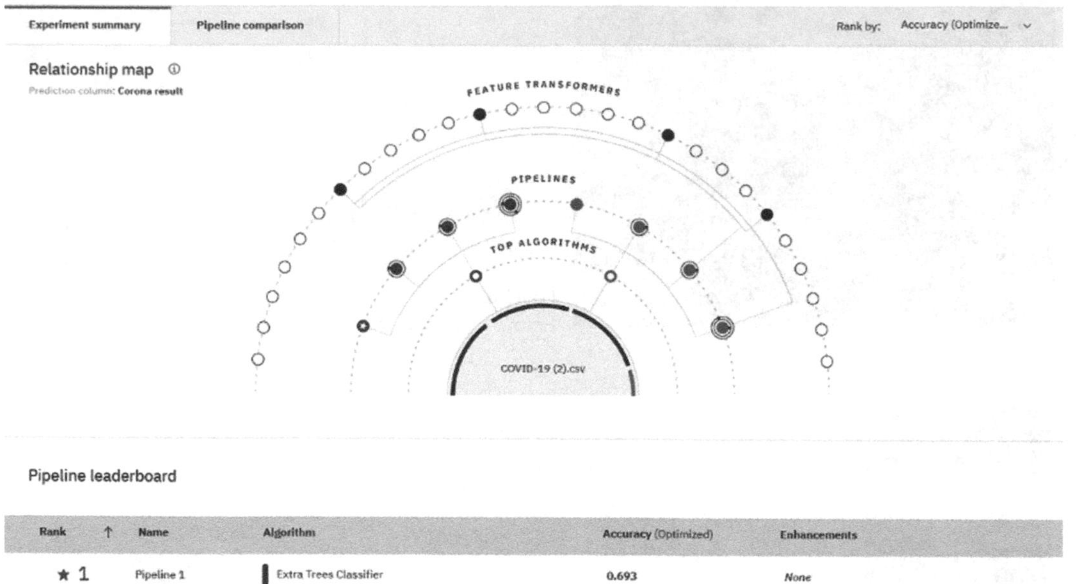

FIGURE 18.4
Machine learning model training.

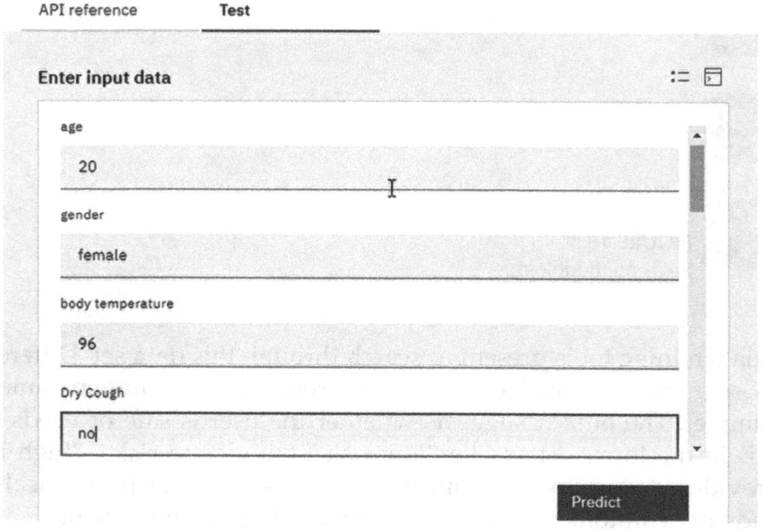

FIGURE 18.5
Input screen.

4. On the basis of the processed image, the message is given to the user about a mask on or off.
5. The user is given a message to wear a mask if he has been found without a mask. He is prompted to capture the image again after wearing the mask.

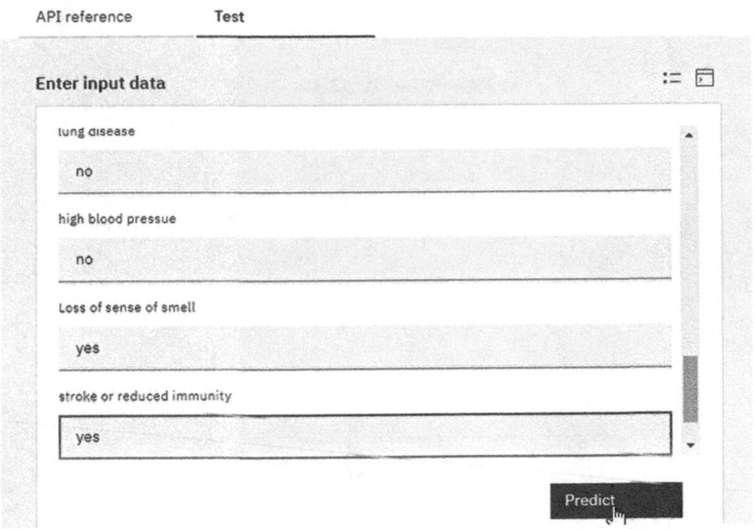

FIGURE 18.6
Input screen.

The mask detection system using the Cloud can be divided into three parts:

Detect whether someone has a spot on a mask,

The event collection and distribution to a Google Cloud Engine, and

The further processing of the events.

The PostgreSQL in the Cloud is the SQL database used for storage. Further processing is done on the Cloud for the separation of events. On the Cloud, an alert service is activated for incoming events in PostgreSQL and a notification is generated which will notify the user about not wearing the mask.

18.3.4 Social Distancing Using Bluetooth

1. The user needs to grant the app the necessary permissions like Bluetooth, location, etc.
2. A BluetoothServerSocket is created to listen for connection requests from different devices.
3. Contacts can be found out after a very short interval.
4. These contacts are serialized into a Gson file for every contact. This Gson file is converted to Json and sent to the Cloud server to cache user information.
5. The number of addresses in the contact list is displayed in everyday's score.

Exposure scores give us the total count of people in the vicinity.

The Bluetooth helps to send the contact tracing feeds to the Cloud, thus assisting in giving social distancing alerts to the user.

When a device comes within contact, i.e., in a radius of 6 feet or less for 30 seconds, a record of all other active Bluetooth devices seen in real time is stored on the device. This log syncs with the Cloud application, providing data that is used to determine potential exposure and to notify the user to take necessary precautions (Figures 18.10 and 18.11).

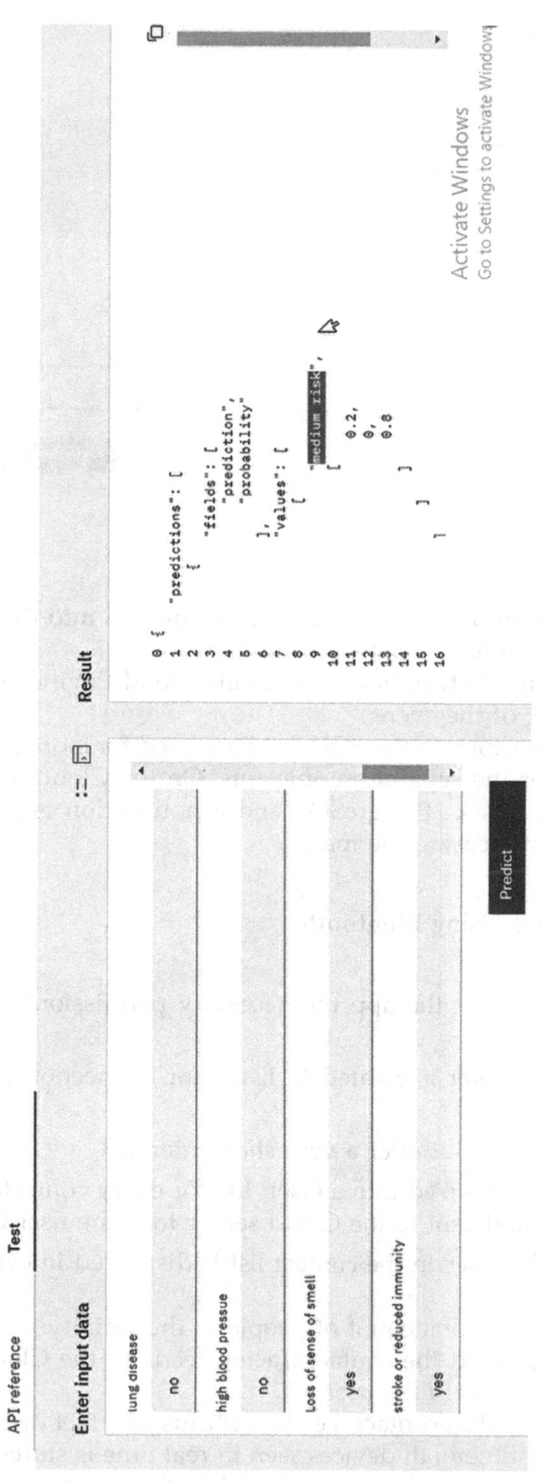

FIGURE 18.7
Moderate risk test case.

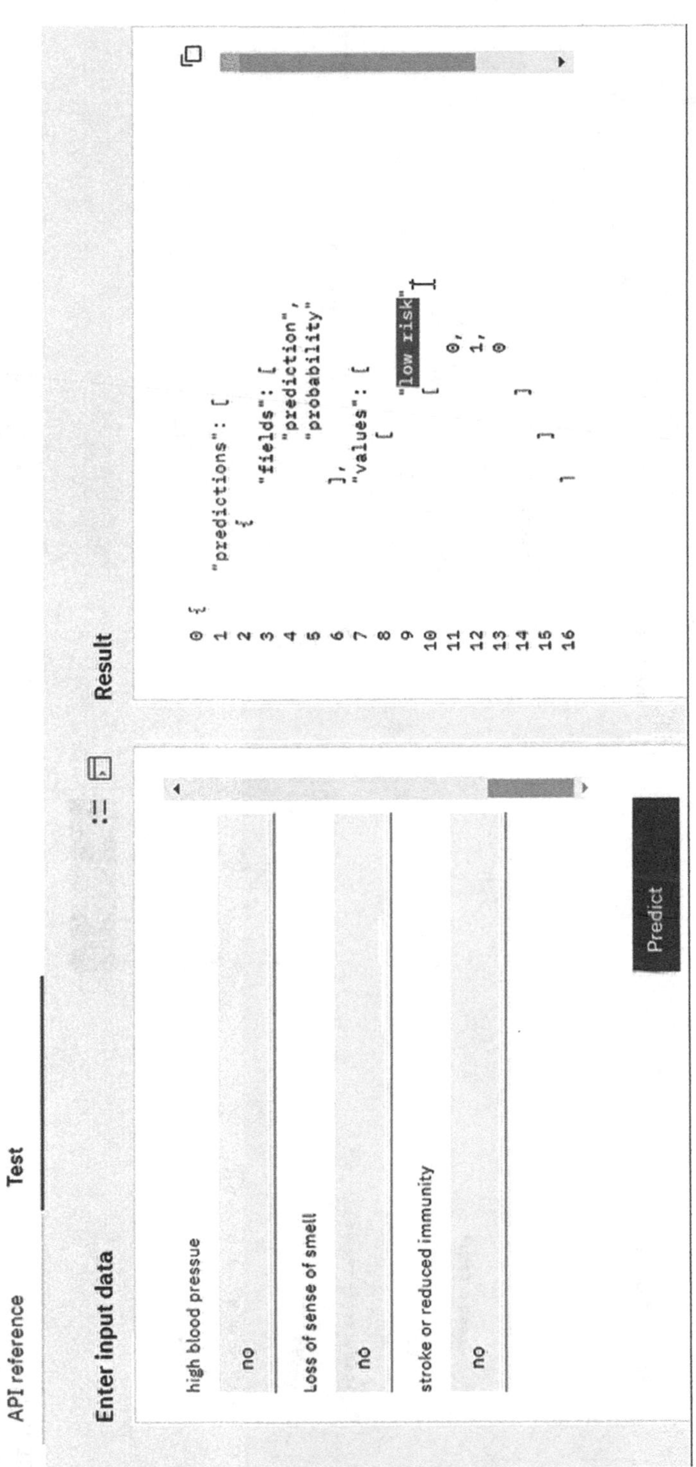

FIGURE 18.8
Low risk test case.

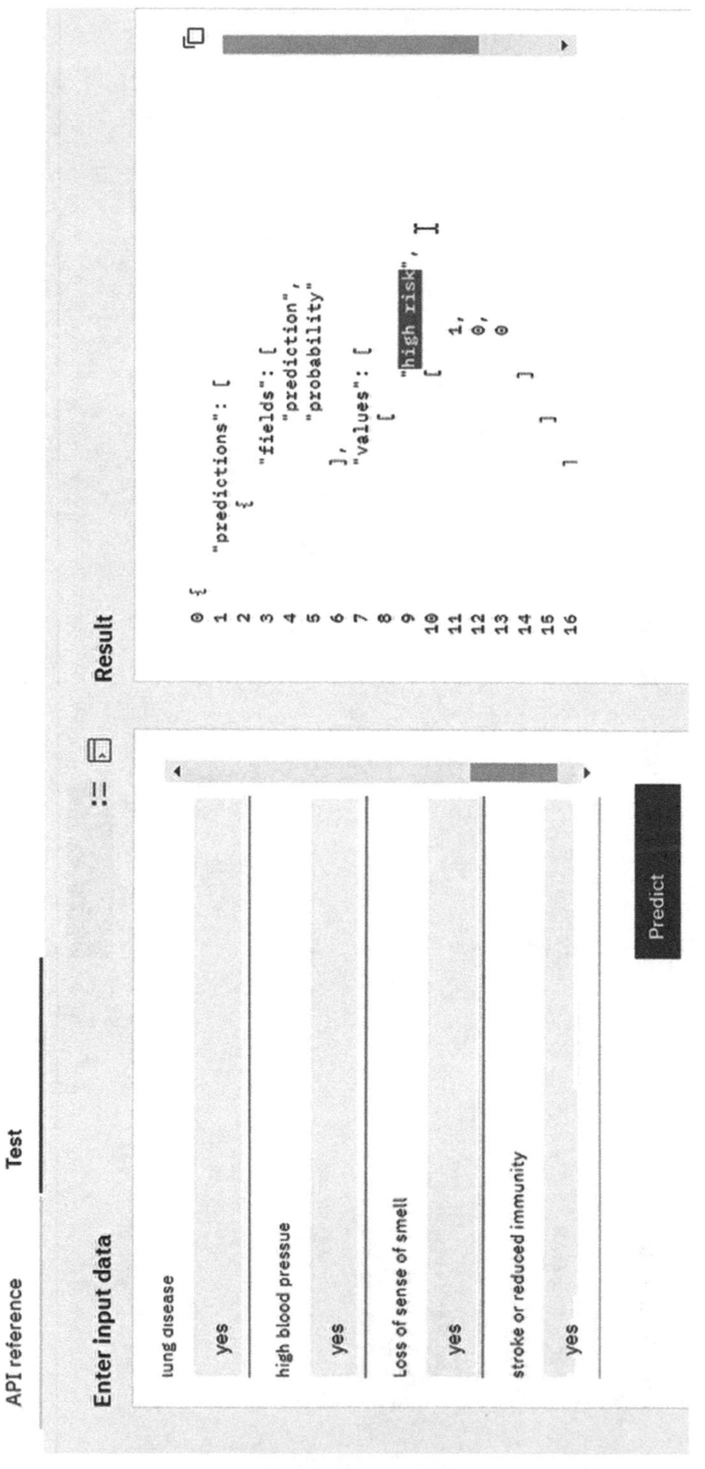

FIGURE 18.9
High-risk test case.

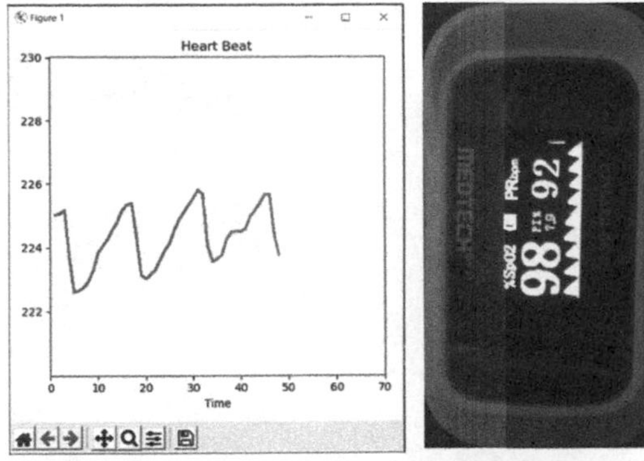

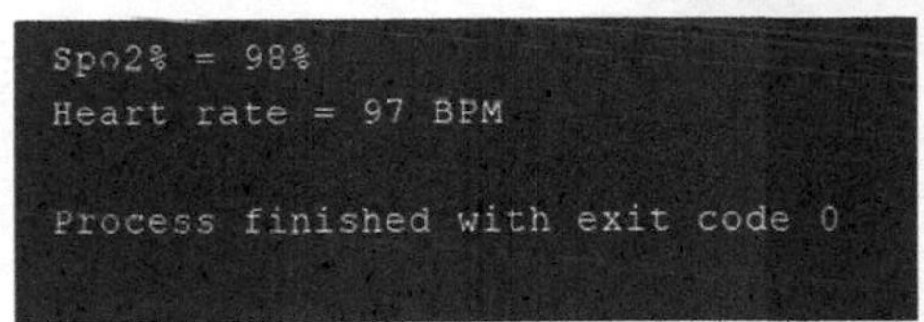

FIGURE 18.10
Test case 1.

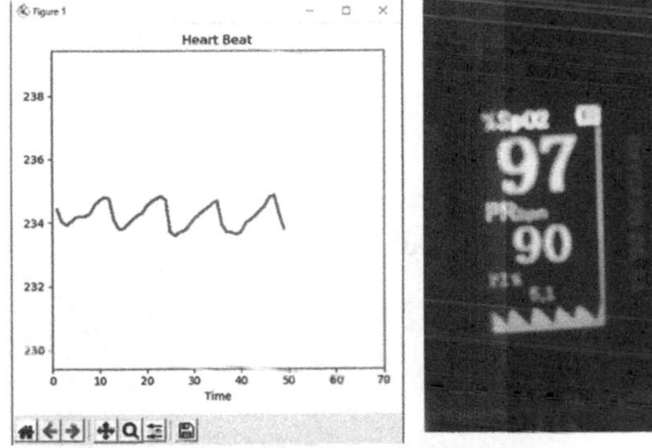

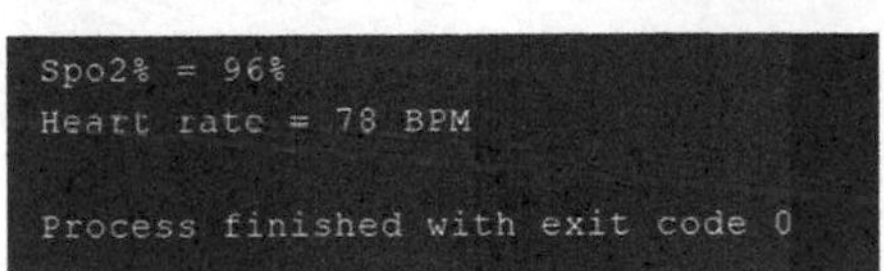

FIGURE 18.11
Test case 2.

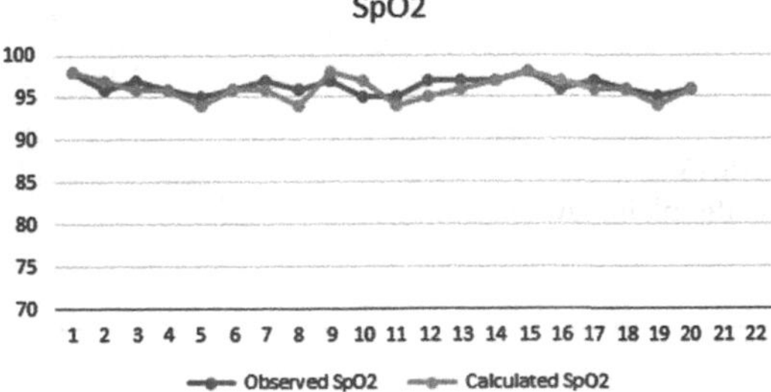

FIGURE 18.12
SpO_2 graph.

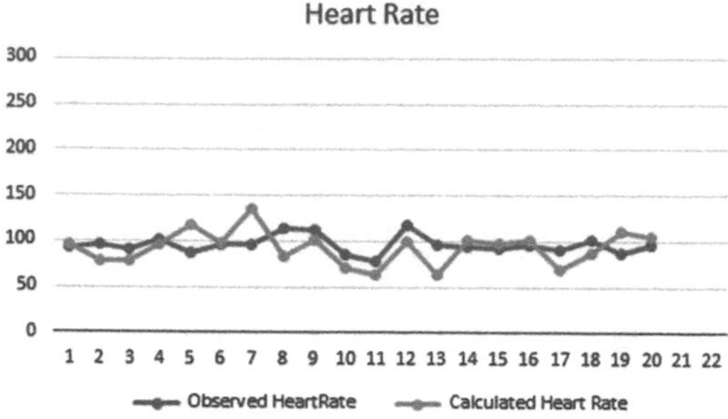

FIGURE 18.13
Heart rate graph.

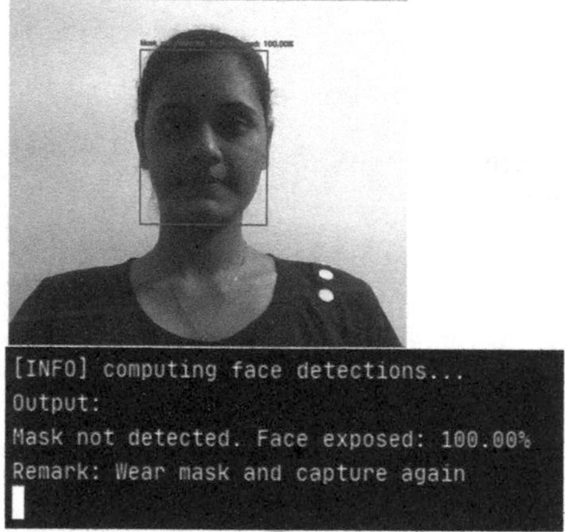

FIGURE 18.14
Without mask: Not accepted.

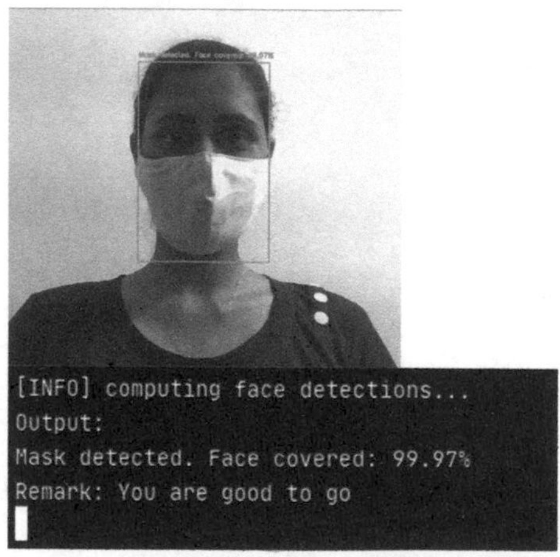

FIGURE 18.15
Mask (white/plain): Accepted.

18.4 Results

The maximum difference between the SpO_2 measurement through the application and pulse oximeter is found out to be +-2. The root mean square error is 1.049 (Figure 18.12).

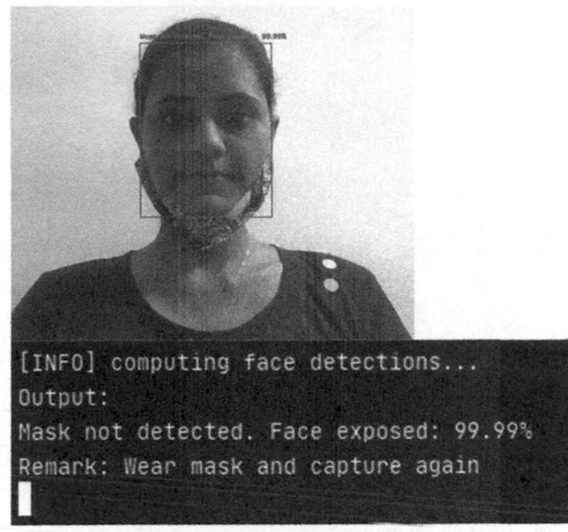

FIGURE 18.16
Mask not worn properly: Not accepted.

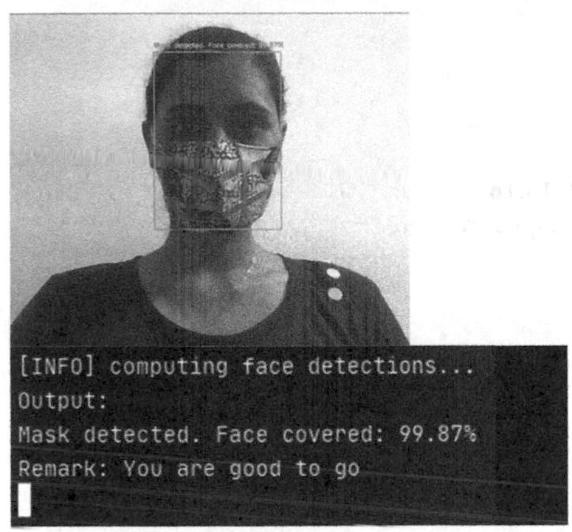

FIGURE 18.17
Mask (printed/colored): Accepted.

The maximum difference between the heart rate through the application and pulse oximeter is found out to be +-33. The root mean square error is 18.987 (Figures 18.13–18.19).

- MASK DETECTION
- SOCIAL DISTANCING USING BLUETOOTH

Images below show the mobile screen visible at various stages of the system (Figures 18.20–18.28).

18.5 Conclusion

We have developed a smart system that will mainly focus on detecting the coronavirus in the human body with the help of the oxygen saturation level (SpO_2) and further evident symptoms like cough, difficulty in breathing, fever, tiredness, etc. (Welekar et al., 2020).

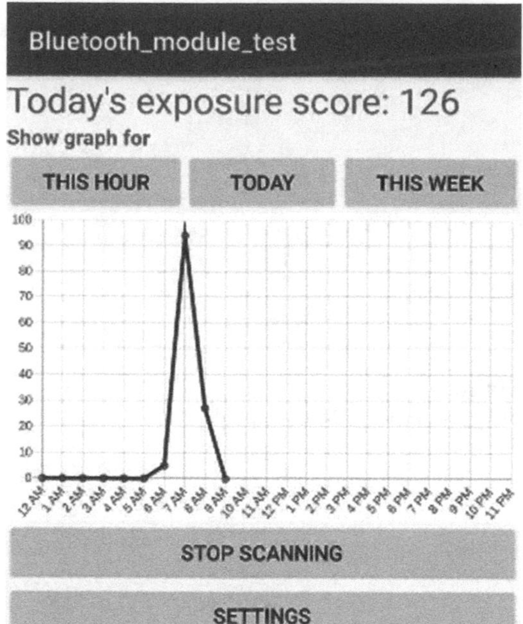

FIGURE 18.18
Hourly exposure score.

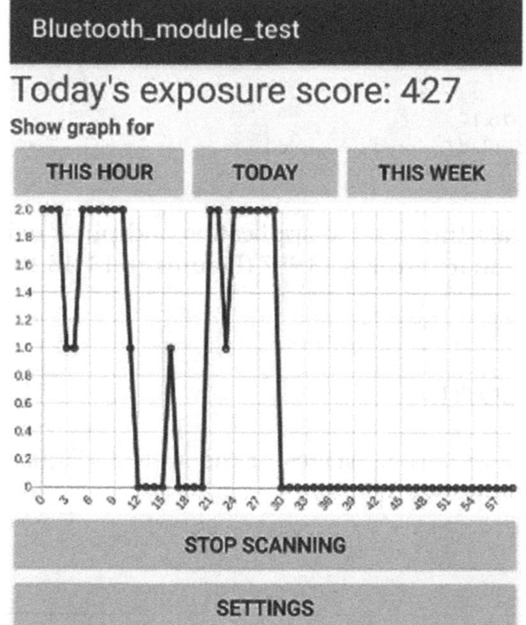

FIGURE 18.19
Day wise exposure score.

Hello
There.
EMAIL
PASSWORD
LOGIN
New Here ?
Create new account

FIGURE 18.20
App screen for login page.

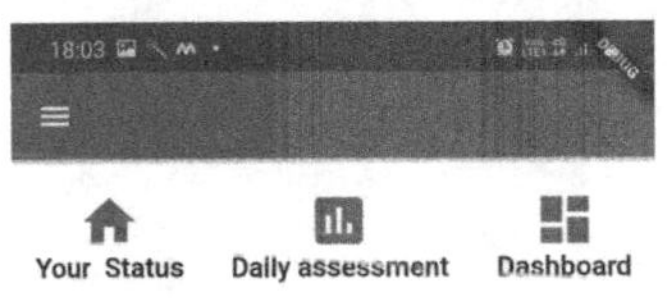
Your Status
Daily assessment
Dashboard
Government Guidelines
Wash your hands for atleast 20 seconds
Wear a face mask compulsorily while going out of your home
Avoid touching your eyes,nose or mouth
If you develop a fever,cough or difficulty breathing,seek medical care as soon as possible
Avoid close contact with anyone with flu-like symptomps.
Avoid travelling as much as possible.

FIGURE 18.21
App screen for government guidelines.

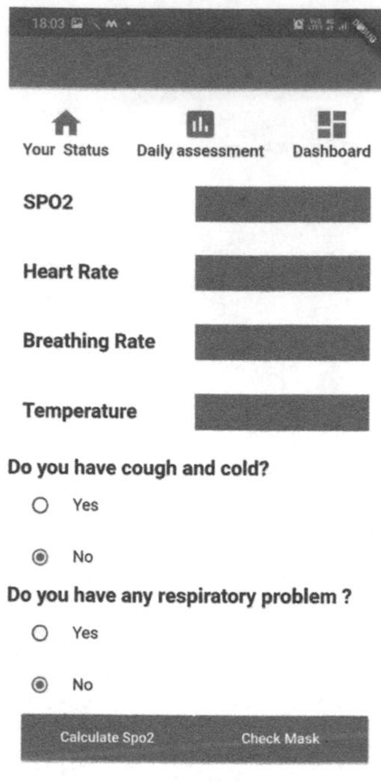

FIGURE 18.22
App screen for dashboard.

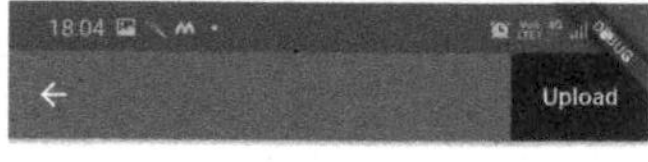

FIGURE 18.23
App screen for user without mask.

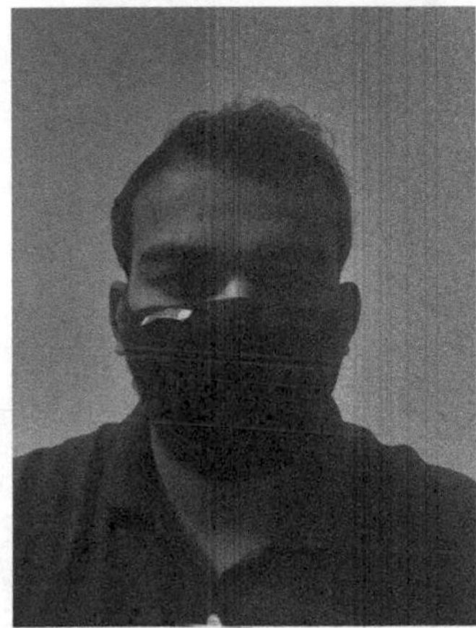

You Are Good To Go

FIGURE 18.24
App screen for user with mask.

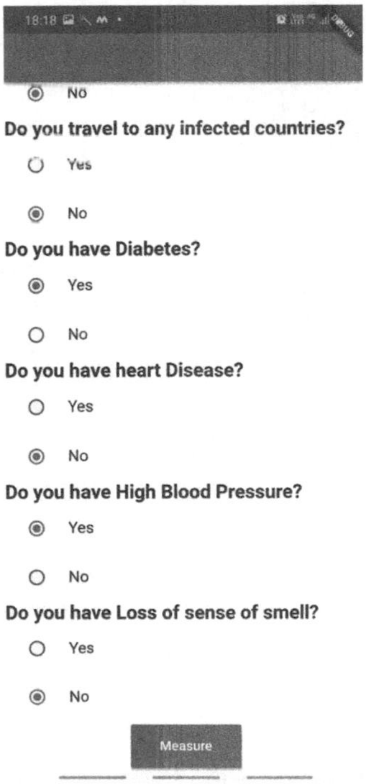

18:18

No

Do you travel to any infected countries?

Yes

No

Do you have Diabetes?

Yes

No

Do you have heart Disease?

Yes

No

Do you have High Blood Pressure?

Yes

No

Do you have Loss of sense of smell?

Yes

No

Measure

FIGURE 18.25
App screen for inputting symptoms.

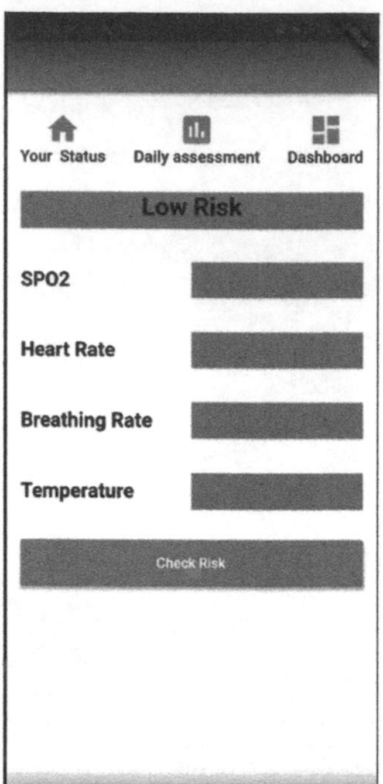

FIGURE 18.26
App screen for low risk.

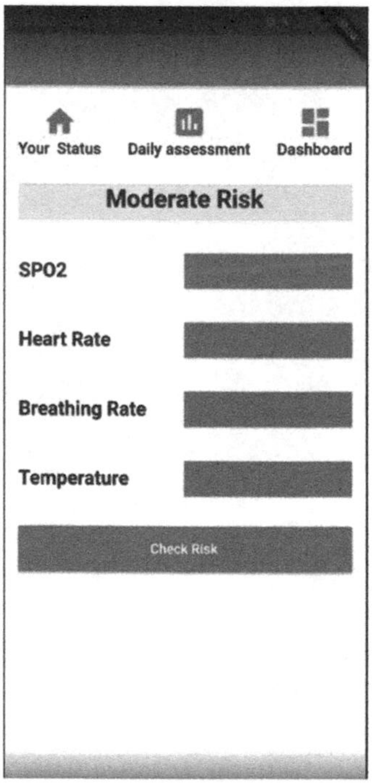

FIGURE 18.27
App screen for moderate risk.

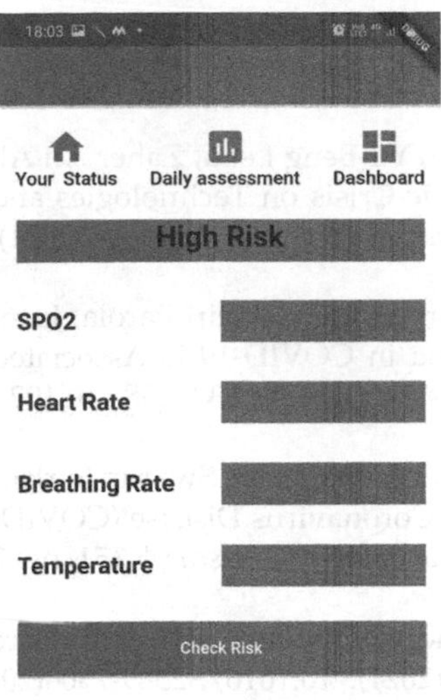

FIGURE 18.28
App screen for high risk.

The other features of our system are verification of user compliance against preventive measures like using face masks while leaving the house and social distancing while moving in public places or crowded areas (Welekar et al., 2020). All of the above-mentioned modules are integrated to develop into a mobile application so that every smartphone user can benefit himself on account of his health without exposing the outside world. The mobile application needs the access of Bluetooth and location of the smartphone. The efficiency of the system is up to 97%. This system is intended to help mankind technologically while such emergency situations that require medical assistance prevail (Welekar et al., 2020).

Acknowledgments

Gratitude to Dr. Ashish Indani, Head, Research and Innovation, Life sciences platforms and medical devices, Tata Consultancy Services for motivating the need to develop technical solutions using IoT or NFC or GPS to reduce challenges at various levels of implementation and guide the development of the SpO_2 oxygen level measurement module.

References

Alashhab, Ziyad R., Mohammed Anbar, Manmeet Mahinderjit Singh, Yu-Beng Leau, Zaher Ali Al-Sai and Sami Abu Alhayja'a. "Impact of Coronavirus Pandemic Crisis on Technologies and Cloud Computing Applications." *Journal of Electronic Science and Technology* 19, no.1 (2021): 100059 ISSN 1674-862X. 10.1016/j.jnlest.2020.100059

Brouqui, Philippe, Sophie Amrane, Matthieu Million, Sébastien Cortaredona, Philip Parola, Jean-Christophe Lagier and Didier Raoult. "Asymptomatic Hypoxia in COVID-19 is Associated with Poor Outcome." *International Journal of Infectious Diseases* 102 (2020): 233–238. 10.102/j.ijid.2020.10.067.

Chatterjee, Pranab, Nazia Nagi, Anup Agarwal, Bhabatosh Das, Sayantan Banerjee, Swarup Sarkar, Nivedita Gupta and Raman R. Gangakhedka. "The 2019 Novel Coronavirus Disease (COVID-19) Pandemic: A Review of the Current Evidence." *Indian Journal of Medical Research* 151, no. 2 (2020): 147–159. 10.4103/ijmr.IJMR_519_20

Cresswell, Kathrin, Robin Williams and Aziz Sheikh. "Using Cloud Technology in Health Care During the COVID-19 Pandemic." *The Lancet Digital Health* 3 (2021). 10.1016/S2589-7500(20)30291-0.

Kanva, Avneendra K., Chandan J. Sharma and Deb Sujay. "Determination of SpO_2 and Heart-rate Using Smartphone Cameras." *Proceedings of The 2014 International Conference on Control, Instrumentation, Energy and Communication (CIEC)* (2014): 237–241.

Welekar, Rashmi R., Manjiri Vairagade, Shreya Rathi, Mohit Sawal, Shrijeet Shivdekar and Siddhi, Belgamwar. "Recent Trends in Intelligent Systems, Data Science, Communication and Computing". *Bioscience Biotechnology Research Communications Special Issue* 13, no. 14 (2020): 193–197.

19

Designing a Policy Data Prediction Framework in Cloud for Trending COVID-19 Issues over Social Media

Shubham N. Ugale, Swati S. Sherekar, and Vilas M. Thakare
Sant Gadge Baba Amravati University
Amravati India

CONTENTS

19.1 Introduction

Network facilities, cutting-edge and latest era, etc., focused to increase user participation in producing and interaction over online social media. Clients get and burn through media substance to a social system, where clients contain the cell phones, which continually create data through an assortment of sensors like cameras, GPS, accelerometers, and so on, and portable applications thus transmit this procured information along with online media (Xu, 2015). Now, online media is an integral and growing part of human lives. Every day the people on social networks share the post and content on YouTube, Facebook, and Twitter. The data transmitted on social networks can stay in the way of clips, pictures, between numerous others. Though the maximum online content does not

DOI: 10.1201/9781003203926-19

spread to many people, some content trends and reaches thousands or even millions of people (Junus and Ming, 2015). Recommendation Technologies (RT) in online networks attract good attention in current years, with the fast growth of data on the Internet. RT allows the customers to discover their favored items efficiently. Collaborative filtering (CF) advice set of rules is one of the maxima generally used advice algorithms (Cao and Ni, 2015). Forecasting the eminence of information performs a crucial part for the pair person and the node of the information. The conventional manner of printing notices in revealed reproduction and its transmitting is an awful lot high priced than publishing online. Automatic social notices that distinguish from conventional information are gradually increasing (Arafat and Sagar, 2019). The speedy improvement of new media has introduced tremendous assurance to the general public in expressing and speaking; however, it has additionally posed demanding situations for policymakers to apprehend and control people's judgment. To remedy those troubles, coverage informatics became presented and has caused remarkable subject lately. Policy data is a subject that has an ambition to search powerful approaches to utilize records and computation to recognize and handle complicated online issues. Policy information popularity prediction becomes a critical factor in current technology due to the fact the amount of information is continuously growing (Luo, 2019).

A current structure thoroughly distinguishes the network areas and categorized the fake and real news articles as well as analyses the equivalence and non-equivalence of the false and true stories. It analyses the similarity between false, true, and mixture stories (Ouyang and Li, 2016). The main aim is to model the vibrant development and it focuses on multiple forecasting levels of social content. The prediction of popularity suffers from one of four stages. The four stages are mainly burst, tall, rise, and valley (Kong and Mao, 2018). A portion of this news will pull in the consideration of countless online clients in a short period and then evolve to a trending subject. These trending subjects might be significant hotspots for people and business associations to calculate the online and offline consequents of the subjects (Liu and Han, 2013). Analysts can construct amazing models to foresee post prominence from different perspectives, like the picture, printed content, sequences, or even brand data. These structures consistently measure the popularity of a post from the perspective of the online media platform (Zang and Li, 2018). A precise forecast of a clip's prominence offers supportive input during making the clip on a specific point and assists to select relevant approaches to advance it (Bielski and Trzcinski, 2018).

Forecasting the fame of social data means simply understanding the bursty video concept which exhibits the immediate growth in online content. An approach is to simply calculate the online importance of clips by utilizing the style grasped from Twitter as an online sensor of video popularity (Roy and Li, 2013). The duty of predicting popularity is achieved by sharing images over social media. Such kinds of functions are known as "Popularity Dynamic Prediction" (Ortiz and Battiato, 2019). In prior years, the intense improvement of multimedia data on the web with quicker and less expensive web access, and individuals have a more grounded interest in online media utilities. To predict the future forecasting of online recordings due to the heavy followed characteristics for online video: most substances get a few perspectives, whereas only a few receive the bulk of the attention (Su et al., 2016). In early social orders, individuals satisfy their requirements by collaborating. Trust is important to face the unspecified whether and that unspecified means another person (Ghafari, 2020). The creator proposed social-driven propagation dynamics-based forecasting techniques that don't need preparing stages or earlier information (He and Lyu, 2017).

A recently arising pattern in information investigation is to depend on online media information for prediction, where the activities of independent internet clients can be appropriately pooled to show the large-scale patterns. However, data from online media may suffer from noise and be sampled because of various factors and the biggest challenge is social media-based data analytics (You and Lio, 2015). Online social stages allow individuals to become acquainted with one another and share things about themselves. Within the sight of OSNs, gigantic substances, for example, recordings and news are sent by clients anytime and anywhere. OSN has enhanced proficient social networks to spread substance-like notices and ads (Jia and Gan, 2018). It presented an innovative framework towards primarily detect an adverse emotion condition that might come about because of devouring false bulletin crossways online media utilizing EEG indicators (Nguyen and Chung, 2019). A fuzzy identification calculation is proposed to distinguish the prominent substance in online media. This procedure is assessed on Twitter online network stage (Nirmala and Babu, 2019).

This chapter discusses five various popularity prediction techniques such as systematic methodology and social forecast algorithm, community-aware iterative algorithm, communities and trust network (CTNRM), novel prediction model, and policy data popularity prediction framework. This chapter proposes the framework for the policy data prediction model, which is used to detect the trending issues of COVID-19 over a Cloud platform, which is the combination of systematic methodology and social forecast algorithm, and policy data prediction framework. It uses three attributes, i.e., social, textual, and contextual attributes, and it uses the prediction evaluation mechanism. It estimates the rewards for better accuracy and prediction model. It introduces a new framework for the Cloud, to predict the trending issues of COVID-19. This model reduces the error rate, time, overhead, and delay to enhance the prediction rate. Those previous methods are problematic toward overwhelming difficulties, and it improves the variety of prediction scheme that is the "Structure for Trending Data Prediction" model proposed here that depend upon the policy data prediction over the Cloud environment.

19.2 Background

Several trainings on the prediction of OSN have been completed to develop the policy data popularity prediction techniques in recent past years. Such techniques include the following.

The popularity forecast is an ongoing investigation subject that is empathetic in what way online networks move the popularity of the media data and use this empathetic to produce great predictions of popularity. This chapter grants a methodical social forecast system called online prediction, which is accomplished towards an estimate of the accurate popularity of video on social media. Dynamic change and developing broadcast designs of clips in online media use situation and context awareness which helps predict the popularity. The popularity estimating stays complete online and then needs no working-out phase or a priori knowledge. These researches display that the projected technique outperforms present view-based methods aimed at popularity prediction.

The service presents a community-aware repetitive procedure toward forecast virility effectiveness about data over online broadcasting utilizing huge information about worker subtleties in online cascades and public framework in online networks. The procedure uses a growing quantity of information to construct self-accurate on the virility timing forecast and advance its prediction (Junus and Ming, 2015).

The author presented an efficient guidance system based on society and prominence networks. In this presented model, the suggested user's neighbor is designated since the handlers in a similar communal as the suggested handler. Analysis of the opinions data set exhibit the possibility and efficiency of a CTNRM. A probationary result checks the efficiency of the projected reference system aimed at cultivating the exactness and boundary evaluation, particularly aimed at sedentary handlers (Cao and Ni, 2015).

The projected method that examines and forecasts the boundaries of news working to foreseen the popularity of news previously drives on online. The projected forecast model remains accomplished toward forecast bulletin content fame which is unpublished. This exploration work trains the model by many limitations aimed at the forecast like a bulletin foundation, bulletin grouping, term article, and subjectivity about bulletin toward a gain in effectual result (Arafat and Sagar, 2019).

The method focuses on the hassle of policy statistics reputation prediction, which could help policymakers to assume the policy information and make better selections. Forecasting the policy facts is a crucial and hard function. That's why the writer proposed a framework for recognizing coverage records. In this structure, the author extracts the attributes of policy records from three measurements, i.e., contextual statistics, social facts, and textual facts (Luo, 2019).

This chapter introduces five popularity prediction schemes, i.e., systematic methodology and social forecast algorithm, community-aware iterative algorithm, communities, and trust network (CTNRM), novel prediction model, policy data popularity prediction framework.

The chapter is ordered as follows.

Section I is the introduction. Section II discusses the background. Section III discusses previous work. Section IV discusses existing methodologies. Section V discusses and analyzes attributes and parameters and how these are affected by popularity prediction models. Section VI gives the proposed method. Section VII gives the stimulation and possible result. Section VIII is the results and discussion. Section IX is the conclusion of the review chapter. Finally, Section X gives the future scope.

19.3 Previous Work Done

In the research literature, many methods studied the policy data of popularity predicting and improving the performance in terms of effectiveness, software reliability, accuracy rate, and lower false and misleading data.

You and Lio (2015) and Xu (2015) has proposed a new model, named the systematic methodology and social forecast algorithm, to figure a dependable projecting scheme for the American presidential voting and American house race. CVAR graphic qualities aided advance the presentation.

Junus and Ming (2015) proposed an innovative popularity prediction model created proceeding community-aware iterative algorithm. Introduce video lifetime by way of a constant in the popularity prediction model also proposes a multi-linear model constructed on the ancient opinion count, upcoming burst state, and video era towards forecasting upcoming video popularity and improvement can be achieved in this chapter with a more precise model between video lifetime and popularity.

Cao and Ni (2015) have proposed CTNRM is presented to expect the result. The twin-attention version includes two parts: the specific interest model and the implicit attention version. These two models take one-of-a-kind levels of records as input, after which they are concatenated by way of a hierarchical shape.

Arafat and Sagar (2019) have proposed a novel prediction model that is essentially a specific approach to social clip popularity evaluation that permits online content creators to expect video reputation and also recognize the effect of its title or video structure on future recognition. The author proposes a self-attention primary build mechanism and gradient weighted magnificence stimulation plots. This method addresses films and pictures and utilizes the secular traits of videos via the self-attention model.

Luo (2019) has proposed the policy data popularity prediction framework primarily depends on how they cope with the exploration breaks, and sooner or later advise a few future routes for researchers on this discipline.

19.4 Existing Methodologies

Many techniques have been implemented over the last several decades for forecasting the popularity of social data. Different methodologies implemented for forecasting the popularity of social media networks are as follows: systematic methodology and social forecast algorithm, community-aware iterative algorithm, communities and trust network (CTNRM), novel prediction framework, and policy data popularity prediction framework.

A. ***Systematic Methodology and Social Forecast Algorithm***

A social prediction process builds a multi-stage recognition forecast in a social style and no longer requires any earlier schooling segment or data set utilizes the powerful changing and developing video transmission designs using web-based media to amplify the forecast compliment. The structured response for determining video popularity completely depends on the situational and logical qualities of online media. Social prediction works altogether on the web media and it doesn't need any earlier preparing information set. Social prediction easily predicts the other trends in social media by exploiting contextual and situational awareness. For the instance of binary fame rank space, the exact benefit work is picked as follows:

$$\varnothing(a_{n'}^{k}, s^{k}) = \begin{cases} 1, & if \;\; a_{n'}^{k}, =s^{k} = Unpopuar \\ w, & if \;\; a_{n'}^{k}, =s^{k} = popuar \\ 0, & if \;\; a_{n'}^{k}, \neq s^{k} \end{cases}$$

where w > 0 is a permanent prize for effectively foreseeing popular recordings and consequently controls the general significance of genuine positive and genuine negative values (Xu, 2015).

B. ***Community-Aware Iterative Algorithm***

Forecast the virility period; this is the main goal of the proposed chapter. This is carried out along a repetitive procedure that examines network shape and online community gestures received from the huge records produced using person interactivity and self-accurate forecast in every repetition. This is the initial try and are expecting a virility period using both online network dynamics and network framework. Their courting with virility timing is described using a representation of ways network framework may be utilized to calculate a virility period.

$$N(t, t') = \sum_{c=1}^{L(t)} n'c(t, t')$$

Here L(t) represents the numeral of networks recognized over current time t. Thus, anticipated virility effectiveness, N(t), represents the earliest time at which N′(t, t′) spread the past a given viral objective N, that can stand being processed by solving the equation (Junus and Ming, 2015).

C. ***Communities and Trust Network (CTNRM)***
The trust calculation module calculates the acceptance as true among customers and the integrity of each person. The community identification unit makes use of the discrete particle swarm optimization set of rules to hit upon groups in the client closeness community. The prominence spread unit determines the client's group of pals and propagates prominence in the trusted community. Community-based belief unit computes the entire agreement with customers and the people agree within the community, and then find the person has depended on the group. CTNRM suggestion unit calculates the anticipated rankings with the content of similarity and accepts them as true among the encouraged user and his companions (Cao and Ni, 2015).

D. ***Novel Prediction Model***
The novel prediction system, to forecast the popularity correlation of social news earlier available in online media. No one calculates the popularity of news content before its publishing. But the prediction model is accomplished to forecast news contents before its publishing. This method, trains the model to use the parameters for the prediction events to get an effective outcome. The popularity of news content is planned and finished the proposed forecast model rendering to training information sets and the era of that news.

$$E = \left| \frac{Real_{Popularity} - Predicted_{Popularity}}{Real_{Popularity}} \right| \times 100\%$$

The accurate measurement of the author's prediction approach is calculated using a general calculation, where E represents the percent efficiency (Arafat and Sagar, 2019).

E. ***Policy Data Popularity Prediction Framework***
The proposed outline for strategy data popularity prediction allows correct forecasting of the popularity of such data by combining multi-dimensional actual qualities into a popularity forecast scheme. It extracts the attributes of policy data from three measurements and conducts an experiential investigation (Figure 19.1).

Using experimental investigation some actual qualities, such as the theme spreading, popularity opposition strength, and hot information significance, are recognized. The

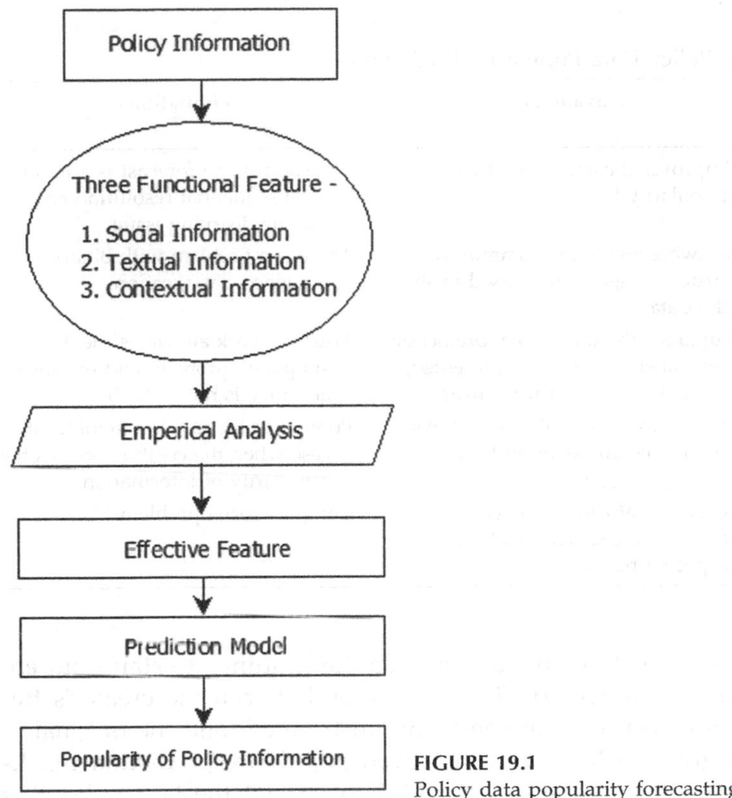

FIGURE 19.1
Policy data popularity forecasting structure.

outcomes display that the address can professionally forecast the popularity of rule data (Luo, 2019).

19.5 Analysis of Methods

The technique focuses on the standardized forecast prize of online prediction. As more video occurrences arrive, the proposed calculation grasps a greater ideal prediction strategy, and subsequently, the forecast benefit upgrades with the number of video cases. Specifically, the presented prediction process can accomplish over 85% of the most ideal award even with a moderately few numbers video examples are available (Xu, 2015). The exploratory outcomes utilizing a genuine data set from Digg demonstrate that the method functions admirably in useful circumstances, in which the forecast mistake is decreased with the past process (Junus and Ming, 2015). The examination of the after-effects of rating inclusion and MAE for the instance of dynamic clients and inactive clients. At the point when w=0.1, the proposed CTNRM has a greater accuracy than different strategies. This demonstrates that the presented CTNRM can prescribe further suitable things to the suggested client than different strategies (Cao and Ni, 2015). The correlation between the creator's frameworks anticipated prediction and genuine prediction. So, the creator effectively checks the prominence of the heading of any news

TABLE 19.1

Comparison Between Different Policy Data Popularity Prediction

Prediction models and approaches	Advantages	Limitations
Systematic Methodology and Social Forecast algorithm	It improves the accuracy of the popularity forecasts.	The social fame forecast is a multi-level sequential resolution and Internet learning issue.
Community-Aware Iterative Algorithm	The awareness of the community structure algorithm is used to share the data.	There is a problem with binary sequence classification.
Communities and Trust Network (CTNRM)	To upgrade the standard of prediction, several strategies were presented, i.e., hybrid CF and trust-aware.	Trust network alleviates the data simplicity problem and enhances accuracy is not so high.
Novel Prediction Model	It calculates the popularity of news content before its publishing.	Popularity lifetime is a significant case when the creator foresees the popularity of information.
Policy Data Popularity Prediction Framework	Recognized attributes incredibly improve the exactness of the expected results.	Complex social problem.

content before distributing. It tends to be handily altered the headings to stand out enough to be noticed through our framework. The correlation between the creator's framework predicted popularity (it was determined before distributed) and the original. It depicts that the framework gives such a lot of improved popularity prediction results (Arafat and Sagar, 2019). The outcomes show that MLP plays out the best validating informational set and the outcome demonstrates that the attribute removed in this chapter are all most successful in the policy data popularity forecast (Luo, 2019; Table 19.1).

16.6 Proposed Methodology

Cloud computing is the transport of various resources through the internet. Nowadays, web-based media is the most widely ordinary environment of interaction over a network. This chapter presents a system for the forecasting of trending issues over a Cloud environment related to COVID-19, and the "Rapid Miner" simulator is used to implement the proposed method. This model uses the Cloud data sets, i.e., Facebook and INvideos data for policy data. Nominal to numerical units are used for interchanging the variety of non-numerical features to the numerical group. This unit is furthermore changing the kind of chosen attribute and plans every benefit of these features to arithmetic utility. The Cloud data sets consist of certain missing values or incomplete data sets so for preparing the complete and meaningful data set the replace missing value mechanism is used and then the meaningful data set is providing the next level. This chapter separates the attributes of policy data from three measurements: social data, textual data, and contextual data. The characteristics of social data incorporate the reproduced time arrangement, opposition strength, and hot data significance. The attributes of contextual data incorporate the title length, word length, the number of images, the season of distribution, date of distribution, creator's authentic mean worth, and creator's verifiable prevalence standard deviation worth. To achieve such functionality, double clustering is performed, i.e., *K*-Means and random clustering is used and it provides the graphs in the form of a sunburst.

Simply, the *K*-Means clustering provides the clustering in three groups and random clustering creates the additional grouping of three main clusters. A random cluster creates features of features, later on, and used an effective feature. The verifiable examination uses a covariance matrix directed to distinguish the successful attributes in the trending issues of COVID-19 across the Cloud environment. Covariance matrix operator, which measures the covariance between every feature of the input contents and restores a covariance framework, offering a proportion of how much two attributes replace cooperatively. According to the investigation, the effective attributes incorporate the creator's recorded prevalence mean value, creator's authentic standard deviation esteem, republish time arrangement, hot data importance, and theme separation, and these attributes are the input of the prediction evaluation stage.

The set role unit builds another feature with the extraordinary role_id. This unit will overwrite a current feature with the role_id and this is utilized to replace the job of at least one feature and then discretize is used to discretize the selected numerical attribute to the nominal attribute. Eventually, the separated attributes are coordinated into an appropriate vector structure, and the information is normalized. The naive Bayes classification technique is used because it utilizes a same model to forecast the probability of various categories depends on different features. It utilizes a comparative strategy to foresee the likelihood of various classes dependent on different features. It just needs a modest quantity of preparing information to calculate the mean and difference of the factors vital for classification. This unit can be provided with a mathematical attribute. Attribute vector data are input to the prediction evaluation to foresee the trading issues of COVID-19 over the Cloud environment.

Framework for trending policy data prediction consists of four phases as follows:

1. ***Policy Data:*** In this chapter, the Facebook and INvideos database related to the COVID-19 are used as policy data across a Cloud environment.
2. ***Nominal to Numerical Unit:*** This operator is utilized for replacing the category of non-numerical features with the numerical category. This unit is furthermore changing the category of determining the attribute; however, it plans every benefit of these features to arithmetic worth.
3. ***Replace Missing Value:*** The data sets consist of certain missing values or incomplete data sets so for preparing the complete and meaningful data set, the replace missing value mechanism is used and then the meaningful data sets provide the next level.
4. ***Three Measurement Attributes:*** It separates the attributes of policy data across Cloud environments using three measurements: social data, textual data, and contextual data. The attributes of social data incorporate the reproduced time arrangement and opposition strength and hot data importance. The attributes of textual data incorporate the title length, word length, the number of images, the season of distribution, date of distribution, and creator's authentic prevalence mean value. K-Means and random clustering techniques are used to achieve the functionality of the three measurement attributes.

5. ***Verifiable Analysis:*** It uses the covariance matrix operator, which measures the covariance between every feature of the input contents and restores a covariance framework, offering a proportion of how much two attributes replace co-operatively. The experimental investigation is directed to distinguish the successful attributes in the policy data.
6. ***Effective Attributes:*** According to the observation, the functional attributes incorporate the authentic mean value, real standard deviation esteem, reproduce time arrangement, hot data importance, and theme dispersion, and these attributes are the inputs of the forecasting scheme. Set role unit builds another feature with the extraordinary role_id. This unit will overwrite a current feature with the role_id and this is utilized to replace the job of at least one feature with the role_id and this is used to change the role of one or more attributes and then discretize is used to discretize the selected numerical attribute to nominal attribute.
7. ***Prediction Evaluation:*** Naive Bayes classification technique is used because it utilizes the same model to forecast the probability of various categories that depend on different features. It utilizes a comparative strategy to foresee the likelihood of various classes dependent on different features. It just needs a modest quantity of preparing information to calculate the mean and difference of the factors vital for classification. This unit can be provided with a mathematical attribute. Attribute vector data are input to the prediction evaluation to foresee the trending issues of COVID-19 across the Cloud platform (Figure 19.2).

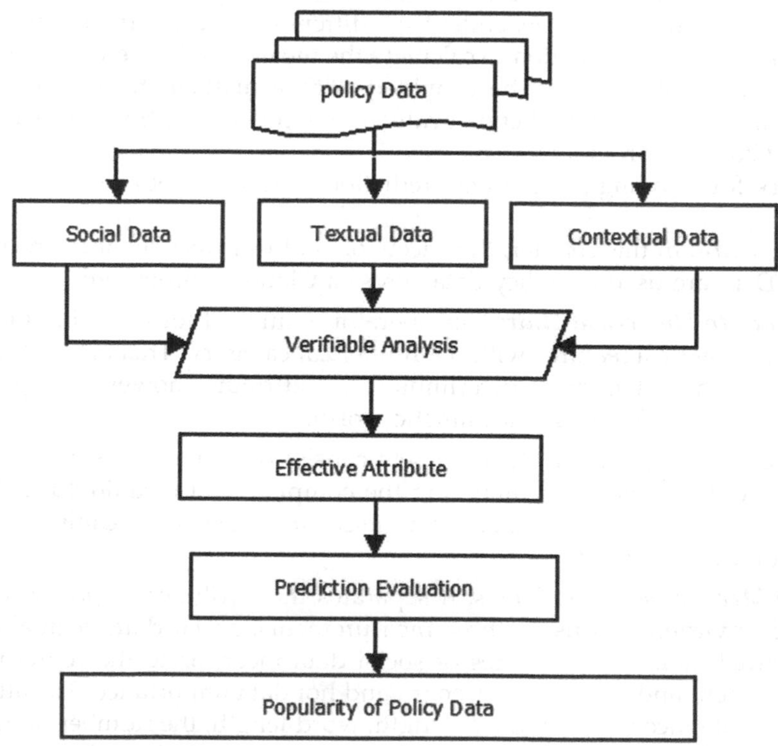

FIGURE 19.2
Proposed framework.

Open in Turbo Prep Auto Model Filter (99,003 / 99,003 examples): all

Row No.	id	userid	cluster	gender = ma...	gender = fe...	gender = NA	age	dob_day	dob_year	dob_month
1	1	range2 [1596...	cluster_1	1	0	0	14	19	1999	11
2	2	range1 [-∞ - 1...	cluster_0	0	1	0	14	2	1999	11
3	3	range2 [1596...	cluster_0	1	0	0	14	16	1999	11
4	4	range1 [-∞ - 1...	cluster_2	0	1	0	14	25	1999	12
5	5	range2 [1596...	cluster_2	1	0	0	14	4	1999	12
6	6	range1 [-∞ - 1...	cluster_1	1	0	0	14	1	1999	12
7	7	range1 [-∞ - 1...	cluster_1	1	0	0	13	14	2000	1
8	8	range2 [1596...	cluster_0	0	1	0	13	4	2000	1
9	9	range1 [-∞ - 1...	cluster_0	1	0	0	13	1	2000	1
10	10	range2 [1596...	cluster_2	1	0	0	13	2	2000	2
11	11	range2 [1596...	cluster_0	1	0	0	13	22	2000	2

ExampleSet (99,003 examples, 3 special attributes, 16 regular attributes)

FIGURE 19.3
Data sets uploaded.

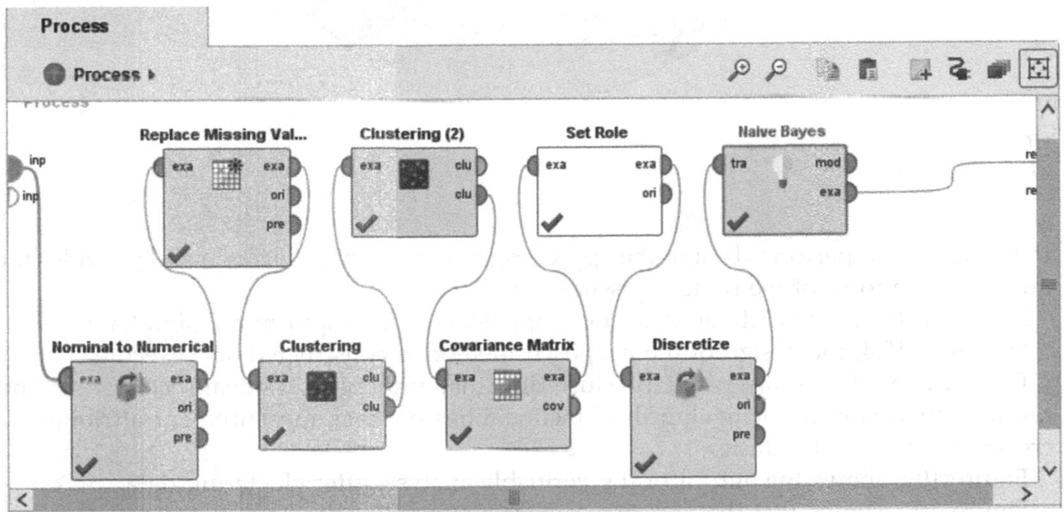

FIGURE 19.4
Proposed framework design.

19.7 Simulation and Results

The evaluation outcomes appear that the direction of the prediction accuracy in the proposed method is satisfactory and its magnitude is proportional to the reliability and accuracy. In this way, it removes the attributes of policy data from three measurement attributes: social data, textual data, and contextual data. The verifiable observation is directed to recognize the functional attributes to forecast the trending issues of policy data. The parcel turns out to be increasingly more refined using the effective feature, and afterward, the feature vector data are the inputs to the prediction evaluation to foresee the

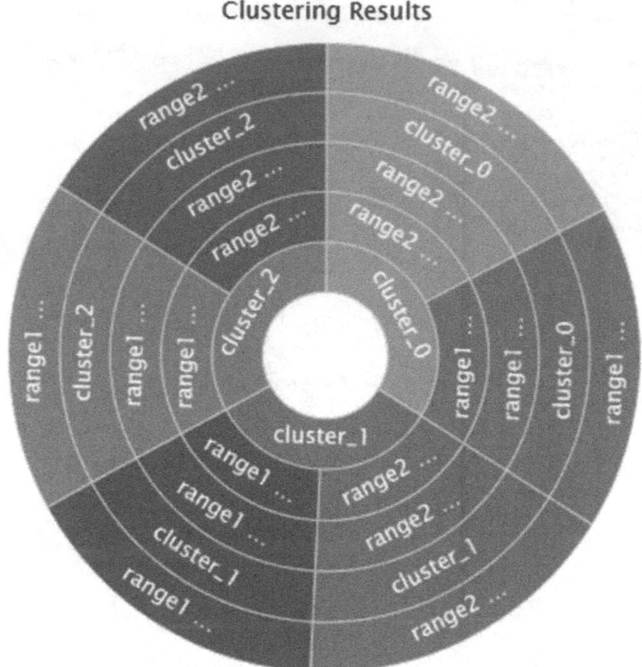

FIGURE 19.5
Clustering results.

trending data. It performs best in the approving informational collection and provides the output in the form of the trending issues of COVID-19.

In Figure 19.3, the Facebook data set is uploaded in the rapid miner simulator.

In Figure 19.4, the design of the proposed method is constructed and executed.

Figure 19.5, shows the result of clustering that undergoes k-means clustering and random clustering for achieving the functionalities of three measurement attributes. It creates clusters of the clusters.

Figure 19.6 shows the output of the verifiable analysis after clustering data.

Figure 19.7 shows that the effective feature among the three measurement attributes and the green portion indicates an effective feature.

Figure 19.8 shows the outcomes of the presented model, and it provides the trending issues of COVID-19.

19.8 Results and Discussion

This proposed method achieves great results in terms of exactness, and simultaneously, forecasting of trending COVID-19 issues exhibits a striking effect in terms of time taken to build the system inside a small time frame.

Figure 19.9 shows the three different clusters of data sets and each cluster predicts the trending issues of mobile visit and www visit in the data set.

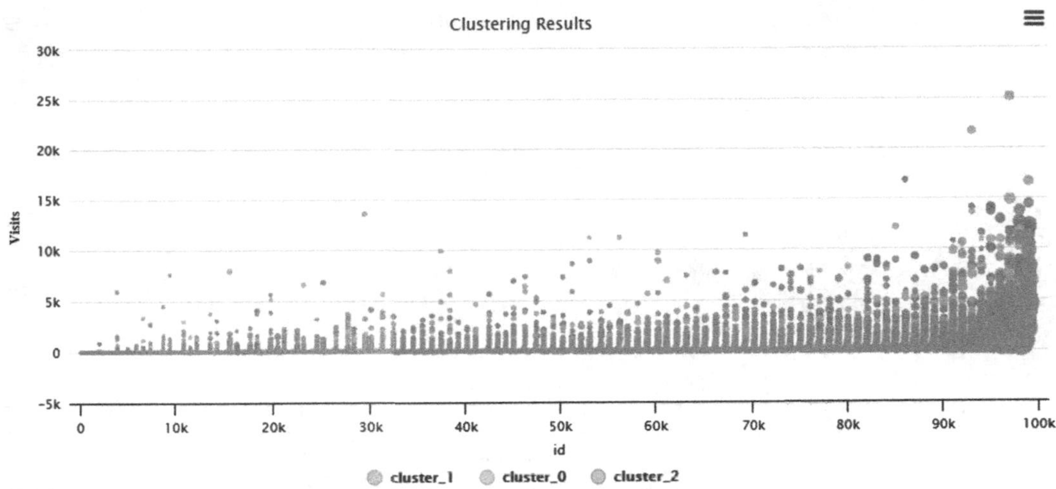

FIGURE 19.6
Clustering results.

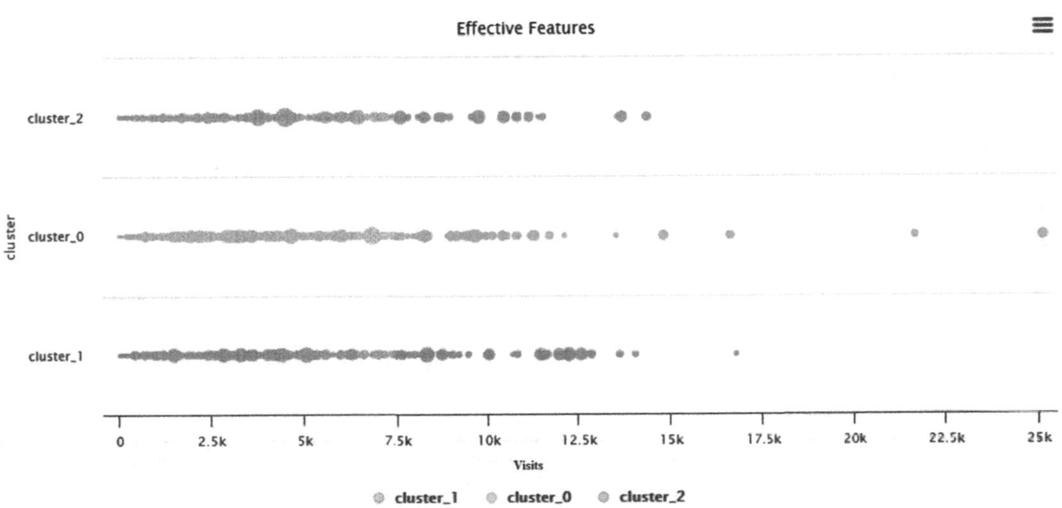

FIGURE 19.7
Effective features.

Figure 19.10 shows that the prediction of the proposed method according to channel titles and trending dates of videos in data sets. It shows that the prediction is using a trending date. The trending date provides the prediction of the last three days, so simply it measures the channel titles' trending issues prediction and provides great accuracy.

Figure 19.11 shows that the prediction of the proposed method according to visits and trending dates of videos in data sets. The above graph shows the prediction result based on three dates concerning the millions of visits.

Figure 19.12 shows that the prediction of the proposed method according to age, mobile visits, and www visits in the data set. The graph shows the efficiency of this proposed

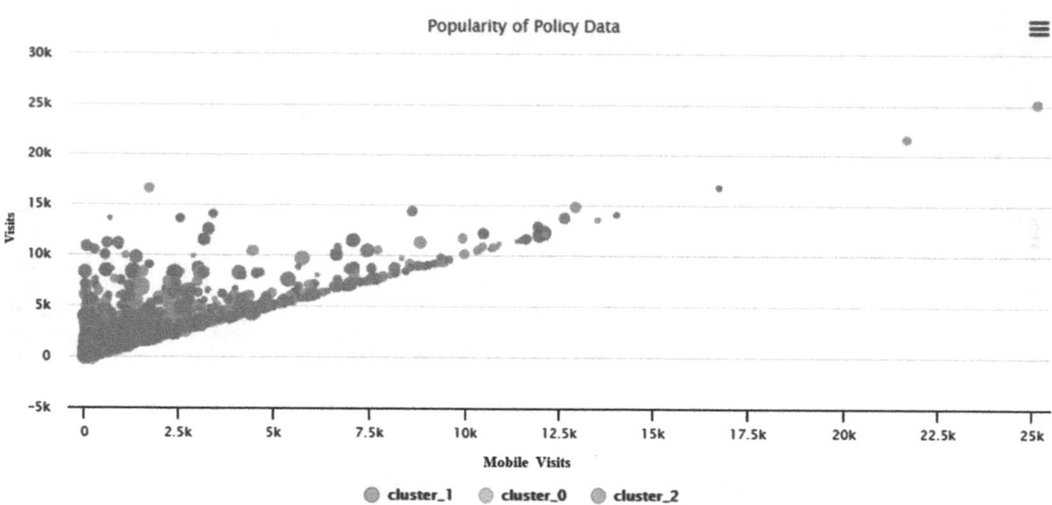

FIGURE 19.8
The admiration of policy data.

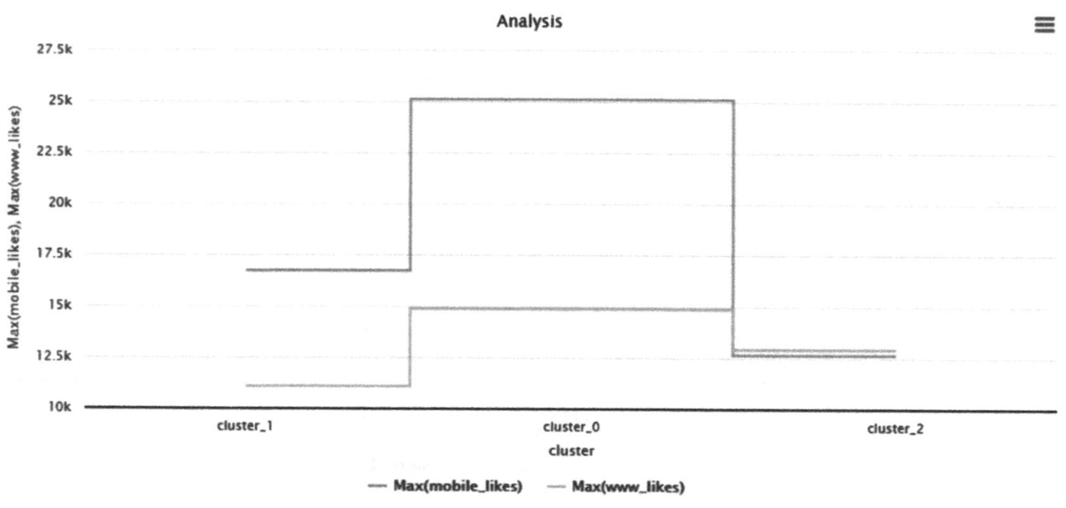

FIGURE 19.9
Analysis of maximum mobile visits and maximum www visits concerning cluster.

method because it provides the exact accuracy between mobile visits and www visits using the age factor.

Table 19.2 and Figure 19.13 show the execution time of previously proposed methods along with the new proposed framework, and the results show that the proposed framework takes less time for execution.

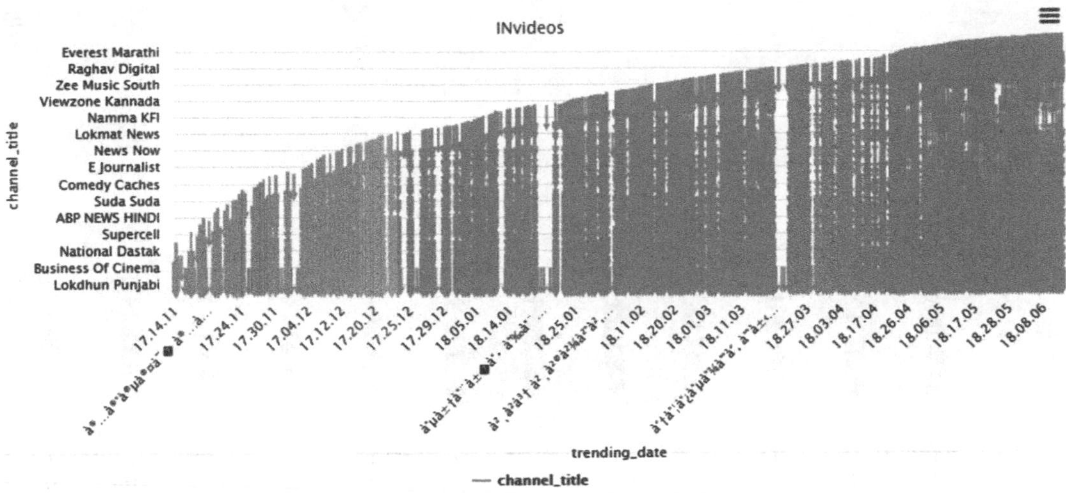

FIGURE 19.10
Analysis of trending date vs channel title.

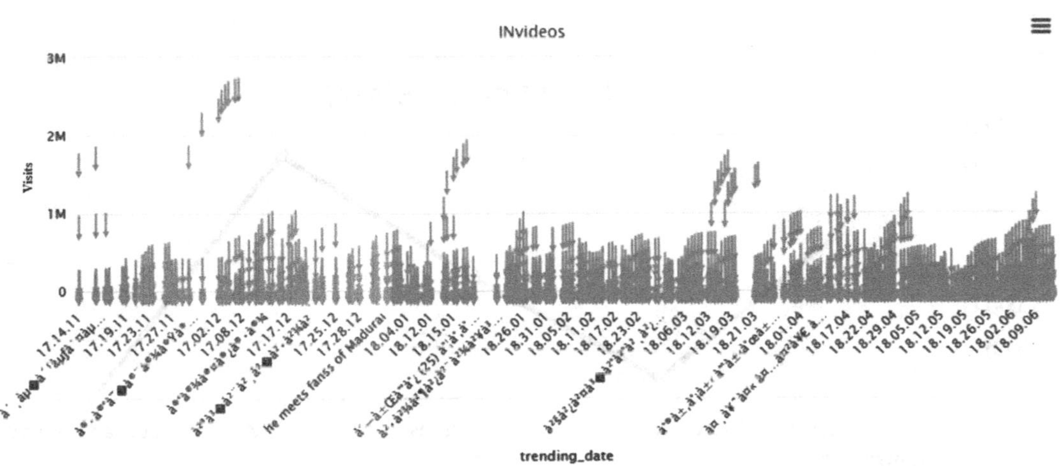

FIGURE 19.11
Analysis of trending date vs visits.

19.9 Conclusion

This chapter is focused on trending policy data prediction across Cloud environments related to COVID-19, and the aim of this model is to forecast the trending issues over the Cloud platform related to COVID-19. The proposed structure is used to forecast the trending issues of the policy data. In this proposed system, the COVID-19 database is added into the model and the method withdraws the attributes of policy data from three measurements: social data, textual data, and contextual data. The verifiable analysis is used to investigate the powerful attributes in policy data forecasting. The effective attribute is provided to the prediction evaluation model to foresee the policy data. Broad

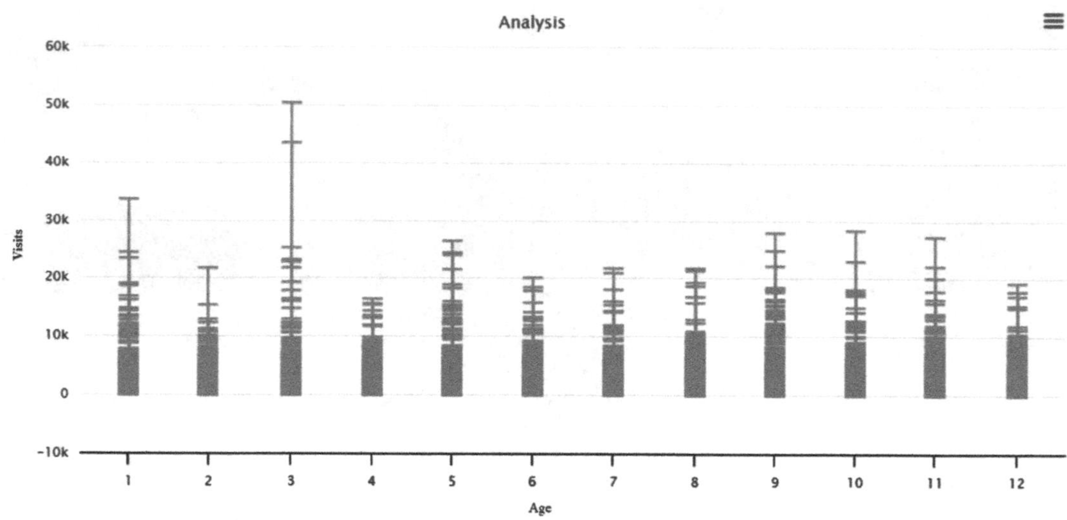

FIGURE 19.12
Analysis of age concerning mobile visits and www visits.

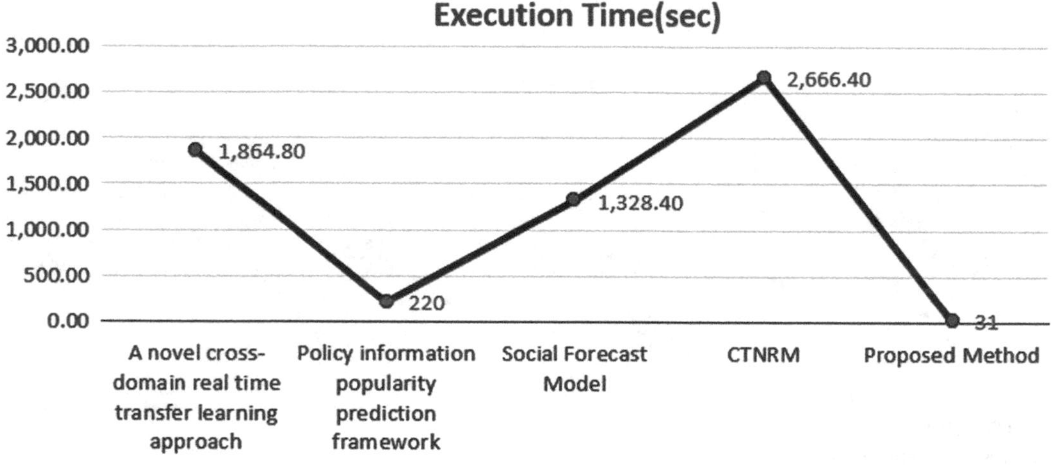

FIGURE 19.13
Analysis of execution time.

TABLE 19.2
Classification Using Execution Time

Sr. No.	Name of the Methods	Execution Time (Sec)
1.	Cross Domain Real Time Transfer Learning Process	1864.80 Sec
2.	Policy Information Popularity Prediction Framework	220 Sec
3.	Social Forecast Model	1328.40 Sec
4.	Recommendation System Depends on Communities and Trust Network (CTNRM)	2666.40 Sec
5.	**Proposed Method**	**31 Sec**

analyses on a genuine world data set show the great presentation of this proposed system, and the withdraw attributes extraordinarily improve the forecasting outcomes. This method provides great efficiency, performance, accuracy, and requires less execution time to predict the data over social media networks related to COVID-19. It can be relevant in online media marketing, brand checking, and political group's prominence prediction. The accurate forecasting of the trending issues of policy data will profit policy producers, permitting them to understand and control people's opinions.

19.10 Future Scope

In the future, course perspective towards utilizing information management of COVID-19 issues over the Cloud environment is toward enhanced precision over foreseeing a prominence connection among the clients. The segmentation of the Cloud is useful for the prediction for trending issues of COVID-19.

References

Arafat, Hossain Md. and Didar Hossain Sagar. "Popularity Prediction of Online News Item Based on Social Media Response." *Joint 8th International Conference on Informatics, Electronics & Vision and 3rd International Conference on Imaging, Vision and Pattern Recognition*, USA (2019). https://ieeexplore.ieee.org/document/8858525 (accessed 07 October 2019).

Bielski, Adam and Tomasz Trzcinski. "Understanding Multimodal Popularity Prediction of Social Media Videos with Self-Attention." *IEEE Access* 6 (2018): 74277–74287.

Cao, Cen and Qingjian Ni. "An Effective Recommendation Model Based on Communities and Trust Network." *IEEE 27th International Conference on Tool with Artificial Intelligence International Conference on Tool with Artificial Intelligence*, Italy (2015). https://ieeexplore.ieee.org/document/7372244 (accessed 07 January 2016).

Ghafari, Seyed Mohssen. "A Survey on Trust Prediction in Online Network." *IEEE Access* 8 (2020): 144292–144309.

He, S. and X. Lyu. "Edge Popularity Prediction Based on Social-Driven Propagation Dynamics." *IEEE Communications Letter* (2017). https://ieeexplore.ieee.org/document/7822896 (accessed 18 January 2017).

Jia, R. and X. Gan. "Impact of Content Popularity on Information Coverage in Online Social Networks." *IEEE Transactions on Vehicular Technology* (2018). https://ieeexplore.ieee.org/document/8276572 (accessed 31 January 2018).

Junus, Alvin and Cheung Ming. "Community Aware Prediction of Virality Timing Using Big Data of Social Cascades." *IEEE First International Conference on Big Data Computing Service and Applications*, USA (2015). https://ieeexplore.ieee.org/document/7184920 (accessed 13 August 2015).

Kong, Qingchao and W. Mao. "Exploring Trends and Patterns of Popularity Stage Evolution in Social Media." *IEEE Transaction on Systems, Man, and Cybernetics: System* (2018). https://ieeexplore.ieee.org/document/8428538 (accessed October2020).

Liu, Y. and Wenji Han. "Trending Topic Prediction on the Social Network." *5th IEEE International Conference on Broadband Network & Multimedia Technology*, China (2013). https://ieeexplore.ieee.org/document/6823933 (accessed 02 June 2015).

Luo, Y. "A Framework for Policy Information Popularity Prediction in New Media." *IEEE International Conference on Intelligence and Security Informatics*, China (2019). https://ieeexplore.ieee.org/document/8823415 (accessed 05 September 2019).

Nguyen, T. and W. Chung. "Negative News Recognition During Social Media News Consumption Using EEG." *IEEE Access* 7 (2019): 133227–133236.

Nirmala, Munirathinam and Babu Madda Rajasekhara. "A Fuzzy Based Fake Information Detection Algorithm to Define the User Trust in Content of Social Network." *IET Networks* (2019). https://ietresearch.onlinelibrary.wiley.com/doi/full/10.1049/iet-net.2018.5208 (accessed 1 November 2019).

Ortiz, Alessandro and S. Battiato. "Predicting Social Image Popularity Dynamics at Time Zero." *IEEE Access* 7 (2019): 171691–171706.

Ouyang, Shuxi and Chenyu Li. "A Peek into the Future: Predicting the Popularity of Online Videos." *IEEE Access* 4 (2016): 3026–3033.

Roy, Suman Deb and Shipeng Li. "Towards Cross-Domain Learning for Social Media Popularity Prediction." *IEEE Transaction on Multimedia* (2013). https://ieeexplore.ieee.org/document/6521345 (accessed 29 May 2013).

Su, Benle, Yumei Wang and Yu Liu. "A New Popularity Prediction Model based on Lifetime Forecast of Online Videos". *IEEE International Conference on Network Infrastructure and Digital Content*, Beijing (2016). https://ieeexplore.ieee.org/document/7974600 (accessed 13 July 2017).

Xu, Jie. "Forecasting Popularity of Videos Using Social Media." *IEEE Journal of Selected Topics in Signal Processing* 9, no. 2 (2015): 330–343.

You, Quanzeng and Jiebo Lio. "A Multifaceted Approach to Social Multimedia-based Prediction of Election." *IEEE Transaction on Multimedia* (2015). https://ieeexplore.ieee.org/document/7293668 (accessed 07 October 2015).

Zang, Zhongping and Jiaxin Li. "How to Become Instagram Famous: Post Popularity Prediction with Dual-Attention." *IEEE International Conference on Big Data (big Data)*, USA (2018). https://ieeexplore.ieee.org/document/8622461 (accessed 24 January 2019).

Index

9781032068039